WILLIAM JAMES

Psychical Research and the
Challenge of Modernity

KRISTER DYLAN KNAPP

THE UNIVERSITY OF NORTH CAROLINA PRESS

Chapel Hill

This book was published with the assistance of the
Authors Fund of the University of North Carolina Press.

© 2017 The University of North Carolina Press

All rights reserved

The University of North Carolina Press has been a member of the
Green Press Initiative since 2003.

Cover illustration: "William James sitting with Mrs. Walden at Séance,"
undated but probably ca. 1909. William James Papers, bMS Am 1092, #1185.1,
by permission of the Houghton Library, Harvard University.

LIBRARY OF CONGRESS CATALOGING-IN-PUBLICATION DATA
Names: Knapp, Krister Dylan, author.
Title: William James : psychical research and the challenge of modernity /
Krister Dylan Knapp.
Description: Chapel Hill : The University of North Carolina Press, [2017] |
Includes bibliographical references and index.
Identifiers: LCCN 2016032974 | ISBN 9781469631240 (cloth : alk. paper) |
ISBN 9781469668758 (pbk : alk. paper) | ISBN 9781469631257 (ebook)
Subjects: LCSH: James, William, 1842–1910. | Parapsychology—History—19th century.
Classification: LCC BF1028 .K53 2017 | DDC 150.92—dc23
LC record available at https://lccn.loc.gov/2016032974

A small portion of chapter 1 appeared previously in a slightly different form in
Krister Dylan Knapp, "James the Flâneur," *American Scholar* 73, no. 1 (Winter 2004): 160.
© 2004 Krister Dylan Knapp.
    Portions of chapters 6 and 7 appeared previously in somewhat different form in Krister
Dylan Knapp, "William James, Spiritualism, and Unconsciousness 'Beyond the Margin,'"
Streams of William James 3, no. 3 (Fall 2001): 1–5. © 2001 Krister Dylan Knapp.

For

MATRONA KAIDA (1926–2011)

and

PAUL KNAPP and TAMARRA KAIDA

CONTENTS

Acknowledgments xi

Introduction Tertium Quid 1

I BECOMING A PSYCHICAL RESEARCHER
1 A Relish for the Non-Normal 21
2 Moral Heroes 61
3 Out of the Egg 101

II PRACTICING PSYCHICAL RESEARCH
4 A Human Rat Hole 139
5 Dramatic Possibilities 172

III THEORIZING PSYCHICAL RESEARCH
6 Consciousness beyond the Margin 211
7 The Unseen World 248

Conclusion Tertium Quid Redux 286

Historiographical Essay 303
Notes 311
Bibliography 355
Index 375

FIGURES

Henry James Sr. 40

James John Garth Wilkinson 49

Henry Sidgwick 66

F. W. H. Myers 74

Edmund Gurney 83

Richard Hodgson 92

William James 95

Mrs. Leonora Piper 188

James McKeen Cattell 202

Hereward Carrington and Eusapia Palladino 290

ACKNOWLEDGMENTS

This book took too many years to complete. Many institutions, organizations, societies, and people helped make it a reality.

Washington University in St. Louis granted me leave from my teaching responsibilities in the spring of 2008 to begin drafting the book. Professor Hillel Kieval, then chair of the Department of History, and Edward S. Macias, then executive vice chancellor, facilitated this leave. Houghton Library at Harvard University provided permission to use the William James Papers, while Bay James, executor of the James Estate, granted the right to quote from that collection. Jim Lawrence, dean of the Center for Swedenborgian Studies of the Graduate Theological Union, granted permission to use and quote from the James John Garth Wilkinson Papers. The Butler Library at Columbia University granted permission to use a photograph of James Cattell.

A host of archivists and librarians at several institutions were also invaluable. Particularly helpful were Leslie A. Morris, curator of Modern Books and Manuscripts, and Susan Halpert, reference librarian, both of Houghton Library, Harvard University; Jocelyn K. Wilk, university archivist at Butler Library, Columbia University; Steven Vance, instructional video and technology assistant at Olin Library, Washington University in St. Louis; and John Hawkins, then the librarian of the Swedenborg School of Religion Library, at that time located in Brighton, Massachusetts. They retrieved numerous archival documents and photographs to give this work historical heft. Numerous reference librarians working at the following institutions filled what must have seemed like an endless series of interlibrary loan requests for arcane works: Indiana University, the University of Massachusetts–Boston,

Boston College, Claremont-McKenna College, and Washington University in St. Louis.

A number of academic organizations and societies made it possible for me to present my ideas during various phases of this project, including at Washington University in St. Louis the History and Philosophy of Science and Medicine Seminar, the Colloquium Lecture Series, the Faculty Workshop Series, and the junior faculty reading group; the European Society for the Study of Western Esotericism; the History of Science Society; the American Association for the History of Medicine; the New England Historical Association; the Northeast Popular Culture/American Culture Association; the Great Lakes History Conference; and the Colloquium Lecture Series in the Department of History at Boston College. Randall Albright, founder of the William James Society, made it possible for me to publish my first exploratory essay in *Streams of William James*, while *American Scholar* allowed me to explore the modernity theme.

No work becomes a book without a press willing to publish it. Special thanks go to Elaine Maisner, my superb editor who believed in this project from the start and never wavered in her support, and the crackerjack staff at the University of North Carolina Press, including Jay Mazzocchi, Alison Shay, and Becki Reibman. Julie Bush saved me from numerous egregious errors, as did Dave Prout, who expertly indexed the book. Two anonymous reviewers provided helpful suggestions that strengthened the work. I alone am responsible for any errors that may remain.

James scholarship is a rich and honorable one. Many fine James scholars have paved the road for this book, especially Ralph Barton Perry, James's first and in many ways still most authoritative intellectual biographer. I owe a debt of gratitude to him and all the others (listed in the historiographical essay and bibliography) who have followed in his footsteps and continue to preserve James's central role in the venerable American intellectual tradition. My agreement with some of them and differences with others should be seen as signs of great respect and admiration for their contributions. If I have succeeded at all, it is because of these scholars.

This book project was supported and nurtured through its many phases by several people, especially Corinna Treitel, who first suggested I look into James's interest in psychical research; Casey Blake, who first recognized the value of this topic and when I doubted myself reminded me to never forget William James and "The Will to Believe"; Lois Rudnick and Alan Lawson, expert mentors who read and commented on early drafts of the work and got me through to the other side; Christine Johnson, Lori Watt, and Ahmet

Karamustafa, warm colleagues who provided perspective and support when the project stalled; Gerry Izenberg, Howard Brick, and Paul Murphy, who read and commented on multiple drafts of my book proposal; and Daniel Bornstein and Liz Borgwardt, superb senior advisers who shepherded me through the publishing process.

The book is dedicated to my grandmother, who unfailingly supported me even though she probably never fully understood what it means to write a book, and to my parents, who taught me to love knowledge, cheered me on every step of the way, and read many chapters. Corinna Treitel, my wife, supported me at every step of the process and usually asked the most insightful questions, indubitably making this a better work, while my daughter, Isabella Rose, light of my life, thought it was "pretty cool" that her daddy was writing a book but never failed to add that she had already written her own book called "All about Fish" by the second grade (true). Finally, special mention should be made about Kroum Markov, my friend since the third grade, who has always been the brother I never had and often asked, "So when is the book coming out?"

I am very grateful to all these fine institutions, organizations, and societies but especially to these people for their assistance and support over the years. Because of them the book is much better; without them it would have never happened. Thank you all.

Introduction

TERTIUM QUID

At approximately one o'clock on a cold, rainy, and blustery New England day, 6 March 1889, Mr. Robertson James ambled up the front stone steps to the grand oak door located at 5 Boylston Place on Beacon Hill near the Massachusetts State House. On the other side lay the offices of the American Society for Psychical Research, where his brother William James, the psychologist and philosopher, and Richard Hodgson, the organization's secretary, awaited him. Robertson had come directly to inform them that the James brothers' aunt—Mrs. Catherine Walsh—had just passed away. Although "Aunt Kate's" death certificate stated that she had died at "about 12 o'clock midnight," her nephew had just been notified that she had passed away about 2:00 or 2:30 A.M. earlier that morning. Robertson, however, had not arrived from the coroner's office, the hospital, the police station, or her bedside. Nor had he spoken with any physicians, nurses, aids, or relatives. Rather, he had just returned from a séance with Mrs. Leonora Piper, the trance medium whose primary control "Dr. Phinuit," purporting to be in contact with Aunt Kate's spirit in the "other world," had announced the news. According to a statement signed by all three men, "Mrs. Walsh has been ill for some time and had been expected during the last few days to die at any hour. This is written before any despatch has been received informing [us] of the death." Mrs. Alice Gibbens James, William's wife and a Spiritualist enthusiast, also had participated in the séance. When she inquired about Aunt Kate, Mrs. Piper replied that "she is poorly" and suddenly threw her head back and blurted out, "Aunt Kate has come." Mrs. Piper informed Mrs. James that when she returned home that evening she would find a "letter or telegram . . . saying she was gone." When the Jameses did return home, William wrote, "I found a telegram as follows: 'Aunt Kate passed away a few minutes after midnight—E[lizabeth] R[obertson] Walsh.'" Later that autumn, after Aunt Kate's "spirit" appeared several more times through Mrs. Piper's control, William remarked that "the 'Kate Walsh' freak" was a "queer business!"[1]

In the late nineteenth century, the "queer business" of the "'Kate Walsh' freak" belonged to a loose category of religious-psychological-philosophical phenomena known as mediumism. Difficult to classify precisely, mediumism was often lumped together with hypnotism, hallucinations, and multiple personalities under the aggregate term "psychic." Psychic phenomena occurred at the borderland of regular consciousness and involved irregular mental activity, which James dubbed "consciousness beyond the margin" and "exceptional mental states," respectively. Because psychic phenomena were so difficult to categorize, precisely define, and reconcile with ordinary experience, a variety of scholars, intellectuals, scientists, ministers, and enthusiasts began to investigate them systematically. An organized pseudoscientific movement known as "psychical research" organically emerged in the Western world, reaching its apogee in fin de siècle England, France, Germany, Italy, and the United States, and it was not unknown in Poland and Russia. Psychical researchers primarily studied two kinds of psychic phenomena: the trance states of Spiritualist mediums and the attendant phenomena such as automatic writing, ectoplasm, and spirit-manifestation, and telepathy and its relations, namely, clairvoyance, telekinesis, second sight, and dream prediction. Spiritualism and telepathy were related because it seemed telepathy might explain the "spirit" communication between the "other world" and this one.[2]

Psychical research permeated William James's life and thought. For nearly thirty years, from the early 1880s until his death in 1910, James immersed himself in the field. His curiosity in matters psychical emerged during his childhood when young William lived in New York in the 1840s and early 1850s and was familiarized with the Spiritualism movement spreading like wildfire across the United States, England, and western Europe. While a medical student during the late 1860s and as a lecturer at Harvard College during the early 1870s, James wrote several book reviews on mental pathology and Spiritualism. His professional commitment to psychical research began during a winter trip to England in 1882–83, when members of the Society for Psychical Research (SPR) befriended him, and in 1884–85, when he expedited the founding of the SPR's sister organization in Boston, the American Society for Psychical Research (ASPR). At that point James became an officer, organizer, financial contributor, and active researcher in the cause of psychical research.

The discovery of Mrs. Leonora Piper by Alice Gibbens James (William's wife), whose séances they attended intermittently from 1885 through 1898, jump-started James's serious investigation of mediumship, while the core of James's fascination with telepathy formed in the late 1880s with his role in experimental and mathematical telepathy, an effort that peaked with his American report on the Census of Hallucinations in 1896. James also used psychical research to augment his theory of consciousness and the transmarginal self. During the first decade of the 1900s, he renewed his interest in Mrs. Piper and Eusapia Palladino, the infamous Italian physical medium whom the SPR investigated on many occasions, and by 1909 he advanced his sublime conscious reservoir theory to explain supposed spirit-return. Throughout it all, James traveled frequently to Europe to discuss matters psychical with his SPR colleagues.

James also debated associates in the scientific community who were bent on discrediting psychical research; reassured nervous Spiritualists who were convinced that psychical researchers were trying to undermine religious faith; engaged in endless committee work; conducted the daily, tedious research; and gave many public lectures. He was a prolific writer, penning six major analytical essays, more than one dozen book reviews, several encyclopedia entries, and lengthy letters to the editors of the scientific and philosophical journals *Science* and *Mind*, the newly formed psychological periodicals *Psychological Review* and *American Journal of Psychology*, and the political, literary, and religious magazines *Nation*, *North American Review*, and *Religio-Philosophical Journal*, respectively. James's psychical research was aimed at the widest possible audience since he also wrote for nonspecialized national publications, including the *Atlantic Monthly*, *McClure's Magazine*, *American Magazine*, and *Forum*, and for scientific laymen in the pages of *Popular Science Monthly*. James bolstered the cause of psychical research by answering calls to write notices and explanations of psychical research in four different Boston newspapers—the *Daily Advertiser*, the *Globe*, the *Evening Transcript*, and the *Herald*.

Finally, James penned more than eight hundred letters on matters psychical to people famous and lesser known, family members and associates, professionals and laymen. None is labeled "psychical research." Only a diligent process of searching through the voluminous James correspondence has disclosed their contents. They vary greatly in length, substance, and style. Some are quite long, detailed, technical, and theoretical, while others are short and make only a passing reference to the topic. Most fall somewhere in between. Some are formal, while others informal. Many reveal James's hilarious wit, while others demonstrate his seriousness. Taken together, these writings offer James's multiple if piecemeal explanations and theoretical speculations of a variety of psychic phenomena, and when examined relationally they show a remarkable consistency in James's thinking about matters psychic.

It is important to clarify at the outset that while James investigated and studied psychic phenomena, he was not a believer or a seeker. Nor was he a practitioner or an apologist for Spiritualism, the religious movement from which mediumship, trance states, and séances first emerged in the early 1850s and that sought evidence for the existence of God, heaven, and the survival of the soul through communication with the departed spirits of loved ones.[3] That is, James did not believe in the survival of the soul after bodily death, that the soul goes to the afterlife (what Spiritualists called "the Summerland"), or that human beings in this world can contact surviving souls in the next one. Since Spiritualists claimed that such events occurred during séances, most of James's psychical research focused on the nature of mediumship and trance states. James was thus not a Spiritualist, though he did encourage his family members and friends to develop their potential mediumistic abilities.

Similarly, James was neither a skeptic nor a debunker. He did not belong to an informal but growing network of self-proclaimed doubters and critics bent on proving Spiritualists' claims false and on exposing mediums as clever charlatans, though he certainly spent a great deal of time separating the frauds and fakers from the genuine subjects worthy of study. His purpose, then, was neither to advance a religious cause nor to undermine one but rather to understand and hypostatize psychic phenomena. Thus, while James noted that "spiritualism is the classic name for the 'soul philosophy,' Spiritism for the medium religion," he typically used "spiritualism" (in both the lowercase and uppercase) to mean mediumistic communication and its religious expression.[4]

What, then, explains James's turn to psychical research? How are we to understand this significant chapter in his extensive oeuvre? While there is a voluminous literature addressing James and psychical research, much of which is quite useful and insightful, not one work fully explains, analyzes, or contextualizes the role of psychical research in James's life and thought. Moreover, none solves the puzzle of what James actually believed, how that belief changed over time, what remained the same, or what issues were left unresolved for him and why. As such, we lack a sorely needed scholarly history of this baffling but significant topic.[5]

William James: Psychical Research and the Challenge of Modernity is the first analytical and contextualized history of James's psychical research.

It offers an original interpretation of the impact of this work on his life and its meaning in his thought. Its purpose is to make good on but also to clarify the promissory note that James's first and still most authoritative intellectual biographer, Ralph Barton Perry, offered in 1935, namely, that "James's interest in 'psychical research' was not one of his vagaries, but was central and typical."[6] While Perry failed to fully expound of what or why psychical research was "central and typical," my extensive research shows that it was significant regarding both the amount of time and energy James devoted to it and the key role it played in his personal and professional relationships. Most important, it informed and was informed by some of his central philosophical, psychological, and religious doctrines, namely, the tough- and tender-minded schemata, the fideism undergirding the will-to-believe argument, the theory of consciousness and of unconsciousness, and pluralism. By contrast, psychical research does not seem to have been significantly related to his pragmatism or radical empiricism. Perry, then, was right in main though not entirely in kind.

Such a finding may surprise some James scholars while pleasing others. The coherence of James's thought is currently unresolved in the pertinent literature. Some philosophers, notably Richard Gale, do not believe all of James's doctrines can be unified into one philosophy because James's self was ultimately divided. Others, such as Wesley Cooper, believe they *could* be given the right framework of interpretation, which he calls the "two-levels view." The nature of this debate is complex, and its outcome hangs on numerous interpretations of many highly technical points in James's pragmatism and radical empiricism, especially whether they are logically compatible. It is a fascinating dispute but one best left for philosophers to work out. This book is a work of social science that engages with known empirical data through textual evidence, not one of hypostatization about Jamesian possibilities above and beyond the text—that is, how his ideas might or might not be related to one another through speculative arguments and ideas invented long after James died and with which he did not engage. For much of what Gale, Cooper, and other like-minded scholars who engage in this form of inquiry do is invent new claims and terms taken out of James's context and time and map them back onto James to "discover" what he "really" meant.[7] Such work might be valuable philosophically but is of little value historically, for it does nothing to further our understanding of the past and of the ideas of James's world taken on their own terms. James's *actual* psychical research thus begs historical explanation and argumentation.

The central argument of the book, then, is that psychical research formed a core part of James's intellectual disposition. While his approach stemmed from his desire to reconcile competing psychological notions, such as normal and abnormal states of consciousness, his penchant was to find alternatives to irreconcilable religious and philosophical dilemmas, often couched as dualisms. In particular, James turned to psychical research to rethink, not reject, the well-trodden approaches to two classic dualisms—the natural versus supernatural and the normal versus paranormal—that many psychologists, philosophers, and theologians had failed to resolve, had thrown up their hands trying to do so, or had discounted altogether. Over time, James's emergent disposition spawned a unique method of inquiry. He did not give it a formal name, but since it sought to find a tertiary synthesis of all dualisms, it might be called his *tertium quid* (whose second *t* is pronounced "sh"), meaning "third way." Its purpose was to reconcile doubt and resolve conflicting opinions beyond what his pragmatic method of meaning and theory of truth were meant to do epistemologically. Since James evolved a third way approach to forming and justifying beliefs about psychic phenomena in particular, the term "tertium quid," which has both naturalistic and supernatural roots, is highly germane.[8]

The term "tertium quid" recalls two stories in the history of Western thought. On the one hand, there is the fable that Pythagoras invented the term to classify birds, which did not fit neatly into his categories of either walkers or flyers (birds have both feet *and* wings); they were thus some "third thing." On the other hand, the term was invoked during the Christological debates in the fourth century C.E., especially by Apollinaris, who referred to Christ as neither human nor divine but some "third thing." Both the natural and supernatural uses were captured in the legal, Latin meaning of the term as a "third something," which after a lull in its etymological development was expanded to mean "failing to fit into a dichotomy." By 1724, the term was used as a noun in modern English and defined as "a middle course or an intermediate component." The meaning of tertium quid, then, has evolved over time to include both the composite of two other things and some third option distinct from the first two choices. James's tertium quid method of inquiry reflected this more modern meaning that combined the positive elements of both extremes while filtering out the negative ones to create a distinct new position, and hence its own "third thing," but also retained some of the medieval meaning with his focus on the supernatural realm.[9]

To grasp the nature of James's third way intellectual disposition, it is useful to understand what it was not. James's tertium quid was not a way of striking an Aristotelian compromise between two extremes. While James once noted that his friend Thomas Davidson "used to crack the whip of

Aristotle" at meetings of the Radical Club in Boston during the mid-1870s, James never championed Greek methodology.[10] It was also not an attempt to find a Hegelian a priori synthesis between thesis and antithesis. James rejected Hegel's system of logic for resolving contradictions and finding underlying commonalities between truth and falsity, once describing it as full of "mental turpitudes and rottenness."[11] Offering eleven clear-cut reasons in "On Some Hegelisms," James stated flatly, "We cannot eat our cake and have it [too]."[12] Finding a third way for James was thus not an exercise in metaphysical synthesis. Neither was it a theory of modeling rational choice in which a finite number of hypostatized actors make "rational choices" based on a number of limited, artificial options. So far removed from the complex and messy realities of experienced life, James found such hypothetical choice-modeling preposterous. Finally, it was not a formal system of philosophical analysis. Although James's pragmatism as a theory of meaning and truth attempted to resolve some epistemological problems in the history of modern philosophy, his tertium quid method of inquiry was less an expression of pragmatism than an attempt to reconceptualize the intellectual underpinnings for which that doctrine was developed to resolve. It was thus not a technical philosophy; it was his philosophical disposition. In my view, this makes it more profound and all the more necessary to understand.

This book, then, belongs to the history of ideas tradition and not to that of analytical philosophy. I treat James not as a professional philosopher but more broadly as an intellectual. As such, it must be emphasized that my argument does not address James's pragmatism understood either as a rejection of classical metaphysical dualisms in the history of philosophy, such as whether the "world is one or many?—fated or free?—material or spiritual?," as James famously put it, or as James's epistemological theories of meaning and truth that rejected the starting points of traditional analytical philosophy.[13] James was a pragmatist, but that is not all he was, and although his pragmatism rejected the premises of classical philosophical dualisms, it should not be assumed that he necessarily applied pragmatism to all binary oppositional categories in all instances. Indeed, a careful consideration of his psychical research reveals that he did *not* reject the premises of the natural-versus-supernatural and normal-versus-paranormal debates so much as try to find a way to reconcile them. This may initially appear less radical than what his pragmatism was designed to do as a "new name for some old ways of thinking," but in fact it was equally if not more radical since it made reconciliation rather than rejection the central starting point of debate while requiring a different kind of mental shift from what pragmatism called for, namely, toward third way thinking. As such, the purpose of this book is to consider the nature of James's thought outside of and independent from his pragmatism to reveal new elements in his intellectual disposition.

James's tertium quid method of inquiry necessitated its own conceptual framework and invoked three essential components. First, it created a way of investigating the world that deemphasized the importance of answering ultimate questions and stressed the means by which we answer them. For James this meant inventing and developing a new deliberative method that stressed that how we understand the world was as important as the understanding itself. The pursuit of meaning and knowledge became process-based, not ends-based; indeed, for James, ends and means could not be separated. Second, as an intellectual disposition it required an attitudinal temperament free of arrogance, dogma, ideology, and especially a priori reasoning. James's goal was not to invent some possible world in which universals were worked out across theoretical notions of time and space but rather to capture all the dynamics of this particular world in the here and now, warts and all. Finally, it embraced change as a metaphysical starting point. The universe for him was full of flux and malleability, not static and fixed, and James conceived of it in very fluid and flexible terms in which knowledge of it was continually created and corrected over time through active engagement with it. Such was James's open-ended and exalted worldview. As Perry put it, "Philosophy, for James, was not an attempt to secure universality, coherence, definiteness, or any other such intellectual end, but to *see* the world as it is in all its fullness."[14] Conceived in this way, my book interprets James as an intellectual whose ultimate concerns addressed something other than his individual contributions to some of his theories and doctrines in psychology, philosophy, and religion. For as significant as they were and remain, his tertium quid method of inquiry was germane to all of them. James's center of vision, then, is best understood as this intellectual disposition and his psychical research as its finest expression.[15]

Of course, James's tertium quid approach to psychical research did not occur in an historical vacuum or in philosophical isolation. Rather, it emerged within and as a direct response to the increasingly hostile conflict between religious belief and scientific knowledge during the long nineteenth century.[16] By the fin de siècle this was a debate that seemed irreconcilable in practice, if not in principle, to many of its participants on both sides of the Atlantic.[17] Such a desideratum cried out for a resolution, and James's writing on religious belief, especially "The Will to Believe" and *The Varieties of Religious Experience*, have been seen as invoking his pragmatism to resolve it.[18] In particular, James sought to address the yawning chasm between agnostics and positivists, such as Thomas Huxley and John Tyndall in Britain, who espoused a scientific naturalism that by the 1860s had little use for a belief in God and human immortality, and defenders of faith such as Bishop Samuel Wilberforce at Oxford and Charles Hodge at Princeton, who combated scientific naturalism by finding ways to make the implications of Darwin's theory of natural selection consistent with biblical scripture and thus rescue the foundation of religious belief.[19] As scientific naturalists and theologians dug in to defend their respective turf, the probabilistic revolution, the rise of statistical thinking, and Darwinism collectively eclipsed the epistemological certitude that both scientists and religious advocates had sought. These developments radically shaped James's intellectual disposition.[20] In entering the fray James's goal was to reconcile the science-versus-religion debate by finding a third alternative to the ontological categories of the natural and supernatural upon which the debate depended. His turn to psychical research was an attempt to develop that tertium quid. Interpreted in this way, the problem plaguing James scholars—that his interest in psychic phenomena seemed "bizarre" and thus unexplainable and unworkable into the pantheon of James literature—can be explained as an instance of his tertium quid method of inquiry. As such, my book corrects the long-standing but erroneous view that James's ideas can be reduced to his personal psychology in which his "ambivalence," as one James scholar contends, led him to "cultivate self[-]conscious impulsivity" and thus to confuse "psychic phenomena, religious belief, and science."[21]

The pursuit of facts was crucial to James's endeavor. Advocates for both science and religion appealed to facts, the former invoking the methodological authority of scientific method, the latter biblical authority. By the late eighteenth century, however, several developments associated with rationalist theology, especially biblical hermeneutics and historical criticism, had begun to undermine religious authority, a process more or less complete by the late nineteenth century.[22] But it was the broad contours of positivism and scientific naturalism, a central tenet of which was the increasingly accepted axiom that for any claim in any field to be considered legitimate it had to be demonstrable and verifiable, that most weakened traditional religion. The achievements in precision measurement, refined instrumentation, advanced empirical testing methods, and new forms of expressing results mathematically created a new and higher threshold. Only after a piece of evidence had been subjected to this rigorous process could it become factual. In this way, James turned to psychical research because it afforded the possibility to redefine the fact.[23] Rational inquiry thus began with a quest for scientifically demonstrable facts. My book shows how James's quest for facts substantiates the radical claim that the "modern fact" was made anew in the nineteenth century through the appeal to, but gradual erosion of, objectivity.[24] Since the unraveling of objectivity led to the crisis of modernity, James's psychical research can been interpreted as one of its pallbearers.

The natural and social sciences dominated this new culture of facts. During the nineteenth century they differentiated themselves from natural magic, natural history, *Naturphilosoph*, and religion, sorting themselves out into their distinct disciplines of physics, chemistry, biology, sociology, economics, and psychology as independent branches of inquiry.[25] Germane to this development in the United States was the first generation of "brass instrument" scientific psychologists, named because their lab instruments were made of brass.[26] Trained by the leading German scientific psychologists Hermann von Helmholtz and Wilhelm Wundt, they formed the front lines of the fact-building mission. Starting in the 1880s, the German model was imported into American research universities when they began to offer PhDs.[27] Lab space, equipment, experimental design, methodology, research protocols, measurement techniques, mathematization applications, professionalization, organizations, periodicals, fund-raising, and the rest of the scientific enterprise became the lifeblood of the new discipline of scientific psychology—a new techno-scientific ideal that drew boundaries from other forms of inquiry that failed to meet the standards of this ideal.[28]

Still, there were many issues of contention. One was the proper object of study. Just what were psychologists experimenting *on*? What *content* were they measuring? What exactly was their phenomenon?[29] James, a founder of the new field, believed scientific psychologists should study the widest possible scope of mental activity, including paranormal phenomena such as Spiritualism, telepathy, haunted houses, and that deemed "occult."[30] But most, including his nemesis, G. Stanley Hall, and other leading figures such as Hugo Münsterberg and James Cattell, working at leading research universities, did not. They believed the proper scope of psychology should be the natural world and vigorously fought James every step of the way.[31] These debates played out in a variety of forums but perhaps most publicly and profoundly at the International Congress for Physiological (later Experimental) Psychology in Europe from the late 1880s through World War I, where at least ten different research paradigms competed for control of the new field.[32] It was the common appeal to facts that eventually made an empirical science out of psychology and allowed it to separate itself from speculative metaphysics and religion.[33] Psychical research was eventually dropped from the program and dismissed as invalid due to methodological and epistemological problems, not to mention widespread fraud and other salient issues. The schism eventually led to two fields of discourse: experimental psychology, practiced at most research universities, and parapsychology (a word not invented until 1925), practiced, for the most part, outside of academic institutions.[34] James's commitment to and defense of psychical research in the late nineteenth century was nothing less than a fight for the very heart and soul of scientific psychology. He lost that debate, but for three decades the future of psychology was open, uncertain, and contested. In this way, psychical research was a stepchild of experimental psychology and for many a "pseudo" science.[35] Scientific psychologists, then, helped establish the fact.

Others, however, fared less well. Liberal Protestants in New England, for instance, where positivism and scientific naturalism overwhelmed Unitarians at Harvard and elsewhere, tried to accommodate their religious beliefs to the culture of facts but eventually fell victim to it instead and wound up hastening the process of religious unbelief in America.[36] Spiritualists, who were spiritual refugees from Swedenborgianism, Universalism, Quakerism, Unitarianism, and Transcendentalism during the "antebellum spiritual hothouse" period, developed a theology that was the logical extension of liberal Protestantism, whose scientific wing hoped to use science to prove the objective reality of spirits.[37] They attempted to compromise with positivism and scientific naturalism by appealing to an "aura of factuality" for which the multiple instances of spirit-return became evidence for their belief, which, in turn, became its own kind of justification, a strategy that failed miserably for Spiritualists in the United States and England by 1900.[38]

Psychical researchers on both sides of the Atlantic worked within the complex matrix of positivism and scientific naturalism on the one hand and the eclipse of liberal Protestantism and traditional religious belief on the other. Many of them were white middle- and upper-middle-class reformed Anglican and liberal Protestant intellectuals who had undergone a crisis of belief characterized by extreme doubt and anxiety.[39] Their experience reflected a larger crisis of cultural authority that produced a sense of weightlessness afflicting the United States. A shift from a Protestant ethos to a therapeutic worldview, which left many yearning for psychic harmony and a new kind of authentic spiritual experience, led to a transformation in the American attitude from a desire for religious salvation to therapeutic self-fulfillment.[40] Key features of this crisis included a religious vacuity and general sense of cultural malaise;

a Hamletian complex brought on by the perception that America was producing weak, indecisive young men trained at the country's leading centers of advanced learning such as Harvard, where Protestantism reigned; and a *tedium vitae* or a cultural lifestyle resplendent with boredom.[41] The cost was a psychological condition known as neurasthenia, an emotional and psychic disorder characterized by easy fatigue, a lack of motivation, feelings of inadequacy, and a host of psychosomatic symptoms that led to a sense of nervousness.[42] Neurasthenia afflicted many American intellectuals and writers such as Theodore Dreiser, William Dean Howells, and Charlotte Perkins Gilman, to name but three.[43] James was no exception. To a friend he once wrote, "I am a victim of neurasthenia and of the sense of hollowness and unreality that goes with it."[44] Neurasthenia—and by extension the larger religio-cultural-psychic crisis—was "the price Americans paid for progress," as one scholar captured it.[45]

The situation clearly demanded reconciliation. The public's turn to Spiritualism and professional scientists' corresponding interest in studying or rebutting paranormal phenomena was but one of many "solutions" to this crisis (three others were the Social Gospel movement, the turn toward "Orientalism," and reformation of traditional Protestantism) in this massive reorientation of American culture.[46] Psychical researchers in particular turned to the fact to try to prove psychic phenomena as another means to reinforce religious faith in place of a failing church. British psychical researchers especially believed that if Spiritualism were proved true, it would lend support for their cherished view of the immortality of the soul. Against this Sisyphean task, the quest for scientifically demonstrable facts offered a glimmer of hope for the religiously minded, crisis-driven intellectual in the nineteenth century bent on proving the survival theory.

James's tertium quid solution to this dilemma was not to take one side or the other. Nor was it to try to strike a compromise between the two that allowed each to coexist side by side without resolving the fundamental principles that divided them. Instead, it was to offer a third alternative that would reconcile science and religion intellectually by finding the kinds of objective evidence that would lend support for subjective belief in psychic phenomena. And it was to psychical research—not to his technical philosophy or scientific psychology, or even to his defense of religious belief—that he turned to try to achieve it. James, then, distinguished himself from agnostics and positivists on the one hand and liberal Protestants and Spiritualists on the other hand, and even from the Sidgwick Group, which was more sympathetic with the believers.

James's tertium quid method of inquiry in psychical research thus shaped his understanding and use of the term "fact." For him, facts were more elastic than what strict scientific naturalists allowed for but more concrete than what religious advocates believed. A fact for James was determined, if it was determined at all, by how well it responded to a mixture of empirical testing and fideistic insight. For James, empiricism consisted of two principles: the traditional one that stipulated that a fact was determined by the use of a scientific method built on verification techniques such as repeated experimental testing and acquisition of large bodies of evidence, and his view that this process must be self-correcting and open to revision over time. A fact for James was objective but never ontologically permanent; it could be modified or even erased as new data poured in, making it a fluid rather than a static concept. James's empiricism thus adhered to scientific methodology.

But in a display of Jamesian paradox typical of his thought and character, he was not consistent in this view. James also believed that *personal* experience as much as scientific experiment accounted for understanding the world. One half of knowing was grounded in personal experience, he argued, because knowledge manifested a *subjective* quality. That is, reaching objective knowledge of any given phenomenon was always dependent to a degree on how any one individual actually experienced that phenomenon. Since a subjective quality permeated the experience-derived knowledge process, knowledge had to contain some subjective elements. For James, this meant the will must somehow be involved in the creation of a fact, which in essence amounted to a kind of fideism, the view that in pursuit of truth one should rely on faith rather than on reason, but also signaled a kind of subjectivity to knowing something.[47] James was a fideist in this broader sense. In other words, his tertium quid approach was both *empirical*, because he held that knowledge derived from experience, and simultaneously *fideist*, because it stipulated that the experience of knowing was ultimately a subjective one, meaning the individual experience of something comprised part of objectively knowing it. This position was an avowedly open challenge to the traditional notion of objectivity, but it was not unempirical per se since it still gave priority to experience broadly conceived.[48] James's psychical research reflected his tertium quid approach since it attempted to use all the accoutrements of scientific practice to systematize the study of psychic phenomena while simultaneously making room for the ever-present subjectivity that permeated the investigator's experience. Since such experience was crucial to deciding whether a given psychic phenomenon had been proven, and because of the incredibly controversial nature surrounding such claims, psychical research was the ideal site to combine scientific practice with personal reflection. James thus found in psychical research a way to study objectively occurring but subjectively experienced phenomena.[49]

James's tertium quid approach to psychical research invoked his famous schemata of the tough- and tender-minded.[50] For James, the "tender-minded" were "Rationalistic, Intellectualistic, Idealistic, Optimistic, Religious, Free-Willist, Monistic [and] Dogmatical," while the "tough-minded" were "Empiricist, Sensationalistic, Materialistic, Pessimistic, Irreligious, Fatalistic, Pluralistic [and] Skeptical." The former reasoned by "principles" and the latter by "facts."[51] One James scholar has argued that James narrowly cast these two types in *Pragmatism* as two sides of our philosophical self—the hard-nosed scientific self and the religious, moral self—and reconciled their differences through his "methodological universalism." The concepts each employed, though seemingly irreconcilable, were in fact reconcilable because they used the same pragmatic theory of meaning.[52] This is a plausible reading in the context of the philosophy of self that deserves careful consideration. But James also *applied* his schemata more broadly. Indeed, one can find his application of the tough- and tender-minded terms and their attendant qualities to what he called the "mental make-up" found in a cast of historical characters beyond a hypostatized, abstract self, referring to "very positively marked men, men of radical idiosyncrasy."[53] Indeed, by offering the phrases "tough-minded empiricist-skeptics" and "hard-hearted scientists," James was more broadly referring to the mind-sets he believed undergirded many positivists, Darwinists, and adherents of the central intellectual principles of the British Enlightenment.[54]

In particular, James identified the American "brass instrument" psychologists such as G. Stanley Hall and James Cattell, and the British scientific naturalists and philosophers Thomas Huxley and William Clifford as prime examples of manifesting tough-mindedness. James found that they were not only skeptical of psychical research but also so adamant in their commitment to scientific method that they often refused even to consider psychical research because it was not scientific enough. Spiritualists and their liberal Protestant supporters, on the other hand, who were prime examples of the tender-minded mental makeup for James, also dismissed psychical research because they believed the attempt to make religious and psychic matters scientific was really an effort to undermine faith in supernatural matters. The tough- and tender-minded dichotomy thus belonged as much to his tertium quid method of inquiry as it did to his pragmatic theory of meaning. It was a way of locating the two extremes against which he needed to find a third way in which James tried to salvage the best of both sides while discarding the worst. In particular, James preferred the factual aspect of the empirical approach and the free-will quality of the religious one but redefined all of them to meet the various intellectual needs via his tertium quid method of inquiry.

James's tertium quid approach to psychical research, then, is best contextualized within four major nineteenth-century developments: the Victorian crisis of religious faith accompanied by cultural malaise and ennui; the rise of Darwinism and scientific naturalism; scientific modernism, or the collective impact of statistical thinking, the probability calculus, exact measurement, and the mathematization of all phenomena; and the professionalization of the social sciences with its attendant rise of experts, specialists, and codified forms of knowledge produced by the educated elite, especially in American experimental psychology. All four developments fundamentally altered belief formation by 1900. This book shows that the rise of psychical research belonged to these major cultural and scientific challenges facing predominantly though not exclusively white male, middle-class, Protestant, transatlantic intellectuals of the Victorian and Edwardian periods.

Ultimately, James's tertium quid method of inquiry is best understood as an expression of modernist thought in the human sciences called "cognitive modernism."[55] Effectively the turn-of-the-century recognition of epistemological subjectivity and uncertainty that nonetheless retained a commitment to scientific investigation, this kind of modernist thought advocated the pursuit of knowledge along German *wissenschaftliche* lines, in which inquiry was secular and broadly methodical and empirical, rather than along the British lines, in which inquiry was also secular but more technical in its methodology and highly narrow in its reduction of all experience to experimentalism. Like British empiricism, it excluded claims to truth based on insights derived from religious, poetic, speculative, or commonsense experience, but unlike British empiricism, it preferred a world of reference to the imagined one created out of pure subjectivity. By emphasizing *Wissenschaft*, cognitive modernism captured the common denominator of many emergent movements of this period—naturalism, empiricism, realism, positivism, pragmatism, and progressivism—while coexisting with political and aesthetic modernism.[56] The former focused on the nature and theory of political, social, and economic structures, which one scholar argues was "socially progressive, rationalistic, competitive, [and] technological," while the latter was "culturally critical and self-critical, bent on demystifying the values of the first." Both kinds of modernism were "conflicting and interdependent," with aesthetic modernism being an artistic form that maintained a dialectical relationship with the second kind.[57] By stark contrast, cognitive modernism held that knowledge of the world was derived primarily from scientific inquiry broadly conceived. If Henry James exemplified aesthetic modernism, then William James, whose tertium quid method of inquiry was steeped in *Wissenschaft*, illustrated cognitive modernism.

While analyses of modernity are typically cast through the prism of Max Weber's haunting phrase "the disenchantment of the world," in which the rationalization of the social, political, and economic spheres creates the absence of meaning in the individual's life and thereby imprisons him in an "iron cage," my book illuminates the way in which James forged a key to freedom. By using psychical research as a crucible to rethink dualistic thinking, James tried to meet the demands brought on by monumental changes in late nineteenth- and early twentieth-century thought. These included the crisis of faith in an increasingly secular world, the problem of individual free will in a deterministic universe, and the relevance of pure ideas in a materialistic cosmos. They also included the maturation of probabilistic thinking in an age of statistical expressions of knowledge claims and the decreasing role of subjectivity, personal experience, and intuition in a world of scientific experiment, empirical methodologies, and mathematical measurement of natural phenomena. The increasing irrelevance of the amateur scientist amid the expansion of formal scientific organizations that fostered rigid disciplinary practices, specialized fields of knowledge, and a coterie of experts rounded out these changes. These developments helped unravel the uncritical acceptance of universalized notions of truth and objectivity and forced many transatlantic intellectuals in the human sciences to make sense of this overwhelming change. While some took refuge in the British empirical tradition, James opted for the German *Wissenschaft*. In this way, James's psychical research can be seen as trying to meet all these demands to become re-enchanted with the world. For James, that meant neither reviving a defense of the old order of unquestioned certainty and objectivity nor blithely accepting the "iron cage" but rather embracing the epistemological uncertainty endemic of the modern condition.[58] Such was the nature of his tertium quid.

That James and other psychical researchers were cognitive modernists reveals the existence of a unique "discourse of community" during the late nineteenth and early twentieth centuries.[59] For psychical researchers in Britain, France, Germany, Italy, and the United States shared a common set of concerns, and they asked the same kinds of questions about the meaning and nature of psychic phenomena. Despite their significant nationalized differences and languages, they manifested a distinct set of values, beliefs, and perceptions that invoked a shared transnational culture of inquiry. Their commitment to progress and truth led them to believe in science's ability to reveal the reality of psychic phenomena. They were thus intellectuals belonging to a broad social class, that is, their shared interest in psychical research did not emerge from a sense of detachment, assumed objectivity, and a reliance on the mind in work and play (though that was not absent from their approach). My argument that psychical researchers made up a distinct set of intellectuals thereby challenges the long-cherished Marxist view that emergent nineteenth-century intellectuals constituted a distinct social type.[60] Instead, psychical researchers as peers engaged in rational discourse steeped in a shared community that manifested historicity, temporality, dynamism, and, above all, contingency. In particular, they took psychic phenomena seriously in their attempt to discover whether the soul survives bodily death. In trying to answer that impossible query, psychical researchers invoked the Enlightenment's commitment to human reason and its insistence that individuals can probe nature with a reasonable degree of confidence and turned to scientific forms of investigation and mathematical expressions of experimental results.[61] In short, James's tertium quid approach to psychical research is best understood as an expression of the uncertainty permeating modernity and thus challenges the view that James was a "reluctant modernist."[62]

William James: Psychical Research and the Challenge of Modernity is divided into three parts. The first third identifies the known and probable origins of James's interest in psychic phenomena and explains how and why he committed himself to psychical research by 1884. Chapter 1 maintains that James's interest in Spiritualism emerged during the late 1840s and early 1850s in his boyhood in New York City and London and shows how it likely derived from his father's and father's friends' investigations of and conversations about Spiritualism. Chapter 2 recounts how James came to psychical research in the early 1880s through a series of friendships and professional relationships he formed with members of the British intellectual aristocracy, especially through participation in their social and dinner clubs. Chapter 3 charts James's contributions to the SPR and ASPR as a researcher, investigator, officer, committee chairman, financial supporter, and cheerleader.

The middle third of the book focuses on his work as a psychical researcher while analyzing the role that his empiricist and fideistic logics played in pursuit of psychical facts. Chapter 4 examines James's role as an investigator of physical mediums purporting to levitate tables and materialize ghostly forms of the deceased and recounts the instances when he revealed several of them to be frauds, including the notorious Eusapia Palladino. Chapter 5 continues this approach by tracing James's role as an investigator of mental mediums claiming to communicate messages from the dead through automatic writing and trance speech. It examines the numerous mediums he studied and shows how and why Mrs. Leonora Piper, the famous Boston Spiritualist medium, convinced him of the "dramatic possibility" that her phenomena were real and genuine.

The final third of the book analyzes the relationship between James's psychical research and his theories of subliminal consciousness and immortality. Chapter 6 examines James's theory of the subliminal self and contextualizes that theory within three competing explanations of the unconscious: German idealism, French pathology, and British materialism. Chapter 7 concentrates on James's theory of immortality, focusing on his explanation of the supposed communications from the dead. In particular, it establishes that his study of trance states in Spiritualist mediums led him to formulate the sublime cosmic reservoir theory, or the view that upon bodily death consciousness melds organically with all previous consciousness and is stored over time in the cosmos, which James called the "mother sea of consciousness."

The conclusion reiterates the book's main themes by way of summarizing the argument that James's psychical research was central and typical of certain aspects of his life and thought. It finds that even after nearly thirty years of dedication to the cause, James was still baffled by psychic phenomena but continued his third way investigative approach in which he maintained that truth would be established in the long run as new empirical evidence accumulated over time and was interpreted through a mixture of objective methods and subjective experience. In short, *William James: Psychical Research and the Challenge of Modernity* shows how and why James's psychical research fostered a new method of inquiry designed to navigate the epistemological uncertainty of the modern age.

I

BECOMING A PSYCHICAL RESEARCHER

one

A RELISH FOR THE NON-NORMAL

"Everything conspired to make William James a pioneer in psychical research. One could almost see it coming a hundred years ahead."[1] The James family history illustrates this statement's prophetic if presentist nature. William's early boyhood developed in an antebellum household in New York City where the unconventional was championed. The standard view of James recounts this legacy. The family heritage spanned from William's grandfather William James of Albany, who, after immigrating to America in the late eighteenth century, amassed a fortune through investment in property and construction of the Erie Canal and governed the family through his authoritative Calvinism, through his rebellious son Henry Sr., the one-legged Swedenborgian theologian who battled orthodox Presbyterianism with his quill and lectern, to William, who, after struggling with this religious heritage, formed a superb career as a professor of psychology and philosophy. In emphasizing the nonconformity of the James family, most scholars have explored its impact on William's psyche. William's identity has been construed in terms of a generational and oedipal conflict, and one chock-full of religious rebellion, psychological crises, and vocational mishaps. A lack of a permanent home and confusion of place due to frequent travel between America and Europe in search of the right kind of education rounds out the interpretation.[2]

The nonconformity of the James family had major repercussions on William's thought as well. William's boyhood encounters with Spiritualism make that evident. Although Henry Sr. frequently moved his family during William's childhood—between America and Europe and among the states of New York, Rhode Island, and Massachusetts—there existed a period of geographical and educational stability for the family. In the years between 1848 and 1855, when young William was between the impressionable ages of six and thirteen, the Jameses occupied one of New York City's newer brownstones at 58 West Fourteenth Street, between Fifth and Sixth Avenues, just several blocks from the Astor Hotel, where William had been born in 1842.[3] During that time William developed what James's first biographer, Ralph Barton Perry, called an immense "relish for the non-normal," that is, an intellectual curiosity to seek out and understand unusual phenomena. William's father was the most immediate source of this habit. A writer and fiercely independent-minded thinker, Henry Sr. was at bottom an iconoclast and maverick. Leisured for life after a prolonged legal battle for his inheritance of his father's sizable wealth, Henry Sr. could afford to pursue his own idiosyncratic interests. Like many cultural radicals of the mid-nineteenth century, Henry Sr. took to reformist and utopian impulses and over the decades championed a succession of social, religious, and political movements ranging from Sandemanianism, Fourierism, and Swedenborgianism to free love, woman suffrage, and abolition, only to dismiss them in turn when they failed to meet his idealization of them.[4] Henry Sr. passed on his hopscotch approach to William, who had a tendency throughout his life to jump from one subject to another, often before finishing the one he started. But this nonconformity also created room for pursuing the "non-normal," which in turn became part of the James family style of inquiry. In this environment, as Perry wrote, normalcy spawned a "shallowness and conventionality of opinion" for young William and only "generated intellectual prejudice."[5] Spiritualism was one such topic to pass through this rarefied air.

Young William's sporadic encounters with Spiritualism over a twenty-year period, from the early 1850s through the early 1870s, sparked a lifelong interest in the topic. They also provided the early foundational elements for his adult commitment to psychical research. These elements were a willingness to take the topic seriously with an open mind, an ability to suspend judgment undogmatically until further investigation revealed ample information, and a resolution to accept that facts were open to revision and even reversal over time. There was, then, an intellectual attitude lurking in William's early experiences with Spiritualism. It was as much a psychological disposition as it was a philosophical position. Indeed, it was something like a method of inquiry that emphasized a posteriori outcomes while allowing for a priori commitments; it brooked no body of ultimate conclusions yet sought out final answers; it took no sides except the side that argues all sides must be considered evenly and fairly; it harbored no ideology except that ideology must not prevail. It was, then, a view that rejected extremes in favor of a third way, and it emerged, at least in part, from his adolescent experiences with Spiritualism.

Two major overlapping and sequential developments contributed to this outcome. The first revolves around indirect textual evidence that suggest likelihoods: his possible witnessing of the Fox sisters, the infamous "rappers" who inadvertently helped launch the mass movement of Spiritualism in the late 1840s; his likely subsequent conversations with many of New York's intellectuals who investigated the Fox sisters in the early 1850s; his interaction with his father, who both participated in these conversations and wrote an essay about Spiritualism in 1852 that young William probably read; and even his possible witnessing of séances in 1855–56 with James John Garth Wilkinson, his father's Swedenborgian friend. Direct textual evidence reveals a second set of developments. These are William's reference to a book on Spiritualism that he read in 1861, a book review he wrote on a Spiritualist tract in 1869, and two letters addressing Spiritualism, one in 1869 to his brother (about the book review) and the other to a close friend in 1874 in which James committed himself to investigate Spiritualism. Taken together, these occurrences reveal a pattern of James's growing interest in Spiritualism that emerged at an early age.

SPIRITUALISM

Spiritualism is the view that the souls of the departed can communicate with the living and that they do so indirectly through some kind of agent, often called a medium. In order to receive such communications, mediums must enter an altered state of consciousness or "trance." Usually seated around a table with the medium, Spiritualists utilize the power of like-minded people concentrating on communicating with the departed souls in a ritual known as the séance. Such rituals for Spiritualists reflect religious piety, not spiritual decadence. Situated somewhat uncomfortably between religion and occultism, Spiritualism has permeated many societies throughout history.[6] Belief in spirit communication and belief in ghosts, with which Spiritualism sometimes overlaps, stretches back to prehistorical oral and written tribal cultures. The ancient societies of Babylonia, Egypt, Greece, Rome, and China have all invoked communication with spirits in some form, and both the Old and New Testaments make multiple references to the influences of spiritual beings on everyday life.[7]

Modern Spiritualism has roots in several eighteenth-century developments. Emanuel Swedenborg, the Swedish engineer-turned-mystic, was one source. In 1745, Swedenborg had a divine revelation: he declared God had chosen him as his messenger. Endowing him with the trance state, Swedenborg claimed God enabled him to travel throughout the ethereal world and communicate with spirits in both heaven and hell. Swedenborg left his post as the assessor for the Royal College of Mines to persuade others of his vision and spent his remaining twenty-seven years in pursuit of mystical truth, writing and publishing copious volumes of philosophical and theological tracts. Swedenborgianism, as his thought came to be called, profoundly influenced liberal Protestants dissatisfied with the orthodox teaching, practice, and interpretation of the mainstream Presbyterian and Lutheran churches. In 1778, a small portion of Protestants broke away to form the New Church in Europe, later called the New Jerusalem, and the New Church in America by 1792. There, it gained a modest following. By 1842 Swedenborgians claimed to reside in all states of the Union but amounted to only five thousand individuals located in scattered communities, occasionally gathering in small convention halls and publishing obscure reports of their meetings. The New Church's greatest impact was from 1835 to 1850, when many of its adherents became Spiritualists. Because many in the New Church also embraced mysticism, an individualist component to Swedenborgianism developed with regard to the notion of postmortem communication. Spiritualists, too, held this view; any person discovering their special mediumistic powers could contact the spirits in the afterlife. For Spiritualists in America, the connection between Swedenborgian mysticism and the Spiritualist séance was thus quite natural. As one enraptured disciple aptly put it, Spiritualism was "Swedenborgianism Americanized."[8]

The possession rituals of the Shaker movement in England during the Quaker revival in the late 1740s were a second source of modern Spiritualism. Known for the trembling they produced due to an excess of religious sentiment, Shakers claimed to have visions and contact with the spirit world while in a trancelike state. At Shaker meetings various individuals began to display a knack for visions, asserting they experienced visits from Noah's spirit and God's angels. By 1837, eighteen different Shaker communities in America were using "mediums" to receive information from the "other world." Their purpose was to verify the qualifications of an applicant to their sect, a sort of theological cousin to the Calvinists' process of manifesting oneself as a member of "the Elect." Although the spirit invasion of the Shakers lasted fewer than ten years (1837–44), it garnered a great deal of (mostly negative) publicity. But it also popularized to a significant degree the possibility of postmortem communication. For Spiritualists, Shakers were a natural ally.[9]

Franz Anton Mesmer, a German priest and physician and the founder of the subsequent movement known as mesmerism, formed a third wellspring of modern Spiritualism. Mesmer claimed his magnets contained "curative powers." Mesmer thought he could "exorcise" the diseased part of the body by using a magnet to restore the proper balance of "magnetic fluid," a process that he called "animal magnetism." While its action-at-a-distance quality smacked of occultism, it was the trancelike states that Mesmer induced in his patients that led to a number of physicians such as James Braid to posit the existence of the hypnotic state, an altered state of consciousness similar to the trance.[10]

Several developments during the nineteenth century created fertile soil for Spiritualism to take root in America. The evangelical revivals of the Second Great Awakening, especially the more emotive wings of the Methodists, Baptists, Presbyterians, and Pentecostals, shared with Spiritualists a dramatic fervor for salvation and redemption. Emerging from the rural areas of Kentucky in 1801 and creeping up the Atlantic Seaboard during the 1820s and 1830s, a zealous piety not seen since the Puritans had dominated New England "burned-over" the American religious landscape, most famously in upstate New York and western Pennsylvania. This exceptionally vivid phrase claimed the souls of the region's inhabitants had been so thoroughly converted during successive waves of conversion that they were saturated with God's healing power. Participants attended camp meetings in secluded, wooded settings where fire-and-brimstone preachers sermonized successively for days at a time only to faint or founder into convulsions. During this period church membership doubled in America. In the "burned-over" districts, more women than men joined; manufacturers enlisted more than laborers; and those in commerce, canal towns, and major seaports remained less affected than those in mill towns and cities of industry such as Rochester and Utica, where master craftsmen and journeymen of the middle class flourished. The underlying message was that salvation was available to anyone (not just the Elect, as Calvinists believed) willing to accept God's grace and eradicate his or her sin. Spiritualists found solace in this "democratic" practice as well; in Spiritualism, everyone was considered a potential medium allowed to communicate with the dead.[11]

By the middle third of the nineteenth century, a number of these practices centered on phenomena involving body convulsions known as fits and mental "possessions" called trances. Both were viewed as some kind of supernormal if not supernatural control from an outside agent, and both allowed room for interpretations that such an agent was either benign or malicious. For some, such "altered states" amounted to evidence of a higher, supreme being who demonstrated his existence by affecting the possessed or entranced individual. These physical and mental states were evidence for mystics, and later for Christian Scientists, who believed in faith healing.[12] For others, however, such phenomena too closely resembled the darker forces associated with fanatics, manias, fads, sects, and cults feared to be lurking in the cosmos. So-called morbid phenomena such as witchcraft, magic, and demonic possession were sometimes offered as alternative explanations and were considered proof that such states were harmful and dangerous, indicating that an individual's soul had been lost to the devil. In a period of fervent religious revival and spiritual awakening, all such phenomena, good and evil alike, typified the emergence of what might be pejoratively called stammering behavior.[13] By the 1850s, many of these developments had moved from the margins to the center of society. In the James household, where they surrounded the family the way water surrounds a fish, Spiritualism most likely made its way into young William's mind, and the Fox sisters would have been the most likely source.

THE FOX SISTERS

Margaret and Catherine Fox, two teenage girls from Hydesville, New York, a small peppermint-farming community located thirty miles east of Rochester, accidentally inaugurated modern Spiritualism. They claimed to be able to communicate with the spirit of a deceased man they dubbed "Mr. Splitfoot" through loud rapping sounds or "knockings" in response to a series of yes/no questions. After being subjected to a battery of tests, sympathetic and skeptical investigators alike failed to find either evidence of fraud or an explanation for the sounds. While the assumption for some was that they emanated from spirits in the other world and therefore proved the immortality of the soul, others were not willing to go that far. As more people inquired, Rochester's newspapers began publishing stories about the Fox sisters and in the process raised the specter of fraud, which in turn led to more investigations. The *Daily Democrat* described one such event: "All agreed that the sounds were heard, *but they entirely failed to discover any means by which it could be done*," adding, "There is some curiosity excited in this community, in regard to this thing, and it was decided ... not to give it up so. These young women will have to be pretty smart, if they deceive everybody!" As the charges of deception mounted, Maggie and Kate, under the management of their older sister Leah, with whom the girls were now living, agreed to give three public demonstrations. Each was supervised by three separate investigative committees and held at Corinthian Hall (Rochester's largest public site) to audiences of four hundred. A group of rowdies offended by the Fox sisters' blasphemous claims broke up the final demonstration. Exiting Rochester in a hurry, Leah took her sisters to Troy, Albany, and New York City, initiating a kind of tour where the girls gave both public and private demonstrations. For eight weeks in July and August 1850, the Fox sisters offered regular sittings to paying customers and made one hundred dollars or more per day. They then moved down the Eastern Seaboard to Philadelphia and Washington, D.C., followed by stints in Buffalo and Pittsburgh.[14]

The Fox sisters thus surreptitiously created the mass movement of modern Spiritualism in America during the 1850s. Indeed, the "Rochester Knockings" inspired the discovery of mediumistic abilities in so many Americans that the 1890s census reported forty-five thousand self-identified Spiritualists residing in nearly forty states and territories, while an informal estimate put the number from a low of several thousand to as high as eleven million (out of a population of sixty-three million).[15] From small towns in Vermont such as Woodstock and Shaftsbury, to medium-sized cities such as Cincinnati in the Midwest and Memphis and New Orleans in the South, to mining camps in Denver, California, and Alaska, Americans organized themselves formally and informally into small and large Spiritualist circles and communities, including those run by James L. Scoot and Thomas L. Harris respectively in Mountain Cove, Virginia. Boston was a mainstay of Spiritualism with the most mediums practicing within a city limit. Numerous Spiritualist newspapers and periodicals mushroomed overnight, including the *Spiritual Telegraph*, the *Spirit Messenger*, and the *Banner of Light*. So, too, did books and pamphlets on Spiritualism, which accounted for the sale of fifty thousand of each by 1871. Whites and African Americans (free and enslaved alike) practiced Spiritualism in the North and the South and were allowed to give demonstrations in each other's otherwise racially segregated churches. Although largely a Protestant phenomenon, a few Catholics and even two Jews (Cora Wilburn and Laura Schlesinger) converted to Spiritualism. Spiritualism also cut across class, ethnic, and linguistic divisions with members of German-, French-, and English-speaking parts of the country practicing Spiritualism. Numerous utopian leaders and communities also embraced Spiritualism, including Richard Dale Owen, a U.S. congressman and the son of Robert Dale Owen, who first formed New Harmony in 1824 on the banks of the Wabash River in Indiana, and John Humphrey Noyes, who led a series of Fourierist "phalanxes" in and around Oneida, New York, where he wove Spiritualism into his eclectic blend of "complex marriage," free love, and "male continence." Many well-known persons in the social reform movements—abolition, woman suffrage, temperance, children's rights, marriage reform, education reform, dress reform, labor rights, vegetarianism, free love, and anti-sabbatarianism—converted to or at least sympathized with Spiritualism. A short but impressive list of high-profile Spiritualists reads like a roll call of American reformists: Harriet Beecher Stowe, Charles and Isabella Beecher, Sarah and Angelina Grimké, Sojourner Truth, Judge John Edmonds (of the New York Supreme Court), U.S. senator N. P. Talmadge, Ohio congressman Joshua Giddings, and Mary Todd Lincoln (who conducted séances in the White House). Elizabeth Cady Stanton and Susan B. Anthony, who identified an egalitarian overlap between Spiritualism and woman's rights, wrote, "The only religious sect in the world . . . that has recognized the equality of women is the Spiritualists." Even Frederick Douglass attended a séance. Perhaps the most famous reformer who was also a longtime devotee of Spiritualism was the fierce abolitionist William Lloyd Garrison. Garrison took Spiritualism seriously from its inception, sitting in 1853 with Leah Fox (the older sister who had discovered her own mediumistic abilities) and still attending séances in 1876, after Garrison's wife, Helen, had died. He claimed to commune regularly with her during these séances, faithfully sharing their messages with his children. The modern Spiritualist movement was so popular that Nathaniel Hawthorne satirized it in *The Blithedale Romance* (1852), and two of America's greatest post–Civil War writers, William Dean Howells and Henry James Jr., William's brother, made Spiritualism the central focus of their respective novels *The Undiscovered Country* (1880) and *The Bostonians* (1886). Indeed, modern Spiritualism was so influential that one scholar has argued that it not only amplified but also helped advance the democratic and egalitarian impulse of republicanism in antebellum America.[16]

NEW YORK CITY STREET LIFE AND THEATERS

Given the immense popularity of the Fox sisters, did young William learn of them during his New York City boyhood years? There is some indirect and contextual evidence suggesting that he may have developed a casual awareness through incidental contact. Throughout their eight-week stay in the summer of 1850, the Fox sisters holed up in two rooms at Allan Barnum's Hotel. Allan was a fourth or fifth cousin of the more infamous P. T. Barnum. His hotel was located in the city's financial district on lower Broadway and Maiden Lane, just four blocks from Barnum's "Great American Museum," which dominated the corner of Broadway and Ann Street. Although the Fox sisters appear not to have performed for large audiences in Barnum's theater, given the Barnum familial association, the close proximity of their establishments, and the girls' immense popularity, it seems not improbable that William could have witnessed them.[17] This possibility increases when one considers the fact that William and Henry Jr. were intimately familiar with the modern entertainment industry taking root in New York City during the 1850s, especially the theaters, concert halls, public gardens, theme parks, and museums situated along Broadway Avenue, the commercial and popular culture center of the city.[18] On Broadway they might have seen the placards and billboards advertising the Fox sisters, since Henry Sr.'s belief regarding worldly knowledge was that firsthand observation was the best way to learn. As such he encouraged his sons to explore the city, sometimes under his watchful eye but more often unchaperoned and trusted with an immense amount of freedom.[19] Henry Jr. later idealized those experiences in two sentimental autobiographical volumes called *A Small Boy and Others* (1913) and *Notes of a Son and Brother* (1914), but the factual content of the locations and events he recalled, albeit with some nostalgia, were nonetheless accurate and thus provide some insight into what they found.[20] Henry Jr. did not mention the Fox sisters by name, but he discussed in flowery detail everything else surrounding them that made those years the source of what he called "Edenic-like consciousness."[21]

The James boys visited many of New York's entertainment marvels. In addition to the many places of worship dotting the city skyline such as Trinity Church and St. Paul's Chapel (located next to the Astor Hotel, where William had been born), Henry Jr. recalled that they patronized the eating establishments Thompson's and Taylor's and shopped at the retail department store A. T. Stewart's. Many evenings they visited colorful theme parks such as Franconi's Hippodrome, where gladiatorial races were staged, and Niblo's Garden, where large fountains splashed amid exotic plants. But their favorite kind of entertainment, Henry Jr. recalled, was found in the many theaters and performance halls. Productions in New York City's theaters ranged widely, from serene opera and genteel renditions of Shakespeare to bawdy song-and-dance routines and dioramas of the deviant performed in theaters along the Bowery, the rougher, working-class part of New York. Young William and Henry Jr. witnessed the entire gamut, attending Burton's on Chambers Street, the Park in Park Row, the Old Broadway, the Palmo Opera House, the Astor at the Astor Hotel, and even Castle Garden at the tip of Manhattan.[22] As Henry Jr. remembered, because William was the eldest he was the first to be taken to the theater by their father and the first to be allowed to go on his own.

William used to attend the theater, Henry Jr. remarked, "quite regularly, on the non-dental [appointment] Saturdays, [when he] repaired to this seat of joy."[23]

Of all the venues Henry Jr. lionized, though, Barnum's "theater" stood out. Famous for his sideshows, innovative entertainment, and gaudy method of publicity, Barnum helped inaugurate early modern popular culture by inventing "a type of showmanship, appealing to public curiosity and thirst for the sensational and the novel."[24] When the James boys attended in the late 1840s and early 1850s, they witnessed a world devoted to boasting a rich and colorful cornucopia of the bizarre and non-normal sides of human life. These included the midget Tom Thumb and his wife, the Feejee mermaid (later proven a hoax); the Shaking Quakers (a group of separatists who agreed to perform their dances in costume for a fee); a dwarf who had ostensibly achieved the rank of colonel in the Union army; the 576-pound woman (Susan Barth); the minstrel-clown known as the "American Hercules" (Dan Rice); the Marinetti family, who performed stage tricks in their leopard-skin leotards; the live 300-pound crocodile "Monster of the Deep," imported from the Nile River; the outstanding gymnasts known as "The Orpheon Family"; magicians like Barney Williams; a Danish albino family displayed in seventeenth-century apparel; and numerous other fantastic phenomena.[25]

This plethora of the bizarre and non-normal sides of humanity stimulated the young boys' imagination. As Henry Jr. summarized it, "The rich appeal of Mr. Barnum, whose 'lecture room,' attached to the Great American Museum, overflowed into posters of all the theatrical bravery disavowed by its title. It was my rueful theory of those days ... that on all the holidays on which we weren't dragged to the dentist's we attended as a matter of course at Barnum's."[26] But it was the total impression of experiencing Barnum's, beginning with its dominating five-story facade, that most impressed Henry Jr. If more genteel garden theaters like Niblo's captured the civilized part of culture, then Barnum's epitomized the ideal visit for observation of the non-normal:

> The Great American Museum, the down-town scenery and aspects at large, and even up-town improvements on them, as then flourishing?—why, they must have been for the most part of the last meanness: the Barnum picture above all ignoble and awful, its blatant face or frame stuck about with innumerable flags that waved, poor vulgar-sized ensigns, over spurious relics and catchpenny monsters in effigy, to say nothing of the promise within of the still more monstrous and abnormal living—from the total impression of which things we plucked somehow the flower of the ideal.[27]

Despite Henry Jr.'s penchant for excessive imagery in his recreation of "Edenic" New York, his autobiographies captured the spirit of the city's antebellum entertainment venues and demonstrate that he and William absorbed much of the emergent modernist culture flowing from them. Since the Fox sisters played a major role in this milieu, it is just possible that as early as 1850 young William became aware of them while wandering New York's streets and patronizing its theaters, museums, and lecture halls.[28]

SPIRITUAL UNCLES

Another possible source of young William's introduction to Spiritualism was New York's Knickerbocker literati, many of whom sat with the Fox sisters to form conclusions about them and Spiritualism. They included the historian and diplomat George Bancroft, editor and diplomat John Bigelow, poet and editor William Cullen Bryant, poet and essayist George Henry Calvert, novelist James Fenimore Cooper, essayist Richard Henry Dana, editor and writer Parke Godwin, editor and political leader Horace Greeley, editor and reformer George Ripley, traveler and translator Bayard Taylor, critic and poet Henry Tuckerman, and poet and essayist Nathaniel Parker Willis. All of these thinkers knew or knew of each other, and they knew Henry James Sr. They frequented the same places, such as the offices of Greeley's *Tribune*, the reading room at the Astor library, the streets and restaurants in the Athenaeum quarter, the public theaters and performance halls, and the grounds of various utopian upstart communities, and were in no small part responsible for creating a literary sensibility in the emergent metropolis.[29] They also congregated sporadically at the James house for dinner conversation. One of the practices that made the James household so unusual was that the children not only were allowed to participate in adult conversation but were required to do so. Indeed, a good deal of the James children's education occurred at the family dinner table, where topics ranging from abolition to Zionism were debated; the more extreme and sensational the topic, the more intense the debate. Spiritualism was one such subject. As Ralph Barton Perry wrote, young William "grew up in a circle in which heresies were more gladly tolerated than orthodoxies. Men like his father and his father's friends, who were attracted to Fourierism, communism, homeopathy, women's rights, abolition, and spiritism, were not likely to have any prejudices against mediumship, clairvoyance, mesmerism, automatic writing, and crystal gazing. From his youth James contemplated such 'phenomena' without repulsion and with an open mind."[30] Participation in these conversations stimulated William's lifelong pattern of free intellectual inquiry and fostered a sense of wonder with "non-normal" matters like Spiritualism. In this way, members of New York's antebellum intelligentsia became William's spiritual uncles.

One especially relevant episode that probably reached young William's ears was a séance that some of New York's literati had with the Fox sisters in June 1850. In attendance were Bancroft, Bigelow, Bryant, Cooper, Greeley, Ripley, Tuckerman, Willis, General Lyman, Rev. Rufus Griswold, and several doctors. According to Willis, who published an account of the event with the pithy title "Post-Mortuum Soiree," their goal was first to witness and second to unravel this new and baffling phenomenon. As was the custom, everyone gathered together in one room with dim lighting and congregated around a table, joining hands together to form a circle. Leah presided as mistress of ceremonies, with Kate and Maggie as the mediums sitting at one end. The group then asked the "spirits" to give a sign of their presence. Initial raps on the table grew louder and appeared to spread to the wall, floor, ceiling, and furniture. These were followed by still louder knockings till none could deny the presence of the sounds. Then, following the usual pattern, Leah asked if the "spirits" were willing to converse with any of the gentlemen present. Eventually, after some confusion, Dr. Marcy inquired about the age of his deceased child (from which nothing satisfactory emerged). Next, Henry Tuckerman asked a series of questions in a kind of test-like, sequential manner to try to determine if the "spirit" with which he was conversing was the one of whom he was thinking. Did he live in New York? Baltimore? Boston? Was he a lawyer? A merchant? A physician? A clergyman? Tuckerman covered age, religion, major character traits, and the number of children and their ages until a familiar portrait of a deceased friend of a family member emerged. At last it seemed the "spirits" identified the Rev. Henry Channing, which Tuckerman indicated was correct. Dr. Hawks took his turn next, but without as much success, followed by Dr. Francis, who used his turn to ask if the "spirits" would converse with any of the others present. When they reached James Fenimore Cooper, they heard loud knocks (Cooper's turn was the most successful of the evening). Through a long and detailed set of yes/no-style questions he acquired enough information to declare the person to whom he was alluding and who the "spirit" had identified correctly was none other than his sister, who had died fifty years prior to that very day, having been thrown by a horse. After several others took their turn, none having achieved as much clarity as Cooper, the knocks began to emanate strongly from the walls, upon which the members investigated their origin but could find no natural explanation for the sounds. The séance then broke up and the evening came to a close.[31]

Evaluations of the séance ranged from guarded open-mindedness to hostile skepticism and from outright amusement to calls for further investigation. Bancroft and Cooper were the most willing to consider the communications. An ardent Democrat known for his ten-volume *History of the United States*, George Bancroft had lost his daughter, Louisa, a few months earlier. She had been his traveling companion and "a very good daughter, as well as an intelligent young person."[32] As with many of the participants in Spiritualism, the loss had affected him deeply, and he may have been hoping for a message from her. In fact, Bancroft had gone to several séances in which his daughter had supposedly contacted him. From some he came away believing the communications were genuine, while after others he was doubtful. With regard to the séance with the Foxes, he was unsure. On the one hand, Maggie Fox's capacity to anticipate the unspoken thoughts of the sitters impressed Bancroft. On the other hand, he had trouble believing the communications were authentic. Still, Bancroft was unable to dismiss them outright.[33] Cooper, the author of the Leatherstocking Tales, told his wife: "I am deep in the Rochester Knockings, which are making a great deal of noise, just now,"[34] but since he did not reveal his opinions about the séance or the Fox sisters, his biographers are divided as to whether Cooper believed in Spiritualism.[35]

By contrast, William Cullen Bryant, the editor of the *Evening Post* (and later memorialized as the "greatest poet of nature"), was openly critical. After the séance, he received a letter while traveling from his friend Richard Henry Dana, who had not been in attendance but knew of Bryant's participation. Keeping him abreast of the developments in New York City, Dana explained that "there is nothing going on here save Spiritual Rappings and their concomitants." In jest and mocking, he added that "one of our judges (an ordinary man) is deep in the matter—*deeper* than he ever was in the law. On this being told to another of our judges, he quietly replied: 'I should advise him to put himself into communication with Judge Marshall or some other able lawyer,'" referring to John Edmonds of the New York State Supreme Court.[36] Bryant replied that "what you tell me of the Spiritualists is remarkable, but does not surprise me. They do not perceive the ridiculous side of their beliefs, and with the greatest gravity say things which strike those who are not initiated as the drollest things imaginable." Finding some hypocrisy among those who strayed from established Protestant sects, he continued, "The most noteworthy thing is their readiness to believe—I mean the readiness of those who have been the most skeptical in regard to the Christian faith." Bryant invoked Robert Owen, the utopian community leader turned Spiritualist: "After he [Owen] became a Spiritualist he believed every alleged revelation coming from that quarter, no matter on whose authority." Offering his own explanation, Bryant concluded, "I regard all this testimony to the natural, instinctive desire of man to believe, on some evidence or other, in a life beyond the grave. If they will not believe it on the authority of the New Testament, they will snatch at anything else which satisfies this desire, however poor the substitute."[37] For Bryant, the will to believe trumped the evidence for belief. George Ripley, the social reformer and literary critic for Greeley's *Tribune*, shared Bryant's skepticism. In a critical review of a book called *Spiritual Communications*, Ripley wrote, "The book affords a fearful example of the danger of substituting the suggestions of personal fancy for the universal principles of morality, and the practical rules for the conduct of the understanding, which have been accepted in all civilized communities."[38]

In contrast to the divide between believers and skeptics, the séance left Willis more amused than anything else. Still, he was willing to suspend belief one way or the other until further séances could be arranged. In a literary interpretation, Willis noted the similarities between Spiritualism and Greek mythology. He likened the ghostly qualities of the spirits to the specter of death who shepherds their souls from this world to the next and remarked wittily that "an electric telegraph across the [river] Styx, before they get one across the Atlantic, would make death less of a separation from friends than a voyage to Europe." Similarly, noticing that the spirits opted to converse with the doctors and novelists instead of the poets and editors, Willis added that "either our trans-[S]tyx geography is wrong—or ghosts have no taste for poets—or newspaper Editors . . . have no immediate connection with Elysium." On a less cagey note, Willis expressed his amazement at how quickly and widely Spiritualism had spread. Convinced the phenomenon could not be ignored, he concluded that "the numerous places in which these Knockings have been heard . . . show that the ghosts have got the trick of it, and the 'demonstration' altogether . . . is of sufficient extent and respectability to warrant grave attention."[39] In other words, Willis implied that a third approach was needed—one that allowed for neither easy credulity nor dismissal but open-minded empirical investigation, a method of inquiry that anticipated James's tertium quid—suggesting that Willis might have been one of young William's more influential spiritual uncles.

Of all attitudes to emerge from the "Post-Mortuum Soiree," Horace Greeley's best exemplified this third way approach. Greeley agreed with Willis that Elysium should be the ambition of Spiritualism but also thought the evidence required a more nuanced analysis. Toward that end, he wrote at length about his experiences with Spiritualism, focusing on his sittings with the Fox sisters. Initially, Greeley deemed the "knockings" inexplicable. He left the June 1850 séance believing there was nothing further to be learned, but his wife was eager for a second sitting. In the off chance that they were genuine, she wanted to communicate with their recently deceased son, "Pickie." Horace reluctantly agreed, but after two or three sittings something must have changed, for the Greeleys invited the Foxes to stay with them for a week to hold many more séances in private (only Kate Fox agreed to come). Greeley reported favorably on most of the sittings, declaring, "I received some response to my questions of a very remarkable character, evincing knowledge of occurrences of which no one, not [even] an inmate of our family in former years, could well have been cognizant." This confirmed some of his findings from a few weeks earlier during a séance in Boston with Mrs. Freeman, a magnetic healer, who had identified accurately his two dead brothers and a sister who had died before he was born.[40]

Bayard Taylor, the noted travel writer who published in Greeley's *Tribune*, attended some of the sittings with Kate Fox at the Greeleys' home in Turtle Bay. He initially believed that he had some success at communicating with Greeley's son: "Greeley's boy has twice sent a message to me from the spirit-world,—at least a request to speak to me. He . . . rapped out on the floor a number of lines of poetry, which are said to be quite good." Despite the boy's known poetry skills, Taylor could not bring himself to believe in a supernatural explanation, declaring, "I will not believe that intelligent souls pass their future lives in such trifling employment."[41] Episodes like these prompted Greeley to reflect on the various explanations for the phenomena. On the issue of fraud, or what he called "trick" and "jugglery," Greeley admitted that cheating undoubtedly occurred, leaving him with "a disrelish for the whole business." But he found the fraud hypothesis wanting because there had been too many times when it could not account for what he had witnessed in séances. This, too, was another remarkable anticipation of James's third way approach. Another explanation bandied about at the time was that of demonic origin—that evil demons were playing tricks on naive and sinful Americans dabbling in the occult. But Greeley rejected that explanation as well, claiming that no devil could be responsible for some of the events he had witnessed.[42]

As Greeley continued to investigate Spiritualism, he developed a distaste for séances. "To sit for two dreary, mortal hours in a darkened room, in a mixed company, waiting for some one's disembodied grandfather or aunt to tip a table or rap on a door, is dull music at best, but to sit *in vain* is disgusting," he recorded. Nonetheless, his investigation led him to a "few general deductions" about "spirit-rapping." First, it was better to live right in this life than to spend one's time "poking and peering into the life beyond the grave." Second, mediums who claimed to be in contact with famous poets were most certainly frauds, for the poetry they reproduced was awful. Third, because the communications in séances, as a rule, were "vague, unreal, shadowy, [and] trivial," it was unlikely that they were messages from departed friends since they possessed none of the qualities in the afterlife that they had while living. Fourth, the mediums' abilities to predict the future should be taken lightly because their knowledge of current affairs was strikingly bad and manifested useless knowledge. Fifth, Spiritualism had not morally improved the women and men whom he had met at séances. Sixth, the evidence for genuine spirit-communication remained very inconsistent. Finally, for all their contact with the other world, which Greeley thought would be a moral place, Spiritualists appeared to be no more tolerant or ethical than non-Spiritualists.[43] Still, it seems Greeley sympathized with the supernatural hypothesis, writing, "Even though the so-called 'spiritual manifestations' of our day should all be proved brainsick phantasies or blasphemous juggles, it will nevertheless be deemed possible ... that some further fresher evidence of the verity and individuality of our friend's existence in the Spirit World should yet be vouchsafed to Man. Faith needs assurance. . . . I am sure they [the raps] cannot be accounted for by merely human agency, [however much they might] confound and mortify their priestly enemies."[44] Alas, the conflicting nature of the evidence has led Greeley's biographers to reach opposite conclusions as to whether he believed in Spiritualism.[45]

So what might have young William assimilated from séances and investigations of them? Being a perspicacious lad, it is likely he would have made several insightful observations. First, the rappings of the kind the Fox sisters produced *might* be proof for existence of what Spiritualists called the "other world" or a world beyond the material one. In the James family household in which Henry Sr.'s preoccupation with the survival of the soul dominated discussion, this possibility would have been familiar and of no small concern. Second, unlike the tenets of liberal Protestantism, which relied on the acceptance of Jesus Christ as one's Lord and Savior, *belief* in Spiritualism was not solely based on faith alone but on empirical investigation as well. Third, the evidence for veracity of the "Rochester Knockings" was shaky at best. To reach a *valid* belief, there was a strong need to establish more and harder evidence, or "facts," as James would later call them. Fourth, despite the need for facts, there remained a personal and thus subjective element to how each individual evaluated the evidence. In particular, persons with recently deceased family members seemed more apt to believe that the communications emanated from their surviving souls in the beyond. Because their grief was so great, they almost seemed to *will* that belief into existence and thus make the communications appear veridical. As such, they made room for the will in empiricism. Fifth, because Spiritualism was highly controversial and its claims hotly debated, an open mind was necessary for avoiding dogmatism, arrogance, and ignorance. Finally, Spiritualism drew on components from religion, philosophy, psychology, medicine, and ethics. Taken together, these observations amounted to a conclusion that neither dismissed nor accepted the phenomenon but instead called for further investigation. This attitude, remarkably similar to Greeley's, was one James wielded in his psychical research from the 1880s onward. As such, it is possible that the conversations young William likely had with Knickerbocker intellectuals—his "spiritual uncles"—may have been one wellspring of his tertium quid method of inquiry.

SPIRITUAL FATHERS

Henry James Sr.

As Henry Sr. sat at the head of his dinner table and listened to these Knickerbocker literati weigh in on Spiritualism, he could not have been pleased. Contrary to what one might conclude from Henry Sr.'s championing of unorthodox causes, his iconoclasm did not automatically translate into sympathy for Spiritualism. In fact, quite the reverse occurred. Throughout the summer and fall of 1850, Greeley had been reporting on the Fox sisters in the *New York Tribune*.[46] Henry Sr., who published some of his essays in the *Tribune*, read those stories as well as Greeley's account of his personal sittings with Kate published in December. They all outraged Henry Sr., especially after Greeley announced that he had had a "conversation with a dead friend (through the medium of a clairvoyant), who disclosed that the late Mr. [Edgar Allan] Poe was presently residing in the 'third society, second sphere.'"[47] It was common for mediums to channel famous personalities, and Poe, having just passed away in 1849, was in vogue. Henry Sr. thought this was both a ludicrous and a dangerous claim because Greeley was not only muttering gibberish but also dabbling in the occult. As such, he challenged Greeley by firing off several letters of criticism to the *Tribune*.[48] Their content read like a response that he might have given at the dinner table, where along with young William his guests discussed their experiences with the Fox sisters:

> Hands off, gentlemen! You may be very proper persons, but I insist upon seeing my company. You have uttered a great many elevated sentiments, no doubt; but sentiment is cheap on this side of the Jordan [Christendom], where we chiefly value deeds. Now if you will only *do* something for us . . . we shall welcome you with all our hearts. . . . Give us an invention like the electrical telegraph, or the spinning Jenny. Give us a solution to some of the great questions of the day—the questions of finance, of an increased agricultural production, of the abolition of poverty and crime. Give us an improved medication, say a cure for smallpox, scarlet fever, gout, or even a tooth-ache.[49]

As Henry Sr. made plain, Spiritualism must be useful to be valuable. In case Greeley and the others failed to heed him, he warned them of the dangers to their mortality: "We have all heard of tender and devout persons who having through some foolish asceticism . . . come under the influence of this attenuated despotism, have at last got back to their own firesides, so spent with suffering, so lacerated to the very core, as to be fit . . . only for the soothing shelter of the grave."[50]

Henry Sr.'s letters attacking Greeley and like-minded defenders of Spiritualism raised two main objections. First, Spiritualism at a minimum was banal. While Henry Sr. admitted freely that spirits from the other world existed and operated in this one, trying to get in touch with them through séances was disgraceful since all the messages had proved useless. For a practical man like Greeley to succumb to a *spirit*ualism that served no useful function was embarrassing. Second, Spiritualism was both medically and morally dangerous. The "spirits," he wrote, "were likely to prove malignant." What frightened Henry Sr. so much was that the "spirits" seemed able to access human memory—to read it "like a book," as he put it. Once inside the human mind, "spirits" induced large quantities of guilt, especially in those minds that were weak and temperamental. Even more than that, however, Henry Sr. believed firmly that the "ghosts" of Spiritualism were wicked and intent on destroying the minds of those who conjured them. Indeed, he was convinced that those who dabbled in Spiritualism were quite likely to go mad. Given Henry Sr.'s penchant to share his views with his sons, it is probable young William knew of his father's letters to the editor of the *Tribune* in 1850.[51]

In 1852, two years after the Fox sisters left New York, Henry Sr. published a scathing essay condemning Spiritualism, written in response to Willis's "Post-Mortuum Soiree." Building on his objections to Greeley, Henry Sr. argued that Spiritualism was simultaneously theologically wrongheaded and morally if not mortally dangerous. The first objection stemmed from Henry Sr.'s rejection of professionalized religion, which he called "the devil's masterpiece for ensnarling silly, selfish men." The ritualism of organized religion in particular was to blame, especially regarding Catholicism but also evangelical orthodoxy and liberal Protestantism. Excessive devotion, formalized rituals, and public piety were each spiritually worthless, he argued. To this list he added the séance of Spiritualism. Unlike his father's family, Henry Sr.'s had no family pew, belonged to no church, practiced no formal religion, and received no visits from clergymen. Instead, Henry Sr. took it upon himself to initiate his children in what he called the "interior truths of the Scripture" and in so doing challenged the orthodox conception of God, calling him a "bogey." "I . . . raise my gleeful fist, I lift my scornful foot, I invoke the self-respect of my children, [and] I arouse their generous indignation," he shouted at the world.[52] Indeed, as Henry Jr. later recalled, the children got "plenty" of religious instruction in their father's theology. It is likely such initiation would have included Henry Sr.'s views about Spiritualism, which suggests that Spiritualism popped up again in William's life in 1852.[53]

Henry Sr.'s interpretation of the scriptures was grounded in his deeply held theological principles that he had acquired from Swedenborg. Asserting that the Spiritualists misunderstood the true nature of Christianity, Henry Sr. maintained that Spiritualism was a dangerous prophecy. It shared in common with orthodoxy a fundamental interpretation of the Bible, especially the Old Testament, that the spiritual world was a *place* positioned in time and space "remote from the natural one." For Spiritualism and orthodoxy alike, "spirit" or "soul" was envisioned as a *thing*, however noncorporeal, that *existed* in the other world. According to Henry Sr., this view revealed a fundamental misunderstanding of Christian theology, namely, it relied on a literal interpretation of the Old Testament that posited God as an actual *entity* and heaven as a *locality*. But Henry Sr. argued (as did Swedenborg, transcendentalists, and pantheists alike) that spirituality existed *outside* of time and space: "Intellect and affection are purely subjective existences; they are not *things* visible to the senses; they are forms of life." In other words, for Henry Sr., the Bible had to be read only as an allegory. Certainly any religious life founded on it, including all types of private experiences, contributed to this subjective form. Thus,

HENRY JAMES SR. (1812–1882), ca. 1855. Contrary to the view presented in most James family histories, Henry Sr. actually opposed Spiritualism. Dubbing it "spiritual dilettantism," he found Spiritualism to be morally bankrupt, medically dangerous, and religiously vacuous. *William James Papers, MS Am 1092.9 (4597.2), by permission of the Houghton Library, Harvard University.*

a "flimsy and gossamer quality" gimmick like a séance was so theologically miscued because it took its "hobgoblin demonstration" as literal proof in an afterlife that supposedly existed in some place, called the "other world." Like the old theology of orthodox Protestantism before it, Spiritualism was thus superstitious. As such, it had to be rejected like so many "miracles" before it. If Spiritualism was "fraudulent" for Henry Sr., it was in this sense, not in an evidentiary one.[54]

To comprehend the full scope and power of Henry Sr.'s stringent objections to Spiritualism, it is instructive to explore his theology in more detail. The bulk of Henry Sr.'s writings were devoted to the defense of religious doctrine whose central theme was "creation," meaning the "divine natural humanity" or the "immanence of God in the unity of mankind."[55] His works were abstruse and argumentative and challenged Christian orthodoxy, especially the Presbyterian faith. As one biographer noted, "[Henry] James spoke the language of metaphysical theology in a day when there were few who uttered or comprehended it." In orthodox theology, the concern had been "given the creation, find the Creator," as one astute commentator put it, but for Henry Sr. it was "given the Creator, find the creation."[56] In Henry Sr.'s theology, his main goal was to explicate the "true relation ... between mankind and its creator."[57] Thus, Henry Sr.'s pursuit of salvation and immortality began with finding the true nature of "man."[58]

Toward this end Henry Sr. developed his own idiosyncratic blend of Swedenborgian and orthodox theological principles, including the doctrines of correspondence, creation, spirituality, immortality, revelation, and regeneration. Borrowing directly from Swedenborg, Henry Sr. first invoked the doctrine of correspondence. It posited the view that for everything that exists in the natural world, there corresponds an equal and more perfect part in the spiritual one. For Henry Sr., "man" dwelled in the natural world, having been provided with subjective existence and inalienable self-consciousness by the creator. Unlike in traditional Christianity, which maintained "man" was composed morally, his goal was to realize himself spiritually, meaning to discover God's nature within him. According to Henry Sr., this act could not be intuited; it had to be revealed. For Swedenborgians, revelation was the process whereby "light" from the spiritual world shed itself upon the natural one. Revelation became *possible* given the doctrine of correspondence, and it was *knowable* by man's reason. Reason alone, Henry Sr. argued, was not enough for salvation, but it was possible to achieve "light"—to be en*light*ened—by revelation. For Henry Sr., this process had taken many historical forms and was still ongoing; revelation was active. While there had been many kinds of revelation, the greatest form was Christianity. According to one James scholar, Henry Sr. defined this as "the doctrine of the eternal and perfect union of God and man in the person of Jesus Christ."[59]

In Henry Sr.'s theology, then, regeneration amounted to a kind of ladder by which man climbed up, arduously but steadily, from the natural to the spiritual world. The contrivance Henry Sr. invoked for the climb he called the "conscience." Unlike contemporary psychology, which located the faculty of reason in the deliberative and intelligent consciousness, Henry Sr. argued that conscience amounted to an instinct. For Victorians like Henry Sr., the mind was a composite of multiple parts located at the higher and lower levels. He called them "degrees," and man had three of them: in ascending order, the senses or instincts (where passions rule), morality or reason (where the intellect rules and perceptions of ideas occur), and spontaneous life or the soul (where the true individual emerges in the pursuit of spirituality). In this sense, the conscience was not an expression of revelation of the senses or reason but an "instinct of the soul." Self-denial, or learning to unlove ourselves before we begin to love others, triggered the process of regeneration. As the process evolved, the instinct and reason would begin to serve the soul. Freedom, or true spiritual life as Henry Sr. defined it, transpired when the process was complete.[60]

Compared with traditional theology, the problem of evil for Henry Sr. did not pose a huge dilemma. He admitted that evil existed but only in man's relation to God, not in the natural world. For Henry Sr., sin was limited to this relationship, not to man's behavior. This made the nature of moral acts a very different type of thing from what orthodox theology posited. In Henry Sr.'s view, moral actions were exclusively confined to the relationship between man and God in his pursuit of spirituality. Evil erupted as a challenge to this process, the only remedy for which was belief. We had to believe, he argued, "[in] an infinite Goodness within us which is striving to woo us into harmony with its own deathless perfection," or, in other words, immortality. Only "by means of regeneration," he concluded, "[do] we realize immortality."[61]

When examined through his theology, Henry Sr.'s objections to Spiritualism crystallize. To begin with, Spiritualism bypassed man's ascent of the regenerative ladder. In place of a challenging process to true spirituality or "freedom," Spiritualism offered a too-easy path. It circumvented revelation with a quick and direct method—the séance—that did not require any effort on the sitter's behalf. It also substituted the rappings from the other world for man's awareness of the natural world, and it avoided entirely the problem of evil. In short, Spiritualism short-circuited man's moral responsibility for his own salvation. Thus, Henry Sr. concluded Spiritualism may have appeared to share a kind of correspondence with his Swedenborgianism, but in fact it was peddling a false notion of redemption. As Henry Sr. put it most forcefully, "*Post-mortem* consciousness is not immortality."[62] What a poor and perverted substitute Spiritualism made for a genuine life of spirit. How Henry Sr. must have writhed, then, when he read Willis's "Post-Mortuum Soiree"!

Henry Sr.'s second main objection to Spiritualism was that its practices were morally dangerous. He argued that Spiritualism corrupted morality by attacking the higher faculties of the mind. Victorians conceived the human mind in terms of composite faculties, divided into higher and lower categories, each one consisting of a certain function necessary for human health, especially for salvation, and each one associated with a particular moral quality. The higher faculties—the intellect, understanding, will, and imagination—were considered especially crucial since they made up the seat of ultimate goodness. A human whose higher faculties suffered was considered in danger of losing his or her moral bearing, something of grave consequence to Victorians, since without a working moral compass one's soul could be lost forever.[63] But despite his embrace of fringe theology like Swedenborgianism, even a maverick thinker like Henry Sr. failed to break away from certain Victorian beliefs such as the primacy of the moral self. Indeed, Henry Sr.'s convictions acquired the language of condemnation characteristic of mid-nineteenth-century moral reformism in which Spiritualists and their sympathizers were judged alike. On the other hand, Victorian morality was so tinged with sentimental religiosity that it tended to produce the frame of mind that was receptive to such views like Swedenborgianism, not to mention Spiritualism. The problem that Victorians like Henry Sr. faced was how to sort out mere sentimentality from genuine theological insight. Answers to this challenge turned on various nineteenth-century conceptions of the mind. Like other Victorian theorists, Henry Sr. maintained that the intellect, the understanding, and the affections were purely subjective forms. The problem with Spiritualism was that it appealed to humankind's "timorous and servile senses." It reduced humans to "below the level of the brute," a state of existence eschewed by Victorians who used animal metaphors frequently to demonstrate the morally debased quality of a person's mind. Henry Sr. was no exception in this regard. "'Spirits,' rather as so many vermin," he wrote, "[make] my will servile to a foreign inspiration." In other words, Spiritualism appealed to the base sides of the soul rather than to its higher faculties; it had the opposite of its intended effect. How, Henry Sr. implored, could Spiritualism be moral? Spiritualists did not edify, they tore down; rappers did not uplift, they degraded.[64]

Building on this corruption argument, Henry Sr. maintained that the "spirits" of Spiritualism controlled memory and corroded the imagination. He worried especially that memory—another higher faculty—was especially vulnerable to spirits since they infected our natural ability to recall events correctly. Following Swedenborg's view that ghosts invaded the memory of an individual and reaped havoc with his character, Henry Sr. noted that they read the memory of a person "like a book." Relating the rise of Spiritualism to the religious revivals, he described Spiritualism much the way he did evangelicalism—as a "fierce cannibalism." To these venomous words, Henry Sr. added that "all those phenomena of a morbid conscience which we see in 'revivals' . . . grow out of their infernal tampering of ghosts with one's memory." Like the transcendentalists, Henry Sr. believed the imagination was the highest and most exalted mental faculty because it was the seat of creativity. Indeed, creativity was seen as a necessary vehicle for linking man's soul with God. If the imagination was to deteriorate, all hope at transcendence was lost—"losing our wits," as Henry Sr. expressed it. Séances, he argued, caused endless torment to the soul where one's wits became "irreparably shattered."[65]

Expanding the argument still further, Henry Sr. thought Spiritualism tried to "affix guilt to the soul."[66] Because Spiritualism trafficked in ghosts, it necessarily brought the world of the supernatural closer to a person's daily life. In Henry Sr.'s personal experience, that came in the form of frequent nightmares after his "vastation." In 1844, just after his evening meal, Henry Sr. penned these now famous lines of his own ghostly encounter:

> I remained sitting at the table after the family had dispersed, idly gazing at the embers in the grate, thinking of nothing, and feeling only the exhilaration incident to a good digestion, when suddenly—in a lightning-flash as it were—"fear came upon me, and trembling, which made all my bones shake." To all appearance it was a perfectly insane and abject terror, without ostensible cause, and only accounted for, to my perplexed imagination, by *some damned shape* squatting invisible to me within the precincts of the room, and raying out from his fetid personality influences fatal to life. The thing had not lasted ten seconds before I felt myself a wreck. . . . I felt the greatest desire to run incontinently to the foot of the stairs and shout for help to my wife . . . but by immense effort I . . . determined not to budge from my chair till I had recovered my lost self-possession. This purpose I held to for a good long hour, as I reckoned time, beat upon meanwhile by an ever-growing tempest of doubt, anxiety, and despair, with absolutely no relief from any truth I had ever encountered. . . . I resolved to abandon the vain struggle, and communicate without more ado what seemed my sudden burden of inmost, implacable unrest to my wife. (emphasis added)[67]

A vain struggle like Henry Sr.'s with an unseen but overwhelming perceived "shape" would have left most God-fearing Christians of the mid-nineteenth century in a "state of abject terror" as it did Henry Sr., but it would also have left them wanting to know more. Swedenborgianism offered an answer: Henry Sr. had had a "vastation" or mystical experience. This experience was tantamount to Henry Sr.'s own religious awakening, and it led him to studying and writing about Swedenborg.

In light of Henry's later encounters with Spiritualism, however, what looms large in this account is the *shape itself*. In fact, the shape continued to haunt him. "After my religious life dawned," Henry Sr. later wrote, "my day was turned into hideous and unrelieved night by tacit ghostly visitations." Since Henry Sr. believed in the existence of ghosts, the possibility that they might be visiting him forced him to admit the reality of Spiritualism. But since the "ghosts" of his vastation experience harmed him psychologically, he was also forced to ponder their intentions, and for Henry Sr. the issue was not whether ghosts existed but whether they were benign or malicious. Since Henry Sr.'s "vastation" indicated the latter, he extrapolated that the "ghosts" of Spiritualism must also be dangerous. Spiritualist deism, then, amounted to nothing less than "spiritual dilettantism."[68]

Henry Sr.'s third major objection to Spiritualism, then, was that its moral bankruptcy could lead to insanity. He knew from his personal experiences with close acquaintances that it could even be fatal. He had witnessed its pernicious effects on the family doctor, Joseph T. Curtis, whom he discovered had been practicing Spiritualism when the Jameses lived in New York City. Curtis was a successful physician who had a thriving practice and had compiled a renowned manual for homeopathic procedures. He treated Henry Sr.'s rheumatism and bilious diarrhea as well as the children's bouts with influenza and other maladies. But Curtis also dabbled in Spiritualism, and he possessed two fundamental and related flaws: he had a tendency to go blind from time to time, and he suffered immensely from voices in his head, which he claimed came from the spirit world. Henry Sr. had witnessed Curtis's mental demise during the 1850s. Although Curtis was at first able to maintain his practice and frequent visits to the James house, he was committed twice to an asylum for treatment; the voices in his head had become demonic. Curtis said the voices were those of the "great society of illuminati" from the afterlife, which he said guided humanity, and that he had been picked by this society to be the savior of his age. As the affliction increased, he informed Henry Sr. that the voices had instructed him to kill his own children! Curtis's tale of a great society of illuminati that chose a leader for each era horrified Henry Sr., not only because he had endangered his own children by placing them under Curtis's care but also because it distorted the higher faculties of the human mind like the imagination. When Henry Sr. wrote that "supernatural communications... prove injurious to the understanding," he was probably thinking of Curtis.[69] In 1857, after a twenty-four-hour bout with the voices, Curtis succumbed, shooting himself fatally in his heart with a pistol. How horrified yet vindicated Henry Sr. must have felt when he heard the news. While Henry Sr. admitted that the voices Curtis heard were "dangerous, demonic, and real," he also made the startling claim that Curtis had been "no more insane than I am at this moment," suggesting the difference between them was that until Curtis began trafficking in spirits, he had been fine.[70]

For Henry Sr., then, the popularity of Spiritualism went beyond mere parlor jugglery; it was a matter of life and death, an evil imposition on humanity. That one of his friends, Temple Chapman, also suffered from "demonical possession" in which evil appeared to reign "supreme & resistless in the Universe" only confirmed Henry Sr.'s belief in the very real dangers of Spiritualism.[71] For Henry Sr., this type of mental demise was a degradation of the worst kind. How could Spiritualism not be blamed? While it is probable that Curtis was suffering from a *psychological* disease like schizophrenia rather than demonical possession, for Henry Sr. the connection between the power of "spirits" in a séance and the spiritual degradation of Curtis's soul was indisputable. Expressing his vitriol, he summarized his objection this way: "I vehemently discredit the prospect of any positive good [coming out of Spiritualism]." In short, Henry Sr. believed that Spiritualism's "spirits" were really demonic ghosts. Their purpose was to control the mind, invade the memory, attack the imagination, and induce guilt. To engage with ghosts regularly as Spiritualists did reduced people to the "gossip of the other world... [that would] gradually inflame our ascetic ambition" and drag men down into moral degradation and even kill them.[72]

By the mid-1850s, then, Henry Sr. concluded that nothing good came from Spiritualism. As such, when one biographer determined that "nothing could have been more proper" for William James later in life than to hold a séance in his library under the portrait of Henry Sr., he could not have been more mistaken.[73] Clearly such an act would have horrified William's father. However, given Henry Jr.'s statement that the boys were regularly schooled in their father's theology, it seems highly likely that while young William was informed of his father's negative conclusions about Spiritualism, he did not accept them. In fact, he rejected them in favor of a far more sympathetic understanding. Evidence for this comes from William's association with James John Garth Wilkinson, a kind of second father to young William during his boyhood years in England. That is, if Henry Sr. believed Spiritualism was a false theology that could lead to insanity, Wilkinson, his intimate confidant and fellow Swedenborgian, held the opposite view. During the mid-1850s, Wilkinson believed Spiritualism provided evidence for revelations and possessed healing agents for the mentally ill, an approach to pathology William later adopted. As Ralph Barton Perry put it, "As one who approached psychology from the side of medicine[,] he gave attention to the pathology of mind."[74]

James John Garth Wilkinson

James John Garth Wilkinson, best known for his edition of William Blake's *Songs of Innocence and of Experience* (1839), was trained in orthodox medicine. In 1834, he was elected to the Royal College of Surgeons of England and became a licentiate of the London Apothecaries Society, but by the 1840s Wilkinson began to chafe at some of the practices of allopathic medicine. Like a number of physicians, Wilkinson turned to homeopathy because he found it less invasive than vaccinations and more efficacious than heavy drugging and extreme bloodletting. Inveighing against the medical establishment, he wrote homeopathic works such as *The Human Body and Its Connection with Man* (1851) and *Divine Revelation and Its Works and Sciences* (1876). Wilkinson believed that homeopathy respected the patient's rights that orthodox physicians overlooked. Indeed, for him, homeopathy limned democracy: all patients had an equal right to humane treatment.[75] By the 1850s he had committed himself to homeopathy, and in the 1860s he denounced the Contagious Diseases Prevention Acts, which he called "an outrage on womanhood at the instance of the medical profession." During the 1870s Wilkinson condemned the compulsory vaccination of children, claiming before the House of Commons Committee on Vaccination that it was nothing less than "blood assassination and the homicidal insanity of a whole profession." He even opposed licensed medicine, arguing that it advanced the profession but not the well-being of the patient. He also opposed vivisection.[76]

But Garth had the temperament of a mystic. According to family lore, the idea of death had preoccupied Garth from early childhood. Sensing that trait, George Blakiston Robinson, Garth's maternal uncle, introduced Garth to Swedenborg's writings. In the 1830s, Wilkinson converted to Swedenborgianism and began a lifelong project of translating the mystic's copious and abstract treatises (Garth had taught himself both Icelandic and Swedish).[77] The work was part of a larger effort as Wilkinson's work in homeopathy,

Swedenborgianism, and Spiritualism amounted to an epistemological interest with the fundamental nature of matter, especially as it developed in the nineteenth-century debates between materialism and idealism. Wilkinson saw matter as simultaneously physical and spiritual and considered dangerous the attempts by materialists to divorce the two. As such, Swedenborg's doctrine of correspondence helped maintain their indivisibility by conceptually blurring the boundaries between the two and then claiming their relationship was too complex for human comprehension. This was an argument, in effect, for the existence of the spirit world.[78]

Wilkinson explored Spiritualism in this vein in a detailed correspondence with Henry James Sr. from 1844 through 1858, the heyday of early Spiritualism.[79] The letters reveal a steady evolution in Wilkinson's thought regarding the supernatural. In one instance he reviewed a book about ghosts, informing Henry Sr. that "certain kinds of Supernaturalism . . . [are] setting in here [England]" and that the book gave "an account of the leading examples of Supernatural Appearance in old & modern times."[80] At bottom, Wilkinson, like so many scientifically minded Victorians suffering a crisis of faith in the mid-nineteenth century, was searching for an evidential basis for religious belief.[81] Toward that end, he focused his efforts on finding a relationship between homeopathy, Swedenborg's notion of correspondence, mesmerism, hypnotism, and various altered states of sleep such as somnambulism. Wilkinson thought that if mesmerism, hypnotism, and "sleep" were three logical places to look for the crystallization of men's souls, then Spiritualism represented a fourth one. Since all these practices required the patient-practitioner to enter into an altered mental state, understanding each could help reveal the nature of the soul. But to make the connection between the two worlds, Wilkinson needed to establish the reality of "ghosts" or spirits. He chastised scientists of the "inductive school" for scoffing at this possibility, because he believed that "of all things in the world . . . [ghosts were] a thing proved equally with any fact in existence by all the laws of human evidence; & yet dismissed with one supercilious grimace & one shrug by the pretended men of facts."[82] To verify his adamant belief in ghosts, Wilkinson needed evidence and a concrete method to show *how* there could be a corresponding spirit in the afterlife. To Wilkinson both seemed possible prima facie, arguing that since "mesmeric effects pass from person to person through space," it ought to be possible for forms to correspond with those in the "plastic spiritual world."[83] Toward that end, Wilkinson imagined a clever thought-experiment in which mesmeric transference could be captured on a daguerreotype. The details of the experiment he would leave to others, but he was committed

JAMES JOHN GARTH WILKINSON (1812–1899), undated. In contrast to his close friend Henry James Sr., Wilkinson supported Spiritualism. He found in it evidence for revelations and a potential healing agent for the mentally ill, inventing the term "spirit cure." *Henry James Papers, MS Am 1094 (2245) f.6a.3, by permission of the Houghton Library, Harvard University.*

to it, confessing to Henry Sr. that "I decidedly cherish the possibility of the thing somehow."[84]

Wilkinson's interest in Spiritualism crystallized in conjunction with Henry Sr.'s and the New York Knickerbocker literati's discussions of the Fox sisters in the summer of 1850. Reading of the events that had "sounded so far & wide through the [British] Newspapers," he requested that Henry Sr. send him "Mysterious Knockings," an account of the events at Hydesville, admitting, "You know I have a certain interest in quaint things."[85] Despite its lofty appeals to enlightened science, the pamphlet disappointed him because of its pretentious comparison to works by famous scientists like Galileo and William Harvey and because of its excessive length in which very little was actually established.[86] Wilkinson remained interested in what Spiritualism could teach him, but he would not accept speculation and assumption in place of sound science and medical experiment. To Henry Sr. he argued that the "spiritual world, & its forces are very differently useful for different people," but too many people generalized too liberally on too few instances of supernatural experiences for Wilkinson's liking. For the instances where spiritual healing occurred, he wrote, "These are [the] rare exceptions, medical & supernatural . . . and though they require [to be] tenderly cared & legislated for, yet it will not do to make their exigencies the rule [for] the treatment of the existing mankind."[87] One particular element of the pamphlet, however, intrigued him. Wilkinson thought the spiritual telegraph method, which substituted the use of the alphabet in place of yes/no knocks, was quite clever since it made the "ghosts" of Spiritualism more intelligible, whereas before "when a ghost came, he was as good as dumb." Now, his "knocks are as good as movements of the telegraph needles."[88] In the spiritual telegraph, then, Wilkinson detected the possibility of proving the reality of spirits.

By 1854, Spiritualism was sweeping England. As Garth explained to Henry Sr.,

> Nothing is talked of here but table movings & spirit rappings. There is, so far as I know, no class of persons of importance who are not penetrated with this odd-looking movement. . . . I really could not have credited that so vast a state of mind could have come over a nation, as this which has come to England by this simple means. All classes are opened now about spiritual intercourse; and we are beginning to learn that the other world is human in its good, bad, & indifferent [ways].[89]

The following year he echoed his increasing enthusiasm for Spiritualism, writing, "The Spiritual Manifestation Movement is shaking all minds here. I know it is the Earthquake of this Age."[90] Those tremors did not fail to reach Wilkinson. Indeed, although he maintained that he had not been "near the spirits," he was "quite convinced, & would avow it publicly that the present movement is Providential in its best parts."[91]

It is possible that young William James experienced some of those tremors during the winter of 1855–56 in London, where Henry Sr. had moved the family to find suitable education for his children and to continue his conversations about Spiritualism with Wilkinson. After a brief stint in Berkeley Square, which the James boys dubbed "Thackeray's London" due to the family's socializing with William Makepeace Thackeray, Thomas Carlyle, and other English literati, Henry Sr. moved the family to St. John's Wood, a short distance from Regent's Park,, where the James children took countless walks and explored the Zoological Gardens. Most important, they lived close to the Wilkinsons, whom Henry Sr. noted "are as full of kindness and hospitality as they can be." Henry Jr. recalled this period as one of "sublime synthesis."[92]

Bordering Marylebone, St. John's Wood was a questionable area in the minds of the moneyed class but a focal point for free thought and fertile ground for an informal colony for bohemian types and liberal-minded reformers during the nineteenth century. Some residents also participated in Spiritualist circles.[93] One of these was a loose group of middle-class professionals including Dr. Ashburner (a Royal Physician and advocate of mesmerism), Mrs. Sophia De Morgan (wife of Augustus De Morgan, a logician and professor of mathematics at University College in London), Mrs. Newton Crosland (the writer known as Camilla Toulmin), and Garth's brother, William Wilkinson, and his wife. The circle also included Florence Theobald (wife of Dr. Robert Theobald, a member of the Royal College of Surgeons), who was a close acquaintance of the Wilkinsons' and whom Garth had introduced to Spiritualism, as well as her friends William and Mary Howitt. The Howitts were neighbors of the Theobalds, who were neighbors of the Wilkinsons. Given the degree of social intimacy of this group, it was only a question of time before they would discover their own mediumistic abilities. Florence became one of the first, developing into an accomplished medium, being especially adept at automatic writing. Some of the others, such as Mrs. William Wilkinson, followed. They all attended séances at the Theobalds' home on a regular basis. The group produced a small body of Spiritualist literature reflecting Swedenborg's notion of "correspondence."[94]

Spiritualist circles like the one at St. John's Wood brought immense cultural and philosophical change to the theological landscape of mid-nineteenth-century liberal Protestantism. Garth recognized this almost immediately. Like most converts to Spiritualism, he and his group found in Spiritualism proof of the scriptures. To Henry Sr. he argued that séances provided evidence for the prophecies made in Revelation and maintained that the "gassy" philosophers, atheists, and materialists all failed to appreciate this connection. They had also failed to grasp Swedenborg's principle of "Influx," as had both the New Church and orthodox ministers. As if lecturing at a revival meeting, Garth thundered, "Revelation and Influx . . . [are] taking place now; & of course, as best as it can: just as the Bible took place." The theological proof for Spiritualism came in the "knocking at the door [which] is the beginning of intercourse between adults; & our own bible tells us, that the Lord stands at the door, & 'Knocks.' This means [spirit-communication] is therefore verified both spiritually & socially."[95] Garth pursued this literalist interpretation in a volume of 110 divinely inspired poems called *Improvisations from the Spirit*. His purpose was to illustrate the power of spirit through God's mediation. The central motif was a dream or trance state in which unusual events happened or insights occurred to the narrator, such as visiting fairies and wizards as well as the discovery of patience, peace, and solitude. He wrote of body parts like the hand, eye, and ear; of concepts like newness, uncertainty, and life; and especially of individuals who had influenced him in some meaningful way, including, Immanuel Kant, Edgar Allan Poe, and Carlyle. The poems that stand out in relation to spiritual healing are "Hahnemann," "Mesmer," "Healing," "Madness," and "Spirit." In these Garth reasserted his belief that Spiritualism affirmed his Christian faith.[96]

With the James family en route to London, he declared to Henry Sr. that "all Metaphysic & Schematology are the soughing of distant winds to me, in comparison with the tremendous forces which this world—Old Realism, now being manufactured into great guns, is exerting & will exert. My life lives in it & receives a New Mission of Vigour from it. I hope in the Lord's name to be one of its Soldiers yet." He was so convinced that he decided to publicize his views. To Henry Sr. he continued, "I have . . . in one of the daily papers, recorded at length my experiences of the spirits," adding that he was done with "General Propositions" (meaning he was finished with exploring the logical possibilities of Spiritualism) and that he wanted more "practical reforms" (meaning he wanted Spiritualism to be medically useful). By the time the James family had reached St. John's Wood, Wilkinson had demonstrated his desire to make Spiritualism personally meaningful.[97]

Somehow having failed to grasp the full extent of Garth's conversion before, Henry Sr. was distressed upon arrival in London to find Garth deeply immersed in Spiritualism. To Ralph Waldo Emerson he confided his acute disappointment: "He is so eaten up with the spirits and all that [and] [h]is imagination is so vast as to dwarf all the higher faculties.... One can't endure the nonsense they talk ... but when one considers the dear human meaning and effort that are struggling at the bottom of all that nonsense, you can't feel any personal separation from the men." As such, Henry Sr. hoped Wilkinson might outgrow his pursuit of Spiritualism the way an adolescent outgrows his indiscretions. "Wilkinson's sarcasm is awful and on the whole he seems to be sowing his intellectual wild oats at present, and will grow more genial in good time," he wrote. "This is it: I think he is now finding his youth." Ironically, Henry Sr. had forgotten his own period of "kicking up his heels," for during the late 1840s he had tentatively embraced the mesmerist clairvoyant Andrew Jackson Davis, known as the "Poughkeepsie Seer." Of course, it was equally possible that Henry Sr. was projecting his own youthful enthusiasm onto Wilkinson and assuming a similarly mature rejection later.[98]

But Garth's interest in Spiritualism outlived youthful indiscretion. For him Spiritualism not only reaffirmed Christian theology but also contained medicinal benefits. In 1857, Garth published a small pamphlet that argued Spiritualism could be used for the therapeutic treatment of mental illness, which he called the "spirit-cure."[99] Following the first principle of homeopathy that like cures like, Garth wanted to find something mirroring the mental states of the insane. He reasoned that if a drug like belladonna could help cure a physical malady like poisoning, then something resembling insanity could likewise cure it; for Garth, that something was Spiritualism. He pointed out that Spiritualist trance states had two stages. In the first, a state of extreme exaltation was reached due to the impact of conversing with spirits. This threw off-balance the medium's mind and caused a state resembling temporary insanity, which wore off in a matter of minutes or hours. In extreme cases it took days or weeks. This was the insanity that Henry Sr. had seen in Dr. Curtis and others, and in the first stage it resembled the crisis-state of mesmerism. But in crisis there was hope, for in the second stage a "great quietude was produced which left the medium feeling quite serene and even blissful." Henry Sr. had failed to observe this. Garth thought the first stage of crisis resembled that of insanity in the patients he treated at asylums, and the second resembled recovered health. Their parallel was uncanny. Spiritualism, he wrote, was "one of the Lord's plants for curing insanity." In short, Garth argued Spiritualism could be used to treat the insane.[100]

To begin the process of healing, Wilkinson suggested that spirit-mediums who practiced automatic drawing should be brought into the asylums to show the patients, physicians, and staff how the procedure worked. Next, the patients would be given pencils and paper to begin their own automatic drawing, which he admitted would be slow in the beginning with only a small number patients being able to produce involuntary writing, such as a few words and primitive figures like circles and ellipses. Once they fully relinquished their wills, however, their production would develop rapidly. He believed their ability would expand to other forms of creative spirit expressions such as composition and poetic writing (like Wilkinson's own *Improvisations*), speaking and singing, music and modeling, and dance and even spirit-driven crochet, which he called "spirit-art."[101] The effect on patients' minds, Wilkinson argued, would follow that of the already established psychological law of transference. As the patients improved, they would realize that their healthy spirit had been displaced with an evil one. In turn, it would be brought to the surface of awareness and gradually transferred out of their minds, with their "spirit-art" becoming the "scapegoats of their states." Occupational therapy was a leading form of treatment for the insane during the mid-nineteenth century, so the idea was not without theoretical foundation. For Wilkinson, their occupation should be the production of "spirit-art." After a six-month period, Wilkinson claimed that patients would be cured and could be released from asylums: "All the madness will be on the move, struggling, fermenting, [and] heaving with sanity. The asylum, no longer a swamp of incurables, will be a burning fiery furnace in which souls and minds are being purified. One of the busiest scenes probably on earth!"[102]

Garth maintained the benefits for science would be immense. Using the "spirit cure," medicine would accumulate a detailed catalog that could be used to chart the method's effectiveness and thereby find ways to improve it. This record would constitute an archive, providing what Wilkinson called a "gallery of states" of the "spirit-experience," which, in turn, would attest to the reality of the spirit-world. Moreover, Wilkinson argued optimistically that the method of spirit-cure could be used to treat cretinism and idiocy as well as the dumb and deaf. In short, his proposal offered mental science a lesson in Spiritualist education. As Wilkinson wrote, "God's law [of] Spiritualism will cure Insanity." There was a catch to the efficaciousness of the spirit-cure, however. Wilkinson was sure to remind his readers that his method would work only if the patients already believed in God. If they did not, using Spiritualism to treat insanity would only worsen their condition.[103] Wilkinson's method was not theoretical. He reported using it on a friend (perhaps Florence

Theobald after one of the séances held at St. John's Wood) and also on the son of the American novelist Nathaniel Hawthorne, who was visiting London in 1857 and who reported favorably on Wilkinson.[104]

In the London winter of 1855–56, when William James was but thirteen years old, he could not possibly have understood either the intricacies of Swedenborg's doctrine of spiritual creation or the two conflicting interpretations of it advanced by his father and Garth Wilkinson, respectively. What he would have likely grasped was that the nature of spirit was contested and that Spiritualism was central to the debate. He might have even understood that the debate invoked a central metaphysical problem. As William put it to his sister years later, "Father would find in me today a much more receptive listener—all *that* philosophy has got to be brought in."[105] The key question worth asking, then, is whose views on Spiritualism had the most impact on young William: Henry Sr.'s or Garth Wilkinson's? Was Spiritualism theologically bankrupt and both mortally and morally dangerous, as Henry Sr. argued, or was it a kind of spiritual medicine used to heal the sick, as Wilkinson maintained?

Conventional wisdom holds that family relationships pull more weight with regard to shaping one's intellectual views, especially when the relationship is a father-son one (all seven major biographies of William James devote several chapters to Henry Sr.'s influence on William). Thus the natural tendency, then, would be to argue that Henry Sr. was more influential on his son than Wilkinson was. In the case of Spiritualism, however, that conclusion would be a mistake. As evidenced by his adult commitment to alternative healing methods, William followed Wilkinson's scientific approach to the study of spirit instead of his father's theological one. In particular, he turned to the medical study of the human mind rather than to the metaphysical probing of one's spirit. Indeed, William chose medicine instead of theology as a career in the 1860s, and he specialized in the pathology of mind rather than in the metaphysics of morals. From the 1860s onward, William's fascination with alternative treatments of the mentally ill burgeoned as he read up on and explored mesmerism, hypnotism, and mind cure. These formed some of the basis of his interests in the scientific investigation of "non-normal" phenomena in the 1870s and led to his study of Spiritualism during the 1880s and 1890s. In fact, it was from his psychical research that James would make many new friends with similar interests, form new scientific organizations devoted to the study of psychic phenomena, and discover trance mediums that provided him with enough data for his investigations. Henry Sr.'s Swedenborgianism may have provided the foundation for such a chain of events to develop, but

Garth Wilkinson's "spirit-cure" was the cause that precipitated it. Thus, while it is true Henry Sr.'s pursuit of spirit engendered in William a lifelong quest to understand the mind, the similarity stops there. By the time he was an adult, William not only rejected his father's arguments against Spiritualism but also actively pursued investigating Spiritualism in the hopes that it might, in the words of one influential James scholar, yield "a more kindly treatment of humanity."[106] Clearly that approach describes Garth Wilkinson's toward Spiritualism and indicates quite strongly that it was he, not Henry Sr., who most influenced William. Indeed, it suggests young William was learning a great deal about the trance's hypostatized curative power during the London winter of 1855–56.

TERTIUM QUID RISING

In 1861 William James entered the Lawrence Scientific School at Harvard College to study chemistry. At first the labors overwhelmed him. In a letter to his parents that fall, he grumbled, "This chemical analysis is so bewildering at first that I am entirely 'muddled and beat.'" William's reference was to a Spiritualist story called *Essay on Spirit-Rapping* in which the protagonist known as "the Linconshire boor" ended his life with the declaration: "What with faith, and what with the earth a-turning round the sun, and what with the railroads a-fuzzing and a-whizzing, I'm clean stonied, muddled and beat."[107] At nineteen years old, this was William's first known reference to Spiritualism.

But it was hardly the last. Eight years later, in 1869, when James was twenty-seven years old and on the verge simultaneously of earning his MD, joining the Metaphysical Club, and descending into a major psychological crisis, he received a letter from Henry Bowditch, his friend and fellow medical school colleague. From Paris, Bowditch described a short pamphlet on Spiritualism he had been reading called *Études expérimentales sur le fluide nerveux et solution définitive du problème spirite*. "Modest title isn't it?" he mused and then recounted the author's conclusion regarding how the medium used his own will to drain Chevillard's nervous fluid out of his body and into the table, thereby making it tip off the ground as if a spirit had done so. Bowditch suggested that William read it to "amuse you for 1/2 an hour as it did me."[108] What Bowditch did not know was that James was writing a review of a book on Spiritualism called *Planchette; or, The Despair of Science*.[109] It marked James's first major foray into the topic. To his brother Henry Jr., who was studying abroad at Oxford, he announced excitedly, "I wrote a notice of a book on spiritualism (*Planchette*) for the [Boston] *Advertiser* and got

$10.00!!"[110] A deft sense of irony and wit, cunning sarcasm, razor-sharp analysis, and frequent historical and literary references permeated the review.

> This pretty little book ... is a brief general history or treatise of so-called spiritualistic phenomena ... [that] is entertaining, and characterized by a perfect freedom from extravagance of manner or opinion, its content mainly consisting from other writers—either reports of "manifestations," or discussions polemical and speculative as to their cause. The author himself, to be sure, appears at intervals, corroborating "things seen and heard," or applauding and reinforcing, sometimes with a good deal of epigrammatic force, the theoretic arguments of the authorities on whose shoulders he seems to have preferred to rest the burden of his case; but his mind is not through the book, as if it had grasped the subject as a whole with any degree of energy.[111]

Such left-handed compliments—one that defended the worthiness of the subject while severely criticizing its author—afforded him the possibility to take the phenomenon seriously without having to reach a definitive conclusion. Commentaries like this one became his modus operandi that demarcated his attitude to Spiritualism for the remainder of his life.

The review also revealed James's earliest attempt to formulate some of the key elements of his tertium quid method of inquiry. It indicated James's predilection for a scientific method of investigation rather than one based on hearsay, secondhand accounts, and "epigrammatic force." As James put it, "A reader of scientific habits would have been more interested by very few cases described by the author over his own signature, and with every possible detail given, in which pedantically minute precautions had been taken against illusion of the senses or deceit."[112] However, while empiricism defined James's approach to Spiritualism, he did not reduce his interest to it. In the same review, James expressed intellectual contempt toward a total reliance on absolute scientific dogma:

> From his snug home in an atmosphere in which pianos float, "soft warm hands" bud forth from vacant space, and lead pencils write alone, the spiritualist has a right to feel personal disdain for the "scientific man" who stands inertly aloof in his pretentious enlightenment. Scientific men seem to demand that spiritualists would come and demonstrate to them the truth of their doctrine, by something little short of a surgical operation upon their intellects.

> But the spiritualist, from his point of view, is quite justified in leaving them forever on their "laws of nature" uncovered, since he no way needs their countenance.[113]

In other words, James strongly believed that Spiritualism ought to be investigated empirically, but he loathed an absolute reliance on scientific method because it disregarded the Spiritualist's worldview. James argued that Spiritualists, like individuals of any other religious faith, were entitled to their convictions, and no man of science had the right to dismiss them simply because his beliefs in the "laws of nature" dictated otherwise. This tension in James's approach—part reliance on scientific method, part skepticism regarding its capacity to explain all phenomena—reflected his tertium quid approach to psychical research and is best explained as James's earliest attempts to formulate a unique method of inquiry by using Spiritualism as a testing ground.

James did not abandon his interest in Spiritualism or its scientific investigation after this review. Neither did he waver from his unique approach. In 1874 James attended a Spiritualist séance (perhaps his first but certainly one of dozens throughout his life) and afterward announced his intention to study it. To Katherine Havens, an accomplished pianist and one of William's many female confidants to whom James often offered his most closely guarded thoughts, he wrote,

> Being desirous of "investigating" spiritualism I went a few days ago to see a medium who was said to raise a piano in broad daylight. She was a deceiver, performing the feat by means of her wonderfully strong and skillful knee. If I go on investigating I should make anyhow an important discovery: either that there exists a force of some sort not dreamed of in our philosophy, (whether it be spirits or not)—or, that human testimony, voluminous in quantity, and from the most respectable sources, is but a revelation of universal imbecility. I hate to settle down into this last conviction, and so would like to give the thing more of a trial than I have done yet. Have you seen any manifestations?[114]

In other words, James simultaneously revealed his skepticism of Spiritualism but his compunction to investigate it fairly and with an open mind. It was an indication, then, that James wanted to seek out some middle path between the two bifurcated extremes of absolute rejection and too-easy acceptance or, as he would later use the phrase in a different context, between the tough- and tender-minded.

"Everything," then, had not "conspired to make William James a pioneer in psychical research."[115] Several interlocking elements, however, had made that outcome seem more prophetic. The information James acquired from his probable knowledge of the Fox sisters during his New York City boyhood in the early 1850s through his first séance attendance at the onset of his professional career at Harvard in the early 1870s reveal three major conclusions. First, James's curiosity in Spiritualism began much earlier than scholars have heretofore recognized.[116] Second, James's interest did not wane but waxed. This suggests his interest in Spiritualism was not an exceptional or unique event in his early life but rather an ongoing if fragmented one. Indeed, William returned to Spiritualism on several occasions during his intellectually formative years. His path to Spiritualism most likely began on the streets and in the theaters of New York and probably continued in conversations with Knickerbocker literati at the James family dinner table. There, some of the best minds and writers of the mid-nineteenth century probably engaged him in discussions of their sittings with the Fox sisters and Spiritualism. In Europe, William's knowledge seems to have proceeded apace with the family's six-month stay in London in 1855–56, where he was likely aware of the Spiritualist circle run by the Wilkinson family in St. John's Wood. The path almost certainly then snaked through William's immersion into Henry Sr.'s wildly abstruse Swedenborgian theology, including his vitriolic attack on Spiritualism for being both a medical danger and a theological absurdity, but would have been counterbalanced by the more sane though no less adamant Swedenborgian Garth Wilkinson, Henry's Sr.'s friend and defender of alternative healing methods from whom William probably learned of the spirit-cure. Given young William's exposure to something as "non-normal" as Spiritualism, then, it is hardly surprising that he developed a relish for it. Indeed, James "was confident," as his first biographer put it, "that orthodoxies, respectabilities, schematisms, unities, architectural symmetries, always missed the native quality of existence."[117] Finally, the lessons the adolescent James learned about Spiritualism shared much in common with the approach he brought to bear on his adult psychical research. In so doing, they served as a touchstone for James's unique intellectual attitude. These elements began with the will to investigate more mediums and expanded to studying Spiritualism systematically. They emphasized keeping an open mind during investigations while allowing the facts to decide the outcome's veracity. And they indicated that a study of Spiritualism should be scientific but mindful of religious faith.

In sum, during the first three decades of his life, William James learned not only to marvel at Spiritualism as something "non-normal" but also to see it as worthy of serious intellectual engagement. In the process, he turned away from the more rigid ideals of his father's outdated theology and toward the more flexible one of his emergent tertium quid method of inquiry that harbored sympathy for both religious and scientific ideals.

two

MORAL HEROES

By the time William James began teaching at Harvard in 1874, he had pledged to investigate Spiritualism. But over the next eight years he did not pursue it. Instead, James busied himself with getting married, starting a family, and settling into a career as an academic. Then, a series of events led him back to the subject. While visiting his brother Henry Jr. in England in 1882, James met a remarkable circle of men and women who, like James during the 1860s and 1870s, had been informally investigating Spiritualism on their side of the Atlantic. They were launching an organization called the Society for Psychical Research, whose purpose was the formal study of Spiritualism and related psychic matters. Upon learning of James's interest, they befriended him and asked him to join the SPR. From the early 1880s onward, James formed dynamic friendships with the circle's principal male members—Henry Sidgwick, F. W. H. Myers, and Edmund Gurney, later dubbed the Sidgwick Group—that lasted their lifetimes.[1] In so doing, he developed an admiration of their intellectual acumen and personal traits, and they, in turn, a fond appreciation for him that bonded them to psychical research. Their friendships made James fiercely protective of them and their common cause, one that he defended against all critics. As James's first biographer wrote, "Gurney, Myers, and Sidgwick became his intimate friends, and loyalty to them implied loyalty to their cause."[2]

James's fidelity to these friendships took root in two significant developments of the long nineteenth century. The first was the rise of an intellectual aristocracy, or a new class of transatlantic and transcontinental intellectuals that challenged the socio-politico-economic status quo of the ruling classes, especially in Britain, where emergent middle-class Victorian families accessed elite universities like Cambridge and the civil service in order to reform the rigid class hierarchy and replace it with a meritocracy. The second was a religious challenge in which these same intellectuals experienced a crisis of faith and began to look away from the Anglican Church and toward science for assurance of their cherished view of the survival of the soul. Such a romantic vision of the afterlife characterized the Victorian mind.[3] Those involved in the Sidgwick Group exemplified these two developments, and they turned to psychical research for solace precisely at the moment that James joined them. James for his part was a member of a rising American intelligentsia with one foot so comfortably planted in the Old World that he took easily to the British intellectuals. Like them, James had suffered his own crisis of faith in the late 1860s and early 1870s, and although his had been more psychological than religious, the experience of profound doubt bonded him to these men.

Closer to home, James formed his most intimate friendship with Richard Hodgson, Sidgwick's Australian-born protégé whom the SPR sent to America to help James run the American Society for Psychical Research in 1887. Unlike the friendships James had formed with those in the Sidgwick Group, the friendship between him and Hodgson did not emerge in the context of the British intellectual aristocracy, though Hodgson was certainly intellectual, and it was not steeped in a crisis of religious faith, which Hodgson had not undergone. Rather, the two men manifested something akin to Aristotle's theory of virtuous friendship, which held that complete friendship was based on the virtue of good people acting in a like manner.[4] It was almost as if his friendships with the Sidgwick Group and Hodgson recalled those of his Knickerbocker "uncles" one generation before. Indeed, James seemed to be drawing on the past by creating his own community of discourse of psychical research.[5] As such, James found trusted allies with whom he could pursue his boyhood interests in the "non-normal" to develop his tertium quid method of inquiry.

THE SIDGWICK GROUP

Formed in 1874, the Sidgwick Group comprised the Cambridge philosopher Henry Sidgwick and his wife, Eleanor, and two of Sidgwick's students, F. W. H. Myers and Edmund Gurney, who had urged him to start the group. It also included Arthur and Gerald Balfour, William Gladstone, and Lord Rayleigh, four high-profile members of Britain's ruling class.[6] The nucleus of the group—Sidgwick, Myers, and Gurney—hailed from what Noel Annan famously dubbed Britain's "intellectual aristocracy," a new class of intelligentsia that emerged in the early nineteenth century.[7] Its members were mostly middle and upper-middle class and, with a few notable exceptions, not of the ruling class (though occasionally they married into it, as did Henry Sidgwick). Their parents tended to be skilled laborers, tradesmen, ministers, bankers, and even shorthand writers who nevertheless produced children who worked primarily with their minds: scholars, teachers, school inspectors, museum curators, and civil servants. Although professional, they were not of the narrowly professional class as lawyers were. They wrote for the new periodicals but were neither of the elite professoriate (except in the case of Sidgwick) nor of the lowly Grub Street hacks. Instead, they criticized the views of the ruling class and helped form the opinions of their own class through public writing and activism. Their families tended to intermarry, more so by the end of the century as increased taxation reduced their wealth. They were of three reformist religious traditions: evangelical Anglicans (the Sidgwicks), Quakers (the Gurneys), and Unitarians, from which a number of their cherished intellectual positions flowed. Politically they were all unified on one of the most important issues of the day—Home Rule, all being opposed to it—but diverged thereafter into three main camps: Liberal imperialists, Conservative reformers, and Fabian socialists. But all believed in the need for social change and manifested two main goals: "intellectual freedom within the universities" (they went to Cambridge rather than Oxford where reform was more possible) and a fairer social structure based on merit in which "the creation of public service [was] open to talent." In other words, they challenged the ruling aristocracy's long-held power over education and civil service.[8]

Regarding the former, they educated their daughters as much as their sons. Literature was their forte even as their relationship to art was ambivalent. Since the principle of Beauty was too abstract to be useful, they did not accumulate objets d'art but rather packed their houses with books, journals, periodicals, and newspapers. On the other hand, they did not belong to bohemia and chose philosophers such as John Stuart Mill and Thomas Hill Green, who wrote for their causes. The new class consisted of "men of good intellect" who sacrificed themselves to their class, believed in the value of competition, especially in regard to education such as fair examinations, and adhered to the Victorian gentleman's code of ethics, behavior, and practice. In this way, the new "aristocracy of intellect" created a tradition of men (and a few women) moving to the forefront of literature, science, and scholarship, and thus "positions of cultural hierarchy," by working their way into mainstream institutions such as the universities and civil service, which they then sought to reform for the betterment of their own class and the ideal British society. In so doing, they created social status for their class while never confusing their status with "the real nobility and the ruling class." Well-known intellectual aristocratic families included the Huxleys, Stracheys, Macaulays, Wedgworths, Darwins, Maynards, Scotts, Haldanes, and Stephens, as well as the Sidgwicks and Gurneys. Indeed, Annan specified that the Sidgwick family was "the prototype of the new academic class."[9]

Shared experiences in education were especially pertinent to the formation of the Sidgwick Group. Sidgwick, Myers, and Gurney all attended Blackheath boarding school, to which they had been shipped in early childhood due to the premature deaths of their fathers. The Balfour brothers, the Myers brothers, and Gurney attended Trinity College at Cambridge during the 1860s and 1870s, when Sidgwick was establishing his reputation. Arthur Balfour and Frederic Myers were the first to earn a degree in Moral Tripos (classics, philosophy, and religion) under Sidgwick's tutelage in 1869. Gurney, Arthur Myers, and Gerald Balfour followed with degrees in classics in 1871, 1873, and 1875 respectively. Gerald introduced Sidgwick to Frederic Myers, and the Balfour brothers introduced Sidgwick to their sister Eleanor, whom he later married. All four Balfour children had been interested in ghosts, and all members of the Sidgwick Group were brought up with an avid interest in human immortality. The bonds they formed provided a gateway to their interest in psychical research during the 1870s and 1880s, thus making their membership in the intellectual aristocracy a major reason for the rise of psychical research.[10]

The Sidgwicks

The son of a minister who died when Henry was just three years old, Henry Sidgwick had a precocious intellect and an ambition to be a scholar from the beginning. In 1855, at age sixteen, he entered Trinity College and in 1859 graduated with the highest honors in classical studies. That same year he was hired as a fellow at Trinity in Moral Tripos, where he taught courses, supervised theses, examined students, and performed the usual administrative services. He held that position for a decade until he resigned it in 1869 over the issue of religious testing (he was against it), though he maintained his lectureship, switching from classics to moral philosophy, which he held until his death in 1900. Like most members of the intellectual aristocracy, Sidgwick participated in a number of professional and social organizations, including the Apostles Society, whose goal was to encourage full and frank discussion of every possible question; the Metaphysical Society, which discussed philosophical issues; the Synthetic Society, whose purpose was to facilitate the reconstruction of essential religious beliefs; and the SPR.[11]

Sidgwick was an invaluable member of all these societies but most crucial to the SPR, which would not have garnered much support from the intellectual aristocracy or the ruling class without him. In fact, Arthur and Gerald Balfour, William Gladstone, and Lord Rayleigh made Sidgwick's presidency a precondition of their membership. Sidgwick, who served as the first president of the SPR (1882–85 and again 1888–92) and as the editor of the *Journal of the Society for Psychical Research* (1885–86), possessed a sweetness of nature and a well-developed sense of humor that made him a kind leader.[12] He was known among his friends for his brilliant repartee and good-naturedness. Henry James Jr., who introduced William to Sidgwick in 1882, noted that "there is something exceptionally pleasant about him."[13] Similarly, the American philosopher George Howison, who was a mutual friend, once remarked that Sidgwick had spoken "warmly" of him in return.[14] The central members of the group recognized his pivotal role, with Frederic Myers dubbing him the "captain in the great enterprise" and maintaining there was "no other man [who] could have filled that post so well as he."[15]

Oliver Lodge, the knighted physicist and university president who eventually became a prominent member of the SPR, wrote, "It was because of Henry Sidgwick more perhaps than to any other single influence, is the comparative success of our movement due." In fact, Lodge credited the early success of psychical research to the "serene sovereign wisdom of Henry Sidgwick. Perhaps than to any other single influence is the comparative success of our movement due."[16] Frank Podmore, a civil servant who became a prominent researcher at the SPR, echoed Lodge. He noted that in addition to Sidgwick's service and commitment to provide his personal funds for studying subjects, analyzing data, offering sound advice, and presiding over the SPR council, the success of the SPR was "due, in the largest measure, to the wisdom, the clear insight, the 'particularly sane intellect' [quoting Sidgwick himself] ... and, above all, to the preeminent justice and veracity of our first president."[17] Sidgwick's main contribution to the SPR, then, lay less in his skill as an investigator (though he was quite adept) and more in his service, reputation, and leadership. His experience in political matters taught him the skills needed for creating a positive public image for the SPR.[18] As James put it, Sidgwick had an "extraordinary gift of inspiring confidence in diverse sorts of people. Such tenacity of interest in the result and such impartiality in discussing the evidence are not once in a century found in an individual."[19]

HENRY SIDGWICK (1838–1900), undated. Sidgwick was chosen to be the public face of psychical research in England because of his wisdom, intellect, and leadership skills. *Henry James Papers, MS Am 1094, box 1, p. 26, by permission of the Houghton Library, Harvard University.*

But Sidgwick was eccentric. He often jogged through the streets of Cambridge in his academic gown and was noted for his absentmindedness, once carrying a cup of tea with him to chapel as he talked.[20] Younger students often complained of his cold teaching manner and his indifference to their needs. One even criticized Sidgwick's unfortunate habit of "eating his beard,—shoveling it by the handfuls into his mouth, while he gazed coldly thro' half shut eyes at the Freshman opposite him [creating] a feeling of uneasy dislike rising in the most sensitive among them to actual hatred."[21] Sidgwick was not universally liked by his peers, either. Conservatives objected to his calls for university reforms, and some orthodox scientists scoffed at his work in psychical research. Some thought him too earnest, splitting moral hairs in favor of ethical high-handedness and exuding an overbearing spiritual pride, while others found him obstinate, as reflected in his foolishly consistent adherence to public rights (Sidgwick once decided to smoke in the presence of two women in a carriage, despite their request that he refrain, merely because it was a "smoking carriage"). The two most substantive charges leveled against Sidgwick were that he was ineffective as a teacher and administrator and that, for all his learning and influence in Cambridge, he failed to found a school of thought.[22] In addition, because of his penchant to examine all sides of an issue, he never developed answers to his questions. To some, it seemed tragic that he died without ever having found a satisfactory answer to even one of his religious, philosophical, or psychical inquiries.[23] Even Sidgwick indicated as such, confessing on his deathbed to Myers that "as I look back on my life, I seem to see little but wasted hours." However, Sidgwick's purpose had been to aspire to ideals and to give priority to process over results. "I cannot be sorry that you should idealise me," he also told Myers, "if that shows that I have made my ideals in some degree felt. We must idealise, or we should cease to struggle."[24] Perhaps more than any other attitude, this one typified that of the British Anglican intellectual aristocracy.

Sidgwick devoted his career to a combination of lecturing and publishing in philosophy, classics, and psychical research. He was deeply learned in history and theology, the latter of which inspired him to master both Arabic and Hebrew, and wrote in the fields of politics, economics, psychology, and philology. Henry also possessed advanced literary and poetic skills, making him one of the last Renaissance men of the nineteenth century. Indeed, Lodge once called Sidgwick a great "storehouse of literary memories." Mostly, though, Henry's major focus sprung from his interests—both personal and professional—in moral and ethical questions, such as proper human action and the possibility of human immortality.[25] A prodigious scholar, Sidgwick wrote a number of books in philosophy, especially in political economy and ethics, including *Principles of Political Economy* (1883), *Elements of Politics* (1891), and *The Methods of Ethics* (1874), for which he is most well known. It sought to reconcile the utilitarian and intuitionist schools of thought to show that Immanuel Kant's principles provided a rational basis for morality, exemplifying the nineteenth-century tradition that sought to supply a rational foundation for ethical belief and practice, that is, one *not* founded on religious principles. Sidgwick also published many articles on politics and social issues in journals like *Mind*.

Like many intellectuals of his generation, Sidgwick followed the broad contours of Enlightenment thought: that human beings were inherently good; that mankind could use its natural reason to discover the universal laws and thereby reveal God's rational and ordered cosmos; that such knowledge could be put to practical use, which over time would advance civilization; and that scientific method, experiment, and observation constituted a thoroughgoing empiricism, which would reveal truth. Sidgwick took that quest with the utmost seriousness. As Lodge noted, "It [was] a privilege to be permitted to bear witness to the eminently scientific type of mind which he possessed."[26] But Sidgwick also believed in common sense and was quite cautious about reaching conclusions before the evidence warranted them, shunning dogmatism with disdain. In this sense, Sidgwick was cautious like James, remaining open to new evidence and interpretations. But when two opposing viewpoints clashed, he had a hard time reaching a final opinion. In this sense, Sidgwick exemplified the dilemma endemic of the late Victorian mind: the cleavage discovered personally and intellectually between religious faith and scientific knowledge. That is, Sidgwick manifested the deep uncertainties and incurable reservations over the long-standing debate between two irreconcilable systems of knowledge. Ultimately, his attitude hampered him and nurtured his doubts that philosophy could ever reconstruct the foundation for a rational religious faith. As Sidgwick put it in a moment of self-reflection, he was always worried about "standing for some false, impossible shore."[27]

Nonetheless, throughout all his philosophical circumspection and scientific exploration, Sidgwick was hopeful, even optimistic. He once wrote that he felt "with something of a profound hope and enthusiasm that the function of the English mind, with its uncompromising matter-of-factness, will . . . [put] the final question to the universe with a solid, passionate determination to be answered, which must come to something."[28] Myers best captured his mentor's complex and rich philosophical attitude, writing that Sidgwick "was not only cautious, systematic, self-controlled, he was also unresting, undeviating, inwardly ardent to the end."[29] Above all else, Sidgwick was a man of high moral fiber. Myers again captured this best when he wrote in memory of him that Sidgwick was a man with the "moral qualities" of patience, caution, and urbanity "and above all a certain doggedness and fixity of resolve. . . . [He] possessed, in an almost unique degree, that motive for dogged persistence which lay in a deep sense of the incurable incoherence of the intelligible world."[30] Sidgwick's fundamental attitude toward the world, then, lay in his attempt to pursue large philosophical questions framed in ethics that he knew lacked clear and ultimate answers but that he nonetheless believed worth pursuing.

Sidgwick brought this attitude to psychical research. Reflecting the open-mindedness of James's tertium quid, it made the two philosophers natural allies. As James put it, Sidgwick pursued psychical phenomena "with a single-minded desire to ascertain the facts, and without any foregone conclusion as to their nature."[31] This shared intellectual commitment became the basis for their professional relationship that helped bring James into the fold of British psychical research. And it also became the basis for their friendship. In reference to their attendance at the International Congress of Physiological Psychology in Paris in 1889, James told his wife that "I am quite thick now with Sidgwick, whom I like amazingly."[32] This was quite fortunate because James did not care for Sidgwick's utilitarianism or his theory of ethics. Having just "finished with great delight this morning the long-postponed Sidgwick's *Data of Ethics,*" he once confided to his colleague Josiah Royce that "of all the long-winded, copious, flexible-minded, dispassionate cusses, he is the worst." And at Sidgwick's worst, James lambasted him as "the most incorrigibly and exasperatingly critical mind in England."[33] But he liked the man and his intellectual disposition toward psychical research.

In 1876, Henry married Eleanor Mildred Balfour. It was a complementary match in almost every way. Due to the restrictions placed on women, "Nora," as she was called, did not attend university but was every bit as educated and talented as Henry and her more famous brothers. She was especially adept in mathematics, a skill that enabled her to assist the work of Lord Rayleigh (her brother-in-law), with whom she coauthored several articles. Eleanor might have become a professor of mathematics at a leading institution of higher education had she been born a century later. Instead, she pursued education administration, helping to found Newnham College for Women in Cambridge, of which she became its principal from 1892 to 1910. Eleanor's marriage to Henry connected him to the ruling class and her to the intellectual aristocracy while equally cementing their commitment to university reform. They both believed that women ought to be allowed to earn advanced degrees (though Henry had mixed opinions on coeducation) and that colleges should abolish religious testing for entry into university (James shared the Sidgwicks' views on women's education, arguing, unsuccessfully at first, to get Harvard, not just Radcliffe, to confer PhDs on his female psychology students, an issue that further bonded James with the British intellectual aristocracy). Eleanor also became a leading psychical researcher, and in some ways her contributions surpassed those of her husband. For one thing, she outlived him by thirty-six years and was thus able to work at it much longer, serving as the editor of the *Proceedings of the Society for Psychical Research* and the *Journal of the Society for Psychical Research* from 1888 to 1897 and as the joint honorary president (with Oliver Lodge) in 1932–33. From 1907 through 1932 she was the society's "Honorary Secretary," which in effect meant that she ran the organization for twenty-five years. An admirable administrator, Eleanor saw all the SPR's major works into publication; an accomplished researcher, she published numerous papers in the SPR's periodicals; a founding member who far outlived the rest, she was the one constant to whom new members turned for guidance and wisdom.[34]

Like her brother Henry Jr., Alice James, who lived in London from 1884 until her death in 1892, also served as James's pro tem family contact with the Sidgwick Group when William was in absentia. The Sidgwicks took kindly to Alice and became favored guests during her periods of convalescence, at which time they swapped each other's work. Alice admired Mrs. Sidgwick's writing style (though she deplored her psychical research material), recording in her diary, "Mrs. Sidgwick sent me a paper upon *Madame de Sévigné*, the best thing I have read of hers. The dear lady is human, like the rest of us." The "human" part was written in jest as those in Alice's circle liked to joke about Eleanor's lengthy reading lists. Katherine Loring, Alice's "Boston marriage" partner, once told a friend who had inquired of Alice's ability to read after one of her bouts with neurasthenia that in fact she was able to do so. "Oh, yes, I suppose Mrs. Sidgwick gave her lists of books," was the reply. Whatever else the Sidgwicks were, they were foremost an intellectual pair dedicated to solving problems and approaching the world through their minds. As William put it, "The Sidgwicks are the incarnation of pure intellect." After the Sidgwicks visited her for Easter in 1890, Alice concurred. She called Henry "the most fascinating talker in England," noting that she had been inspired by his "flow."[35] William agreed, once explaining to his wife, Alice, that a friend "read aloud Mrs. Sidgwick[']s essay on apparitions of the dead in the last Report of [the] London S[ociety] for Psych[ical] R[esearch]. Tonight we continue."[36]

Like James, the Sidgwicks' turn to psychical research in the 1880s stemmed from their interest in Spiritualism that had permeated British culture across class lines at midcentury. Very much unlike James, though, whose curiosity in Spiritualism had sprung from the peculiarities of his family and its championing of the "non-normal," a distinct religious component marked the British intellectual aristocracy's interest in Spiritualism. As early as the 1850s, Henry Sidgwick had been driven by a concern for teleological necessity to support his religious faith; like other members of the group, he needed some sort of reasoned proof for his belief in God and human immortality. This took him in several directions, including his decision to join the Ghost Society at Trinity, which concerned itself with exploring haunted houses and searching for ghosts. During the 1860s, Henry, like many liberal intellectuals of that stormy decade, experienced a crisis of faith, causing him to pursue further avenues to reaffirm it. The investigation of Spiritualism was one such effort. "You know my 'Spiritualistic' ghost-seeing tendencies," he confessed in a letter to his sister in 1867. These "tendencies" became lifelong pursuits. Like his interests in ethics and theology, though, his opinions of them were absorbed quickly into his open-ended and process-oriented style of inquiry, leaving him in doubt as to their exact nature. "I have been inquiring into Spiritualism, but it has not come to much," he recorded in his journal. "I can get to see and hear very astounding things in the dark with people I do not know, but I can never get conditions to satisfy me."[37] The 1870s became Sidgwick's "decade of spiritualism." During this period, he devoted himself to investigating it with the same seriousness he had brought to his theological concerns during his religious crises of the 1860s. In his journal he wrote, "I have now gone in for the investigation of Spiritualism in real earnest; not (so far) with much result of a kind interesting to outsiders; but to me the interest of the inquiry grows with every step." Sidgwick indicated his sincerity in the pursuit, writing, "As for Spirit-rapping, I am exactly in the same mind towards it as towards Religion. I believe there is something in it; [I] don't know what: [I] have tried hard to discover, and find that I always paralyse the phenomena."[38] Before marrying Henry, Eleanor had a similar trajectory for similar reasons. Indeed, she had introduced both her brothers and her sister Evelyn (eventually Lord Rayleigh's wife) to the study of ghosts and Spiritualism in the 1860s and 1870s. For Sidgwick, then, a crisis of faith led him to psychical research.[39]

Frederic Myers

Of all the members of the Sidgwick Group with whom James became friends, no one personified the view that the goal of psychical research was to demonstrate human immortality more than Frederic William Henry Myers.[40] With the personality of a poet and the education of a classicist, Myers, being "morally too uncertain and emotionally too sensitive to confront life without the larger hope," as one scholar captured it, exemplified the romantic ethos of the Victorian mind.[41] Like Sidgwick, Myers was the son of a minister who had died when Myers was still a boy at age seven, which also like Sidgwick landed Myers in Blackheath boarding school. Myers attended Cheltenham College from 1858 to 1860 and then moved on to Trinity from 1860 to 1864, where Sidgwick was his tutor and where he won many prizes for his outstanding poetry. From 1865 to 1872, Myers worked as a lecturer in classics at Trinity, passing his degree in Moral Tripos in 1869. Frederic married Eveleen Tennant, the daughter of Charles Tennant (an old friend of his father's), in 1880 and subsequently moved to Cambridge, England. Myers's career roughly mimics his developing intellectual interests and can be divided between his poetry years (1867–82) followed by his psychical research years (1882–1901), though his interest in Spiritualism began in the early 1870s when he became part of the Sidgwick Group. From 1872 until his death in 1901, Myers worked as a school inspector, but the job's low demands and the financial comfort his marriage to Eveleen afforded him provided ample time to serve the SPR as both secretary (1888–99) and president (1900), write numerous articles on psychical research, and pen one of the field's most important books, *Human Personality and Its Survival of Bodily Death* (1903).

Like the other members of the Sidgwick Group, Myers experienced a crisis of faith in the 1860s for which he turned to Enlightenment thought and the scientific method to prove the existence of the afterlife. And also like the others, Myers passed through several phases of scholarly and personal interest—in his case Hellenism, Christianity, and agnosticism—before discovering psychical research. Throughout all of them he expressed his views in poetic form, publishing most of his verses in magazines. After Myers died, some of these were brought together in a pamphlet called *Fragments of Prose and Poetry* (1904), a rather accomplished set of literary pieces whose style a friend and professor of literature praised as a "promise of all the major virtues, a sure mark of the distinguished mind . . . [that] carries on the noble traditions of our literature."[42] Something of an original thinker with acute, thoughtful, and subtle ideas to which Myers gave eloquent expression, he was known among his close friends as a man of many intellectual gifts. But his "most striking characteristic," as one of them put it, "was the eagerness and ardor with which he identified himself with all matters great and small that had a real interest in the average human being."[43] A prominent Myers scholar concurred, writing, "Myers was in general kindly and courteous, and he possessed great social gifts. But he was none the less extremely reserved, and he shared his innermost feelings only to a small circle of close friends," echoing Gurney's view that "only Henry and I really know what he is."[44]

At the same time, Myers possessed a number of traits that earned him the disdain of some in Cambridge. To begin with, he could be forceful, ardent, and excessively intense. He also had a tendency to turn intellectual disagreement into personal distrust that invited scorn in return. During his early school years, he was arrogant, ambitious, selfish, and even proud—behavior unbecoming to the intellectual aristocracy's value of self-sacrifice and a cultivated aloofness. During his youth Myers committed not a few follies, and there was some lingering doubt regarding the originality of several lines from a poem he wrote that won him the prestigious Camden medal at Trinity. Myers also had a tendency to drift toward the extremes, which in the words of one historian of psychical research made it "difficult [for some] to believe that his extravagant sentiments and astonishing beliefs could be genuine." Indeed, Myers's dramatic style and manner frequently bordered on the theatrical. A former student of Myers once wrote, "Frederic Myers rang, perhaps, the most sonorously of all, but to me he always rang a little false."[45] His poetic style, with its rich cadences, was just a little too contrived, even for late nineteenth-century British intellectuals.

Most egregiously, Myers failed to suppress in public his excessive fondness for beautiful women. Two highlighted episodes include his three-year-long affair with Annie Marshall, a woman unhappily married to one of Myers's cousins, who eventually committed suicide, and his marriage to Eveleen Tennant, whom he married mainly for her looks and wealth. He also shared an obvious fondness for Arthur Sidgwick's and Oliver Lodge's daughters. Myers's animated passion for beautiful women could border on unbridled lust and sometimes failed to keep his Victorian code of behavior in check. It was also bound up with his philosophy of life that included his views on psychical research. As he once put it to James, his "principles" were an "endless life & a merry one! Girls & Ghosts & and plenty of them!," though Myers insisted that he was a "lover of life" and that the "tenacity" with which he felt things was "organic," not "ethical."[46] Others, however, were less forgiving. The philosopher F. H. Bradley, for instance, doubted Myers's intellectual integrity, once

F. W. H. MYERS (1843–1901), undated. Myers personified the hope that psychical research would provide scientific proof for the afterlife. *Henry James Papers, MS Am 1094, box 1, p. 24, by permission of the Houghton Library, Harvard University.*

confiding to James that "a man who starts by writing semi-erotic pseudo-Xtian poetry & then develops [*sic*] ... himself by spirit-rapping with silly women is not very likely to have truth for his main object."[47]

Myers had his defenders, though. Oliver Lodge, for instance, admitted to having become "rather intimate with him," upon Gurney introducing Lodge to Myers. After sharing a series of conversations about psychical research, Lodge discovered that for a man lacking formal scientific training, Myers had a remarkable grasp for scientific research, explanation, and theory:

> I never knew a man more receptive, nor one with whom it was a greater pleasure to talk; his grasp of science was profound ..., even into some of the more technical details ..., [although] it was not a detailed knowledge of science that he possessed, of course, but it was ... a philosophic grasp. ... He was laying the foundation for a cosmic philosophy, a scheme of existence as large and comprehensive and well founded as any that have appeared. ... With Myers the word science meant something much larger, much more comprehensive: it meant a science and a philosophy and a religion combined. It meant, as it meant to Newton, an attempt at a true cosmic scheme.[48]

These words of high praise, from a respected man of science who usually curbed his language, indicated he believed Myers had truly earned them. Indeed, on many occasions Lodge expressed his admiration for his "intimate friendship" with Myers, once writing, "I esteem it one of the honours of my life." Over the years Lodge did not fail to signal the importance of Myers's role in his life. For instance, during a séance following World War I when the soul of Lodge's son, Raymond, supposedly made its first contact from the "other world," it was ostensibly through a message from the soul of Myers (who had died in 1901). This greatly impressed Lodge, noting that it "was only the last of the many benefits that I have derived from my friendship with that remarkable man. He it was who first broke down my skepticism, and impressed me with the reasonableness of the hypothesis of survival." Actually, it was not the last benefit. In 1928 Lodge told an unidentified friend, "I am glad to hear that you have such an admiration for Myers. It is difficult to exaggerate my admiration for him and his special form of genius."[49]

Myers's personality, then, was rife with tension and pregnant with ironic contradiction. As one scholar put it, Myers "was endowed with a remarkable, indeed dangerous, assortment of seemingly irreconcilable qualities—with an enquiring mind and a profound need for the security of a religious belief; with the crassest sensuality and the bodiless yearnings of a mystic; with the most unruly of emotions and affections, and an uncommon capacity for scrupulous self-questioning."[50] Lodge's description of Myers's personality captured its more extreme qualities: "His was a keenly emotional nature. What he felt, he felt strongly; what he believed, he believed in no half-hearted or conventional manner. When he doubted, he doubted fiercely; but the pain of the doubt only stimulated him to effort, struggle. . . . He was content with no half-knowledge, no clouded faith, he must know or he must suffer, and in the end he believed that he knew."[51] Myers's philosophical disposition thus starkly contrasted with Sidgwick's and James's tertium quid, which advocated compromise, moderation, and open-ended possibility.

Nowhere was that difference of intellectual style more apparent than in how each thinker approached psychical research. Myers's fascination with matters psychical stretched back to his boyhood years when his father and some of his acquaintances had dabbled in mesmerism.[52] During the 1870s, Myers, like Sidgwick and others of the intellectual aristocracy, turned his attention to ghosts and Spiritualism. But the Spiritualists disappointed him as he recalled finding "little of real companionship in the small sect of Spiritualists," even though they were "at that time almost the only seekers and transmitters of knowledge from a field wider than they knew."[53] By contrast, the friendships he began forming with future members of the SPR sustained him. During his days at Trinity, he found Sidgwick and Gurney the "veritable incarnation of beneficial wisdom ... [each having] met with a wisely cautious sympathy my eager joy."[54]

Myers's friendship with Sidgwick began at the end of the 1860s when he was Sidgwick's student, at which time they discovered each other's aspiration to seek hidden knowledge to support their belief in human immortality. Seeing more in Sidgwick than some other students had, Myers discovered Sidgwick's appreciation for matters spiritual "in a star-light walk" when he asked him "whether he thought that when Tradition, Intuition, Metaphysic[s], had failed to solve the riddle of the Universe, there was still a chance that from any actual observable phenomena,—ghosts, spirits, whatsoever there might be,—some valid knowledge might be drawn as to a World Unseen" and found in Sidgwick's answer that he "thought that this was possible."[55] Myers's recollection is remarkable for its utter candor that such knowledge was not only a theoretical possibility but a practical reality as well. That night "Sidgwick and I caught together the distant hope that Science might in our age make sufficient progress to open the spiritual gateway which she had been thought to close;—to penetrate by her own slow patience into the vestibule of an

Unseen World." For his part, Sidgwick's feelings regarding Myers, and the hopes for the role of science to unravel the mysteries of the "Unseen World," were equally felt. In fact, he had not only moved beyond his desire to merely not lose sight of Myers like a "rising sun" but also believed that Myers's determination would help lead to solutions to "the riddle of the universe."[56]

James first learned of Myers through his brother. In 1879, Henry Jr. described Myers to a mutual family friend as "a very pleasant, gushing aesthetic Briton, but not powerful." William experienced Henry Jr.'s observation that Myers felt his beliefs intensely, even if he did not express them vigorously, and also Myers's two-ness. To Henry Jr. he described one of his European itineraries: "I shall very likely sail in the *Lucania* with Myers, though I shrink from such close companionship with him, for so long feeling that our differences are more deep-down than our resemblances."[57] James had several opportunities in the coming years to test this hypothesis during his visits to Cambridge and London, but it was at a shared panel on psychical research at the International Congress of Physiological Psychology in Paris in 1889, where James had cemented his friendship with Henry Sidgwick, that James and Myers also formulated a bond. "It has been a true happiness for me to feel this new friendship," Myers told James. "I regard it as a boon," adding that he thought their "sense of fellowship culminated" in their stroll on the Champs-Élysées, where a "radiant carolling creature" sang at a charming café.[58] But James was less sure. To his wife he confided that although "Myers is a good looking fellow . . . a figure s'what like mine . . . , [he is] taller, and [has] a very intense and energetic character, suggesting despotism, meanness and all sorts of things lurking in the background, which I didn't altogether like."[59] Three years later James remained unsure what to think about Myers's complex personality. "F. W. H. M.," he told his wife, "is a queer fellow—such intensity in his own line, or lines, I never knew."[60] Not surprisingly, when these sentiments reached Henry Jr. through the family grapevine, he agreed with William: "You are very interesting about Myers—and very véridique [truthful]—there is a wholly disagreeable social & human element in him of which I have been always uncomfortably conscious."[61] William, who was traveling in France at this point and socializing with Myers, pondered this and confessed to Henry Jr. that "it is queer to find a man with such unusual gifts, and for whose *function* I have such respect, and yet who arouses so little personal admiration."[62]

James's lingering doubts about Myers never fully dissipated, but they affected him less so over time. In 1893, Myers circulated a partial autobiography called *Fragments of Inner Life*, of which only twenty-five copies were printed. He distributed ten of them to his "intimate friends," including Sidgwick, Lodge, and James. The contents addressed his family background and childhood, his education, his intellectual journey that stretched from classics and religion to agnosticism, and his eventual turn to science and psychical research. A number of poems flanked the text, including "Mourning" (a tribute to Annie Marshall, his mistress) and "Marriage" (a tribute to Eveleen, his wife). One chapter discussed the role of friends, while the concluding one was appropriately called "Final Thoughts."[63] James, who read drafts of *Fragments of Inner Life* before it was printed, hoped to unravel Myers's mysterious and complex personality. Writing to his wife, he described the work as "short but eloquent" and portrayed Myers as one "whose desires are so imperious, whose movements so impatient, and whose interests at bottom so egotistic in their nature. [He is] a unique individual for the intensity of his life."[64] To Myers, James made the rather praiseworthy but startling claim "I have been through the proof with renewed feeling of its eminence as literature and of its value as psychology."[65] He probably thought the work valuable as psychology as much as it was a portal into Myers's interior world.

The offered hand of friendship in both the poem "Friends" and the book profoundly affected James's estimation of Myers. "By the way, my dear Myers, in which you make me your confidant," he wrote to Myers in comparison, "contrasted as I am in so many ways with yourself—democratic, misanthropic, cold-blooded, hollow-hearted, neurasthenic above all, and abstract where you are concrete. But out of such twinings strong ropes may be made, and if you get *any* such enlargement of *glimpse* through me as I get enlargement of *view* through you, the partnership will be hallowed."[66] Although Myers's intellect (as James understood it) was clearly different from James's preferred tertium quid, his high regard for Myers revealed a budding friendship between the two men whose bond strengthened over time and eventually reached that same "thickness" that James and Henry Sidgwick had established. One week later, after a dinner party, James described Myers's face as "phosphorescent with spiritual light and human geniality."[67] And although more than three years elapsed until James next wrote "a word of friendliness," he confessed that "the struggle for existence seems to reduce all of articulation to the mechanical expression of immediate wants. But now that the New Year is beginning, I feel moved to waft towards you a sentimental greeting."[68] Even Sara Whitman, a James family friend whom William had recommended to Myers, had found that she liked him.[69]

In the winter of 1900, James and Myers spent six weeks together at Charles Richet's Château de Carqueiranne Var, located just east of Marseilles along the Mediterranean Sea. Richet, a French philosopher with an avid interest in psychical research and an active member of the British SPR, had moved his family to Paris for the colder months and had offered his summer residence to the Jameses and Myerses for the winter, which both couples accepted.[70] In anticipation of the upcoming vacation, James wrote with glee to Wilber Baldwin, a fellow physician traveling in Italy at the time, "We have been offered Charles Richet's chateau..., and shall take it & share it with my friend Frederic Myers and his wife, if the conveniences seem good."[71] Myers fawned at James's acceptance, telling him that Richet would be pleased, while James tried to entice the Sidgwicks to join the two families (they declined).[72]

The Jameses were also going for William's health. "Richet's hospitality just at this crisis [of nervous fatigue] has been a most extraordinarily friendly and beneficent thing for us both, and in particular exactly the kind of abode that my condition required," he told Karl Stumpf, a German psychologist. Stumpf was one of many sounding boards James used for psychical research, even though Stumpf was more skeptical than he.[73] A more sympathetic voice was Théodore Flournoy, the Swiss psychologist at the University of Geneva whom James met and befriended at the International Congress for Physiological Psychology in Paris in 1889. "In order to get an out-of-door life consistent with passivity," he told Flournoy, "I am going to Costebelle near Hyères, where Myers also expects to be, and where Richet has very generously offered both of us his 'Chateau de Carqueiranne.'... When I once get there I will send you my news."[74]

But Flournoy was more than sounding board. He was a kindred soul who became one of James's closest European friends. They shared remarkably similar heritages and fortunes (both came from Protestant families that immigrated to new countries—the United States and Switzerland—where their grandfathers amassed wealth), education (through Harvard and the University of Geneva), culture (a passion for reading and discussing high literature, poetry, and the arts), politics (both sided with Alfred Dreyfus and opposed the Spanish-American War), and professional development (both studied with German psychologists, earned MDs but never practiced medicine, and taught physiology before moving on to psychology and philosophy). They also shared a similar temperament (both manifested a strong sense of fair play and a willingness to suspend doubt), a romantic sense of humanity (both felt a great deal of sympathy toward human suffering), and a passion for nature (both enjoyed mountain hiking and the outdoors). Most germane, they had an open-minded intellectual attitude, especially toward psychical research. Flournoy was not a member of the SPR, but he conducted his own extensive research on Hélène Smith, a medium who claimed to be the reincarnated Marie Antoinette and a visitor to the planet Mars, whom he wrote about in *From India to the Planet Mars* (1899). James reviewed the book favorably, and Flournoy repaid him with glowing reviews of his books. Finally, the two men were victims of neurasthenia, which was not only the immediate cause for James's informing Flournoy of his plan for convalescing at Richet's chateau but also emblematic of a large correspondence that lasted two decades. A large chunk of it was devoted to discussing psychical research, making Flournoy an equally intimate psychical friend, if not more so, as the Sidgwick Group members. Indeed, the two men were so close that James told Flournoy, "There is hardly a human being with whom I feel as much sympathy of aims and character, or feel as much 'at home,' as I do with you."[75]

After settling in, William began writing letters to family members and friends in which he described his good fortune as a "godsend."[76] Not surprisingly, the countryside relaxed James. Two or three times per week they took "the *calèche de louage*" (carriage for hire) to the villages of either Toulon or Hyères or back into the country. "The latter is indescribably beautiful," James gushed, adding, "Great are the advantages of the territory of France in having a New England (Normandy) and a California (Provence) only 18 hours asunder." It was so magnificent that James could only in jest find something wrong: "The worst of it is that one begins to grow accustomed to the ignominious pottering and dawdling through the day ... and forget that one ever had a higher vocation."[77]

But if the chateau was "a perfect God-send," as he told a family confidant, some of James's doubts about Myers remained, as he added, "If I can only bear the talking to the Myerses without too much fatigue!—But that also I am sure will come."[78] Still, the Jameses and the Myerses seemed to interact quite well in the first few weeks. "We are trying co-operative housekeeping with the Myerses and it works very well," James told Josiah Royce, his philosophy colleague. "M[yers] [is] revealing an exceedingly gentle and patient side of his character."[79] Their relating must have gone well enough, for although the Myerses had initially planned to stay for a month, they wound up staying six weeks.[80] However, at one point their close interaction tested James as he once complained that although "the Myerses form a good combination ... , Mrs. M[yers] is rather a spoilt child."[81] The extended visit strained Alice as well. "Your mother is extremely rosy and well," William told their daughter, who remained at home. "She has no complications now that the Myerses and the medium are gone."[82]

The medium James referred to was Mrs. Rosalie Thompson, a merchant's wife and a new potential talent for the SPR whom Myers had found.

In addition to resting and recovering, they had all come to Carqueiranne to test her. The Jameses and Myerses held séances at the chateau with William and Frederic analyzing the event while Alice and Eveleen compared their own potential mediumistic abilities to Rosalie's. The sittings convinced James of her mediumistic talents. After describing Richet's house and surroundings to F. C. S. Schiller, a British philosopher, friend, and member of the SPR who developed a version of pragmatism called humanism, James mentioned the sittings and concluded that he had found "Myers's medium ... extraordinary."[83] To another family friend, James recounted the same set of events, describing Mrs. Thompson as a "charming woman whom he lately discovered to have mediumistic gifts, and who has let him study her as Hodgson studies Mrs. [Leonora] Piper. Hers is a much better case, all [a]round, than Mrs[.] P[iper]'s."[84] Apparently Mrs. Thompson's sittings were good enough to convince Myers as well. To Wincenty Lutoslawski, the Polish philosopher and psychical researcher, James wrote that she had "convinced Myers." Oddly enough, though, James added that while she may have been a better case than Mrs. Piper, she also confused him because the sittings left him even "more perplexed about spirits." Nonetheless, what James called Hodgson's "idiotic prophecy"—that Mrs. Thompson would not become a medium worth studying—never materialized: she became the SPR's focal point during the first two decades of the twentieth century.[85]

The events at Carqueiranne thus cemented James's and Myers's friendship. Despite their very different personalities, and in spite of the two radically different approaches the two men took—Myers's romantic search for immortality, James's tertium quid—they used their investigations to form a mutually beneficial and often rewarding bond that simultaneously advanced the cause of psychical research.[86] In this way, their relationship became one more entry point of James's honorary membership in the British intellectual aristocracy. As Myers once put it, James had become "as dear and intimate as the friends of boyhood."[87] Given the extremely closed nature of British Victorian social structure, this remark is exceedingly telling of just how important James was to the Sidgwick Group.

Edmund Gurney

If James's friendship with Sidgwick had been based on mutual respect, and that with Myers steeped in guarded curiosity, then the one with Gurney was formed through a shared sense of profound personal suffering. Edmund Gurney was the fifth child of eight. His childhood mirrored that of Sidgwick's and Myers's: his father was a minister (rector of St. Mary's), though many family members had made careers in the law as well. His father had died when Gurney was ten, and he too was sent off to Blackheath boarding school. Like Sidgwick and Myers, Gurney went to Trinity College (1866–71), on a minor scholarship, where he won a few prizes and excelled at sports. He also had a passion for music, art, and aesthetics, but also like Sidgwick and Myers he chose classical studies. Gurney was a very attractive man. George Eliot was so taken by his charm and good looks that she confessed she could think of nothing else for several days, writing that "his mind was as beautiful as his face." Eliot eventually used him as the model for her protagonist Daniel Deronda in the 1868 novel of the same name. In the story, Deronda is a man of the highest ideals (as Gurney was) and sympathetic to the heroine, Gwendolyn Harleth, who is trapped in an unhappy marriage to the wealthy but tyrannical Henleigh Grandcourt. Through her relationship to Deronda, though, she is able to develop her higher moral faculties, thus manifesting the ideals of Victorian womanhood. If Gurney was at all like Deronda, then Eliot's praise for him was indeed highly estimable. Similarly, Gurney was also quite gentle and friendly, as well as likable and sympathetic. He had many friends, and everyone liked to hear him laugh. Jane Harrison, who knew Gurney during his student years, recalled him as perhaps "the most lovable and beautiful human being I ever met."[88]

Although charismatic, Gurney was a depressive. Like James, he suffered periodic mental breakdowns, including a yearlong one while an undergraduate. His peers described him as "sensitive" to suffering—his own and others'. Indeed, it was the sense of hopeless suffering at which he most despaired. Unfortunate family events intensified this sensibility. In 1875, when Edmund was twenty-eight, his three sisters died in a tragic boating accident on the Nile. The event sobered Gurney for life. Many found him cold and aloof, and his conversation and manners tipped toward the sarcastic. This disconcerted some, even to the point of disbelief. Lady Battersea, for instance, quipped, "Mr. Gurney talks too much of humanity really to care for it."[89] Indeed, Gurney confessed to James that "the mystery of the Universe and the indefensibility of human suffering" were always with him.[90]

In addition and related to his mental health problems, Gurney lacked a profession. He tried four different ones, which can be divided roughly into four time periods of his adult life: music (1872–77), medicine (1877–81), law (1881–82), and psychical research (1882–88). Gurney was a diligent worker, committing himself to each new field with an intense fervor and seriousness, often investing long hours of arduous labor (perhaps even to the point of

EDMUND GURNEY (1847–1888), undated. Gurney was the most prodigious researcher of the Society for Psychical Research but also a depressive. It was through him that James was introduced to the Sidgwick Group. *Henry James Papers, MS Am 1094 (2245), f.49.2, by permission of the Houghton Library, Harvard University.*

mania), but failed to convert his energy into a concrete end point. The one he loved the most was music; Gurney desperately wanted to be a concert violinist, but despite long hours of practice and dedication, he had neither the skill nor style. Gurney then turned to medicine and completed most of the requirements for a degree but could not endure the suffering of the preoperative room. And his mind was far too creative and his personality too restless to withstand the confines of rule memorization that the legal profession required. By the time he quit law school in 1882, he was thirty-five years old and had published one book, *The Power of Sound* (1880)—a philosophical treatise on the aesthetics of music that argued the strongest effects we feel for music are consistent with a scientific study of their condition—that garnered little attention from either philosophers or art critics and left Gurney casting about for something at which to excel.

At this point Gurney turned to psychical research. Like the others, though, his interest in it stretched back to 1874, when he had joined Sidgwick and Myers in their early investigations of Spiritualism. Like them, Gurney was drawn first to psychical research for religious reasons but perhaps even more than them sought empirical evidence for the survival thesis in the face of a crisis of belief.[91] It also offered a solution to his crisis of profession. Gurney formally joined the SPR in 1883, becoming its secretary for six years (1883–88), an unpaid position that his family finances afforded him but that also required extensive labor such as copious letter writing, bookkeeping, researching, and frequent travel. He was also the editor of the SPR's *Proceedings* and *Journal* (1886–88). Gurney's main areas of interest were hypnotism and telepathy. They stemmed from his reading of medieval literature on hallucinations, about which he collected and examined between two and three hundred books. Like the others, he eventually concluded that all such information had to be considered hearsay and unsubstantiated since it could not be verified by subsequent scientific testing. Indeed, it was Gurney who convinced the others that they would have to collect new data under laboratory conditions to make valid epistemological claims regarding psychic phenomena.[92]

James met Gurney though his brother in the winter of 1882–83. By this point Henry Jr. was thriving in England and had made his own connections with the British intellectual aristocracy through literary and social circles. William had received an invitation to several British debate societies and men's clubs, and he turned to his brother for proper introductions. One was the elite Philosophical Club (founded 1847), a dining and discussion group of forty-seven men associated with the Royal Society that invited distinguished foreigners as guests. It boasted such names as Balfour, Gladstone, Huxley, and Tennyson.[93] James also met members of the Aristotelian Society for the Systematic Study of Philosophy, a technical group founded in 1879 by Shadworth Hollway Hodgson (no relation to Richard Hodgson), a leading British philosopher who enamored James, and of the Metaphysical Society, which was in the words of its historian "a symbol of the last great effort of the European mind to find a universe of discourse."[94] These associations were the exclusive province of middle- and upper-class men, professionals and autodidacts, and experts and aristocrats and were designed to foster good fellowship and philosophical discussion. Meetings were held at a senior member's residence or private club where discussion could develop over the course of a long dinner at which banter and witticisms mingled with serious dialogue. An esprit de corps fostered strong and loyal bonds between its members that were reinforced over time with the discovery of similarities of one's likes and dislikes in philosophical outlook, intellectual style, and personal integrity. Despite the exhaustion his participation cost him, James thrived in this environment, once writing, "I'm getting into the thick of philosophic society here," and at another time, "I went to the Aristotelian Society last night and had an instructive time."[95]

These societies had overlapping members who knew one another, and it was through an informal dinner club called the "Scratch Eight" that James was introduced to Gurney and eventually to the rest of the Sidgwick Group. Established by a core of intellectuals calling themselves the "Sunday Tramps" because of the long walks they took to talk philosophy, the Scratch Eight met irregularly for provocative discussion during the 1870s. In addition to Gurney, the eight "tramps" were the philosophers Shadworth Hodgson and George Croom Robertson, the legal historians Frederic William Maitland and Carveth Read, the psychologist James Sully, the jurist Frederick Pollock, and the essayist Leslie Stephen. The activities of the Scratch Eight reflected what Erasmus Darwin (Charles's grandfather) at a similar group called the Lunar Men a century earlier had called "a little philosophical laughing."[96] Theirs was a kind of semisocial, semiprivate behavior of intellectual misfits and geniuses who found a secret pleasure by confidently advancing their iconoclasms in the company of like-minded and sympathetic men.

In December 1882, when James was visiting his brother in England, Gurney invited him to a Scratch Eight dinner and repartee. "They meet once a month during the winter months, to dine and then discuss some philosophical subjects," he explained, "so you would be in for a considerable amount of 'shop'—I very much hope that you may be disengaged."[97] The invitation delighted James, and in preparation for meeting Gurney he readied himself by reading *The Power of Sound*. "I've been all the morning . . . trying to read [the book] . . . against meeting him on Sunday," he told his wife, who frequently served as William's confidant.[98] After the first gathering, he wrote, "Last night I dined at Gurney's with the 'Scratch Eight.' Gurney . . . proves to be one of the first rate minds of the time, a magnificent Adonis, 6 feet 4 [inches] in height with an extremely handsome face, voice, & general air of distinction about him, altogether the exact opposite of the classical idea of a philosopher. I felt quite at home among them, [and] was asked to the next meeting."[99] The meeting so impressed William that he enclosed the invitation to Alice and rushed back to his room to finish the book.[100] After another dinner two weeks later, he described his "delightful evening last night at the Scratch-Eight. Charming fellows all. Gurney strikes me as a big man with any amount of loose power about him. The evening at Gurney's was first-class, he is a wonderful creature, with no end of mental power."[101] Indeed, Gurney and others impressed James so much that he told Alice that "I have decided to stay till the end of the week for the 'Scratch Eight' dinner."[102] However, as much as James enjoyed the personal rapport and intellectual debate, the exhilaration exhausted him. "London does thoroughly disagree with me," he told Harry. "I am in a state of acute brain-fag, although I've done a mere minimum of work. I am only staying out the week on account of a philosophical dinner which takes place on Friday, this being Monday."[103]

Like most informal fledgling dining and discussion clubs, the Scratch Eight had a short life span. Gurney was the first to notify James of the society's shaky status: "I don[']t know whether we shall resume scratch 8s, at any rate before next year. Robertson . . . is an EXCELLENT chairman, with a sympathetic eye all round . . . [and possesses] the faculty of never losing his way in a discussion."[104] The impetus to continue was clearly in doubt, but Gurney later claimed James had helped keep it alive. "We have had no more Scratch 8s, since the evening when you were central," he told James.[105] But Robertson was a bit more optimistic, explaining to James that "our Scratch 8 *may* resume its work next winter. At present the elements have broken far too loose to be drawn together in a hurry: Gurney [is] now interested in you know what [that is, psychical research]," and the others were absorbed in their own special projects (Stephen was giving lectures on literature at Cambridge and working feverishly on the *Dictionary of National Biography*, of which he was the editor, and Pollock was engaged in his duties as an Oxford law professor).[106] But whatever else happened to the Scratch Eight, James knew that his life had been enriched though his participation and responded that he had been "filled with the liveliest admiration of the energy and intellectual temper of Gurney." Indeed, James confided to another tramp, "You know that, to quote what Gurney said one evening, to attain to assimilating your thought is the chief purpose of one's life."[107] These were neither idle nor overly sentimental thoughts. With four of these men—Gurney, Robertson, Hodgson, and Sully—James would become friends and colleagues, maintaining lengthy correspondences, and with Gurney and Robertson in particular he would develop especially close relations, admiring their dynamic minds and devotion to humanity. Gurney especially made the biggest impression upon James's heart as any man ever would with his unwavering dedication to psychical research.[108]

Despite the intimacy James developed with the Scratch Eight, he wrote to his brother that he had failed to make an impression. "Gurney," he complained, "whom I should most have liked to know, has taken no notice of me."[109] But James was mistaken. The admiration was mutual. Later that year, Gurney gushed to him, "Your letter was a GREAT delight. I echo, from heart as well as brain, every word you say as to kindred idiosyncrasies,—such kinships being the rare & precious things in the revelations of which one is occasionally made to feel that Providence is giving one one's turn. I certainly don[']t mean to let this particular turn be a short one."[110] Such exchanges warmed both men. "Your last letter was a very great delight to me," Gurney told James. "Full sympathy comes to us but rarely, in fact *such* sympathy *never*, & is all the more invigorating. I hope we shall get on in time."[111] Gurney's sentiment was highly understated. Their friendship not only matured but did so especially because of a shared understanding about human vulnerability. Both had experienced the anguish that their fragmented and delayed careers had caused them, both periodically suffered from mental breakdowns, and both sought intellectual outlets to address their afflictions—James in the study of psychology, Gurney in the pursuit of aesthetics.

Although James and Gurney found much in common personally, it was their shared interest in psychical research that sustained the relationship. "So you are really going to interest yourself practically in 'psychical research,'" Gurney exclaimed. "It is almost too good to be true."[112] Over time, psychical research afforded plenty of witticisms germane to men like James and Gurney, with the latter once making the double entendre that "you [James] have been constantly in my thoughts, however little telepathy may have revealed the fact to you; & on my permanent consciousness of you."[113] On a more serious front, their correspondence reveals that the two men cushioned the pain of mental anguish with their pursuit of matters psychical. "I wish to goodness you were not severed by that intractable Atlantic," Gurney once exclaimed.

"I don[']t believe there is any one of any repute in England, except Robertson, & the people in the SPR itself, who would walk across the street to see the results [in an article on hypnotism in the *Proceedings*] I wrote about."[114]

James read carefully everything Gurney wrote, especially *Phantasms of the Living*, the SPR's tour de force book on telepathy and hallucinations. Coauthored with Myers and Podmore but really the brainchild of Gurney, *Phantasms* was significant for several reasons. The first of the SPR's major works, it pointed to the importance of unconscious mental processes in the production of trance phenomena and expanded the methods used to induce hypnosis, thereby revealing the role that memory played in the hypnotic state compared with that in normal waking moments of consciousness.[115] Although parts of the book were based on faulty data and marred by invalid generalizations, it was otherwise a formidable piece of scholarship. Gurney, however, harbored great doubts about the merits of his work, which he shared with James upon finishing it: "[As] far as I can sum up my impressions, I should say that if I met the book as the work of a stranger, I should be almost completely unimpressed by it, and that I should be wrong. I don[']t even know whether I have at all succeeded in giving, by my tone, the sense that I really have of the insecurity of much of the evidences as regards detail; which does not imply insecurity as to the essential point of the various items."[116] James understood Gurney's insecurities instantly, as he was then wrestling with writing *The Principles of Psychology*.

James liked the book immensely. His approval provided great relief to the frazzled Briton, not least because a fire at the publisher's printing shop had burned the entire manuscript, forcing Gurney to reread all 1,400 pages of the original draft to prepare it a second time for publication.[117] "Your letter about my book was a *very solid pleasure*," Gurney told James. "The approval of one such as yours means, for me, that the book *has succeeded*, however much it may be damned and ridiculed. I do not the least know as yet what its reception is likely to prove to be or have been. Except for the little paragraph in 'Mind,' there has been only one notice of it which has given me any satisfaction; but it is perhaps significant that the [London] 'Times' should have ventured to treat it with some degree [of] respect."[118] No letter from James is known to have survived, so his opinion about his validating all of Gurney's efforts is unknown.[119] What is known is that James was willing to go on the public record in his admiration for and defense of Gurney and *Phantasms*. In fact, taken as a whole, *Phantasms* nearly overwhelmed James in its originality and brilliance. "Have you seen Gurney's two bulky tomes?" he excitedly queried his friend and fellow psychologist Karl Stumpf. "[It is] an amazingly patient and thorough piece of work[.] I should not at all wonder if it were the beginning of a new departure in natural history.... I think Gurney worthy of the highest praise for his devotion to this unfashionable work. He is not the kind of stuff which the ordinary pachydermatous fanatic and mystic is made of."[120] It was true: Gurney was no ordinary man, but as will become clear, James had overstated Gurney's abilities.

Although Gurney's commitment to psychical research enamored James, it was his general philosophical attitude that most impressed him. In particular, James saw in Gurney something akin to his own approach to psychical research. Indeed, it seems likely that one source of James's tertium quid approach emerged from a review he wrote of one of Gurney's earlier books by the very same title: *Tertium Quid, Chapters on Various Disputations* (1887), a two-volume work of critical essays on topics of a broad and philosophical nature that Gurney had written during the 1880s, featuring titles such as "The Human Ideal," "Natural Religion," and "A Chapter on the Ethics of Pain."[121] Getting paid "ten dollars" for his review in the *Nation*, James told his wife on at least three separate occasions that he had struggled mightily during that winter to read the book, make sense of it, and write his review.[122] In one instance, he noted "that impossible review" required him "to take a cup of coffee to do it on" (James generally disdained stimulants, though he tried a number of them on several occasions). But after a solid afternoon of writing, his efforts led to success, with James explaining that once "my pen got in to a eulogistic turn..., I let her run. All the better for G[urney] & no worse for the Nation readers."[123]

Despite these complaints, which were quite typical of James's letters, his review was quite glowing. He found two admirable qualities: the fair and balanced method of seeking truth that echoed the notion of a tertium quid, and his final assessment of the book, which praised it as first-rate. Of the former, James noted that Gurney "loves truth almost too much." Of the latter, James concluded "that *if there be* an invisible order continuous with the present order of Nature and enveloping it, our attempts at solving the religious problem rationally may be postponed till the facts of the invisible order are known.... [M]r. Gurney's intellectual fiber is at the furthest imaginable extreme from credulity. Balanced states of mind like his are growing commoner.... Altogether these volumes can rank among the subtlest and sincerest pieces of critical work of our time."[124] Ironically, although James's accolades "surprised and delighted" his friend, Gurney noted in his final letter to James the book's "complete failure, as regard sale."[125] Still, James's review revealed his philosophical disposition, especially the idea that truth could be found by steering a middle course such as the one Gurney recommended between "Nature" and "the religious problem." James's conclusion captured his views about what attitude human beings should take when making inquiries into the world: a fair and balanced one that was not a priori trapped into accepting a dichotomous conceptual framework and that thus allowed for some "third thing." In other words, James's friendship with Gurney was but another source of his emergent tertium quid. As he put it to a dying Henry Sidgwick, "Our hope of you had, I confess, been infinitesimal, but you know what Gurney wrote . . . about the difference between a life with an infinitesimal hopeful possibility in it, and a life with no possibility at all."[126]

During the 1880s, then, James had discovered, explored, and established a profound fraternity with intellectuals on the far side of the Atlantic. His participation in the Scratch Eight in general and his friendship with Gurney in particular not only immersed him in British intellectual and associational life but also, more importantly, formed the portal to James's formal entry into psychical research by introducing him to members of the Sidgwick Group, which, in turn, provided him with an outlet to develop his tertium quid method of inquiry.

Richard Hodgson

Of all the psychical researchers James befriended, he was closest with Richard Hodgson. Hodgson differed from the other core members of the Sidgwick Group in several significant ways. Considerably younger than the rest, he was neither the son of a minister nor of a statesman, his father did not die when he was a boy, and although of English origin he was born in West Melbourne, Australia (his father was an importer who had emigrated from Yorkshire). Most important, Hodgson was not educated at public (that is, "private") schools but rather attended common ones, followed by several years at the University of Melbourne, a state-sanctioned institution. In many other ways, however, Hodgson had much in common with the Sidgwick Group. Like Henry Sidgwick, he was quite prodigious from the start. In 1878, by the age of twenty-three, he had earned an LLD (before that, Hodgson got his BA in 1874, an LLB in 1875, and an MA in 1876). Like Gurney, he played the violin and was interested in aesthetics, and like Myers he wrote poetry (though not as eloquently). Upon the completion of his doctor of laws degree, Hodgson left Australia and sailed for England to enroll at St. John's College, in Cambridge, where he studied classics with Sidgwick, eventually earning a degree in Moral Science in 1881, as the others had. Of them all, Sidgwick thought Hodgson his best student, and through their relationship Hodgson became an honorary member of the British intellectual aristocracy.[127]

Unlike them all, though, Hodgson was a manly man. He possessed a muscular physique yet was light on his feet, and although he smoked incessantly he had a zeal for sports, fervently lifting weights, boxing, swimming in the ocean, and playing racket sports. He was also a member of sporting fraternities, the forerunners of modern sports enthusiasts who loved to attend sporting events for the male camaraderie and shared excitement but also, as scholars of sports have shown, as a refuge from femininity, domesticity, and the pressures of the workplace in the demanding industrial economy and competitive marketplace.[128] Henry James III, William's son, provided one of the more detailed accounts of Hodgson's personality, describing him as "very observant," having a "sharp eye," and possessing a "serene, untroubled countenance." He considered him "picturesque," noting his "booming voice" and "hearty laugh."[129] Hodgson liked to argue, enjoyed repartee, and gesticulated frequently during conversation. He also possessed a kind of "great animal spirit," frequently using words like "splendid" and "glorious."[130] To a great extent, Hodgson was something of a maverick. He wore a brown suit instead of a black one, refused to kneel (in symbolic protest) during his degree ceremony, and carried a pesky parrot on his shoulder when frequenting his private club. Although not an atheist, Hodgson did not experience the crisis of faith that plagued Sidgwick, Myers, and Gurney. However, he did have premonitions and came to believe in extrasensory perception. Unlike the others, Hodgson never married, but like them (Henry Sidgwick being the exception), he held the Victorian view that women belonged to the domestic sphere.

Hodgson's curiosity in matters psychical developed during his youth in Australia, but it was through his association with Sidgwick, Myers, and Gurney that he decided to devote his career to studying them. Hodgson joined the SPR in either late 1882 or early 1883, and despite his age and class differences with the Sidgwick Group and the fact that he was not a founding member, Hodgson became an integral participant. He was also the only member of the SPR to make his living through psychical research (though the others devoted as much time and labor to it). Indeed, Hodgson was the only paid member of the SPR, serving as an investigator (1883–87), secretary of the ASPR (1887–90), and secretary-treasurer of the "American Branch" of the SPR (1890–1905). His many areas of interest in psychical research led him to study Theosophy, telepathy, double personality, and trance mediumship.[131] Initially, Hodgson played the bogeyman. In 1883 he was sent to India to

RICHARD HODGSON (1855–1905), undated. Sidgwick's Australian accolade, Hodgson was the backbone of and tireless researcher for the American Society for Psychical Research and a fervent supporter of Mrs. Leonora Piper. *Henry James Papers, MS Am 1094, box 1, p. 17, by permission of the Houghton Library, Harvard University.*

investigate Madame Blavatsky and her Theosophy troop, which he exposed as fraudulent.[132] This earned him the reputation of being a scrupulous researcher who combined the right blend of curiosity, skepticism, detective skill, and patience. In 1886, with the help of S. V. Davey—a professional "conjurer" who shared his secrets with the SPR—he exposed the slate-writing medium William Eglinton as a fraud and demonstrated the role that incorrect observation and memory lapse played in the investigation of psychic phenomena.[133] Hodgson went on to uncover Eusapia Palladino's trickery and cast doubt on Myers's favorite medium, Mrs. Rosalie Thompson.[134] And he edited Myers's *Human Personality*, a book that had been more or less complete when Myers died in 1901 but that needed shaping before publication. In 1887, the SPR sent Hodgson to the United States to study Mrs. Piper, the famous Boston trance medium, which he did for almost two decades, publishing two lengthy articles on her. In the first, Hodgson concluded that the evidence for the survival of the soul thesis was inconclusive, but in the second, after five more years of study, he decided that nothing other than this thesis could adequately explain her abilities.[135] Hodgson was at work on a third article when he died quite unexpectedly while playing handball in 1905. Despite his feverish but meticulous work, he never tabulated his findings in book form, leaving untouched most of his post-1898 material.

Upon arriving in the United States in 1887 to assume his position in the ASPR, he began a friendship with William James that lasted nearly two decades. At first William was hesitant and even a little suspicious because he had read some of Hodgson's early philosophical articles and found them wanting (during the 1880s, before Hodgson devoted himself to psychical research full-time, he published a few pieces in *Mind* and *Contemporary Review*). With Sidgwick's financial backing and pedagogic blessing, Hodgson had been sent for six months to study German philosophy in Jena. While grateful for the education, Hodgson always remained faithful to his first philosophical love, Herbert Spencer, whom he declared "the greatest thinker the world has ever seen."[136] In one of his more strident attempts to defend Spencer from attacks by T. H. Green (Spencer's nemesis) in the pages of *Contemporary Review*, Hodgson resorted to attacking Green, which drew a venomous reply. A similar flare-up occurred in the pages of *Mind*. Upon reading Hodgson's second article during the summer of 1885, James declared it "muddled, clotted, dusky, and ineffectual, save for a gleam or two of light."[137]

When the Sidgwick Group heard of James's doubts from Croom Robertson, they immediately tried to quell them. Gurney spearheaded the effort, writing to James in praise of Hodgson, "I think, when you see something of him, you will be struck by his really remarkable thoroughness & acuteness in the sort of work he is now doing. His qualities are *absolutely invaluable*; & psychical research ought to insure his life for about a million pounds. His intellectual honesty is quite complete; & he combines the powers of a first-rate detective with a perfect readiness to believe in astrology. (*Don[']t quote this*, as it might be misunderstood. I should pity the astrologer whose horoscopes he took to tackling.)"[138] Gurney's high esteem of Hodgson stood in for Sidgwick's view, since there existed something of a father-son relationship between the two, with Sidgwick subsidizing Hodgson's trip to Jena and peddling Hodgson's early philosophical articles at *Mind* and Hodgson once praising Sidgwick as an "able man" for his ability to run the SPR.[139] Upon learning that Hodgson would be welcomed into the Sidgwick Group and offered as the ASPR's new secretary, James wrote to a friend that "Sidgwick & [G]urney have taken him up because of his leanings or more in their 'Psychical' direction."[140] It was at this time that Sidgwick had assigned Hodgson to investigate the Theosophy "business" in India. Of those efforts, Gurney had nothing but additional praise. In some of the last words ever penned to James, Gurney wrote, "It *is* a mercy that Hodgson exists; I cannot help being glad that he is likely to stay a bit longer with you, though he will be very welcome when he returns."[141]

James's worries subsided upon meeting Hodgson in 1887. Almost immediately the two men developed a near daily working relationship. But it was not because of the intellectual aristocracy that James and Hodgson became friends. Rather, it was through a shared ideal of virtuous friendship steeped in Victorian manliness. Both valued investing an immense amount of time and effort in psychical research. In fact, with the exception of family members and possibly certain faculty members at Harvard such as Josiah Royce, James spent more time with Hodgson during the late 1880s and all of the 1890s than any other person.

They met frequently at a number of locations. One was the ASPR offices on Boylston Street near the State House in Boston; another was at Hodgson's apartment right around the corner on Charles Street. "I went again to Hodgson's. . . . Thence to Hodgson's . . ." after visiting the "offices of the [A]SPR," he scribbled to his wife once, and later, "I spent a couple of hours with Hodgson." On another occasion he noted he was even completing the very letter he was writing to her in "Richard Hodgson's rooms."[142] James also dined with Hodgson at various men's clubs. "I have been dining with [Hodgson at] the 'Liberal Union Club' [organized by the philosopher Francis Ellingwood Abbot to promote in part the separation of church and state],"

WILLIAM JAMES (1842–1910), 1887, when he first met and befriended Richard Hodgson. Photo by the Pach Brothers. *William James Papers, MS Am 1092 (1185.56), by permission of the Houghton Library, Harvard University.*

he told Alice, where Hodgson spoke on psychical research. "Hodgson talked very well. Many stories by many members. I put in a word for planchette." On another evening, he noted that he would "have supper with Hodgson and not get home until after eight." And while giving the third of six lectures on abnormal mental states at the Brooklyn Institute, he wrote to Alice to say that "I just caught a [trolley] car, and found Hodgson lunching with a great crowd at the Tavern Club." For all of these public appearances, James observed that unlike himself Hodgson was quite comfortable and confident in unfamiliar venues. "R[ichard Hodgson] is very good with strangers, & shows his best side—he ought to see no others," he told Alice.[143]

Hodgson also frequented the Jameses at their home at Ninety-Five Irving Street in Cambridge, just a short walk through the woods to Harvard Yard. Mealtimes were often the occasion for discussing psychical research. To Alice, James noted he had "had lunch with . . . Richard Hodgson." Once Hodgson came for tea "weary with the Leonora Piper agency," while another time James said he "saw Hodgson and [they] had lunch with Jim Putnam." Hodgson and James spent so much time talking psychical research at James's house that William once inquired of Harvard president Charles William Eliot whether "Hodgson could use a room at Harvard, where he would sometimes sleep," and not have to travel back to Boston late at night. The positive impact of all these meetings led James to confess to George Dorr that Hodgson was "showing himself [to be] absolutely good tempered and reasonable."[144]

James and Hodgson also traveled together for matters psychical or met up in major metropolises such as New York or at vacation spots such as Newport, Rhode Island. Describing one itinerary to Alice that involved investigating some new mediums, William wrote that he was "to leave for Newport at 11:40, in co[mpany] with Hodgson," and two days later wrote again that he and Hodgson were departing for Manhattan, after "a pleasant thirty hours in Newport." Apparently, they traveled by steamer instead of rail, for James noted that "Hodgson & I started in the rain . . . [in] a rather rocking boat last night but slept well in a beautiful clean stateroom, and saw the wonderful approach to the city between six & seven [the following morning]." Despite the growing bond, James made light of Hodgson's inability to replace the company of his wife, writing, "I don't know whether I told you that I was going to take Hodgson mit [German for "with"]. What a fate!—to own an Alice Gibbens, and yet to have to put up with the company of a Hodgson instead! [W]hat mockery!"[145] The jest worked in both directions.

Even when James and Hodgson were traveling abroad separately, they sought out each other. In one case, there were near visits in England and Italy.

To his friend James Jackson Putnam, William wrote, "You will miss Hodgson. I am hoping to see him before the end of the month, at Cambridge, where I may be able to make a little visit at the Myers'es [sic]." But the Jameses left for Rome before Hodgson arrived in England, of which James disclosed to Hodgson that he was "desolated that there is no chance of my seeing you before you leave." After they left and Hodgson had reached London, James expressed his relief that Hodgson had arrived safely: "Glad you are safe over. I am hoping to see Myers here in a few days.... I wish I *could* join you, but of course I can't. Why not come *here*???" To persuade Hodgson, Alice added a note of her own personally requesting he come to Rome. The "two weeks," she teased him, would be a "liberal education for you." Apparently Hodgson was unable to get away from England, for he responded that he wished James could come there instead. He added that William should introduce himself to George Frazer, Hodgson's friend, who was staying at the same hotel as the Jameses and wanted James to "convert" him to psychical research.[146]

James and Hodgson also traveled together in the more remote parts of New England, such as to Bar Harbor, Maine, where they visited with the Dorrs. George Dorr had been a student at Harvard in the late 1880s and because of James's example took up an active interest in investigating Spiritualism. On several occasions he summoned James to his home to conduct séances. In one instance James replied that he could not come this time but that Hodgson, who had just arrived in the United States, would come in his place. "I am glad you are going to have Hodgson, who is a trump, in spite of his clothes," James joshed. Dorr grew to like Hodgson as well and even agreed to pay Hodgson's salary of "1500 dollars" when psychical research in America was floundering financially, which James lauded as "quite reasonable."[147]

Perhaps the most cherished visits occurred when the two men adjourned to the countryside. One favorite spot was "Putnam's Shanty," a collection of cabins located in Keene Valley, Vermont, jointly owned by James, Putnam, and others. Sigmund Freud once visited and participated in séances with Putnam while Putnam cemented his loyalty to Freud and his commitment to psychoanalysis.[148] James and Hodgson hiked vigorously together throughout the Green Mountains, where James admired Hodgson's vitality, once writing to his daughter that in going up a hill he had to "follow in the wake of Hodgson" and instructing her "to pardon me for leaving him to [sic] unprotected to the enemy—meaning the jeunes filles [young girls]." When it threatened to rain too much to climb "the Giant," they opted to "scamper up the mountain across the valley & back." James also "took Hodgson to the Ausable River," as he told Alice, "and up the new carriage road towards the ponds—not nearly such a vandalic innovation as you might suppose." On the rainy days they used the time to enjoy a "reading aloud of Spencer by Hodgson" so that on the sunny days the two could discuss it, which, as William told Alice, "was continued well up the mountain side" the next day. After another visit years later, James told Hodgson he hoped he had "enjoyed" Keene Valley.[149]

James also invited Hodgson to his country house in Chocorua, New Hampshire, where James brought only his most trusted friends and family members. In addition to discussing psychical matters, Hodgson played at length with James's sons, who adored him, acting as a lovable uncle. As William once told his two boys, "Hodgson is here, as 'ribald' as ever."[150] Indeed, Henry III provided the most colorful and extensive portrait of Hodgson during the Chocorua days:

> I recall that he used to have big pockets made in the lining of his jackets, something like the pockets in a gamekeeper's coat, although he told me they were conjurer's pockets. Out of them he would fish cork balls for palming tricks, tobacco pouches, pipes, papers, books, almost everything. In those days, he used occasionally to spend a week or so with the family at Chocorua, in New Hampshire, and we boys used to trail around at his heels as much as he would let us. He used to take us out swimming, and taught us to fish.... He would enlist us boys or any other duffers who happened to be guests in the house, fill a row-boat, and infect everybody with something of his own manly spirit. He filled us youngsters with enthusiasm, and under such circumstances was not only willing to put up with our society for hours, but made us feel as if we were all playmates together. He used to play hide-and-seek with us in the woods, and amused us with sleight-of-hand tricks. I still cherish with a good deal of sentiment a fly-rod which he brought to Chocorua one year, and of which he was evidently proud.... My father hated fishing and was never with us on such occasions; and according to fishermen they ought to have been silent for hours, but Hodgson talked a great deal about whatever caught his eye.... Sometimes he would hum a tune, sometimes quote poetry, of which he was great reader.... I realised that he never pitched his reflections or talked above the level of our young heads. We were fascinated.[151]

Although it is mildly perplexing that James disliked fishing—since it was a manly activity and he appreciated nature perhaps more than anything or anyone else—he nonetheless felt deeply that Hodgson was good for his sons. In fact, he held up Hodgson as a model human being for his sons to emulate. "The *man of men* is he who in the army, at sea, or on any arduous expedition," he explained to them, "keeps up the spirits of the crew by showing good cheer and turning things into a joke himself. To be known as such a man is to be recognized for having the root of human character—helpfulness and steadfastness. Hodgson & Nichols are such men. I wish the James boys might be known to be such."[152] Could any other statement indicate such deep admiration for this man and his appreciation of Hodgson's manliness? Even Putnam, who also got to know Hodgson during their long hikes, confirmed such sentiments, recalling that of all the men and women of the SPR, James counted among his personal friends "especially Richard Hodgson."[153] Upon Hodgson's leaving the Jameses's house in Chocorua, William explained to Flournoy his admiration: "Hodgson left us this morning after a visit of ten days. It is a pleasure to see a man in such an absolute state of moral physical health. His very face shows the firmness of a soul in equilibrium—another proof of the strength which a belief in future life may give one!"[154]

As the foregoing indicates, the central members of the Sidgwick Group played significant roles in James's life. With them James formed intimate friendships that lasted two decades and were some of the closest relationships he developed with any persons outside his family. As James put it, "Wherever you are it is your own friends who make your world."[155] James shared several significant features with these friends, including a similar family and social background; a style of candor, wit, and straightforwardness; and a deep intellectual curiosity for matters psychical. These friendships were not transient but deep and sustaining, and they nurtured him through his doubts regarding the progress of psychical research and comforted him during its triumphs. Moreover, they were not born of mere chance but rather out of a particular attitude toward life steeped in personal experience. With Sidgwick he shared an appreciation for rational thought and patience toward the open-ended data revealed from their investigations. With Myers he shared a passion for the possibility that such data might someday amount to solid evidence for a belief in human immortality. With Gurney he shared empathy for the needless suffering in the world but also the necessity to persevere with one's life nonetheless. With Hodgson he shared a respect for a rugged, manly approach to life. And so together they became brothers-in-arms, forming what Ralph Barton Perry called a "moral comradeship."[156] It was partly because of this brotherhood that James decided to take seriously his youthful interest in Spiritualism and to commit himself to psychical research for the rest of his life. For James, this was nothing short of a moral act. As he once exclaimed to Hodgson, "You and I must be moral heroes, especially you.... [Others] will wish on the day of judgment that they had put themselves on record with our quintet (Oliver Lodge, Frederic Myers, Mrs. S[idgwick], you and I) in order to be then sharing our prominent position of honour and profit."[157]

This was quite a statement, since James was more inclined toward careful consideration than dogmatic pronouncements. Thus, when Perry wrote that James's "loyalty to them implied loyalty to their cause," we can see he did so without irony or hyperbole.[158] We can also see that while those friendships were formed to address specific intellectual problems, they were grounded in class, religious, and gendered developments of the late nineteenth century, and particularly within a Victorian transatlantic community of discourse in which a group of intellectuals struggled with their faith while wrestling for their place in modern society. Ultimately, they provided James with the freedom to develop an intellectual attitude toward matters psychical that became his tertium quid method of inquiry.

three

OUT OF THE EGG

The dynamic brotherhood that William James and the Sidgwick Group created became the informal basis for James's tertium quid approach to psychical research. But it was not alone sufficient to sustain his efforts. Something more formal was required, namely, officially organized bodies that investigated psychic phenomena. These became the central purpose of two small associations in 1882 and 1884 respectively, the British and American Societies for Psychical Research (SPR and ASPR). Similar groups formed on the European continent. Taken as a whole, they manifested distinct spatial dimensions in Western scientific culture during the late nineteenth and early twentieth centuries whose institutions were demarcated geographically. A notable pattern developed along east/west and north/south axes from Poland to the United States and from England to Italy respectively, with Boston/New York, London/Cambridge, Amsterdam/Utrecht, Berlin/Munich, and Warsaw/Krakow forming the longitudinal axis between 50 and 55 degrees, and London/Cambridge, Paris, Geneva, Milan, Genoa, Turin, Florence and Palermo forming the latitudinal axis from 0 to 15 degrees, with the SPR in Cambridge forming its epicenter at Greenwich Mean Time. In other words, psychical research between the 1880s and 1920s was a transatlantic, transcontinental, and trans-European development consisting of primarily white, educated, Protestant, middle-aged men (and a few women) trained mostly in medicine, philosophy, and the emergent social sciences who formed new official dues-paying organizations replete with established periodicals, annual meetings, and membership roles, all of which relied heavily on the finances of a few well-heeled individuals to fund and sustain their cause.[1]

James's psychical research emerged within this institutional nexus. He joined the SPR in 1884, facilitated the launch of the ASPR in 1884–85, and assumed many duties in both organizations from there on, helping to build their missions, sustain membership levels, raise operating funds, chair investigative committees, conduct research, write articles and review others for their periodicals, pen letters to other members, answer inquiries from an expectant public, justify the work to skeptics, and defend their reputations from critics. In addition to these services, James sat on the ASPR council (1885–87) and was elected vice president of the ASPR (1887–90), vice president of the "American Branch" of the SPR (1890–1906), which was established after the ASPR was later subsumed into the SPR, and president of the SPR (1894–95). Like the moral comradeship he developed with the Sidgwick Group, James's formal role in organized psychical research societies occurred within two significant developments of the long nineteenth century. The first was the emergence and spread of learned societies in the West, especially transcontinental and transatlantic scientific ones that fostered modern disciplinary practices, specialized fields of knowledge, and a coterie of experts. The second was the advent in the United States of voluntary associations in which Americans sought democratic harmony through participatory membership in communal organizations whose function was to offset the rise of a corporate society and hierarchical culture. The SPR and ASPR modeled themselves in the fashion of scientific societies and the ASPR in particular of associational life.

James maintained his active membership in the ASPR to the end of its life in 1906 (as the "American Branch" of the SPR) and in the SPR to the end of his life in 1910. But he did so very reluctantly because in spite of his commitment to psychical research, he harbored a strong aversion to organizational life. While the SPR and ASPR remained small and relatively insignificant compared to major scientific societies such as the British and American Associations for the Advancement of Science, they aspired to structured organization. James's reluctance to participate in psychical research societies arose from the tension between his philosophy of individualism, which championed the heroic role of the individual to follow his or her own experience, and his distrust and even disdain for institutions and their highly formalized, bureaucratic, and administrative procedures, which he felt quashed individual initiative, creativity, and spontaneity. In particular, James found that his desire to be loyal to the men and women of the SPR and ASPR conflicted directly with the very organizations they created for the purpose of pursuing psychical research. Because of this incompatibility, James hesitated to accept any of the responsibilities of organizational work.

Nonetheless, James summoned his energy for it and dutifully performed his tasks. And he did so because he realized that ultimately his role in these organizations offered the best chance to investigate the "non-normal" *systematically* in ways that an individual or even a loose cadre of them, such as his Knickerbocker "uncles" or even the Scratch Eight tramps, could not. However reluctantly, James participated in psychical research societies to foster his tertium quid. Ironically, then, James became what his first biographer called "a partisan of psychical research, both as officer and as soldier in the ranks."[2]

THE SOCIETY FOR PSYCHICAL RESEARCH

From its inception in 1882, the SPR exhibited a strong sense of purpose and high-mindedness.[3] While it was not the first serious body in England to investigate psychic phenomena, it was the first scientific and long-lasting investigative society.[4] Its objective was clear: "to investigate that large body of debateable [sic] phenomena designated by such terms as mesmeric, psychical and spiritualistic without prejudice or prepossession of any kind, and in the same spirit of exact and unimpassioned enquiry which has enabled Science to solve so many problems, once not less obscure nor less hotly debated."[5] The first of many such lofty statements, the SPR promised to make a systematic attempt to unlock the mysteries of psychic phenomena. James supported this approach, though he made more moderate statements in its defense. To Karl Stumpf, a German psychologist and friend, he wrote, "I don't know whether you have heard of the London 'Society for Psychical Research,' which is seriously and laboriously investigating all sorts of 'supernatural' matters. . . . I don't know what you think of such work . . . , but I believe there is no source of deception in the investigation of nature which can compare with a fixed belief that certain kinds of phenomena are *impossible*."[6] Stumpf thought James's interest in psychical research was unworthy, but James disagreed.[7] Along with the SPR, he maintained that psychic phenomena belonged to the natural realm and that empiricism would unveil their properties. It was the perfect starting place to apply his tertium quid since it neither accepted nor dismissed the "non-normal" outright but instead offered a philosophical justification for its systematic investigation.

The SPR was steeped historically in two groups, one informal and secretive and one formal and scientific, namely, the Cambridge Apostles and the British Association for the Advancement of Science. The former was the philosophical and moral model and the latter the scientific and organizational one. The relevance of these two societies to the SPR is most apparent through Henry Sidgwick's leadership roles in all three. In 1820, several St. John's College undergrads founded a conversation club formally called the Cambridge Conversazione Society, or the Cambridge Apostles, which quickly became a secret society for the elite intellectuals at Trinity and King's Colleges that produced members of the Bloomsbury circle and the Cambridge spies. Lord Tennyson, Erasmus Darwin, and James Fitzjames Stephen were but three early notables. The philosophers G. E. Moore and Bertrand Russell were also prominent members. So, too, was Henry Sidgwick, who claimed his immersion into it during the early 1860s "had more effect on my intellectual life than any one thing that happened to me afterwards." Developed in the context of the Victorian Platonic revival that championed dialogic reasoning in which the pursuit of truth trumped all other concerns, the club functioned much like the Scratch Eight and other philosophical discussion societies. Sidgwick described the club as "the spirit of the pursuit of truth," in which every member was encouraged to be "perfectly frank . . . , [and where] absolute candour was the only duty" enforced. The point was to discuss matters of grave importance, not for the sake of debate itself or the "love of paradox." The Apostles was a perfect fit for young Sidgwick and an ideal precursor to the SPR since he believed both societies addressed the "deepest problems of human life." Indeed, since the SPR's guiding purpose was to find evidence for the survival thesis—itself a pursuit of fundamental truth about human nature—the SPR became the logical successor for Sidgwick's ultimate search for "the secret of the Universe."[8]

If the Cambridge Apostles served as the intellectual inspiration for the SPR, the rise of learned societies in the nineteenth century, especially provincial and disciplinary ones with their sole mission of knowledge advancement, served as the organizational model. Their origins stretched back to the mid-seventeenth century when something akin to a scientific community had emerged with the advent of national scientific societies such as the Royal Society of London (1660) and the French Académie des Sciences (1666).[9] These early scientific societies had several intellectual origins, each related to Lord Bacon's empirical program.[10] Structurally, they were metropolis based, preprofessional and highly bureaucratic, and warranted by the monarch's political and social charters. Membership was limited to the aristocracy and a few gentry, and they pitched the work in nationalist themes designed to further the aims of the state.[11]

The SPR was also rooted in provincial scientific societies that emerged in the late eighteenth and early nineteenth centuries. In contrast with national societies, provincial ones did not espouse a national mission or owe their existence to a monarch and thus did not require a charter. They also offered membership to men (and once in a while a woman) of learning beyond the aristocracy and gentry. The science practiced at provincial societies was designed to meet the social needs of their members in that it was generally more loosely organized and eclectic, and vocational interests of the amateur researcher were encouraged through prizes and service awards. Provincial societies were in principle distinguished from professional societies whose main purpose was maintaining standards and establishing scales of remuneration.[12] Provincial scientific societies took their cue from the tremendous growth of literary and philosophical societies, which together formed at a rate of between five and twenty per decade such that by the end of the nineteenth century, there existed more than one hundred in the British provinces. Most of the scientific societies consisted of amateurs, industrialists, and men from the professions who were tied to industry and interested in advancing scientific knowledge primarily for economic development. Membership ranged from one hundred to five hundred, or about that of the Royal Society two hundred years prior. Nationalist, specialist scientific societies also emerged in this period, including the Linnaean Society (1788), the Geological Society (1807), and the Chemical Society (1840), which challenged the metropolitan Royal Society.[13]

Since amateurs conducted much of the research in provincial societies, and since much of that work was geared toward industry and advancing the interests of the nation-state, it was felt that a society was needed, in the words of one historian of science, to "unite scientists throughout the country [to] promote British science."[14] That organization was the British Association for the Advancement of Science. Founded in 1831, the BAAS was modeled after the German national scientific society which the natural philosopher Lorenz Oken helped establish in 1822. Charles Babbage first floated the idea while attending a German meeting in Berlin in 1828.[15] The BAAS took itself very seriously from the outset, founding a mission and a set of rules, electing officers for distinct periods of time, creating a council, developing both a journal where members could publish findings and an annual report that contained meeting notes and news of the profession, and establishing an annual presidential address to summarize scientific advances.[16] The BAAS had two distinct features, namely, recognized specialists who delivered regular reports from the various fields and the formation of individual sections replete with committees whose purpose was to undertake assigned tasks.[17] The BAAS became the organizational model for the SPR, partly due to the influence of

William Barrett, a prominent physicist who was an active member of both and one of the SPR's founders.

The BAAS emerged in a period of social and political reform between the 1820s and the 1840s that gave rise to the "middling classes." This middle class, which was taking root in the provinces, was invested in Britain's imperial project and believed that the advance of science and technology would help further that cause. Although "democratic and provincial" in appearance, the BAAS was actually run by a few well-heeled and interlocking Cambridge men known as the "Gentlemen of Science" whom Samuel Taylor Coleridge famously dubbed the new clerisy, though it was William Whewell who coined the generic term "scientist" in 1833 as a way to separate those researchers from philosophers and to signal that their subject matter was material nature. In the words of this society's historians, "men of knowledge found new importance" during this period when industrialization "increased income, travel, [and] easier communication" and a "revived interest in formal higher education" helped define the new scientific intelligentsia, thus giving rise to peripatetic associations like the BAAS (it met in a different provincial capital each year) and thereby helping foster a sense of "geographical union." Cambridge, where the SPR would be based, became a major center of reform, and its colleges became the focal point of the BAAS, which was run by the "Cambridge Network" at Trinity, where the majority of the "Gentlemen of Science" worked. Moderate by temper, BAAS leaders mostly belonged to the liberal Anglican Church (Broad Church) and tended to be political centrists (mostly Whigs) who were opposed to Home Rule. They were largely composed of a number of ordained ministers, many of whom became leading professors and researchers. And they were also the main office holders of the BAAS, four of whom were eventually knighted. Membership was exclusive. Pointedly, "no Jews, Roman Catholics, Methodists, Congregationalists, Baptists, diehard Tories, Utilitarians, or proponents of socialism" were found among them. In short, the BAAS was the culmination of two centuries of evolving scientific organizational structure that reflected the middle class's reformist impulse.[18]

The scientific clerisy of the BAAS and intellectual aristocracy of the SPR also overlapped with regard to key individuals, goals, and purpose. Sidgwick, Barrett, Oliver Lodge, and William Crookes were prominent members of both, both organizations made truth their highest aim, and they shared a similar passion regarding their singularity of purpose. As two BAAS historians have summarized it, "The Gentlemen of Science saw themselves not as spokesmen for a narrow interest ..., but simply as the anointed interpreters of God's truth about the natural, and hence, moral world."[19] The SPR had the same goal but with one significant and controversial modification, namely, to include psychic phenomena within the scope of the natural world. With this crucial caveat, the SPR became a notable focal point for the next generation of educated intellectuals to sponsor psychical matters.

The SPR, then, modeled itself after the BAAS, which itself was a descendent of national, provincial, professional, and disciplinary learned societies. However, while the SPR aspired to scientific research and practice, it did not neatly fit into any of the classic taxonomic categories of scientific societies. Rather, it was a hybrid that combined significant features of all four types—national society, provincial society, professional organization, and disciplinary organization. Although neither chartered, controlled, supported, nor financed by the government, nor officially enlisted to serve the interest of the nation-state, the SPR sought to advance the cause of psychical research in order to benefit British subjects. In that sense it was like a national society. Given that the SPR was a more informal, loosely organized social club based in Cambridge and not in the nation's capital, it partially fit the description of a provincial society, too. Since its members were trained professionally, albeit not in the natural sciences, it manifested some features of a professional organization. And because the SPR developed its own specialized field of knowledge ("psychical research") that required expertise (though no separate training) and created its own publications, membership, and funding, it was a kind of disciplinary organization as well.[20]

Nonetheless, in almost every way the SPR mimicked the organizational structure of the BAAS. This was the case from the wording of its founding mission, the election of officers, and the creation of a council, to the establishment of research committees, the advent of serial publications, and the delivery of the presidential address at the annual meeting. First, the SPR elected officers. Henry Sidgwick served as its first president. The original vice presidents were Barrett; Arthur J. Balfour, the prime minister of Great Britain from 1902 to 1905; Harvery Goodwin Carlisle; John R. Holland; the Right Reverend Bishop of Carlisle and Minister of Parliament Richard Hutton; the essayist Roden Berkeley Wriothesley Noel; the physicist John William Strutt Rayleigh; the physicist Balfour Stewart; the philologist Hensleigh Wedgwood; and William Stainton Moses, clergyman and eventual Spiritualist. The SPR quickly built up a significant body of members and associates as well. Beginning with fewer than three hundred members in 1882–83, the SPR more than tripled its roll to approximately one thousand a decade later in 1893, with its numbers multiplying thereafter.[21] Several notable "honorary members" included influential professionals such as the chemist and physicist Sir

William Crookes, the naturalist Alfred Russel Wallace, and the British prime minister William Gladstone. Indeed, the SPR membership rolls read like a "Who's Who" of British intelligentsia. In addition to those mentioned, a number of high-profile names stand out. From Britain: Gerald Balfour, minister of Parliament and nearly prime minister; Leslie Stephen, author and critic; John Addington Symonds, poet and literary critic; Alfred Tennyson, poet; John Ruskin, art critic and author; and Lewis Carroll, mathematician and author. From France: Charles Richet, physiologist; Ambroise Liébeault, neurologist; and Pierre Janet, psychologist. From Germany: Heinrich Hertz, physicist; Albert von Schrenck-Notzing, psychiatrist; and Max Dessoir, psychologist. From Italy: Cesare Lombroso, sociologist. From Russia: Alexander Aksakof, civil servant. And from the United States: G. Stanley Hall, psychologist; Edward C. Pickering, astronomer; and Henry P. Bowditch, physiologist.[22] As the stature of these names suggest, engaging in psychical research during the late nineteenth century was neither academically dishonorable nor politically embarrassing. On the contrary, being a member of the SPR became a kind of calling card of the transatlantic intellectual aristocracy. As Gladstone put it, psychical research was "the most important work, which is being done in the world . . . , by far the most important."[23]

Second, like the BAAS, the SPR created separate investigative committees whose ranking member supervised the research. These included the Committees on Thought-Transference (Telepathy), Hypnotism (or Mesmerism), Apparitions and Haunted Houses (Ghosts), Physical Phenomena (Spiritualism), and Reichenbach's Experiments (Magnetic Sense). Third, again following the BAAS, the SPR established two periodicals in which to publish members' research. The *Journal of the Society for Psychical Research* (*Journal*) was a private publication only for members of the SPR and served as a review forum. It was the first place researchers pitched their arguments and where members made suggestions for improvement before the work was published in their official and public record, that is, the *Proceedings of the Society for Psychical Research* (*Proceedings*), though naturally there was some debate over which research to publish where, such as in the case of Eusapia Palladino.[24] In these ways, then, the SPR successfully adapted the organizational model of the BAAS.

Not surprisingly, the SPR faced many of the challenges of learned societies. Raising an ample amount of funds to pay for its work and sustain its existence was the most prominent. It was also one of the major ways in which the SPR failed to mimic the BAAS. Whereas the latter dealt in hundreds of thousands of pounds, the former could barely raise thousands. Finances were needed to pay for the periodicals, public announcements, office space, secretaries, assistants, supplies, and travel expenses. For start-up funds, Edmund Gurney used £17,000 of his sizable inheritance from his grandfather who had been Baron of the Exchequer. Sidgwick, who married into wealth, used both his wife's family money (Eleanor was a Balfour daughter) and that which his salary provided. So, too, did Frederic Myers (their lectureships at Trinity College paid £500 per year). Such wealth was not excessive but did allow these men to bankroll the SPR to the amount of £600 or £700 per year—a large enough sum with which to start a small scientific organization.[25] But these sources were not adequate enough to sustain it, so the SPR turned to trusts and personal endowments. For instance, Myers's mother left £200 for psychical research, and his brother Arthur bestowed £3,000 upon his death in January 1894.[26] Later, Sidgwick and Myers also entrusted sizable sums for the cause (Sidgwick left £12,000 upon his death in 1900 and Myers £37,000 upon his in 1901).[27] But the SPR's biggest windfall came when Marie Sinclair (d. 1895), the Countess of Caithness and a writer on religion and the occult, bequeathed £13,000 (nearly her entire estate) to the SPR. However, since she had refused to put any "money *down*" before her death, the windfall was to be kept quiet; Myers wanted Richard Hodgson to know this information, but it was not for "talk beyond our own group."[28] Trusts and bestowments thus greatly supplemented SPR funding and even helped it incorporate by 1895.

Lodge, however, was keenly aware that the continued funding shortages would be a major problem in the long run. According to F. C. S. Schiller, a British pragmatist who had joined the SPR and also become one of James's trusted confidants, Lodge proposed a permanent endowment of £200,000 as a remedy. But that level of funding was simply not available. Instead, he had to settle for a goal of £8,000 earmarked for scholarships to anyone, "irrespective of sex" or nationality, willing to devote himself or herself to psychical research.[29] Schiller, for his part, thought the American private sector should be tapped. When James informed him of his impending trip to Stanford University in 1906, Schiller suggested that James encourage the Stanfords to donate some of their "boundless wealth" and prodded him to "hint" to Mrs. Stanford, who was a devotee of Spiritualism, that "a permanent endowment is greatly needed at the S.P.R."[30] It is unknown whether James sought her out, but the reality remained the same: the SPR was perpetually short of operating expenses, forcing it to seek creative ways to fund its enterprise—a crucial difference from the financial success of the BAAS.

If raising adequate finances was a constant challenge, then performing the day-to-day labor was terribly tedious. This was similarly true for BAAS administrators, but since the SPR had far fewer resources, this became a much more burdensome task. Gurney, who had become the SPR's secretary, an unpaid position he held from 1883 to 1888 at which he labored dearly, described this reality to James: "The fact is that 'psychical research' is a large business, and I doubt its compatibility, at any rate with my upsettable constitution & easily fagged brain, with any serious daily professional work, for chance of success in which I am already very late in the field."[31] Gurney wrote up to fifty letters per day. "I have been tremendously busy all the winter with psychical matters.... It is a rather demoralising *sort* of work," he complained to James. "One lives in a whirl of sporadic interests & small excitements."[32] The SPR members made a fetish of the minutiae that challenged even the most patient of researchers.[33] Still, James believed that they were the new pioneers of psychology. To George Croom Robertson he wrote with shock at the lack of progress in experimental psychology and offered a "humiliating confession": "I'm afraid your *psychical researchers* really are the hold of the torch at present among you!"[34] By contrast, he believed the French and Americans were doing fine, explaining to his brother that "three first class works, in point of both originality and of learning, have appeared here within 4 months. Stanley Hall's and mine will make five. Meanwhile in England they are doing little or nothing. The [']Psychical Researchers' seem to be the only active investigators."[35]

A third major challenge the SPR members faced was potential damage to their careers and professional reputations. Although many intellectual aristocrats joined the SPR, being a scientist who belonged to both the BAAS *and* the SPR posed problems. Since many scientists were highly skeptical that psychic phenomena belonged to the study of nature, they tended to scoff at brethren who crossed that philosophical line. As such, the SPR had to work constantly to garner their respect. James maintained a reputable standing in both scientific and academic circles, but his more skeptical colleagues constantly stymied his efforts to enlist their support for the SPR and ASPR. As such, accepting elected office and publishing research in publications such as the *Proceedings* incurred significant risks.

The case that gave James pause was the one that hardened the skeptics at the Royal Society and the BAAS, namely, that of Sir William Crookes. A highly accomplished chemist and physicist, Crookes built his reputation for his work on the element selenium in the 1850s and on his discovery of the element thallium in 1861, for which he found the atomic weight in 1873. He also conducted significant work with radioactive matter, inventing several key instruments like the radiometer in 1876 and a high-pressure vacuum tube, called the "Crookes tube," used in the discovery of X-rays. Crookes also experimented with gases and rare earth material, and testing with radioactive matter and X-rays led him to believe he had discovered a fourth dimension, which he dubbed "radiant matter." Crookes possessed several other talents. He wrote on politics and economics, served as an adviser to the British government, and belonged to and was president of many scientific organizations, including the Chemical Society, the Royal Society, the BAAS, and the SPR. For his outstanding contributions and service to science, Crookes was knighted in 1897.[36]

But Crookes's scientific acumen lay more with inventing ingenious experiments and instruments than in applying sound philosophy. Crookes advanced the theory of "psychic force," the view that a noncorporeal form of causation explains hidden psychological action. After studying Daniel Dunglas Home, the levitating medium, Crookes declared him genuine and concluded that "certain physical phenomena such as the movement of material substances and the production of sounds . . . occur under circumstances in which they cannot be explained by any physical laws at present known."[37] Crookes's problem was not that his theory was unsound per se, especially as a variant of the ether theory that was then in vogue, but rather that his willful belief and his personal involvement with mediums clouded his judgment.

Most damaging to his reputation in this regard was his support of Florence Eliza Cook, the physical medium at whose séances full-length human outlines appeared to the sitters. Cook's most famous materialized spirit-control was "Katie King," the supposed daughter of John King, a pirate who made frequent appearances as a "spirit" in her séances.[38] In 1873–74, Crookes proclaimed her authentic in a lecture he gave to the Royal Society and subsequently published his findings in the prestigious *Quarterly Journal of Science*, a journal he once edited. Much to the annoyance of his skeptical and orthodox colleagues, though, Crookes relied more on his status as a respected scientist than on sound evidence.[39]

While Crookes's psychical research alienated much of the larger scientific community, it impressed many in the Sidgwick Group. In the late 1870s, Sidgwick, Myers, and Gurney held sittings with Florence and her sister Kate, who also claimed mediumistic abilities. These investigations revealed the value of scientific method. The theory, however, was another matter. While Henry Sidgwick was less convinced by Crookes's notion of "psychic force," Myers was less cautious, maintaining the Cook sisters manifested supernatural abilities and that "Katie" was a genuinely materialized spirit. For him, the investigations of the Cook sisters provided solid evidence to believe in human immortality. Crookes impressed Charles Richet as well, who maintained to the end of his life that of all the investigations into physical mediums, "certainly the most celebrated and certainly the most decisive are those of Sir William Crookes which it seems it is impossible to doubt."[40]

Myers and Richet, however, were unaware of a probable conspiracy to deceive psychical researchers and the public. Circumstantial evidence suggests that Crookes used his endorsement of Florence to cover up his probable affair with her. In return for her sexual favors, Crookes recommended her to Charles Blackburn, a wealthy businessman and credulous Spiritualist who was seeking his own private mediums to communicate with his dead family members. Led by their mother, Emma (her husband had abandoned the family), the Cook sisters were seeking material gain. In return for their mediumistic services, they convinced Blackburn to provide for their well-being. As long as Crookes verified Florence's veracity, Blackburn agreed to support the Cooks, but over time the Cooks exploited Blackburn. In fact, the financial "arrangement" was so great that the Cook women eventually forced their way into living at two of Blackburn's elegant houses in London, from 1883 to 1887 and again from 1888 to 1891, at considerable expense to Blackburn.[41] Amazingly, the sordid affair did not end Crookes's devotion to psychical research as he continued to investigate and publish in psychical matters into the twentieth century.[42]

James and Gurney do not appear to have known about the details of Crookes's private life, but they did witness the tarnishing of his professional standing for backing Florence Cook and Dunglas Home. Worrying about their own reputations, Gurney wondered whether his decision to become the SPR's secretary might be "disadvantageous," fretting, "There is a further risk—that in ten years['] time the subject will not be visibly advanced & time will seem thrown away; but the risks must be faced." More crassly, Gurney invoked John Tyndall's phrase that in the eyes of the scientific world, psychical research amounted to little more than "intellectual whoredom."[43] James agreed, once remarking to a friend, "We [that is, psychical researchers] shall be lucky if our scientific names don't grow discredited the instant they [skeptical scientists] subscribe to any 'spiritual' manifestations." This sentiment was wishful thinking, though, since James likened the chance of Crookes's thoroughly tarnished reputation undergoing a positive recovery to that of French military officer Alfred Dreyfus getting off: "It would be like the Royal Society 'acquitting' Crookes."[44]

Ultimately, though, both men accepted the risk, with Gurney confessing to James, "You, at any rate, are not among the friends who will be quite confident that I am or rather that we are making an egregious blunder," and James later staking his reputation on Mrs. Leonora Piper, the famous Boston Spiritualist medium.[45] Even so, James thought that because of their training and methodology, scientists rather than philosophers or theologians or "literary men" were the best-equipped professionals to objectively investigate psychic phenomena, noting that the latter group was "much easier to discredit."[46] That, after all, had been the fate of the London Dialectical Society; it was not scientific enough. In spite of all these drawbacks and risks, then, James realized the SPR offered the best chance to pursue psychical research, and he promptly tethered his tertium quid approach to it.

THE AMERICAN SOCIETY FOR PSYCHICAL RESEARCH

Whatever the idiosyncrasies of the SPR, it was not alone. During the late nineteenth century, voluntary psychical research societies emerged in France, Holland, Germany, Switzerland, and Italy.[47] And the rise of these hybrid organizations was not limited to Europe. In 1884 the Americans decided to join the fray, but the impetus came from the SPR. That autumn William Barrett sailed to the United States to arouse interest in New York, Philadelphia, and Boston. Regarding James, he pointed out that "Professor James" is "already acquainted with our hon[orable] sec[retary], Mr. Edmund Gurney, and has read the earlier parts of our *Proceedings* with much interest."[48] On the initial crossing, Barrett gave a lecture on psychical research to members of the BAAS, many of whom, including Barrett, were on their way to their annual meeting in Montreal. On the return voyage, he chatted with fellow passengers on the nature of psychical research and found that while some people would always be wary, dismissive of the methods, or convinced psychic phenomena were the result of trickery, others were quite impressed and became dues-paying members on the spot. Summarizing his trip, Barrett recorded that "the net result of these cross-Atlantic passages may be said to be information given, misconception removed, interest awakened, [and] new allies made." Indeed, Barrett's sociability, professional connections, and scientific standing helps explain how he was able to convince so many American scientists and men of social position, including James, to form what came to be called the American Society for Psychical Research.[49]

Forming organizations was deeply embedded in the American grain, and James's participation in the ASPR was not at all unusual. Although historians have attempted to show more recently that associational life in America has been more of a variable than a constant, there still remains a consensus that the United States witnessed the most growth of voluntary associations in the second half of the nineteenth century than in any other period.[50] Indeed, most Americans during this period joined a society, group, or club when voluntary associations emerged by the hundreds to offset the rising power of hierarchically organized corporate bodies. Attempting to foster communal harmony and a sense of fraternity, Americans of all classes, races, creeds, and genders came together in democratic fashion to advance their special cause. Organizations designed for every societal niche—professional, civic, political, religious, moral, cultural, charitable, labor, self-improvement, and benefit—sprouted up. By 1820, for instance, citizens in the Commonwealth of Massachusetts formed organizations at the rate of eighty-five per year. Most associations were small, local, and organized exclusively around a central theme or common concern, such as temperance or abolition. They were often established by like-minded citizens who came together freely in intimate settings such as churches, town halls, and libraries.[51] As Alexis de Tocqueville put it famously, "In no country in the world has the principle of association been more successfully used, or applied to a greater multitude of objects, than in America."[52] If America in the nineteenth century had been a "nation of joiners," as Arthur Schlesinger Jr. captured it, then intellectuals who joined learned societies formed their own particular version of voluntary associations.[53] James's decision to join the SPR and ASPR, as with those who joined the Aristotelian Society and Scratch Eight in Britain and the Metaphysical Club in the United States, then, typified this larger nineteenth-century American tendency.

Like the SPR's relation to British scientific societies, the ASPR bore some relation to the advent of American scientific societies, which served as the main form of knowledge advancement, like their counterparts in the Old World. As part of the seventeenth-century tradition, British subjects in the New World established a number of learned societies, such as the ill-fated Boston Philosophical Society (1683), led by Increase Mather, one of the most venerable of all early "American" intellectuals. Although the Royal Society served as the colonists' main learned society through the 1770s, the successful revolt for independence guaranteed that royalty would not support the creation of subsequent organizations such as the American Philosophical Society (1745) and the American Academy of Arts and Sciences (1780). Nonetheless, the American penchant for organizing, then, had its roots in the experiences of British colonists.[54]

The first two-thirds of the nineteenth century witnessed the rapid rise of national learned and scientific societies in the United States and mirrored the country's larger tendency for nationalism. Like the British pattern of this period, Americans formed a large number of provincial societies, in their case at the state and local levels, especially the northern and eastern states (slavery and the southern way of life retarded their growth in the South). Scientific societies and specialized ones in particular led the way, such as the Linnaean Society of Philadelphia (1806) and of New England (1814) and the Washington Botanical Society (1817). Also like the British, the Americans formed national scientific societies during this period, including the National Institution for the Promotion of Science (1840), the Smithsonian Institution (1846), the National Academy of Sciences (1863), and most notably the American Association for the Advancement of Science (1848). But, unlike the British, the Americans often had troubled either forming or sustaining national societies, especially those that were government supported, since that notion violated nineteenth-century liberalism.[55] Nonetheless, the advent of scientific societies such as the AAAS helped launch American science.

Down to its name, the AAAS was modeled in almost every way after the BAAS. Because of the nature of American life, though, there were important differences, most notably its "democratic" quality in which anyone interested in science could join, serve on its committees, and vote in the election of officers. This meant that amateurs played a much larger role in the AAAS compared with the BAAS. The American suspicion of elitism during the age of Jackson, then, fostered this egalitarian spirit, though it should be noted that elites still ran the organization and produced the most formidable science, including Henry Rodgers, Dallas Baches, Benjamin Peirce, and Louis Agassiz, who as a prominent member of the BAAS was most responsible for creating the AAAS in the image of the BAAS, even though Rodgers drafted the AAAS constitution.[56]

American science during the late nineteenth, when the ASPR was formed, was marked by three major traits: specialization, national centralization, and the rise of technological societies. This period also witnessed the emergence of the modern research university, at which specialists and experts taught, conducted research, and produced the future generations of scientists. Not only was specialization the norm, but "specialization within specialization became the rule."[57] Scientific societies followed this pattern with hundreds continuing to develop at the local, regional, state, and national levels. There were scientific organizations for just about every branch of scientific pursuit: agriculture, biometrics, botany, chemistry, climatology, forestry, geography, geology, mathematics, naturalists, optics, physics, zoology, and so forth, each with their own national organization and many with state, regional, or local ones. The social sciences created national organizations as well, including the American Political Science Association (1903) and the American Sociological Association (1905). Since the American Medical Association (1847) was one of the first prominent professional organizations to form, it quickly followed the subspecialization pattern with societies for dermatology, gynecology, neurology, oncology, ophthalmology, pediatrics, and so many others. Experimental psychology also emerged in this period and shared some semblance with the social sciences, forming the American Psychological Association in 1892, which James helped create. Psychiatry, a hybrid of medicine, experimental psychology, and philosophy, formed societies in New England, Boston, and New York. And mental hygiene, their distant cousin, did so as well.[58] In an era of specialization, one statistical study of learned and scientific societies in the United States found that compared with fewer than 100 societies formed from the seventeenth century through 1860, in the forty-year period from 1860 through 1900 there were over 300, a 200 percent increase over a much shorter period.[59] It was within this context that the ASPR formed, being one of 21 new organizations to emerge in the 1880s and one of 130 of all learned societies during that decade—the period with the single largest growth (the 1870s was the next closest with 80).[60] In other words, the ASPR was part of a matrix of learned and scientific societies of the late nineteenth and early twentieth centuries that embodied the organization of knowledge.

Individuals and their ideas came together in these societies as well as in the modern research university. They were primarily white middle-class, college-educated men (and a few women) who cultivated the notion that the advancement of knowledge and the building up of societies and institutions was for the public good. In his Stanford Founder's Day speech, James noted the impact this development was having on the pursuit of knowledge at American universities in particular, singling out "our extraordinary American reliance on organization."[61] But the specialization that occurred in the United States was somewhat different from that of the United Kingdom in that America was a highly decentralized, pluralistic, and egalitarian country that was suspicious of elites, experts, and central authority, thus requiring institutions and their leadership to be more flexible, open, and ad hoc in the organization and pursuit of knowledge. The emphasis placed on the PhD, for instance, created tension within the ideal of a "society of equals."[62]

James was a perfect embodiment of this tension. On the one hand, he was elite. He came from a family with means, had earned both college and advanced degrees, and was highly cultured. As a professional, he helped create modern methods of inquiry, founded and participated in several learned and scientific societies, and worked in what became a leading research institution. He also helped develop several specialized forms of knowledge in psychology, philosophy, and religious thought—fields requiring experts like him to interpret and analyze them. On the other hand, James loathed the world of elites and those who used their status to justify their actions or intellectual positions. James led a comfortable bourgeois life but was not class oriented, and he disdained class snobbery. He thought a college education ought to be available to those beyond his own class, including women, blacks, and Jews (though James held boilerplate Progressive Era attitudes about their supposed inherent limits). He taught graduate students and helped confer PhDs on them (including these minorities), but he loathed the requirements of the degree and thought that the expert status and specialization it created were bad for American life because it violated the country's value of individualism. "Is individuality with us [Americans]," he wondered, "also going to count for nothing unless stamped and licensed and authenticated by some title-giving machine?"[63] And although an expert and specialist, James went to great lengths to make his ideas accessible to the educated public, giving numerous lectures that tried to explain his principles and positions on a variety of topics using everyday metaphors, similes, and comparisons.

Most important, James sought to ground in lived experience everything he did, from the personal to the intellectual. Throughout it all, James frequently championed the "little guy" and never missed a chance to disdain the members of the privileged class that he belonged to who used their station and advantages in life in ways that violated his commitment to pluralism, egalitarianism, and a moral sense of fairness. This was especially true with regard to his defense of psychical research. Explaining to readers why he included a major article of his on psychical research in *The Will to Believe*, he wrote he had been "attracted to this study [for] some years by my love of sportsmanlike fair play in science," adding that "I have seen enough to convince me of its great importance, and I wish to gain for it what interest I can."[64] In short, James benefited greatly from the elite organizations to and for which he belonged and worked, but his heart belonged to the democratic world in which he lived and that he sought to understand. His desire to find a middle ground between his elite intellectualism and his democratic personality thus exemplified his tertium quid and help explains why he joined the ASPR.

Toward that end, on 23 September 1884, James agreed to meet at the Boston Athenaeum Club with several prominent men of learning, including G. Stanley Hall, Henry Bowditch, Edward Pickering, and Charles Minot, a physician, for "the purpose of considering the advisability of forming a Society for Psychical Research in America [and] a committee with full powers."[65] Among other resolutions, they decided to invite "scientific men" like themselves to join the society, of which eighty responded favorably.[66] *Science*, the leading journal of scientific research in the United States, published announcements to help attract qualified participants and wrote up a favorable review.[67] After gathering several times in October and November, the ASPR held its first formal meeting on 18 December 1884 and passed a constitution, boasting ten articles, that James helped draft. Article I, Section 1, dubbed the organization the "American Society for Psychical Research," and Section 2 established its object: "the systematic study of the laws of mental action."[68] Another statement described the ASPR's purpose as "making an exact study of that border-land of human experience."[69] The terms "systematic" and "laws" reflected James's preference for the empirical aspect of his tertium quid, and the council's wording—an "urgent scientific need" to undertake "the exact study of this border-land of human experience"—indicated James's likely influence on the ASPR's direction.[70]

Following the SPR, the ASPR formed five separate investigative committees: those on Thought-Transference, Hypnotism, Apparitions and Haunted Houses, Physical Phenomena, and Reichenbach's Experiments. Separate, smaller committees were also established to investigate divining rods and to perform the society's literary work. To its councilmen and members, the officers issued a circular, hoping that enough volunteers would be "forthcoming to form committees whose personal composition will be a guarantee of the character of the investigation performed by them." Without them, the council worried "the American Society for Psychical Research may fail to justify its foundation."[71] By early January 1885, the ASPR's Committee on Thought-Transference called for volunteers to participate in the first ASPR experiments, and that June the committee began to present its findings.[72] In October, Bowditch gave a follow-up report about additional experiments on which James commented.[73] Finally, in early January 1886, just one year after the ASPR's inception, James gave a report as chair of the Committee on Hypnotism.[74] In reference to the Committee on Mediumship, on which James also sat, the ASPR's overall mission became crystal clear: to establish scientific facts. "Neither the gathering of testimony from others, nor the mere gaining of personal conviction satisfactory to ourselves [will be enough]," the council stated, "but rather the ascertainment of facts [is what we need].... We seek, in other words, evidence, that is, facts, so ascertained and recorded as to be open to but one interpretation."[75] James would have likely bristled at the rigidity of the last claim, but he agreed that establishing facts was paramount. For the next five years, James labored almost continuously in search of them by conducting research, writing reports, chairing meetings, responding to numerous inquiries from individuals seeking to be tested for their special abilities, penning articles for both the ASPR's and SPR's *Proceedings* and *Journal* respectively, and by writing essays for mass consumption in more popular magazines such as *Forum* and *Scribner's*. Indeed, from 1885 through 1890, James engrossed himself with psychical research.[76] In this way, James's tertium quid approach leaned toward the institutional trappings to which hybrid societies such as the ASPR aspired.

It was clear from the outset that the ASPR would mimic the SPR's organizational structure while manifesting the American pluralistic and egalitarian impulses. First, it voted in twenty-one officers to serve as members of the council for terms of one, two, or three years, depending on the member's preference. Elected to the council through 1885 were George Frederick Barker, physicist; Moorfield Storey, lawyer; Charles Caroll Everett, professor of theology at Harvard; John Trowbridge, physicist; Samuel Hubbard Scudder, naturalist; William Watson, engineer and author; and Coleman Sellers, engineer. Elected through 1886 were Bowditch, James's old medical classmate and now a professor at the Harvard Medical School; Minot; Charles Cabot Jackson, businessman; Simon Newcomb, astronomer; Thomas Wentworth Higginson, reformer; William Henry Pickering, astronomer and Edward's brother; and Nathaniel Dana Carlile Hodges, librarian. Elected through 1887 were Hall; Edward Pickering; George Stuart Fullerton, philosopher; Robert Pearsall Smith, businessman; Major Alfred Alexander Woodhull, military surgeon; James Mills Peirce, mathematician; and, of course, James himself, who was to "hold office [as an elected councilman] till October, 1887."[77]

Simon Newcomb, America's leading astronomer, served as the ASPR's first president. James recognized his importance, claiming he was an "uncommon hit" because of his accomplishments in astronomy and his status as a natural scientist. But not everyone agreed. John Wesley Powell, the naturalist, ethnologist, and explorer of the American West, thought the choice "to be ridiculous in the highest degree."[78] Hall, Fullerton, Bowditch, Minot, and Edward Pickering were chosen as five vice presidents, and William Watson, an engineer, served as treasurer in 1886. James once asked him to send along checks from Catherine Walsh (his own "Aunt Kate") and Mary Tappan (a family friend), whom he had recruited as two new associates of the ASPR.[79] Although not initially a vice president, James was elected as one in 1887. Other significant individuals affiliated with the ASPR included John Forrester Andrew, son of the one-time governor John Albion Andrew and a Boston lawyer, politician, and unsuccessful candidate for governor of Massachusetts in 1886. Forrester was elected to the council in early January 1887 to replace some of the departing councilmen. Minot Judson Savage, a Unitarian clergyman, became a member of the ASPR and later founded his own organization for Spiritualists, the American Psychical Society, along with Amos Emerson Dolbear, an educator and inventor. George Bucknam Dorr, a student of James's at Harvard in the early 1870s and again in the late 1880s, took an avid interest in psychical research because of James's influence and became a major supporter of the ASPR. Samuel Pierpont Langley, an astronomer, joined the ASPR in 1889, becoming a vice president of the SPR from then onward, and later served a key role in the American Branch of the SPR. Finally, James Hervey Hyslop transformed the defunct American Branch into the newly organized American Society for Psychical Research in 1906, moving its offices to New York City and reinvigorating its mission, member base, and endowment.[80]

Like the SPR, the ASPR tried to move beyond its fledgling status by building up its base. It had roughly 250 members and associates in 1885, 300 in 1886, and just over 400 by 1889.[81] Trying to drum up interest, James recruited Mr. Russell Whitman, a lawyer in Chicago. "He is a superior man—or *was* when I had him in College a few years back—in every way," he told a friend, and "is a member of the Soc. For Psych. Research, anxious to do work."[82] James also inquired of Thomas Davidson if he knew of "Col. Bundy of Chicago," wondering whether he carried social status. "W[oul]d he be a dangerous member . . . of the Soc[iety] for Psych[ical] Res[earch]? We must go cautiously."[83] Davidson, a Scottish-born writer, was seeking new edifices upon which to build a religion devoted to moral reform. He founded the Fellowship of New Life in London in the early 1880s and a similar group in New York in 1884, which showed some interest in Spiritualism. As he was living in Orange, New Jersey, during this period, it is possible that he was connected to the New York City branch of the SPR as well. James once asked him if he could "tell me aught of your mysterious 1/2 million rival society[?]"[84] He also informed his sister, Alice, that "I stopped over night here [Pelham, New York] to see Kitty [Katherine Prince], & a certain Woodhull who lives [at] night, & with whom I have some business."[85] James had arranged a meeting with Major Woodhull, the husband of the notorious Spiritualist and radical feminist Victoria Woodhull, to discuss his becoming a member of the ASPR, which he did for a brief time.[86]

The ASPR also created the *Proceedings of the American Society for Psychical Research* to publish members' research. Despite James's efforts, however, it did not generate a *Journal* in the early years.[87] As soon as word reached the shores of England, the SPR waited eagerly for the first publication of the new organ. "How *lovely* it will be when we get your 'Proceedings'!" Gurney exclaimed. "*Do* cook [up] a number quick." James, though, doubted its overall value. Having mailed to Robertson a copy of "Part II" of the ASPR's first issue, he blushed that it was "a rather sorry 'exhibit,' from the 'President's address' [on] down. There is no one in the Society who can give time to it, and I suspect it will die by the new year." His pessimism must have been somewhat disheartening for the SPR members on the other side of the Atlantic who had been so enthusiastic about the ASPR's efforts to establish its own periodical.[88] Charles Renouvier, the French philosopher whom James credited with having helped him believe in free will, shared James's pessimism regarding the quality of psychical research journals, once writing to James that he hoped the "publications of the Society for Psychical Research will show less credulity than those that appear in the February 1886 issue of *Revue Philosophique*."[89]

Nonetheless, with all of the organizational apparatus in place, James began promoting the ASPR. To Shadworth Hodgson, the Scratch Eight philosopher who had most stimulated James, he announced that "we have been stirred up by the English Society for Psychical Research's example, to start a similar society here." Although guardedly optimistic that the ASPR would find competent subjects to study, James admitted that the "returns come slowly.—I mean stuff to inquire into comes slowly; and altogether my small experience has filled me with a prodigious admiration of the devotion and energy of Gurney, Myers and others with you. Something will come of it all, I am sure."[90] James also announced to Robertson, another Scratch Eight philosopher, that "we have started a [S]oc[iety] for Psychical Research in Boston, in which I have been somewhat interested; you know I don't quite share your hardness of heart in reference to the evidence for telepathy, & even ghosts—or has your heart softened in the last year or two?"[91] Robertson had been skeptical, but after reading early SPR reports he changed his mind, replying to James that "Edmund Gurney and other psychical researchers have it right."[92]

The editors at *Science* heartily agreed with this sentiment. After dismissing the "men of this 'dark-age' of mind" who could not accept any data that might lead to established facts about matters psychical, they noted how much "deep-seated interest" there was in psychical research and added that "in spite of a healthy skepticism . . . there is no longer a feeling that such matters can be laughed out of court."[93] For his part, James remained confident that the ASPR would at a minimum establish some facts that would win the organization respect among scientists. As he put it to Robertson, "Once these facts show themselves susceptible of serial, & statistical, and other modes of treatment familiar to scientific men, the barrier will fall at a stroke, and we shall hear much less about their rarity and the difficulties of ascertaining them accurately [and more about] their analogy with other natural processes, conditioned by general laws."[94] In other words, when psychical research used empirical methods to establish facts about psychic phenomena that normalized them within accepted scientific knowledge, it would establish itself successfully as a legitimate science, and the ASPR would establish itself as a respectable scientific organization. But James was soon forced to temper these uncharacteristically dogmatic claims. Regarding the future of the ASPR, James cautioned a friend that it was much too soon to think they would be successful. "The [American] Society for Psych[ical] Research isn't out of the egg yet. Its success will wholly depend on whether any individuals be forthcoming who will give their whole time to it—as Gurney et al. have done in England."[95]

As it turned out, however, time was not friendly to the ASPR. From its inception it faced a series of organizational challenges that eventually led to its downfall. First, the society began hemorrhaging its researchers almost immediately. Most officers and councilmen, including Barker, Storey, Jackson, Hodges, Hall, Peirce, Woodhull, and both Pickerings fled the ASPR as soon as their terms expired or shortly thereafter. Several more left after the ASPR was subsumed into the SPR in 1890 as the "American Branch," including Scudder, Sellers, and Higginson. Only Newcomb, Langley, and Fullerton stayed the course through the 1890s, despite their skepticism and concern about their reputations. Bowditch retained his affiliation into the early 1900s, while only Everett and James remained active members until their deaths in 1900 and 1910 respectively.[96]

Second, the ASPR fumbled its day-to-day operations. With the quick exodus of Edward Gardiner, the ASPR lacked a competent secretary. In 1887, Richard Hodgson arrived from England to assume those duties. But he was not James's choice, rather Myers's, and there was some debate as to whether he was the best man. It seems that James preferred Joseph Jastrow, a one-time student of G. Stanley Hall at Johns Hopkins who had some training in laboratory psychology. But Jastrow turned it down because he believed, according to Hall, that psychical research was not rigorously scientific.[97]

Third, the work progressed slowly. In 1887, the ASPR was forced to make emergency appeals for subjects and researchers: "The results which the American Society has so far achieved have not been so great as anticipated. [As such] the Council thinks it desirable to circulate a brief account of the lines of research not being investigated by the various committees, and to make an appeal for a more zealous coöperation of the members and associates of the Society."[98] Despite such pleas, James perceived from the beginning that efforts at finding reliable subjects and gathering testimonial evidence were failing and warranted grave concern. Indeed, circulars like this one reached a small number of people and brought fewer replies. Low numbers indicated a modest interest at best, which in turn intimated a possible problem with gathering enough valid data, without which the ASPR had little purpose to exist. Regarding his own committee's attempt to attract more mediums, James confessed to his friend and author Elizabeth Ward, "I am not sure that our circular of inquiry about mediums brought even as many as ten letters of advice—not one was from a medium himself." The circular had made an impression on Ward, though, for she became an associate member of the ASPR and later mailed him an article to read on the "Psychic Wave" sweeping the country, for which James thanked her the following summer, noting that he would introduce it at the next ASPR meeting.[99] Still, the returns were not very promising.

Finally, the ASPR faced immense financial challenges. The problem was extremely burdensome because, unlike some of the SPR members who were independently wealthy and could afford to recompense the costs not covered by member donations, the ASPR core lacked this kind of supplemental income. Also unlike the SPR, the ASPR could not depend on wealthy philanthropists who were keen on discovering the nature of psychic phenomena. As such, the ASPR was forced to rely heavily on subscription fees, on small voluntary contributions, and frequently on the funds of the SPR, especially from the pockets of Myers, Gurney, and Sidgwick and their well-heeled benefactors. In other words, the SPR largely bankrolled the ASPR.

One of James's main responsibilities was to seek out new sources of funding, and he sometimes had to resort to his own bank account. But his efforts paled in comparison to those of the Sidgwick Group. Much annoyed, James told his wife, "$50 [came in the mail] from Henry Wyckoff for the [American] Soc[iety] for Psych[ical] Res[earch]—I had asked him for a thousand!"[100] On occasion someone would donate a somewhat larger sum, such as William Sturgis Bigelow, a Boston physician and trustee of the Museum of Fine Arts, who gave "$1,000 dollars for the ASPR." James thanked Bigelow for his contribution but noted he would prefer to keep it a secret so as to not discourage "small donations," which James believed would cumulatively bring in the most funds.[101] Nonetheless, James was savvy enough to reserve the funds to pay toward Hodgson's $1,500 annual salary—the ASPR's only full-time, paid position. Toward that end, James drew up a flier to garner philanthropic support. It reflected the typical elements of a fund-raising letter but also begged the group's officers and members to continue paying their dues to keep the society afloat. As James explained to his friend John Forrester Andrew, "[The ASPR] has languished in the midst (as I believe) of plenty of material for study, simply because none of its members seem to have time or inclination to work."[102] Despite James's best efforts to drum up support, though, the funding situation remained bleak. "The Treasury is low," James told Myers candidly. "I am going to see if anything can be done, but it[']s 'flogging a dead horse.'"[103]

Flogging dead horses for the ASPR was not only an unrewarding activity for James but also a time-consuming one that he grew to resent over the years. "My interest [in psychical research] however does not go to the length of giving up much time to the business—I cannot," he confessed to Robertson.[104] Of course this was more wishful thinking than reality as James invested a great deal of time and energy to psychical research that year. Nonetheless, even though he believed firmly in its mission, he continued to complain that he lost too much time to it. Again to Robertson, James confided exasperatedly,

> I have wasted a good deal of time on "Psychical Research" during the past year, and Gurney and I have scribbled a number of notes to each other in consequence. "Two lost souls!" you will say,—but that is what remains to be seen. Our poor little "Society" will very likely break down for a lack of a Gurney or Myers to devote time to it. But I feel quite convinced at the end of my year's work, such as it has been[,] that this sort of work is as worthy a specialty as a man could take up; only it *is* a specialty, demanding an enormous sacrifice of time, and in which amateurs will be as inferior to experts as they are in most other departments of experience. Believing this, I shall probably give very little time to it next year, because at the utmost I should be a dabbler and amateur.[105]

Despite such feigned modesty, James was hardly an "amateur" or "dabbler." James also broke his promise to stop devoting so much time to psychical research. On several notable occasions between 1885 and 1890, James continued to grumble that psychical research stole time away from finishing

The Principles of Psychology. "Subjectively," he highlighted for his wife, "my main problem is to get through my psychology [book].... I shan't touch a medium and probably not a mesmeric subject, with the end of a long pole. Psychical Research took up a long time last year."[106] But James found psychical research much too absorbing, its work much too demanding, and its potential for a major breakthrough in mapping the human psyche much too great to keep that resolution. Still, he repeated his complaint to an old Scratch Eight tramp: "I got successfully through the academic year, in spite of the fact that I wasted a great deal of time on 'psychical research' and had other interruptions from work which I would fain have done."[107] In other words, the intellectual demands that psychical research extracted from James continued to prevent him from making the kind of progress he wanted toward finishing *The Principles of Psychology*, but they remained far too important for him to drop them.

In fact, not only did he fail not to "touch a medium," but he also built his daily, weekly, and monthly schedule around psychical research, and he did so despite the tedious nature of the work and the lack of positive results. As on so many occasions, William explained the outcome of his investigations to his wife, Alice, in a spate of letters. "[I engaged in] a great deal of [p]sychical [r]esearch talk—which I confess begins to be rather a bore, as long as it is so inconclusive—and [I did] some negative experiments in the eve[nin]g," read one. On another occasion, he wrote, "[I was] out from town after an evening wasted in would be psychical [r]esearch at Hodgson's room. [The] subject's brother came but no subject." Describing an uninvited visitor who appeared at the James residence and interrupted a letter William was writing to Alice, he complained that the man "hadn't been there three minutes ere he lapsed into a trance state and began to speak 'under control'" and "detained me for a rather tedious half hour with his rubbish, & kept me from outpouring myself." In still another incident, he informed her that he had been visiting Josiah P. Quincy, an author interested in psychical research, where there had been "tedious and inconclusive 'psychic' talk—ah me! to have a *fact* to talk about, instead of hearsays!"[108]

Although committed to psychical research, James detested the demanding work. At times he was ready to give it up entirely. While attending a Chautauqua and spa treatment in Saratoga Springs, New York, he wrote to Alice, "This A.M. I saw 3 other performances, one of mesmerism, the others of so called spiritualism—nauseous! On the whole the sight of the people there was extremely depressing. Intellect down to zero. I'm glad I've seen it, but I don't think I could have stood it another day."[109] Similarly, to his sister, Alice, he confided, "I have been tolerably busy with mediums, a loathsome occupation, and intend next winter to give it up and devote myself to my own work which suffers by this time wasting pursuit."[110] James also despised what he called the "social side" of psychical research. To his brother Henry, he echoed this sentiment, writing, "I *loathe* all this psychical work so far as it had a social side. I must preside over a meeting in Boston, at which [Oliver] Lodge's paper on her [Mrs. Piper] will be read."[111] And he especially reviled all of the professional obligations, stating in his presidential address to the members of the SPR and ASPR that the presidency "resembles a mouse-trap."[112]

Still, James pushed on. For instance, although he changed his mind at the last minute, James initially committed to be the APSR's representative for the Auxiliary Congress of Psychology, which devoted itself to discussing psychical matters, at the World's Columbian Exposition in Chicago in 1893.[113] Another example of his professional duty was to give public lectures on various research programs, such as those at the Brooklyn Institute ("a course of 6 for $300"), that discussed the pathological features of psychic phenomena, as well as his 1896 ASPR presidential address given at Wellesley and Bryn Mawr Colleges. But they left him wanting. "All these public appearances help make me known," he explained to his brother, "even if they don't enrich me."[114] James also published popular articles on psychical research to raise funds for the ASPR. "I wrote an article of (I imagine) beneficial nature to the Forum on the S.P.R. instructing the Editor to forward *both proofs & check to you*," he told Hodgson. "Give $50 to the Society from me, and send the rest . . . to my account."[115] Finally, James supported publicly held séances and related events. On one such occasion, he assisted the performance of Washington Irving Bishop, an American mind reader about which the *New York Tribune* and *New York Times* reported.[116] He thought that by lending his name to the cause he would attract interest and thereby help fill the coffers of the ASPR and thus provide some respect to psychical research.

James's efforts to prop up the wilting ASPR, however, were severely hampered by Gurney's untimely death in 1888. The event sparked a discussion between the two societies as to whether Hodgson should return to England to assume Gurney's secretarial duties or remain at his post in the United States. Hodgson favored the former plan, since he identified more with England than with America, had trained with Sidgwick, and had become accustomed to the members of the SPR. America, by contrast, made him lonely. Myers, however, was against this plan, believing Hodgson's skills were best utilized in the United States. "If Hodgson returned to England to help *our* Society," he explained to James, "I should endeavor to raise a salary to send him out to work for us in *America* in spite of the great personal pleasure & help wh[ich] his presence here w[oul]d give us. It is therefore plain that Hodgson is best placed where he is."[117] As an extra incentive, Myers added that "some of us here would willingly help, if need were, in supplying funds for Hodgson to work on."[118] Once again, private SPR money buttressed the foundering ASPR.

Whether the additional funding arrived is unknown, but it is doubtful that any funding at this point would have helped, or that Hodgson or James, or any of the other prominent council members, could have done anything to save the foundering ASPR. As James put it, "Hodgson is an admirable fellow, but one man can't do everything."[119] Similarly, he confided to his wife, "[I] had lunch today with Richard Hodgson and Henry Bowditch to decide whether to give up the [American] Society for Psychical Research after this year."[120] As early as 1888, James was beginning to see the termination of the ASPR as an independently organized and learned association. But Myers remained adamant; the work of the ASPR must continue. Noting the rising public interest in psychical research and the importance of keeping "charlatan and semi-charlatan bodies" at bay, he stressed to James that "I should extremely lament the collapse of your American SPR. . . . I think that to dissolve the *Society* now would be a deplorable hasty proceeding."[121] Two years later Myers echoed himself, noting how "struck [he was] by the great increase of subject matter [at the ASPR]." The ASPR, he concluded, was most decidedly not "moribund."[122]

Myers's proclamation, however, amounted to little more than wishful thinking. Given the perpetual funding shortages, the demanding nature of the time-consuming work, the skepticism from both the Spiritualist and scientific communities, and the fact that the ASPR was having trouble maintaining its high-profile officers, councilmen, and committee members, it was only a question of time before the ASPR would come to an end. At the time of its inauguration in 1884–85, there had been much enthusiasm and high hopes for success at establishing a new kind of science and a new kind of organization to support its endeavors. But the ASPR, like so many voluntary associations, never gathered enough momentum to support itself. Toward the end of the 1880s, most of the original scientists had left the fold, many of the committees had become defunct, membership roles had stagnated, and funds had evaporated. By 1890, the nucleus of the ASPR amounted to little more than James, Dorr, Hyslop, and Hodgson and his secretary Miss Lucy Edmunds, and it was clear the society was simply not strong enough to survive without James's effort and support. And with so little return for his labor and time, James was inclined to forgo the hard work that was necessary to keep the ASPR running. So, on 14 January 1890, much to the relief of all, the ASPR dissolved itself. It had lasted just five years.[123]

THE AMERICAN BRANCH

The closing of the ASPR did not mean an end to organized psychical research in the United States. Instead, the society was formally subsumed into the SPR as its "American Branch." But the branch's existence was not automatic, and changing the formal status of the society did not resolve the ongoing fundamental challenges facing psychical research in the United States. Indeed, those that had plagued the ASPR continued to swamp the new branch. Especially pertinent were the perennial issues of raising adequate funds and maintaining a steady set of qualified investigators. In fact, these had become so overwhelming that James once confessed to his wife that "I wish the [S]oc[iety] for P[sychical] R[esearch] had no American Branch on the whole."[124] By contrast, the launching of the "American Branch" elated Myers, whose personality predisposed him to make wide-eyed generalizations that were favorable to psychical research organizations, believing that their inevitable success was simply a question of labor and luck.

Myers's optimism rested on the work of a small number of scientists but especially on James's contributions. For instance, he wrote to James that "not one single member of our small group . . .—the group who are going for the discovery of this century, viz., scientific proof of man's survival;—not one single member, I say, is on the whole so well situated as you for the successful pushing of the inquiry."[125] But James, who was committed to his third way, was less sanguine that psychical research could offer such certainty. James also understood better than Myers that Hodgson, Langley, and himself—now the three vice presidents of the branch and only remaining officers—failed to constitute a sufficient research team. Myers tried to buck up James by drawing up a simple table that identified nineteen psychical researchers by country, as if its international dimension somehow guaranteed success:

AMERICA	ENGLAND	FRANCE	GERMANY	RUSSIA
W. James	H. Sidgwick	Richet	Schrenck-Notzing	Aksakoff(?)
Hodgson	Mrs. Sidgwick	Danex(?)		
	Crookes	Pierre Janet	Dessoir	
	Wallace			
	(on the verge)			
	Lodge		Hertz—	
			electrician—	
	F. W. H. M.[yers]			
	Leif		Münsterberg	
	Podmore		Möll	

On paper Myers was right; active researchers from five separate countries existed.[126] But in practice the number was much smaller. Crookes's reputation was in tatters because of his defense of Florence Cook and Daniel Home, Heinrich Hertz never committed, and Hugo Münsterberg eventually joined the growing chorus of scientists hostile to psychical research. But it was an impressive list nonetheless, for it contained some of the leading philosophical and experimental scientists in the industrialized world. Indeed, it anticipated what quickly developed into an axis of psychical research programs in Britain, the United States, France, Italy, and Germany that mirrored a "psychotherapeutic axis" in these same countries.[127]

James forwarded this letter to Hodgson with a handwritten note at the end that read, "Dear H., Read and return. Myers is the stuff out of which world-renewers are made. What a despot! W. J."[128] In slightly more favorable terms, James expressed similar comments to Myers: "Verily you are the stuff of which world-changers are made! What a despot for Psychical Research! I always feel guilty in your presence, and am, on the whole, glad that the broad blue ocean rolls between us for most of the days of the year. . . . Of course I wholly agree with you in regard to the *ultimate* future of the business, and fame will be the portion of him who may succeed in naturalizing it as a branch of legitimate science."[129] Sidgwick, who was closer in temperament to James, was more cautious. To James he expressed his view: "Hodgson's last letter to Myers [which mentioned Myers's letter to James] is very cheerful about the prospects of P[sychical] R[esearch]," he wrote. "I hope his hopefulness has a rational basis."[130] To some extent Myers had been right, since these were some of the SPR's most productive years. On the other hand, Myers had been overly optimistic regarding the American Branch's role. From where was the money going to come?

To address that perennial issue, Myers (with Sidgwick's blessing) proposed a detailed scheme to James. American members would be rolled over into the SPR membership at $3 each. With the rising costs of publishing their periodicals, all dues would be raised to about £7 per member. At the current member levels, he calculated a balance of £75 for other expenses. As Hodgson's salary, secretarial work, and travel expenses amounted to £350, he proposed that SPR general funds be used to cover the balance. But the SPR would guarantee this for only one year, since he and Sidgwick already contributed most of the annual SPR funding (roughly £600 to £700).[131] This proposal, however, presumed Hodgson wanted to continue as secretary of the American Branch, but it appears that he was thinking at that point of pursuing a career in medicine. If he did go in that direction, Myers averred the American Branch would remain in "suspended animation" while they searched for other candidates. In the interim he suggested that James could run the branch for the first half of 1891 and if Hodgson decided to pick up in the second half, the offer to continue paying him $1,500 would still stand. Either way, they needed to find a solution since the 430 members should not be lost to associational vicissitudes.[132] James replied halfheartedly to this new plan: "Our 'Branch,' you see, has tided over its difficulties temporarily; and by raising its fee will enter upon the new year with a certain momentum. You'll have to bleed, though, ere the end, devoted creatures that you are, over there!"[133] Privately, he shared his doubts with his wife that he did not believe the branch would survive the year.[134] His pessimism was well founded. To Langley, he reported that "the [American Branch of the] S.P.R. fund doesn't mount up brilliantly."[135]

In fact, the situation had become even more desperate. During the previous year, James, Hodgson, and Langley had assessed the patient. In a report issued in the *Journal* they maintained the society was doing "admirable work in sifting genuine from spurious psychical phenomena and in establishing beyond question among men of science and non-spiritualists generally, a class of facts." But they also noted a lack of adequate funds to sustain the work. As such, they would have to expand the base. In 1890, there were 425 names on the roll, of which only 90 were full members (indicating a slight increase from the previous year, when the membership of the ASPR had peaked at 400), but the net worth of the American Branch amounted to a mere $2,500. Such a pittance would not cover Hodgson and Miss Edmunds's salaries, office rent, travel expenses, and the like.[136] So the branch issued another circular that stressed its very survival depended largely upon increased voluntary contributions. This new attempt worked temporarily, but by 1894 the branch's treasury had run dry and it had to beg for funds from the SPR. A flurry of letters from Myers recounted the by-now familiar pattern. Myers sent a check for £120 and expressed hope that Sidgwick and SPR member Walter Leaf would match it. But by late 1895 the American Branch had serious liabilities. It owed £80 on the balance of Hodgson's annual salary and £20 to Miss Edmunds. Unless these debts could be paid, the branch would have to be "wound up," as Myers put it, or become an independent entity.

For his part, James worried that while these measures would stop the immediate hemorrhaging, they failed to address the underlying problem. But Myers continued in the same vein. He informed James that Robert Pearsall Smith had raised £170 to pay off the balance due on Hodgson's and Edmunds's salaries as well as to cover the Piper investigations for the rest of the winter.

Hodgson, however, had reached his limit with the year-to-year arrangement and wanted something more permanent. Unless £2,000 could be promised to pay his salary and cover all other costs for the next four years, it appeared the research would cease and the American Branch would have to terminate itself. Sensing the severity of the problem, Myers wrote to James with still another possible solution. He offered £100 of the £3,000 of his brother's bestowment and asked James if he would invest the funds in securities. James agreed to supply him with his "propositions for the future, especially with reference to your poor brother's bequest," and promptly invested the much-needed funds in railroad bonds. Since Arthur had intended the money to be used for psychical research, Myers suggested some of it should go toward funding trance mediumship study, stipulating that the "[Mrs.] Piper inquiry must go on." Myers, who clearly had trouble accepting the futility of such efforts, finally realized that a much larger sum of steadily flowing funds was necessary for the American Branch's survival. James agreed and decided to loan the branch £80 of his own money.[137]

But these amounts were woefully insufficient. Indicating how desperate the situation had become, James told Sidgwick in 1895 that Hodgson was once again without funds and that the ASPR treasury was empty. In fact, despite the money earmarked for Hodgson, James estimated a $1,000 deficit for that year. "Hodgson's salary is 300 dollars now.... Miss Edmunds's [$]35, $100 [for] rent now due on [the ASPR] office, etc.," he noted, adding, "I can advance money for pressing needs." James had written and crossed out "but not conveniently," suggesting just how reluctant he had become to bankrolling the day-to-day operations of organized psychical research. He also noted the slim chance of raising money to keep the branch afloat but said he was not hopeful: "The circular for a 'fund' will be issued after the [Mrs.] Piper *Proceedings* appears. I myself hope little or nothing from it—but miracles sometimes happen, and the only thing is to try." Emphasizing his concern for the survival of the American Branch without such funding, he continued, "I still believe that you will have to decide finally whether to stop the Branch here or contribute at least a thousand dollars a year."[138] And to Myers he reiterated that "you must be ready for another pecuniary disbursement, I fear ere long!"[139]

Seeking other avenues of support, James once asked Charles William Eliot, president of Harvard College, whether "Harvard would accept an endowment for psychical research."[140] But James seemed to doubt his own request, for he added that since the "people in New York [at Columbia] now doubt the value of this [funding psychical research with university dollars],"

Eliot should not "trouble himself further." As a rule, universities in the United States at this point did not fund psychical research, though Henry Seybert had established a commission in his name at the University of Pennsylvania to investigate Spiritualism during the 1880s.[141] James inquired of Horace Furness, a Shakespearean scholar and lawyer who chaired the commission, whether he might help pay for Hodgson's salary, to which Furness replied that he could not because the money bequeathed by "Old Seybert" had been used up.[142] In the end, James thought that while psychical research was certainly worthy of funding, it should come from the private sector "independent of universities."[143] Dorr, who agreed with James, had been surreptitiously supplying Hodgson with $1,500 when the SPR council had stopped paying him a regular salary in 1902. James had been surprised to learn of the arrangement after Hodgson had "quite spontaneously" blurted it out to him, but he also seemed to approve of it since it freed up Hodgson to act "quite independent of their control."[144] Nonetheless, due to Hodgson's good work, Myers thought it necessary for the American Branch to maintain its existence. "Surely," he exclaimed to James, "the Branch can still fight on!"[145]

The American Branch did "fight on" until the unexpected death of Richard Hodgson in 1905. Hodgson had collapsed suddenly while playing a game of handball at the Union Boat Club in Boston, and his passing raised the specter of the branch's survival. Since 1887, when Hodgson had been sent over to the United States as secretary of the ASPR, he had with Lucy Edmunds effectively run the day-to-day operations and performed the lion's share of the investigative and experimental work. Although James had played a significant role, he knew that without someone as good as Hodgson it was highly questionable whether the branch could continue—the intervening two decades having erased his doubts completely about his abilities. "Hyslop hasn't the practical qualities, Newbold can't do it, they have no one to send from England," he explained to a friend. "The fact is Hodgson *was* the 'Branch.'"[146] Schiller, by contrast, continued to advocate for a philanthropic solution. To James he queried, "Can not someone even in America, where every scientific fad finds some one to endow it, be induced to do something for psychical research?" Clearly, though, relying on so few individuals, even good ones like Hodgson, ultimately destabilized the organization. "The diffused interest in knowledge & in scientific investigation of these matters," he argued, "is even yet too slight to support a good man with an adequate salary derived from subscriptions."[147] Lodge understood that reality. Trusting James's judgment, he notified him that the future of the branch "would depend largely on your advice," adding that "you are our sheet anchor over here.... We await your further communication."[148] After weighing the alternatives, James's decision was to advise for closing the branch. To Théodore Flournoy, his friend and Swiss psychical researcher, he wrote, "I suspect that our American Branch of the S.P.R. will have to dissolve this year, for lack of a competent secretary."[149]

On 18 May 1906, the three vice presidents (James, Dorr, and Hyslop) of the American Branch met in Boston with J. G. Piddington, the SPR representative who had been sent over for the occasion. Each signed the notice that stated "after a full and anxious consideration it has been decided to dissolve the American Branch of the Society for Psychical Research at the end of the year."[150] The notice also made four assurances to its members and financial contributors. First, the SPR would carry on psychical research. It planned to conduct cross-correspondence tests between Mrs. Piper in Boston and a new medium—Mrs. Verrall—in England. Second, the records of the ASPR and the American Branch, especially the Piper material, would be relocated to the SPR's possession (part of Piddington's mission had been to collect it and see its safe journey back to Cambridge, where it would be kept for future analysis). Third, a thorough review of all material not related to the Piper material would be conducted and a summary of it published in the *Journal*. Finally, Hyslop would be allowed to commence a new organization (unfortunately also called the American Society for Psychical Research), but it would have no official ties to the SPR. Hyslop would be given a few boxes of newspaper clippings that advertised Mrs. Piper over the years but nothing substantive.[151] James casually summarized the branch's demise to his brother, writing, "Piddington is here and the S.P.R. winding up seems to promise to run sufficiently smoothly."[152] But for him the dissolution could not have come sooner. "To tell the truth," he confided to Flournoy, "I'm rather glad of the prospect of the Branch ending, for the Piper-investigation ... had begun to bore me to extinction."[153] When the American Branch of the SPR finally closed in December 1906, the first wave of formally organized psychical research in the United States had lasted just two decades.

That the first generation of transatlantic psychical research organizations survived at all might be explained by the will and fortitude of a few dedicated men and women struggling to scientifically investigate psychic phenomena. The SPR resorted to the loyalty of its membership and the availability of personal funds, while the Sidgwicks' supportive cheer and research; the scientific skills of Crookes, Barrett, and Lodge; Gurney's dogged pursuit of data; and Myers's uncanny ability to hold the theoretical and popular lines while the others (including James) flirted with abandoning the mission, saw them through. That the ASPR and American Branch survived at all was testament to Hodgson's indefatigable investigations, Dorr's clandestine funding, and James's determined efforts despite his persistent nagging doubts. In this sense, their work seems something of a small miracle.

The demise of early American psychical research societies, however, raises a specter: why did they eventually and perhaps inevitably fail? Seymour Mauskopf, a historian of psychical research, argues that what really consummated the end of the ASPR was not a series of interlocking institutional pressures, as argued herein, but rather a lack of professionally trained scientists who were committed to psychical research.[154] There is a significant degree of truth to this claim, as indicated by the early mass exodus of qualified experts and specialists who might have brought a modicum of success to the work had they remained. But this reason cannot alone account for the relative *success* of psychical research in general or James's commitment to it in particular. That is, it does not explain the fact that James stuck with psychical research throughout his career; that the ASPR paid Hodgson to work full-time; that the American Branch contained more members by the end of 1890 than the ASPR had when it dissolved in the beginning of that same year; that the American Branch continued to find funding, however sparse, to pay Hodgson and carry on its mission while the SPR lacked its own full-time equivalent after Gurney had died in 1888; that the American Branch did some of the SPR's best work between 1890 and 1906; and that the SPR itself had difficulty finding professionally trained scientists devoted to its cause (neither Lodge nor Crookes nor Barrett devoted his career to psychical research) and yet maintained its existence. Thus, the conundrum is not why the ASPR and the American Branch failed but why they succeeded for as long as they did, despite all the hardships. More pertinently, Mauskopf also contends psychical research had been at best a secondary activity for James. But as the foregoing indicates, James devoted so much of his daily, weekly, monthly, and yearly time and energy to psychical research that such statements strain credibility. On the contrary, his first biographer's view that James's interest in psychical research had been "central and typical," not "one of his vagaries," more closely approximates the truth.[155]

However, given that the ASPR and American Branch were constantly on the brink of extinction, it is difficult to understand what motivated James to continue with these organizations. Thus, the underlying quandary is how can it be explained, on the one hand, that James devoted so much of his time, money, and energy to psychical research—at times slowing his work on *The Principles of Psychology* and even endangering his scientific reputation and academic standing—while on the other he constantly doubted the value of the work and predicted the inevitable end of these "hybrid" societies? The answer is locatable in James's desire to find in psychical research a tertium quid to overcome a conflict between his disdain for organizations and their growing role by the late nineteenth century in the structuring of knowledge, and his philosophy of individualism. "As an individualist," his biographer wrote, "James had an antipathy to organization, mechanization, and officialdom," an antipathy that manifested itself in all of James's intellectual interests, including ethics and religion, politics and government, psychology and science, philosophy and mysticism.[156] The same held true for his commitment to psychical research. For each area James found a common denominator, namely, the tendency of modern bureaucratic trappings to overwhelm the individual. In the end, James's ambivalence about his official roles, duties, and obligations in the SPR and ASPR mirrored his ambivalence regarding the place and value of learned and scientific societies. But his greater need for *systematic* investigation of psychic phenomena that only an organized group could undertake helped him overcome that reluctance. Thus, James's decision to join and help run psychical research societies offered him the institutional arrangement to pursue his tertium quid method of inquiry.

II

PRACTICING PSYCHICAL RESEARCH

four

A HUMAN RAT HOLE

During the late nineteenth and early twentieth centuries, psychical researchers on both sides of the Atlantic investigated copious phenomena ranging from mesmerism, hypnotism, and alternative healing to crystal ball gazing, demoniacal possession, and witchcraft. They looked into claims of haunted houses and poltergeist sightings and collected signed affidavits from ordinary citizens professing the ability of "second sight" or who experienced apparitions of the living and the dead. Mostly they investigated Spiritualism, in which they held hundreds of sittings with "mediums" who claimed the ability to communicate with souls in the afterlife and conducted dozens of telepathy experiments in which they tested numerous subjects and random members of the public. Aiming for a scientific inquiry of psychic phenomena, psychical researchers made it their priority to establish a data bank of evidence that they hoped would lead to facts that over time would support theories such as the survival thesis. In the long run they envisioned the discovery of new "psychical" laws, theorems, and axioms against which new evidence could be tested and verified. Facts, then, played a pivotal role in the pursuit of psychical knowledge. William James practiced psychical research along these broad contours. Indeed, if James's loyalty to his friendships with members of the Sidgwick Group and his complexly ambivalent attitude toward scientifically aspiring organizations like the Society for Psychical Research and the American Society for Psychical Research help explain how James became a psychical researcher, then his work as a practitioner of the craft is best described as the empirical quest for facts. "'Facts,'" as he put it, "are what are wanted."[1]

But establishing scientific facts turned out to be much more difficult than James and the other psychical researchers ever imagined. This was for two reasons. First, psychical researchers had immense trouble finding reliable subjects to study. They spent most of their time weeding out genuine from fake phenomena and in the end failed to generate a valid data pool from which they could begin to collect the kinds of evidence they sought. Instead, through their investigations they inadvertently confirmed a rather ordinary fact, namely, that the vast majority of their subjects possessed no unusual ability whatsoever. A substantial number of investigations ended with either a naturalistic explanation, such as coincidence or luck, as with most claims to second sight, or simple misunderstandings, such as the case of the Welsh Fasting Girl, a young woman who hallucinated because she deprived herself of nourishment. The vast majority, however, ended in charges of fraud, especially the investigations of mediums. These subjects amounted to nothing more than deluded persons or garden-variety conjurers playing a good game. Overall, psychical research demonstrated there was nothing unusual about most subjects' abilities; they simply professed the ability to do things they actually could not. For that reason, the "facts" of Spiritualism failed to persuade prominent critics.[2] Psychical researchers thus clarified much of the confusion surrounding psychic phenomena, but their findings were highly ironic since they led to the exact opposite of their intention and thereby undermined their own hypotheses. As Edmund Gurney lamented to James, the pursuit of the "shifting quicksand of facts . . . [has] amounted to a ragged affair."[3]

The other major problem that psychical researchers faced in their pursuit of facts was a conceptual one. What exactly was a fact? Positivists throughout the nineteenth century argued the discovery of facts would advance the historical development of scientific knowledge and social progress, but the precise definition of a fact remained an open matter. Were facts irreducible bits of data that simply exist in the world waiting to be collected, or were they more like pieces of evidence that could be marshaled to support an initial hypothesis? Did they exist independent of the knower and thus were just waiting to be discovered, or were they inextricably bound up with the knower and thus in some way a product of his or her thinking? Could their interpretation be separated from themselves? No psychical researcher wrote a discourse on the nature of facts, and it seems that none gave much thought to these important distinctions. On the whole, it appears that psychical researchers conflated all of these possibilities, assuming in plain positivist fashion that their investigations and testing would almost automatically reveal incontrovertible evidence of psychic forces existing independent of their knowledge of them *and* that that information would justify their belief in the survival thesis. In other words, their use of the term "fact" collapsed its distinct ontological and interpretive meanings. This was a conceptual confusion of epic proportion since it equated measured observation with wishful thinking and careful scientific reasoning with gross religious speculation. Given that the fact has played such a pivotal role as an epistemological unit in modernity, psychical researchers muddled rather than clarified what "psychic" facts might be and thereby left open exactly what kind of knowledge, if any, they offered. But psychical researchers were not alone in this regard; most positivists failed to make these kinds of distinctions in their use of the term "fact."[4]

As a leading member of the ASPR, James investigated a number of mediums in America, such as Mrs. Diss Debar, Miss Helen Berry, and Mrs. Hannah Ross, and he critiqued the SPR's investigations of those in England and India, including Henry Slade, William Eglinton, Charles Foster, Madame Blavatsky, and especially Eusapia Palladino. Through his unabashedly empirical approach, James helped the ASPR and SPR expose these mediums as frauds. In so doing, he faced mounting criticism from both extremes, which he categorized as the believers who too easily accepted the reality of mediumship and the skeptics who just as easily dismissed it. Spiritualists made up the former group and in James's view were too naive. Many scientists constituted the latter group and were far too cynical for him. Both shared a dogmatic tendency. They bore much likeness to the two intellectual types—the tender- and tough-minded—that James captured in his famous taxonomy in *Pragmatism* and may have even been its inspiration since they predated his use of the term there. The former were "idealistic" and "optimistic," while the latter were "materialistic" and "pessimistic."[5]

Tender-mindedly, Spiritualists objected to the reliance on demonstrable scientific facts. What they sought in mediumship, indeed from religious faith in general, was not so much scientifically proven facts but an "aura of factuality" that made their experiences meaningful. Facts were supposed to substantiate their predetermined vision of cosmic order and a divine plan, not challenge that coherence or undermine the foundational tenets of religious faith, especially that which required a certain amount of unquestioned belief. When scientific facts and the aura of factuality clashed, Spiritualists objected that their belief was under attack and thus criticized psychical researchers for trying to undermine their faith.[6] On the other hand, many scientists objected in tough-minded fashion that psychical researchers did not go far enough. Experimental psychologists in particular claimed psychical researchers' methodology and mathematical analyses were flawed and that their evidence was not factual since they were trying to scientifically understand something that was ipso facto unscientific. As G. Stanley Hall once dismissively put it,

"Spiritualism, in its more vulgar form, is the sewerage of all the superstitions of the past."[7] For Spiritualists, then, psychical research was too positivist; for scientists, it was not positivist enough and could never be even in principle.

James's empirical approach to psychical research tried to strike a balanced, middle path between these two extremes and thus exemplified his tertium quid method of inquiry. To the Spiritualists and believers, James insisted that without scientifically demonstrable facts, the public and especially scientists would never accept the reality of their phenomena. A certain amount of verifiable facts was necessary, and psychical researchers were the ones to establish them. To the critical scientists and skeptics, James maintained that a certain amount of respect for raw phenomena was equally necessary. To an extent, he agreed that most mediums were of the "dark-sitting and rat-hole type," as he put it, but he felt strongly that refusing to even study mediums or dismissing the data without even looking at it, as Hall and others did, was unempirical and thus violated a central canon of being a good scientist.[8] To claim a priori understanding before investigation was for James tantamount to epistemological suicide. By contrast, James maintained that in order to know whether such phenomena were genuine, researchers had to be as vigilantly empirical in their investigation as any scientist would be in studying his or her chosen topic. He thus advocated complete a posteriori understanding of all phenomena. This meant that regardless of how idiosyncratic mediumship might seem compared with the known body of facts about the natural world, its investigation should go forward, and no amount of speculation as to its nature should be ventured upon until the data were gathered in the most systematic way. As Ralph Barton Perry put it, "James felt that the critics of psychical research . . . were obeying the dictates of a 'theoretic creed,' while he, on the other hand, was 'baldly empirical.' The rejection of phenomena for methodological reasons is an inversion of the rightful priority. We should never regard phenomena as 'impossible.'"[9] It was this very sense of allowing for the possibility of the impossible that James brought to the quest for facts in his investigation of mediums. In so doing, James's tertium quid method of inquiry dictated a thoroughgoing empirical approach to psychical research.

EMPIRICISM AND THE SEARCH FOR FACTS

The SPR's and ASPR's empirical program is best understood as part of nineteenth-century positivism, but their quest for facts exemplified a fetish for them that had been present in modern Western thought since Francis Bacon defined facts as the basic units of systematic knowledge. With its roots in the scientific revolutions of the sixteenth and seventeenth centuries, positivism simultaneously narrowed and fulfilled the Baconian program by maintaining that science was the only valid form of knowledge and facts its only valid object of study. In the eighteenth century, Saint-Simon and his followers advanced a philosophical system of progress that hailed the steady accumulation of facts as necessary for the advancement of both practical or applied and theoretical or speculative knowledge and denied the intelligibility of all approaches that superseded the factual claims of science. Positivists of all stripes disdained all metaphysical, religious, and ethical claims that could not be verified by scientific methodologies while simultaneously holding that these speculative, rationalistic, and emotive disciplines would eventually become scientific once they were firmly positivistic. Auguste Comte expanded positivism to include a history of science by arguing natural sciences like astronomy had inevitably and irreversibly developed through three conceptual stages (theological, metaphysical, and positive) and that this demonstrated the historical progress of the human mind. Upon this edifice, Comte sought to formulate a science of society. John Stuart Mill, a onetime devotee of Comte, challenged Comte's system by adding introspective psychology (which Comte had inexplicably left out) and by arguing that there was nothing inevitable to the social sciences leading to laws about human nature. Instead, Mill maintained that rational men were needed to intervene to ensure social and political progress. In addition, Mill and his utilitarian colleague Jeremy Bentham stipulated that facts could be the basis for a science of the mind, and Bentham went so far as to advocate for a fact-based "exact science" of all human endeavors. And although Nicolas de Condorcet did not actually argue that progress conceived as factual science would historically lead to a perfect society, the idea seemed to imply this utopian ideal. Each of these historicist positivists, then, built upon the Enlightenment's view that reason would trump superstition and argued the empirical methods of the natural sciences could be used to create a social science that would to varying degrees advance knowledge and society.[10] By the twentieth century, philosophers of science had identified the crucial dimensions of the scientific fact, including invariance, stability, and standardization, that made it a powerful epistemological and social unit of scientific knowledge.[11]

Although James rejected Comte's positivism as "too sharp and definite," he and the other psychical researchers worked within this general paradigm.[12] But, like many positivists, they differed in their assessment of progress. Some, such as F. W. H. Myers and Oliver Lodge, were more utopian and believed psychical research would inevitably demonstrate the survival thesis.

Others, such as the Sidgwicks and for a time Richard Hodgson and Frank Podmore, were cautiously hopeful. James, with no inclination toward the survival hypothesis or personal need for religious belief, emphasized the need to ensure the work was first and foremost thoroughly empirical. Only a rigorously scientific investigation would yield useful facts—an approach that was evident from the very moment James became a psychical researcher. As the ASPR's Committee on Mediumship (of which James was a leading member) stated, its mission was "to test and determine the existence of these facts and phenomena."[13] It hoped to investigate these mediums the way a botanist would study a plant species—through something akin to the modern scientific method in which the logic of discovery and the evaluation of evidence was subjected to rigorous testing and verification. James led this effort and was thus committed to establishing scientific facts about mediumship. However, James used his own particular empirical criteria in the committee's evaluation that were grounded in his tertium quid. That is, James hoped to find a third way between the critics who closed their minds to even the possibility that physical mediumship might contain genuine psychic phenomena and the believers whose minds were so wide open to accept all the phenomena without any kind of verification process. This much is evident from the committee's statement of purpose, which stipulated that psychical researchers "must, on the one hand, overcome the natural tendency of all persons to desire and believe the marvelous without thorough investigation, and on the other hand they must not through a too narrow conservatism close their eyes to facts which are inexplicable by ordinary causes."[14]

James's appeal to facts can be understood through his interpretation of philosophical empiricism. Steeped in the tradition of modern European empiricism, James believed all knowledge is derived a posteriori.[15] Like most other empiricists during their respective eras, such as John Locke, David Hume, and Mill, James tailored a version to meet the philosophical challenges and pace of the new scientific knowledge of his age. For James, a robust empiricism possessed two central axioms. The first stipulated that although knowledge is not limited to that which the scientific laboratory delivers or the scientific method renders, it is best *tested* by these processes. James identified five conditions to this process. The systematic acquisition of data had to be gathered in an impartial manner. It became evidence only when a large enough body was accumulated, rendering it analyzable for consistent patterns. The evidence became fact only when the patterns detected were achieved consistently through multiple, repeated testing (or verification). Only when enough solid evidence was produced could theories, purporting to explain any phenomenon, be offered. Finally, attempts to theorize before the first four conditions were met were premature and thus non-empirical and indicated that either rationalism or dogmatism had contaminated the process and thereby invalidated any knowledge claims. Moreover, theories unsubstantiated by facts were to be avoided at all costs. Since a hypothesis was only as good as the evidence it was built on, theories for James amounted to little more than shorthand for empirically established facts. As his first intellectual biographer put it, "The *purpose* of theoretic invention was economical and useful description of fact. Theories are to be judged primarily not by their logical consistency or aesthetic symmetry, or by other formal criterion, but by their factual relevance. They are at best a substitute for something better, namely, first-hand observation.... In brief, a scientific theory was for James essentially a hypothesis."[16]

The second main axiom specified that all knowledge gained through the process of the first axiom was subject to revision by all future evidence *as experienced by the experiencer*. It was this final provision that made James's empiricism robust. As James once put it, a philosophy is called "empiricism... [when] it is contented to regard its most assured conclusions concerning matters of fact as hypothesis liable to modification in the course of future experience." In short, James's empirical conditions for knowledge hinged on the ever-changing quality of experience.[17] Thus, something that was not a fact could become one for James if the right kinds of empirical evidence were found experientially. It was precisely this kind of approach that guided James's tertium quid search for psychical facts.

On numerous occasions James encouraged members of the Sidgwick Group to be more rigorously empirical. For instance, publishing the results of some new investigation merely for public exposure, as Myers frequently did, was shortsighted and annoyed James. "What we want is facts, not popular papers," he thundered, "and until the facts thicken, papers may do more harm than good." Myers thought the orthodox scientific community might be persuaded to take psychical research more seriously if the public were persuaded first, but James retorted that "'professional' opinion won't be conciliated by popular expositions, but only by S.P.R. Proceedings."[18] James also encouraged psychical researchers to avoid the temptation to reach conclusions or speculate prematurely on the meaning of some recent discovery, again as Myers was wont to do. "We are getting lots more evidence of various kinds," he reported to James. "[Charles] Richet has just been staying with me,—much stirred (tho' this is private as yet) by some *spiritualistic* phenomena in Russia with no paid medium,—very good evidence."[19] But James was not impressed since the "evidence of various kinds" was too vague and thus not factual. To Myers he replied, "The facts are *so* discontinuous so far that possibly all our generation can do may be to get 'em called facts."[20] Indeed, while writing his SPR presidential address, James confided to Myers that he had been "ultra-non-committal as to our evidence." Although he admitted that his strategy was partly due to "thinking it to be good presidential policy" and that he "may have overdone the impartiality business," he was mostly using his empiricism to guide his tertium quid method of inquiry into psychical facts.[21]

While James was pushing the SPR to be more rigorously empirical, others such as Thomas Davidson were admonishing James for being overly empirical. A Scottish-born writer, self-styled philosopher, and educator of Greek and Latin, Davidson was a towering man with bright blue eyes and a hearty personality. Seeking employment, he left Scotland in the 1860s for a series of mostly high school teaching positions in London, Ontario, St. Louis, New England, and New York City. He was also an intellectual traveler, traversing a number of schools of thought ranging from positivism to Kantian idealism to Aristotelianism in his early days, to Rosminian Catholicism in his middle years, to Fabian socialism in his penultimate phase. Throughout each, Davidson remained optimistic, believing that truth came to him no matter what creed he adopted. Mostly, though, Davidson was a radical individualist. He sought a kind of spirituality that favored the claims of the intellect, especially those that manifested ethical conduct, but one that did not lapse into authoritarian secularism, a view he called "apeirotheism," which amounted to pluralistic idealism that blended Platonism, rationalism, and pantheism.[22] But Davidson also held an egalitarian view of the universe, one full of immortal spirits whose chief purpose was to love and aid one another. As he put it, "'Creeds are nothing, life is everything. . . . The divine . . . is a republic of self-existent spirits, each seeking the realization of its desires through love, through intimacy with all the rest, and finding its heaven in such intimacy.'"[23] Davidson promulgated these views at his philosophy camp, Summer School for Cultural Sciences, which was located at his home ("Glenmore") on East Hill, Hurricane, in the New York Adirondacks. James sometimes lectured there, as in 1903 when he was working out his doctrine of radical empiricism, or after spending time at Putnam's Shanty in Vermont, where Davidson sometimes joined James and others for philosophical bantering and rigorous hiking.

James first met Davidson at the Radical Club in Boston in the mid-1870s, at whose meetings James recalled, "Davidson used to crack the whip of Aristotle over us." Davidson occupied a special place in James's heart. Not only had he introduced James's future wife to him but he also possessed a "genius for friendship" and was "one of the purest of human beings" James ever met. Although the two men disagreed philosophically (James thought Kant dogmatic and pretentious), they developed a mutual admiration for the other's abilities and especially for their shared rugged individualism. Of the twenty maxims James found in Davidson, he was first and foremost a man who believed in absolute self-reliance and who espoused the "energies" of the individual, his self-worth, and the value of understanding the world and human relationships through lived experience. Davidson and James, then, shared significant traits, but unlike James, Davidson's radical individualism led to his problems with authority. Harvard president Charles William Eliot, for instance, rejected Davidson as a job candidate after Davidson published in the *Atlantic Monthly* a set of stinging criticisms of Harvard's Greek department. James, who had recommended him for the position, thought Harvard had lost a "great opportunity" but also realized the outcome was the best one since Davidson loathed "academicism." Still, James admired Davidson's autodidactic style, dubbing him "the knight-errant of the intellectual life."[24]

Where the two men disagreed most vehemently was over psychical research. Davidson thought the psychical researchers' empirical approach was far too narrow. He argued their scientific methodology was "antispiritual" and claimed this bias would never prove the survival thesis, which he believed was neither quantifiable nor subject to verifiable testing in a laboratory. But James thought Davidson had misunderstood his methodology and the actual practice of psychical research. He emphasized the SPR and ASPR had no commitments in any direction other than ascertaining reliable evidence. "As for any 'anti-spiritual' basis of our society," he assured Davidson, "no theoretical basis exists, or *bias*, of any sort whatever, so far as I can make out, exists in it." Psychical researchers, he claimed, should be noted for "their complete colourlessness philosophically. They seem to have no preferences for any general-ism whatever. I doubt if this could be matched in Europe." In case Davidson remained unpersuaded, he reemphasized the urgency of gathering sound evidence to establish scientific facts. "For I take it the urgent thing . . . is to ascertain in a manner so thorough as to constitute evidence that will be accepted by outsiders, just what the *phenomenal conditions of certain concrete occurrences are*. Not till that is done can spiritualistic or antispiritualistic theories be [supported or] even mooted."[25] In other words, James believed that his de-emphasis on theory undermined Davidson's antispiritual charge. The SPR and ASPR in his view were neither antispiritualist nor dogmatic but simply fact seekers. In this sense, James agreed with George Croom Robertson, who maintained that "Edmund Gurney and other psychical researchers have it right."[26] Still, James admitted that while the ultimate purpose was to gather enough valid evidence to test theories, he realized a great gulf existed between those two stages and much work remained, including finding reliable subjects to study. Thus, he and the other psychical researchers began the tedious process of investigating Spiritualist mediums in which the difference between *suspecting* most mediums were frauds and *knowing* they were was paramount to establishing facts.

THE SPR AND PHYSICAL MEDIUMSHIP

Spiritualist mediumship was a transatlantic and transnational development that permeated the United States, Great Britain, Germany, Italy, and France (where it was called "Spiritism" by its founder, Allan Kardec). Hundreds of mediums advertised themselves in the flourishing Spiritualist press on both sides of the Atlantic to hundreds of thousands of readers, followers, and believers of this new faith.[27] By the late nineteenth century, the practice of Spiritualism was wide and varied, but two main types of mediums could be delineated: mental and physical. Mediums of the former type collapsed into a trance state and acted as a supposed conduit between the spirits of this world and those of the next. "Communication" occurred through either acts of speech or writing. Physical mediums produced some sort of materialization that was taken as a sign of surviving spirits of the deceased.[28] Physical mediumship preceded the mental variety historically for the obvious reason that material phenomena offered better proof of the existence of the afterlife and thus provided its participants with an immediate kind of solace. It was also more controversial because of its sensationalized quality. Physical mediumship as an expression of Spiritualism spanned roughly eighty years, from the late 1840s, when the Fox sisters unwittingly inaugurated the modern Spiritualist movement with their famed "rappings," to the late 1920s, when Mina Stinson ("Margery") Crandon was still producing "ectoplasm," a term Charles Richet invented which referred to a gooey substance that emerged out the medium's orifices to form what Richet dubbed "pseudopods" or "spirit-appendages." But its heyday occurred in the late nineteenth century, when physical mediums produced an array of phenomena that ranged from the more mundane instances of table rapping, furniture levitation, and slate writing, to the more complex forms that utilized spirit cabinets, full-form materializations, and body levitation and shrinking. There was hardly a limit to what physical mediums exhibited in their increasingly sophisticated if implausible séances.[29]

The SPR investigated a variety of physical mediums and found all of them fraudulent. These included Henry Slade, a famous levitator, body shrinker/expander, and slate writing master with whom James appears to have once sat;[30] William Eglinton, a skilled manipulator of slate writing who learned his trade from Slade and whom James initially thought might be promising;[31] Helena Petrovna Blavatsky, the cofounder with Henry Steel Olcott of the Theosophical Society, the group Hodgson exposed as fraudulent but that James joined for a short time around 1892, attending a few of its meetings;[32] and Charles H. Foster, who practiced "pellet reading" in which the spirits supposedly communicated by writing their sentiments inside of small, wrapped-up blank pieces of paper resembling small pellets.[33] James played a minor role in all of these cases, but he did follow them closely as the correspondence reveals the SPR informed James about its investigations.[34] It also indicates his reaction to them was consistent with his empirical quest for facts. For instance, after reading Hodgson's articles, James told his philosopher friend Shadworth Hollway Hodgson that "I am glad of his demolition of that jade, Blavatsky."[35]

Eusapia Palladino

After exposing Slade, Eglinton, Blavatsky, and Foster, the SPR's Committee on Mediumship concentrated on Eusapia Palladino. The most studied and controversial physical medium in fin-de-siècle Europe and America, Eusapia claimed she had to cheat on occasions when the spirits did not cooperate but that most times her phenomena were genuine. But how could such a thing ever be verified? The disagreements over this question led psychical research societies in England, Germany, France, Italy, Poland, and America to conduct multiple investigations of her throughout the 1890s and early 1900s. In cities such as Rome, Naples, Turin, Genoa, Palermo, Cambridge (England), Paris, Warsaw, and Boston, Eusapia gave literally hundreds of sittings and séances for investigators, credulous believers, and curious onlookers from every rank of society, making her perhaps the most studied medium during the heyday of physical mediumship.[36]

An illiterate Italian peasant, Eusapia (as she is called in the literature) was orphaned at age twelve and sent to Naples to work as a laundress, where she lived with a family whose members were Spiritualists. They encouraged her to develop her own mediumistic gifts, and by sixteen she claimed the power of self-levitation. In the 1870s, under the patronage of Signor Damiani, Eusapia gained a reputation as an outstanding medium by producing phenomena such as table levitations, the appearance of mysterious lights, and loud detonations that sounded like pistol shots. By the late 1880s, Cesare Lombroso, the Italian sociologist and physician whom James once met, began to study her. Although initially somewhat baffled, Lombroso proclaimed her phenomena authentic and converted to Spiritualism in 1891. His colleague Giordanno Virginio Schiaparelli, an Italian astronomer and member of the Milan committee that investigated Eusapia in October 1892, also wrote a favorable report. Myers encouraged James to sit with Eusapia while in Milan. It is unknown whether James did, but this occasion marked the beginning of his immersion into the Eusapia case.[37]

The Italian reports led to the Polish investigations of Eusapia in Warsaw in 1894, where she reportedly sat forty times for the psychologist Julian Ochorowicz. The results produced charges of fraud as well as bafflement, which led to further sittings that year at Richet's house on Île Roubaud. These sittings marked the beginning of the SPR's investigations of Eusapia. There, Eusapia amazed Richet, Myers, and Lodge—levitating furniture, producing rappings, and moving objects around the séance table and room—all without apparent physical cause. Taking their usual precautions to hold the medium's legs and arms, these sittings persuaded them that she had not been cheating (although Richet noted the sittings took place in total darkness). During these investigations, Eusapia produced her first ectoplasmic "pseudopod," which clutched and pulled at the sitters.[38] As with the other subjects, SPR members informed James of their investigations of Eusapia.[39] Richet, for instance, explained that while "reasoning" convinced him that Palladino's phenomena were genuine, he nonetheless had trouble believing the results that ran "contrary to physics," though he added Myers's and Lodge's abilities to suspend their emotions and to rely solely on reasoning for their judgment impressed him.[40] For Myers's part, "reasoning" convinced him that the phenomena were genuine, confiding to James that "there is *no doubt* as to this business."[41]

Myers was so impressed with these sittings that he coaxed Henry and Eleanor Sidgwick to join him at Richet's "newly bought" chateau in Carqueiranne for some additional ones where they could judge for themselves. He then informed James that the SPR planned a special *Proceedings* issue devoted to Eusapia.[42] Although the group could not get Lord Rayleigh to come have a look, as he was too busy "discovering a new gas,"[43] Ochorowicz and Albert von Schrenck-Notzing, the German psychical researcher, did participate in these sittings. Upon their completion, everyone weighed in with their initial impression. Myers told James that the Sidgwicks agreed with Myers and Lodge that Eusapia produced some genuine phenomena and that Lodge planned to report them as indisputably genuine at the next SPR meeting.[44] Hodgson, who had not yet witnessed Eusapia but had been kept abreast of the developments in America via post, remained skeptical of his colleagues' glowing reports of her. After some discussion, it was agreed that she would come to Cambridge for further sittings in the winter of 1894–95 and that Hodgson would be paid to come over to observe and form his own opinions. These developments suited James, as he informed Alice that Hodgson was immediately leaving for England to "study Palladino" and that he was pleased the matter was "being pushed." For his part, Hodgson thought he would be able to show that Palladino was the next Blavatsky, that is, nothing more than a very clever conjurer.[45] Before coming to Cambridge, though, Eusapia was to go first to Munich so Schrenck-Notzing could study her more thoroughly. As far as Myers was concerned, though, it did not matter where she gave sittings; the location should not affect the outcome.[46]

But Myers was wrong. The sittings in Cambridge, which were delayed by a few months until the late spring and early summer of 1895 because Sidgwick and Lodge had the flu, proved a bust for Eusapia and her supporters and a boon for Hodgson and her detractors.[47] Hodgson exposed her in a *Journal* report that indicated Eusapia was using a free hand or leg in the dark to move objects and to make sounds and concluded that "nothing but trickery had been at work."[48] Myers was later forced to recognize this when he told James that Hodgson had given an excellent speech about Eusapia.[49] Sir Joseph J. Thompson, then master at Trinity College, had attended some of the sittings. He recounted an incident in which Eusapia supposedly made a small melon levitate and move from one table to another without apparent physical support or causation (so-called telekinesis). Illuminating Myers's gullibility, Thompson offered an explanation for the mobile melon that did not invoke occultism. According to Thompson, Myers had a habit of encouraging mediums by pretending some phenomena had happened to him such as being "hit in the ribs." With that, Thompson explained, "the circuit [of the sitters' clasped hands around the table] was thus broken and it was perhaps a minute before it was re-formed. . . . What had happened was quite obvious: while the circuit had been broken and Eusapia was free she had reached out, got the melon, sat down and put it on her lap, intending to kick it from her lap on to the table."[50]

Hodgson's and Thompson's conclusions irritated Myers, not to mention Lodge, Richet, and Ochorowicz, who initially thought Eusapia was genuine. They each admitted that while the phenomena produced in Cambridge in 1895 had not been as spectacular as that in southern France in 1894, where the test conditions admittedly had been more lax, they were convinced nonetheless that Eusapia had not been cheating. Even if they could not prove it, they simply saw things they believed could not be fraudulent. Apparently they had failed to learn from Hodgson's investigations of Blavatsky that showed mal-observation (when people mistakenly report events they do not actually observe) accounted for her apparent genuineness. In response to Hodgson, whom they thought too skeptical anyway, each wrote a report in the *Journal*. Myers, in particular, perhaps because of his initial enthusiasm, defended her (and himself) most stringently by arguing that Eusapia's behavior in Cambridge, where she had been caught cheating, and her behavior in southern France, where she had not, were completely separate and thus unrelated events; the former could not be used to discount the latter. Myers, Lodge, Richet, and Ochorowicz also wrote responses to Hodgson's arguments.[51] The Sidgwicks, however, believed they had been duped and immediately reversed course. Confident in Hodgson's investigative skills and their own eyewitness accounts of her in that second and less successful set of sittings, they abandoned their support for her. This caused some tension within the SPR leadership, with Hodgson and the Sidgwicks on one side and Myers, Richet, and Lodge on the other. That the phenomena had been far less convincing in Cambridge also resulted in a minor setback for psychical research writ large, since several leading scientists such as Thompson and Francis Darwin (Charles's cousin), whom they hoped to bring into the fold, had been in attendance and were unimpressed by the phenomena.[52]

The central members of the SPR, then, divided over Eusapia. The height of the disagreement occurred on the eve of James's assuming the SPR's presidency (1894–95). As one of the president's functions was to arbitrate disagreements over which material belonged in the *Proceedings*, James immersed himself in the controversy. His efforts reveal his commitment to empiricism and to his tertium quid. Examining the various reports and letters on Eusapia, he corresponded with the key members from both sides of the debate. James discerned that Lodge and Myers supported her and favored producing a special issue devoted to her phenomena while Hodgson and the Sidgwicks did not and were against it. The issue centered on Lodge's desire to publish his findings from the November 1894 *Journal* as matters of fact, an event that never materialized but not for lack of Lodge's efforts. Toward that end, he composed a long letter to James that discussed his work and why he thought some scientific journals should devote a special issue to Eusapia. He hoped to garner support and to acquire submissions from Richet, Sidgwick, Myers, Ochorowicz, Lombroso, and Dr. George Finzi (an honorary member of the SPR living in Milan) and explained to James that there had been a "good deal of discussion as to how it [the Eusapia material] was to be published." Lodge was concerned that Spiritualists like William Thomas Stead, a British journalist and then editor of *Borderlands* (a periodical devoted to spirit prints) who had conducted séances with Eusapia, would "garble" the information. Instead, Lodge thought it would be "wise to storm the scientific citadel" by publishing the results in *Nature*, the scientific journal of the British Association for the Advancement of Science.[53]

Anticipating James's preference for facts, Lodge explained that Eusapia's case showed that objects can be "moved without ordinary kinds of contact," that is, she possessed telekinesis. To bolster his point on this highly controversial claim, he added, "As to the explanation of comm[unication] we grope, . . . the direction I like best to grope in is a semi-metaphysical[,] semi-psychological [and] semi-biological one." Almost as if he doubted this claim upon putting ink to paper, he added parenthetically, "probably because I am ignorant of all this science." This was a strange remark for Lodge to make since he was an adept scientist and usually did not pretend at modesty. Still, he added that "it feels to me as if the idea of a movement could sometimes take effect & produce an objective physical result. As if what we do when we will to move a finger could be extended so as to effect the movement of a distant chair or book." Lodge explained further that his description of the events accounted for the facts, but he was hesitant to offer a theory. From a physicist's perspective, he remarked, "[It] is the Philosophers who must find us a theory . . . , & we shall look to you for help."[54]

That Lodge thought James could be that philosopher reveals he did not understand James's empiricism. But James made it clear to him in his own lengthy response. Indicating he had received a copy of Lodge's report from Hodgson, one he admired because it was written by "*a man* dealing with *facts*," which was "refreshing after the pedantry and pretentious timidity of orthodox deliverance," he advised Lodge against publishing the report in a scientific journal (though he was not opposed at that point of it going into the *Proceedings*). As for "storming the scientific citadel," James thought this an even worse idea, writing that he was "extremely averse" to seeing it in journals like *Nature* or *Science* since nothing would be gained by it. He was concerned for Lodge's reputation, not to mention that of the SPR's, much as he had been for Gurney's the previous decade. James argued the effort would amount to nothing more than "another Crookes case to be deplored" and that Lodge would be regarded like that of James's "soft headed friend Brackett." Scientists, James warned Lodge, "will make pious exclamations of pity, deplore your 'vagueness,' etc., etc.," disparaging the report's "breadth and philosophical character" for want of scientific worth. In other words, without further research to verify Lodge's data on Eusapia, James thought the results were not yet scientific and thus not facts.[55]

James knew that personal experience more than anything else convinced people of a medium's veracity. He also knew that sentiment was not a sufficient substitute for scientific research. Explaining the dilemma to Lodge, James noted how the ever-shifting linguistic standards affected Spiritualists, psychical researchers, and the scientific community alike, each using them for their own ends. He now believed that the SPR had landed in the same spot with orthodox scientists that Spiritualists had with psychical researchers just ten years prior, Spiritualists having tried to argue that psychical researchers had to take their experiences at face value and not try to prove them. James recognized this irony by suggesting psychical researchers were now victims of their own strategy; the very language they had wielded against Spiritualists was now working against them in their own attempts to persuade the scientific community. Going public with all the Eusapia material, then, was a grave mistake. Instead, he argued for additional data that in time would bolster the case. "The stuff will keep," he assured Lodge, "and the bigger the bomb to be exploded at once in the [P]roceedings, the greater the shock."[56]

The James-Lodge exchange over Eusapia reveals their different interpretations of what facts were. And James's interpretation would certainly affect his ruling on the Eusapia case. For guidance, James turned to Myers: "I tingle for exact details about Eusapia. You don't even say whether Lodge is absolutely convinced, but I supposed he must be from the general context. I shall have to think over the question of sending his report to Science [magazine] or elsewhere, after seeing it in proof. I don't see what is to be gained in this matter by haste."[57] James's arguments prevailed, for Lodge informed James that "your cordial and wise letter arrived today & your advice chimes in almost exactly with the position into which we on this side [of the Atlantic Ocean] have been drifting."[58] But that did not end the matter, for James was also concerned about Lombroso's desire to march boldly on by publishing his Eusapia findings as facts. Like Lodge, Lombroso had been equally impressed with the 1894 sittings in France. He came to believe that Eusapia possessed an unknown psychic force that she transmitted through the ether. Such appeals to the ether would have impressed Lodge (who believed in the ether hypothesis), but James thought Lombroso something of an ass, exclaiming once, "Lombroso swings fairly round the circle of illogicality and credulity. The vastest donkey of the age." Nonetheless, James's empiricism required that he not dismiss physical mediumship outright, blurting out to Lodge with frustration, "Why are 'physical phenomena' so absolutely baffling?"[59]

Myers continued to keep James abreast of the developments as they carried over into the investigations of Eusapia in Cambridge in 1895. He told James the SPR was going to pay Hodgson forty pounds to come to England to investigate Eusapia and talk other SPR business, including the future of the "American Branch." For her visit, Eusapia lodged with Myers and Robert Pearsall Smith, a situation that James later severely criticized as having contaminated the entire investigation. Myers reported that the "phenomena [were] very good—[and that] all [was] going well." His wife, he explained, spent the days talking with Eusapia, despite the fact that neither one spoke the other's language, and had photographed Eusapia wearing Sidgwick's academic cap and gown. Myers spent his time in the séances "holding Eusapia's feet" though not her arms, but added that "Sidgwick has to *flirt* with her [to try to distract her from cheating]; (this [is] not for Philistine ears)."[60] Apparently the testing environment had been quite lax, making it a clear violation of James's empiricism. Indeed, at the end of Eusapia's one-month stay, Myers sharply reversed his evaluation of her: they had caught her cheating. To James, he cried out, "*Re* Eusapia[,] all goes ill! Although Lodge & I cannot altogether abandon the Islam phenomena [that is, the 1894 sittings at Richet's in southern France], it seems possible that all this Cambridge phenomena have been is fraud." Myers added that Hodgson had been "most useful and helpful" in studying Eusapia but that "we don't want all this talked about at present, until we have given Richet [an] opportunity of seeing her again and considering his position." Myers then revealed how the differences between the SPR members over Eusapia were emerging, concluding that "anyhow, for *evidential* purposes E[usapia] P[alladino] must be dropped,—I fear— Hodgson & Lodge [are] coming into sharp intellectual collision—[which has led to] . . . a fine example of frank single-handed candour on both sides." Because of the fraud and poor evidence, Myers now believed that the idea for "the Eusapia no. [number] of the Proc[eedings] must be dropped" and that they should move on to other cases. Unlike Lodge, Myers at least admitted his mistakes and gave the appearance of learning from such a humbling experience, as James's empiricism wisely counseled.[61]

James, however, was less persuaded by Myers's newfound sobriety. To Sidgwick, James confided his concerns regarding Myers's and Lodge's initial embrace of the material, as well as Eusapia's fraudulent behavior, writing, "I fear the Eusapia business may prove a blow to our prosperity for a while, even though Hodgson's withers are unwrung thereby. It has been a bad blow to my own faith in expertness and the effects of education in those matters, to see Lodge and Myers to precipitate in publication, not to say conclusion."[62] By contrast, James viewed Sidgwick's approach in line with his own empiricism: "You as usual, have saved your self by holding your tongue.... Nobody, not even I, knows what you thought, and I have understood all along that Mrs. Sidgwick was in doubt. The worst of it is that the rabble that now catch up the laugh would have been the first to be deceived had they seen the phenomena."[63] Methodologically, the Sidgwicks and Hodgson were closest to James, the latter of whom James finally revealed his ultimate opinion on the Eusapia material. With regard to testing and taking precautions with her, he wrote,

> I have always all along assumed that E[usapia]'s clothing had been thoroughly searched. I supposed this so obvious that it "went without saying." But it seems probable, after reading you, that that was not done and that if done it would have been mentioned.
> All I can then say is that if Richet & the rest had that woman in their houses all that time *without* doing this, and then came to conclusions, there is no fool's name too hard to be applied to them. It fills one with panic & disgust, the whole episode. It makes one realize also *your* invaluable presence.[64]

James and Hodgson, then, were in perfect empirical alignment on the Eusapia case, and they had not been duped as the others had been.

The SPR's involvement with Eusapia probably would have ended at that point, but Richet, who was the most convinced by her phenomena (and the least persuaded by Hodgson's critical report of her), conducted still further investigations of her in Paris in 1898. This was in keeping with James's empiricism, since it offered another chance to gather additional data and perhaps more facts. The initial results of these sittings were good enough to persuade Myers, who had become rather disgusted by the matter at that point, to come and have yet another look. Apparently Eusapia produced some amazing phenomena, for Myers, who had failed to learn from his gullibility, became persuaded of her genuineness all over again. To Lodge he wrote, "[The] phenomena last night [were] *absolutely convincing.*

Not a shadow of a doubt."[65] After another sitting, Myers returned to England ready to publish a new report in the *Proceedings*. He put his full support behind these new investigations and tried to persuade the Sidgwicks to reopen the SPR's investigation of her. But the Sidgwicks, still stinging from the failure of the 1894–95 investigations, were not budging. Myers's insistence inflamed his relationship with Hodgson, who thought Myers was again being duped. Hodgson described Myers's notes of the sessions as "worthless" and said that he was "absolutely convinced that Eusapia was a trickster from beginning to end."[66]

Théodore Flournoy, the Swiss psychologist and a close friend of James, participated in the 1898 sittings as well. They intrigued him enough to conduct his own, which in turn convinced him the phenomena were genuine. Because of their apparent methodological shortcomings, though, James found them of little value. To Flournoy he wrote, "Bill [James's son] notes that you were again convinced by Eusapia, but that the conditions were not satisfactory enough (so I understood) to make the experiment likely to convince absent hearers. Forever *baffling* is all this subject, and I confess that I begin to lose my interest."[67] After much debate and discussion in closed-door committee meetings, fireside chats at gentleman's clubs, and private letters, Hodgson, with the support of the Sidgwicks, outflanked Myers. Instead of a new report on Eusapia, Myers was rewarded with permission to publish only a letter that explained his own personal account of her. It was printed in the *Journal*, thereby limiting its readership to just psychical researchers, effectively closing the SPR investigations of Eusapia until 1908, when they were reopened by Hereward Carrington, another adamant defender of her, long after most of the original participants had passed away and could not object.[68]

Slade, Eglinton, Foster, Blavatsky, and Eusapia were but a few of the numerous tricksters hawking their trade for a living. With sleight of hand or simply a nimble knee, they duped countless people, including some of the more gullible SPR members. That they succeeded in their legerdemain is testament not only to the high number of credulous believers seeking soothing information from the other world but also to the omnipresence of Spiritualism in the late nineteenth century. That the SPR went to great lengths to expose many physical mediums exemplifies the tenacity of this fledgling organization. And that a small number of its members, including the Sidgwicks, James, and Hodgson (at this point), did not succumb to spiritual subterfuge indicates the centrality of James's empiricism in the quest for psychical facts.

If James had played a relevant but indirect role in the exposure of Slade, Eglinton, Blavatsky, and Palladino in England and Europe, he immersed himself directly and deeply in the investigations of physical mediumship in America. To his cousin Kitty Prince he once described an instance whose location of investigation humored him: "I'm going to see a materializing medium to night,—the most promising we've yet got hold of—in the [Massachusetts] Institute of technology. Don't you think it is a harmonious locality[?] Alice goes with me—the first enjoyment we have had in common for a long time."[69] James presented the results of this and sittings with other physical mediums at the ASPR meeting held on 4 June 1885. "The committee on mediumistic phenomena had made a number of visits to mediums," the secretary's record revealed, "but had nothing of importance to report."[70] Such outcomes frustrated James. As Gurney put it in response to James, "You don[']t tell me what *you* are doing much except in the dreary visiting of mediums."[71] So appalling were most of the physical mediums that during the Eusapia controversy, Myers, perhaps in an attempt to redeem himself with James, suggested blackballing them. But James strongly opposed this tactic: "To a fraudulent medium black list, I should say 'quite impossible.' It is stooping too low, even if the terrific practical difficulties and responsibilities were overcome."[72] This was a noteworthy admission, since numerous conjurers existed in America for whom such a list could have easily been composed, made up of those James had investigated, including Mrs. Diss Debar, Miss Helen Berry, and Mrs. Hannah Ross. Like those in England, the results of these investigations revealed that these three were frauds. None are as infamous as Eusapia, but they are central to the story of James's empirical approach to psychical research.

Mrs. Diss Debar

Mrs. Diss Debar was one of the most outrageous fraudulent physical mediums of the late nineteenth century. Born around 1849 to Professor John Solomon of Kentucky, she used a string of aliases such as "Ellora," "Madame Helena," and "Swami Viva Ananda" throughout her criminal life. Beginning as an impersonator during the 1870s, she collected money as Editha Gilbert Montez, the daughter of Lola Montez, the courtesan. In the 1880s she formed a Spiritualist mediumship partnership with "General" Joseph H. Diss Debar and was sentenced to six months' imprisonment for fraud. In 1898 Diss Debar married Frank Dutton Jackson of New Orleans, and the two ran a fraudulent mediumship parlor in Jefferson Parrish called Orders of the Crystal Star. They were arrested and served a short prison sentence, but there were allegations of sexual misconduct as well. Resurfacing as Frank and Laura Horos in Europe in 1899, they stole the rituals of S. L. Gregor Mathers's Hermetic Order of the Golden Dawn and passed themselves off as leaders of the Koreshan Unity. They also worked in Cape Town, South Africa, where they ran a series of swindles in which Laura pretended to be a swami mistress of occultism. After establishing their College of Life and Occult Sciences in Britain in 1900, the Jacksons used their courses on magnetism, mediumship, and clairvoyance as a front to rob and rape gullible young women until 1901, when the Jacksons were arrested and convicted. Frank served fifteen years and Laura seven, effectively ending their notorious careers.[73]

When James investigated her during the late 1880s, Diss Debar was operating a colorful salon in New York in which she provided much high drama and sensationalism. Since the phenomena were so obviously faked, even to the undiscerning eye, a visit to Diss Debar's shop was more like watching a vaudeville show than participating in a séance. In this regard Diss Debar drew from a class of mediums for whom Spiritualism was a form of Barnumesque entertainment. But she also had nefarious intentions. Although most mediums did not get rich, several convinced wealthy benefactors to support them, find clientele, and even provide homes at their expense. These included such leading social figures and businessmen as Cornelius Vanderbilt, Charles Partridge, and Henry Seybert. In her case, Diss Debar swindled Luther Marsh, an elderly attorney, to hand over his private residence in New York.[74] Such practice was common enough in the late nineteenth century that Hamlin Garland, the popular novelist and follower of psychical research, portrayed it in his semifictionalized novel *The Tyranny of the Dark* (1905).[75] The book depicted Viola Lambert, a young, beautiful medium who falls under the control of the sinister and ex-minister-turned-rabid-Spiritualist Anthony Clarke. Because of Viola's mediumistic talents, she is patronized by the rich and powerful banker Simeon Pratt, who, late in life, loses his wife and two daughters in a drowning accident when their steamer sinks in a cross-Atlantic voyage. In great grief, Pratt turns to Viola, whom he feels is able to produce communications with them. In return, he moves her (and Clarke and Viola's mother, a true believer) into his mansion and provides them with a lavish lifestyle. Meanwhile, Clarke has become convinced that he possesses the talent to make Viola commune with the spirits. He tries to force her to marry him so he can control her, but she resists. It is only at the hands of Morton Service, a rational scientist and secular man who has fallen deeply in love with Viola, that she is finally rescued, though what becomes of her life thereafter Garland left open. During the research stage, he wrote to James requesting material about mediumship and Spiritualism, to which James steered him to the SPR's *Proceedings*. "They and Myers's Posthumous book on 'Human Personality,'" he told Garland, "were the repertory."[76]

Diss Debar's entertaining performances amused James. In April 1888, after James and Hodgson first investigated Diss Debar, he told his wife that she gives "the most extraordinarily described physical performances. We found the old girl herself, a type for Alexandre Dumas, obese, wicked, jolly, intellectual, with no end of go and animal spirits, who entertained us for an hour, gave us an appointment for a sitting on Monday, and asked us to come and see Mr. March to night. What will come of it all I don't know. It will be baffling, I suppose, like everything else of that kind."[77] Whether it was because James enjoyed discovering Dumasian characters or because he treated Diss Debar, like all other mediums, as a potential source of data, James returned three days later. To Alice he wrote, "Hodgson and I are now going to Dis de Bar's [sic].... I think I may go back to night," but he learned nothing new because the next day "Mme. Dis Debar [sic], as I foresaw her, was 'too ill' to see us."[78]

Perhaps because of Diss Debar's frivolous nature, James used her entertaining though clearly fraudulent performances as a kind of benchmark against which physical mediums had to improve. For instance, upon investigating Mrs. Horace W. Cushman, he wrote in disgust to his wife that he was "in bed at 11:30, after the most hideously inept psychical night in Charlestown over a much praised female medium who fraudentlently [sic] played on the guitar." He was so frustrated with the ridiculousness of the performance that he quipped, "A plague take all white livered anaemic flaccid weak-voiced yankee frauds! Give me a full-blooded red-lipped villain like dear ole Dis Debar [sic]—when shall I look upon her likes again?"[79] More seriously, he noted to Hodgson that if Cushman could be shown to be a fraud, then what were they to make of the testimony of Harry Place and Elliot Coues, who were treating her phenomena as genuine?[80] Would not his empiricism require that he too make a wholehearted attempt to take physical mediumship seriously? Whatever the case was, there were many other such characters, including the Eddy brothers and J. V. Mansfield, both of whom the Spiritualist press lost face in defending because of their fraudulent practices. Another was a medium who went simply by the name "Jesse." As James told Hodgson, "What a pity it is in North Dakotah [sic], for Jesse seems to be a regular Eusapia. She gives a lot of witnesses['] names, and I have asked for the document immediately back."[81] For James, then, mediums such as Diss Debar and her ilk were mostly used for entertainment rather than serious research.

Miss Helen Berry

If James had been persuaded to compose a blacklist, it would have included the names of Miss Helen Berry and her sister.[82] He helped expose them as frauds, and his experiences with them reflected his empirical approach to psychical research and his tertium quid method of inquiry. James's introduction to the Berry sisters began in 1886. As George Palmer, James's philosopher colleague, recalled, "He and I, as members of a Committee of the Psychical Society [ASPR], attended 'cabinet séances' every Saturday for an entire winter, and at the close reported in our opinion all the materializing phenomena were fraudulent." Palmer was particularly impressed with James's cautious empiricism, adding that James "never concealed from himself how large a part fraud and self-deception play[ed] in spiritualism."[83]

In March of that year, James wrote to Horace Howard Furness, a Shakespearean scholar and lawyer at the University of Pennsylvania who had become a ranking member of the Seybert Commission at that university, whose purpose it was to investigate Spiritualism. His two sons were taking courses with James at Harvard and had volunteered to participate in James's studies on hypnotism. James asked if Furness knew of the Berry sisters and whether he might like to come to Boston to investigate them, to which Furness replied that he would be happy to meet James and study the "spirits."[84] Furness seemed to share James's sense of caution and counseled the necessity of relying only upon the evidence of clearheaded persons who were on location, so it is likely that James saw in Furness a level-headed empiricist and fellow adherent of the third way. When Furness inquired whether James himself had been to visit the Berry sisters, he exclaimed, "I have been 12 times!" He also stated that while some parts baffled him, "the whole arrangement seems to reek of fraud. I wish I could organize a raid which would capture the whole gang. What I have seen requires *at least* six confederates. But I haven't yet a good conscience about rejecting off hand *all* the stories the other sitters tell of unquestionably identifying the forms by face and what they say."[85] Despite what appeared to be convincing evidence, James's reluctance to allow himself to conclude the Berry sisters were out-and-out frauds indicates his cautious empiricism. At the very least, he sought sufficient proof one way or the other. But his hopes were in vain, since on another occasion he noted that not only had he gone twelve times but friends and relatives had gone twenty-three times and still "no spirit form came directly to any one of us."[86]

It is likely that Hodgson would have found enough evidence in all these visits during that half year to conclude the Berry sisters were frauds and to include them on Myers's proposed blacklist. James himself certainly came close when he indicated his desire to set a trap to catch them. Clearly he witnessed what he thought was an elaborate ruse but could not be sure. Of "Miss Helen Berry," he wrote disappointedly, "there is little to say." He noted that most of the test conditions had not been sufficient to rule out fraud and by implication had failed to demonstrate it, too. On one occasion, however, when he and Minot Judson Savage, who was serving on the ASPR's Committee on Mediumistic Phenomena, were allowed to sit behind the cabinet and examine its contents (they found nothing including no evidence of a trap door), two forms did emerge. But he could not explain this and other phenomena other than to say that it was their first sitting with Miss Berry and they could not call the experiment satisfactory because the test conditions had not been met. James concluded on the empirically somber note that since "no spirit form came directly to any one of us ... , we offer no opinion regarding the phenomena."[87] James's open-ended conclusion paid dividends since it led other committee members to investigate further. By 1889, Dr. Joseph Weatherhead Warren, the ranking committee member, decided that the Berry sisters had amounted to a waste of time because their reputations had come "'under a cloud'" for associating with known frauds. He reported, "At least seven materializing and etherealizing mediums ... have come to grief here in Boston during the past two or three years. Such a state of things hardly tends to encourage ... [the] committee in active pursuit of this class of phenomena."[88] In this Jamesian way, the Committee on Mediumistic Phenomena concluded the Berry sisters were most likely frauds.

Mrs. Hannah Ross

Hannah V. Ross was a popular physical medium in New England during the mid-1880s. She gained notoriety through advertising her services in the *Banner of Light*, the leading Spiritualist newspaper in Boston. According to the *Banner*, the first widely reported sittings in which Hannah produced materializations and at which her husband Charles assisted occurred in Providence, Rhode Island, in 1883. On the tip of a suspicious sitter, the Rosses were raided soon afterward, and Mrs. Ross was seized by investigators. Upon her release, Hannah and Charles moved to Boston, where they rented parlors, held séances anew, and established a rapport with the local Spiritualist community.[89] James was made aware of the Rosses through Alfred Russel Wallace, the naturalist and codiscoverer of evolution, in 1886. News of Mrs. Ross's phenomena had reached Wallace upon his invitation to give the Lowell Lectures in Cambridge. As part of his itinerary Wallace had arranged for several sittings with the Rosses and took the opportunity to write to James to request that they investigate the Rosses together.[90] Supporting the plan, Myers had sent a letter of introduction to James, saying, "You will find him greatly interested in the psychical matters which we are both of us working at."[91]

Upon arriving in Boston six months later, Wallace sent a note to James that included a set of instructions from Mrs. Ross indicating the terms of the sitting. To avoid offending her, Wallace argued against a thorough exploration of her personal background, though he agreed reluctantly to a light search of her rooms to show that she was not cheating. To reassure James, Wallace provided some basic background information on the Rosses and noted that "the arrangements at the Ross's [sic] are the simplest conceivable."[92] Although clearly not empirical evidence, James accepted the conditions. After the sitting, the *Banner of Light* published a story, reporting that six women and ten men of social distinction (two of whom were Wallace and James) attended a séance on 27 December 1886 (the second meeting occurred the following evening). It claimed the arrival of a spirit called "Bertha" who moved about the room from one sitter to the next while attracting much attention and described her as a "youthful beauty" possessing "child-like affection." Although Bertha "came" to Wallace, who convinced him of Ross's genuineness, she did not approach James, who remained cautious.[93]

Given their differing investigative styles, it is not surprising that Wallace and James reached different conclusions. The other sitters were even more suspicious and suspected the Rosses of cheating. In a raid one month later, the authorities seized several "spooks" (coconspirators draped in gauze-like robes) and in the process revealed Mrs. Ross's fraudulent practices. On 4 February 1887, the *New York Times* reported the raid on its front page. The article described the nature and details of the raid and how authorities caught the counterfeiters:

> It was agreed that at a certain moment each member of the party should seize one of the "spirits," as well as the mediums and her husband. A moment or two before the signal was given[,] one of the party was conversing with a materialized spirit. The young man seized the shadow by the hand, and with a firm grip, and yanked it into the middle of the room. At the same instant the light was turned on, a stalwart man seized Mr. Ross in his arms, just as that gentleman pulled his revolver, while others securely held Mrs. Ross, as well as several "spooks" in the cabinet.[94]

That Mr. Ross felt compelled to carry and draw his gun suggests just how contentious séances could become. Inspection of the cabinet revealed four boys and a little girl, a trap door, and various mechanical devices. The Rosses had been running nothing more than an elaborate ruse, but it is doubtful that James was the one who notified the authorities. To William Sturgis Bigelow, a trustee of the Boston Museum of Fine Arts who had an interest in Spiritualism, James explained there was nothing yet on Mrs. Ross except for a student of his who fell into a trance in his study and had agreed to try to develop with her. Why, then, would he want to expose Mrs. Ross when she might produce genuine phenomena on other occasions?[95]

Not understanding James's empiricism at all, the *Times* missed this crucial point. Much to James's dismay, the newspaper used his remark that Mrs. Ross was "among the wonders of the nineteenth century" to imply that he thought she was genuine. A week later, on 12 February, the *Banner* reported its account of the raid as well. It likewise quoted James and offered him as a respected man of science who purportedly attested to the "genuineness of the manifestations at Mrs. Ross's." Unlike the *Times*, though, the *Banner*'s intent was to support Mrs. Ross by offering, in effect, an apologia. The *Times* was poking fun at James-the-scientist, while the *Banner* was criticizing him for the same qualities. The two similar quotes were used to support opposite conclusions and thus demonstrated how the media conflated James's words to support their own agendas. While such tactics were daily occurrences in the era of yellow journalism, they irritated James to no end.[96]

In actuality, James's "testimonies" were never meant as an endorsement of Mrs. Ross's genuineness. Nor were they intended to discredit her, for James had not argued or supplied evidence for or against her either way. He had merely attended in the hopes of acquiring data that might reveal some facts. In discussing the problem of mal-observation in *The Principles of Psychology*, James invoked the challenges of investigating physical mediums like Mrs. Ross. "In a dark room a man sees a gauze-robed figure who in a whisper tells him she is the spirit of his sister, mother, wife, or child, and falls upon his neck. The darkness, the previous forms, and the expectancy have so filled his mind with premonitory images that it is no wonder he perceived what is suggested. These fraudulent séances would furnish most precious documents to the psychology of perception, if they could only be satisfactorily inquired into."[97] In other words, materializing spirits satisfied some people's need to believe. For instance, after bumping into Francis Child's wife on Concord Street in Boston, who was in a hurry to sit with Mrs. Ross, James told his friend that Mrs. Child "vanished . . . so abruptly that I hand't even time to feel her pulse. I suppose she is completely converted by this time, and will begin haunting Mrs. Ross. We shall have an interesting talk when we meet."[98] James's empiricism, then, helped uncover Mrs. Ross's fraudulent operations while simultaneously revealing an important fact about human psychology, namely, people's need and capacity for self-deception, a point that critics of Spiritualism such as the brass instrument psychologist Joseph Jastrow had demonstrated as well.[99]

Still, James was none too pleased to read his name "very unwelcomely to myself" in the newspapers. Perhaps feeling more exploited by the *Banner* than by the *Times*, he wrote a balanced letter to the former explaining his actions and positions in the hopes of rectifying the matter. The *Banner* printed it as part of an exchange, which it called "PRO AND CON, In Re Mrs. H. V. Ross: Who Shall Decide When Doctors Disagree." James made it clear that he had made three separate visits (two of them were the private ones Wallace had arranged) and that in order to create more neutral testing conditions he had tried to get Mrs. Ross to have a sitting at a location other than her apartment, but "*she refused to do so at any price*." Instead, they agreed he would sit with her in her own rooms to see if the spirits would come to him. Despite his hunch that she was a fraud, he explained, he was seeking new data. At the first sitting, James did not detect any obvious signs of fraud. He had examined the floors, walls, and so forth and decided that she warranted another visit. But on the next two sittings, he detected so much fraud that he wrote there were "confederates from the back room . . . [making] roguery" evident; the Rosses' séances were clearly designed to deceive. James mentioned several details, including witnessing an adult posing as a child-spirit—"the body was *as unplausible looking a dummy as I ever saw*, slung from the neck of the real person who might have been kneeling on the floor"—and a cabana of other charlatanry involving individuals sneaking in and out of cabinets, oblivious to their detection. After that, James noted that he "resolved not to waste any more time upon performances given at her own house. Good carpentry can make a secret door in any wall." James concluded his letter by stating that he wished to stick to the facts as closely as possible, and he criticized the *Banner* for "defending exposed frauds through thick and thin so as to present a 'solid front' (!!) to your enemy." Instead, he suggested the newspaper might raise funds to help convict the Ross gang. The *Banner* responded in kind, saying that it did not have a policy of defending exposed frauds but merely was following the American tradition of assuming innocence until proven guilty and stating that it had "no favors to ask of Prof. James or his ilk [psychical researchers], and feel that our course is founded in justice and truth." The opportunistic nature of the *Banner* was on full display, as James's status as a "man of science" was now conveniently a hindrance to it and the cause of Spiritualism.[100]

Not surprisingly, Alfred Russel Wallace sided with the *Banner*. By this point, Wallace had long been a committed Spiritualist.[101] Like the defensive posturing of the *Banner*, Wallace's comments were designed to protect the Rosses by reprimanding James. This amounted to nothing more than the rhetorician's trick of attacking one's critic in lieu of offering a substantial point. In his letter to the *Banner*, Wallace took issue with James's evidence that the Rosses cheated. He argued that James's view—that a trap door (through which the counterfeit spirits passed) could have been built easily by a skilled carpenter for the séance and just as cleverly and quickly covered up afterward—did not account for the structure of the wall itself. The problem for Wallace, however, was that when the Rosses were exposed and the wall was examined, he had moved on to lecture in Washington, D.C. How could he have known such details unless someone wishing to protect the Rosses supplied him with them? Were the Rosses, or one of their sympathetic sitters, conspiring with Wallace? Or was he merely trying to distance himself by attacking James? Either way, Wallace appeared rather foolish.[102]

Another credulous Spiritualist who criticized James was Edward Brackett, the uncle of the "spirit" Bertha who had appeared in the séances. He, too, fired off an angry letter to the *Banner*. Brackett argued that James and men of his class who investigated Spiritualism under the guise of science were the problem. Taking a similarly fallacious approach as Wallace had, Brackett assaulted James's abilities as an investigator, writing that he "appears to be singularly unfit to investigate so delicate a subject, for both mediums and the so-called materialized forms show a decided aversion to him." Continuing with his ad hominem attack, he noted that where once James refused to have his name associated with the case, he "now comes forward to strike a woman while she is prostrated by a severe illness, caused by the brutal treatment of men who called themselves gentlemen." Finally, Brackett criticized the rise of modern science and specialists: "With the advance of civilization there has come to the front . . . the class of men known as specialists who cultivate a part of their intellect to the dwarfing of their other faculties. In many things they are the weakest of mortals." Brackett's tact to change the subject indicated there was little material with which to defend such obvious frauds as the Rosses, and indicting James by condemning modern science was not going to save them.[103]

The matter might have ended there except that the Rosses were raided a second time (the third including Providence), vindicating James and indicating the futility of Wallace's and Brackett's defense of them. On 14 April 1887, the Rosses were arrested. Mrs. Ross was released, however, on the common-law ground that for misdemeanor cases involving husband and wife, the wife was presumed innocent on the view that her husband coerced her to act against her will. Mr. Ross was tried by a jury and found not guilty (his intent to defraud could not be proved with the evidence that had been admitted into the courtroom). Despite the favorable outcome to the Rosses, Mrs. Ross ceased advertising her services in the *Banner*. Ten years later, however, when she tried to resume her sittings, the *Banner* did advertise her on several occasions despite the fact that a new editorial board agreed not to promote known frauds. Apparently they found her satisfactory, but during the intervening period physical mediumship had waned and was being replaced by the more popular trance-mediumship.[104]

The impetus for the raid probably resulted from the findings of Horace Howard Furness. Furness had returned to Boston in the spring of 1887 to investigate Mrs. Ross. After his initial sitting, he wrote James to inform him that he had detected fraud. He suspected that the counterfeit "spirits" who claimed to come from the "vast deep" had probably emerged from the back parlor (though he had not yet located the secret door that James would). He also informed James that he had received a tip that the authorities had planned another raid and wondered whether James could not use his influence to prevent it so that Furness could have another chance to expose the Rosses himself. He added that he thought Mrs. Ross had recognized him and that it might preclude him from sitting with her again.[105] It is not known whether James prevented—or even could have prevented—the earlier raid, but Furness opted to sit again with Mrs. Ross. This time he exposed her and her conspirators for the frauds they were. "Has the sun of the Ross's [sic] set? Is that little heaven below broken up?" he asked James. He explained to James that when apparitions materialized from the cabinet "chalk [sic] full of spirits," he stamped on their feet and swept them across their cheeks with his arms, all of which caused them to dance "round with pain like a bear on hot plates." Furness was dismissed quickly from the premises but not before "accidentally" but literally stepping on Mrs. Ross's toes. As to legal proceedings, he added, "I doubt the wisdom of attacking Materialisation in this way. It converts it into Martyrialisation, which never pays."[106]

The following month, Furness informed James of the forthcoming Seybert Commission's report on physical mediumship, which Furness had helped author as chair of the commission. The secretary of the commission, George Stuart Fullerton, a philosopher, cowrote it. While the report focused most of its efforts on Henry Slade, it concluded that Mrs. Ross was a fraud. As for Furness, he was done with investigations. Still, he quipped with his intrepid sarcasm, "What would Mrs. Ross be without Boston? Nothing at all. What would Boston be without Mrs. Ross? Nothinger still?"[107] Relatedly, after James's investigation of the Rosses, the ASPR's Committee on Mediumship held a meeting in late 1887. It recommended against using professional or paid materializing mediums as their conditions "rendered any scientific investigation impossible." Instead, the committee sought "private and unpaid" mediums to investigate, who, they believed, would not bias the data the way the Rosses had.[108] The *Boston Daily Globe* covered the meeting. Its article attested to the fact that despite the outcome of the Ross case (and others like it), the ASPR was still pursuing its quest for quality data—no doubt along the lines of James's empiricism. Once again, however, there was little new evidence to offer, with the *Globe* reporting that "Professor James then said that the laziness of the members of the society was the reason why so few satisfactory results had been obtained. He called on the members to brace up in their contributions of time and money, saying 'We have important work to perform if we can only keep it alive.'"[109]

The *Banner* also reported on the meeting. Having been outwitted by James the previous year, though, it resorted to castigating the ASPR for what it believed was an overreliance on scientific method, which obscured rather than revealed the true nature of Spiritualism. "After all," the editors demanded to know, "what else but failure can be expected from men who have never permitted believing spiritualists to take a leading part in their work?"[110] The editors directed their venom at James in particular:

> We surmise that the Professor is mistaken in this as in other of his conclusions; that the reason of so few unsatisfactory results is that the Society of which he is a distinguished, active member, is on the wrong track: It is searching for fraud, and finds so little that it has scarcely any success to report. It makes the most of what it ferrets out, but that is so infinitesimally small it has to go to outsiders for a supply, and accepts even that grudgingly; but rejects all that savors of sustaining truth. What different results can be expected from such a course, since proofs of the truths of Spiritualism, and of the genuineness of the phenomena, "hang about us like a cloud?"[111]

Resorting to the same ad hominem attacks that Wallace and Brackett used against James, the *Banner* concluded that the ASPR would continue to fail until it "gets down from its high stilts and works out its missions with the people and for the people, rather than for a class of self-inflationists."[112] But the ASPR was unmoved by such populist cant. In early 1889, the Committee on Mediumistic Phenomena issued a second report noting that "at least seven materializing or etherealizing mediums... have come to grief here in Boston during the past two to three years." Nonetheless, the committee was "still ready to examine even these phenomena on the receipt of tangible experiences on the part of trustworthy persons."[113]

That the debates between skeptics and believers could become so heated and involve so many charges and countercharges was nothing new. If anything, the exchanges over the Rosses' case exemplified the growing schism between secular scientists and religious advocates in the late nineteenth century. They also indicated how all sides faced serious risks in defending or advancing their cause. Spiritualists needed new instances of spirit contact to support their belief system. The editors at the *Banner* thus defended mediums like the Rosses on loyalty grounds: even if they were cheating, the price of abandoning them equaled an admission that could weaken their faith. Since Spiritualists *believed* that spirits of the dead return from the other world and converse with the living, they did not need science to demonstrate it as a fact; their own experiences confirmed it. Spiritualism was religion in their eyes, and the Rosses helped build up an "aura of factuality" for the belief in spirit-return just as any religion required of its faith. Whether there existed cases of fraud was simply irrelevant. Their view, then, was that while some mediums were fraudulent, others were genuine; the cause of Spiritualism could not be impeded. Thus, the editors at the *Banner* argued that psychical researchers not only were far too cautious but also lacked all "comprehension of spiritual laws and forces," seeking instead to "drag everything down to the requirements of the science of muck."[114]

Psychical researchers also defended their belief system. In principle, they agreed on an empirical approach. Where they disagreed was on how stringent that approach should be. James and Hodgson (and Gurney at times) were more cautious, while Myers and Lodge (and Richet at times) were more cavalier. The Sidgwicks leaned more toward James's view but were not unsympathetic to Myers's. Whatever their individual positions, as aspiring positivists they agreed that success hung on the accumulation of facts, not on a mere aura of factuality. The problem they all shared, though, was that they could not generate facts because they could not find even one honest subject on whom to collect data. If psychical researchers established any facts in their investigations of physical mediums, it was the rather simple and obvious one that most mediums cheated, a point that critics like Jastrow delighted in making.[115] As James nicely captured it, "Falsus in uno, falsus in ominibus" (Once a cheat, always a cheat).[116] In this sense, their work had useful implications for the future of psychical research, but it was extremely disappointing for the Sidgwick Group, which was bent on proving the survival thesis.

For James, however, the outcome of the SPR and ASPR's investigations of physical mediumship was not a disappointment but a reaffirmation of his empirical project. Since he was not so much interested in proving the soul survives bodily death as he was in following the dictates of scientific methodology, establishing that mediums cheated was not a fatal blow. Rather, the findings amounted to a few good data points on what was sure to be a long continuum of them. As he put it in his 1896 SPR presidential address, he "appreciate[d] what solid progress we have made. Disappointing as our career has doubtless been to those of our early members who expected definite corroboration or the final *coup de grâce* to be given in a few short months to such baffling questions as that of physical mediumship, to soberer and less enthusiastic minds the long array of our volumes of *Proceedings* must suggest a feeling of anything but discouragement." But blowing into the sails was only so effective, for it did not resolve the issue. In particular, James found that the SPR had "left matters as baffling as we found them; neither more nor less. For if on the one hand we have brought out new documents concerning the physical miracles of Stainton Moses, on the other hand, we have by the Hodgson-Dav[e]y-experiments and the Pal[l]adino episode very largely increased the probability that testimony based on certain sorts of observation may be quite valueless as proof. Eusapia Pal[l]adino has been to us both a warning and an encouragement."[117] In other words, the investigation of physical mediumship validated James's empiricism.

Gurney was one of those "early members" who had been disappointed from these investigations. Because finding decent facts turned out to be much more challenging than he had initially realized, he confided to James that "I am afraid I do not think it by any means certain, as you seem to expect, that the evidence will now flow in more easily. I am not sure that the collection of facts will not be *harder*."[118] But harder, for James, was simply another way of saying more empirically rigorous, which would have made him smile in agreement with Gurney. Indeed, James embraced the harder path, avoiding the extreme pitfalls of the credulous Spiritualists and their ilk at the *Banner of Light* and even the more pleasant advocates of spirituality by the likes of

Thomas Davidson, on the one hand, and the hard-boiled skeptics and cynics in the form of G. Stanley Hall and Horace Howard Furness in the scientific and philosophic communities on the other. Such tender- and tough-minded types, for James, approached physical mediumship wrongheadedly because they were either too willing to believe in any phenomenon paraded before them or too adamantly unwilling to consider the possibility that any phenomena might be genuine. Both extremes represented a kind of closed-mindedness that James abhorred. James also had to navigate a modest middle path within his own ranks, helping to keep the more gullible Myers and impatient Lodge, and occasionally the Sidgwicks and even Gurney, more toward the center. Throughout it all, James maintained that the best approach was a thoughtful, nuanced, and above all genuinely open-minded one. Only with this attitude could any investigator hope to find a critical mass of facts. In short, James's firm commitment to a robust empiricism steered him through the challenges of investigating physical mediumship and in so doing revealed his tertium quid method of inquiry that should have made most positivists blush.

Despite the foregoing, a recent critic has argued that James was a poor psychical researcher, that his empiricism was vapid because he was gullible to conjurer's tricks, that he "believed in an afterlife," and that "he did not once devise or even consider devising a sting operation to expose mediums as hucksters."[119] The preponderance of evidence presented in this chapter, however, explodes these claims and indicates the exact opposite was the case. As James once expressed to Hodgson, "My mind goes back . . . to the 'moral miracle' of those people with the possibilities of fraud before their minds for so many years, not smelling the real state of things. . . . Duffer as I am at observing, I feel absolutely certain that I should know that trickery was going on."[120] And he was right. So the question is not why was James naive (he clearly was not) but rather why after exposing so many frauds did he continue with psychical research? The answer lies in the "dramatic possibilities" he found in the mental mediumship of Mrs. Leonora Piper.

five

DRAMATIC POSSIBILITIES

While the exposure of fraudulent physical mediums weakened the cause of psychical research, the study of mental mediums bolstered it. This was especially true for William James, who once called the investigation of physical mediumship "a human rat-hole life."[1] Unlike physical mediums, mental mediums did not rely on materializations and props but rather fell into a trance in which their "control" utilized speech acts and automatic writing to communicate with the sitters. The Society for Psychical Research investigated a number of so-called trance mediums such as Mrs. Rosalie Thompson and Mrs. Margaret de Gaudrion Merrifield Verrall and found that while some communications could be explained away, others could not. But the most famous and productive trance medium was Mrs. Leonora Piper, a one-time Spiritualist whom the SPR and the American Society for Psychical Research studied for more than three decades, from the mid-1880s through World War I, during which time as their exclusively paid subject she gave hundreds, perhaps thousands, of sittings to numerous persons on both sides of the Atlantic. Compared with all other mediums of both kinds, Mrs. Piper produced such high-quality results that psychical researchers believed she was no ordinary subject, and for James especially she appeared unique. Indeed, while he did not uncritically accept the evidence at face value and was reluctant to hypostatize its meaning, James came to believe Mrs. Piper represented an extraordinary opportunity to demonstrate the reality of psychical phenomena. As his first biographer captured it, "James had a hypothesis for which he claimed a 'dramatic possibility'—an impression of things left upon his mind by his familiarity with the phenomena . . . , [and] Mrs. Piper . . . played so important a part in the unrolling 'drama' of psychical research."[2]

Steeped in the nineteenth-century positivist view that science and scientific method could deliver ultimate truths about the human condition, the ASPR and SPR generated mounds of data in the form of stenographic reports and personal accounts of sittings with Mrs. Piper and other trance mediums. James maintained that only rigorous empirical criteria could validate this data, but in the case of trance mediumship, where the evidence was much better than the physical kind but still inconclusive, James offered a second kind of argument to justify his belief in the legitimacy of the phenomena, namely a fideistic one. Often used as a pejorative term about the role of faith in justifying knowledge in Catholicism and later Protestantism, fideism was the view that faith, not reason, leads to religious truth. Taking broad cues from both the Pauline and Augustinian strands of fideism, which held that reason was either irrelevant to faith (St. Paul) or at best informed faith (St. Augustine), James invoked fideistic logic that gave priority to the will over the intellect and to belief of all kinds, not just religious faith, over reason. Influenced in particular by Christian skeptics such as Blaise Pascal as well as by skeptical empiricists such as David Hume, both of whom emphasized the role of human psychology in relation to belief formation (Pascal as a form of justification, Hume as form of causal explanation), James stipulated that belief and the believer could not be separated. In particular, he argued the subjective quality of personal experience *as experienced by the experiencer* played a role in justifying belief. In other words, through psychical research James took a derisive theological term and made it a neutral philosophical doctrine.

James invoked fideistic logic most famously in support of religious belief in the much lauded though frequently misunderstood essay "The Will to Believe." In defense of the tender-minded, James tried to counter the rising tide of late nineteenth-century scientific naturalism and to keep at bay extreme skeptical empiricists such as Thomas Huxley and William Clifford, who argued that every person has a duty to be a religious agnostic because the evidence for God and the afterlife was inconclusive and did not admit belief, a view James found intolerant since it was too tough-minded and therefore did not allow for the possibility of the universe to surprise us.[3] What is less known but equally notable is that James also invoked fideism repeatedly to support his work in psychical research, especially in favor of forming a belief about the evidence that trance mediums such as Mrs. Piper produced in their sittings, including one supporting the survival thesis. As such, the will-to-believe argument addressed not only religious faith but also psychic phenomena. It is even likely James invoked fideism to justify belief in such phenomena since he referenced them in "The Will to Believe" and related essays, in letters to family, friends, and colleagues, and especially throughout other psychical research writings of the same time period such as "Notes on Automatic Writing" (1889), "A Record of Observations of Certain Phenomena of Trance" (1890), "What Psychical Research has Accomplished" (1892), and his SPR presidential address (1896), which repeatedly invoke fideistic logic in support of the study of mediumship. In other words, James may have appealed to fideism to buttress religious belief against the rising tide of scientific naturalism, but he simultaneously expanded and exemplified it through his investigation and subsequent defense of Mrs. Piper.

James sat with Mrs. Piper two dozen times in 1885–86, when he formed his initial opinion that she was worthy of scientific investigation, and at least three occasions in the late 1880s for the Catherine Walsh, Baby Eliza, and Hannah Wild cases, from which he gathered evidence for that belief. After 1890 James sat with Mrs. Piper less frequently and more sporadically, though several key moments stand out, especially a series of sittings James held at his Cambridge house in 1894 where a number of academics and scientists participated, including Nathaniel Shaler, Charles Norton, Wendell Barrett, G. Stanley Hall, James Cattell, and Silas Mitchell, while others such as Josiah Royce, Hugo Münsterberg, and James Baldwin were asked but refused and still others such as John Trowbridge, Charles Jackson, and Horace Furness declared her a fraud. Although the total number of times James sat with Mrs. Piper over the years is unknown and probably unknowable, since there are so many unspecified references to sittings over the years, it was clearly not an inconsequential number since he staked his professional reputation on her. Stretching his empirical tenets, James kept inconsistent records of his sittings, though he often collected ex post facto impressions through others' notes and personal letters. Several James family members each sat one or more times with Mrs. Piper or other trance mediums, including two of his brothers, Henry Jr. and Robertson, as well as his wife, Alice, and two of her sisters, Mary and Margaret, and their mother, Mrs. Elizabeth Walsh, while James's sister, Alice, who deplored mediumship, once tried to trick James by sending a lock of hair to test Mrs. Piper that she professed was hers but was not. The aggregate of these accounts convinced James that Mrs. Piper was not a fraud, that her trances were genuine, and that she possessed some "unexplained abilities." In 1892 he felt a "satisfactory explanation of the phenomenon is yet to seek. It offers itself as spirit-control; but it is as hard to accept this theory without protest."[4] But in 1896, just four years later, he proclaimed her as his "white crow," an anomaly in nature (all crows are black).

As James scholar Robert McDermott nicely put it, "To deserve her status as James's 'white crow,' Mrs. Piper had to be the instrument, agency, or medium of verifiable knowledge which she could not have known from a natural (or normal) channel."[5] In Mrs. Piper, then, James appealed to fideism to confirm the dramatic potential of human nature and thereby continued his quest for facts. In so doing, he used psychical research to further his tertium quid method of inquiry.

FIDEISM

Working within the broad confines of positivism, James's empiricism emphasized scientific methodology. But in a typical display of Jamesian ambiguity and paradox, he was not consistent in this view, and it was not the only epistemology he espoused. James also believed that *personal* experience as much as scientific experiment accounted for understanding the world. One half of knowing was grounded in personal experience, he argued, because knowledge manifested an irreducible *subjective* quality. That is, reaching objective knowledge of any given phenomenon depended to a degree on how any one individual actually experienced it. This view was an avowedly open challenge to the traditional notion of objectivity, but it was not unempirical per se since it still gave priority to experience. In his tertium quid approach to psychical research, James attempted to systematize the study of subjective experience in order to expand what counted as objective knowledge. That is, what James saw in psychical research was that it afforded the possibility to objectively study subjectively experienced phenomena. As McDermott put it, "Psychical research ... emphasize[d] the personal and subjective character of knowledge. James repeatedly criticized the resistance to the personal and subjective dimension of human experience that too often characterizes the scientific ideal. Psychic phenomena, of course, are intrinsically subjective and consequently tend to be regarded by scientists as inaccessible and unintelligible.... James sought to show that by this self-imposed restriction, science risks losing the truth it jealously seeks to criticize and control."[6]

The subjective and personal quality of psychical research attracted James as part and parcel of his fideistic tendencies. Derived from the Latin root *fides* (faith), fideism is the view that "truth in religion is ultimately based on faith rather than on reasoning or evidence."[7] While modern use of fideism emerged in France in the late nineteenth century when two Protestant theologians at the Sorbonne, Eugène Ménégoz and Auguste Sabatier, first introduced the term *fidéisme*, the concept has its roots in medieval theology when St. Paul and

St. Augustine first invoked two versions.[8] The essence of extreme fideism was best captured by Tertullian's expression *credo quia absurdum* (I believe that which is absurd) and exemplified in the Pauline doctrine that faith involves being willing to believe without adequate evidence. St. Paul maintained fideism was central to Christian doctrine and argued that all religious truths were contrary to rational activity. St. John of the Cross took this a step further and stipulated there were super- or extra-rational truths such as mystical or revelatory experiences far beyond what rationality could generate. The Christian skeptic Michel de Montaigne maintained that reason was simply too limited in its ability to ascertain fundamental truths and argued that ultimate principles were always open to question and rational standards themselves were subject to revision. Søren Kierkegaard further advanced this view by contending religious truths ran contrary to rationally guided standards that were merely probable, while Pierre Boyle opposed religious truths to reason, arguing the former were incomprehensible by the latter. Such extreme fideism was aptly summarized by Pierre Jurieu's famous formulation "I believe it because I want to believe it," meaning there simply was no rational justification for the leap of faith that religious belief requires.[9]

Moderate fideism emerged in tandem with but in contradistinction to the extreme form. It is best summarized by the Augustinian phrase *credo ut intelligam* (I believe in order to know). In this tradition, fideism does not reject reason as irrelevant to religious truth but relegates it to secondary status in which faith precedes reason; reason and empirical evidence can play some role in religious truth but only once it is accepted that the pursuit for rational truths is predicated on accepting faith itself. Once this step is made, it becomes possible to argue that commitment to religious truth is itself rational. Thus, rationality is subsumed into religious faith. Pascal's fideism was an excellent instantiation of the Augustinian form. He maintained that our need for ultimate truths but our lack of ability to find satisfactory ones led us to faith. Once that human predicament was accepted, Pascal maintained that the psychological experience of faith became empirical evidence for religious truth. "Such evidence," as the historian of philosophy Richard Popkin aptly captured it, "might then constitute 'good reasons' for believing what one has already accepted fideistically."[10]

Although initially a term of theology referring almost exclusively to religious forms of belief, modern philosophers in the skeptical empirical tradition have offered nonreligious fideisms. Hume, who argued that everybody lives with their own private belief system, offered one of the most popular understandings of fideism in stating that religious belief runs contrary to reason, custom, and experience. As such, rationality could never be used to justify belief, religious or any other kind, but it could be used to explain its cause(s). In this way, Hume maintained it was possible to establish a set of reasonable beliefs that could be used to evaluate other beliefs, which in turn could become reasonable themselves, thereby making the psychological nature of belief part of rationality, which Hume characterized as the nature of all belief, not just of religious faith. Bertrand Russell radicalized Hume's skeptical fideism by arguing that scientific beliefs worked this way as well and that therefore science itself required an article of faith, one that James's colleague George Santayana dubbed "animal faith." As Popkin aptly captured it, "The philosophical tradition emanating from Hume, then, can be considered as a kind of fideism, sharing some of the characteristics of the moderate fideism of the Augustinian tradition."[11] In short, skeptical empiricists took religious fideism about faith and turned it into philosophical fideism about belief.

This tradition greatly influenced William James. But James did not write theologically about fideism, and his fideism was not theological, even though he employed it to justify religious belief. Rather, fideism for him was a philosophical position, much like pragmatism and radical empiricism—that is, names he gave to designate his epistemological and metaphysical doctrines—were. Moreover, while the term has had a largely pejorative connotation in the long and complicated history of Christian theology, fideism as a philosophical position for James was a neutral term that merely reflected a particular theory about the relationship between religion and science. He found it especially useful for establishing justified belief when weighing experienced subjective faith against empirically generated and verified evidence.[12] Since James typically invoked fideism when discussing religious faith, though, his version shared some elements with both the Pauline and Augustinian traditions. The weak version, which James probably owed to discussions with Chauncey Wright, held that once individuals had done all that was ethically required to find evidence to support their religious beliefs, they had a *right* to believe what their volition demanded. In this sense, James agreed with Pascal and Hume that psychological experience plays an indispensable role in how we come to belief and with Russell that scientific belief presupposes some element of faith, which is itself psychologically determined. But unlike the Christian skeptics, James did not start from the view that faith takes priority over reason or that empirical evidence relies on accepting faith as a starting point. On the contrary, as a thoroughgoing empiricist he maintained that rationality required starting with empirical evidence, of which science and scientific method generated the strongest kind, but that when all such evidence could be gathered but had not yielded belief, then it was rational to introduce an element of faith. In this sense, he stood the extreme version of fideism on its conceptual head. Indeed, James's fideism stipulated there were instances in which belief could be justified beyond inconclusive empirical evidence. At the same time, however, James also advanced a stronger version that shared much in common with the more extreme Pauline tradition, a position he seems to have inherited from Charles Renouvier. James held that there were also instances where a will to believe *preconditioned* obtaining the very evidence for belief in question. Here James seemed to be arguing that belief must precede reason in certain instances, including those involving religious faith. Both versions of James's fideism, then, drew on the Pauline and Augustinian traditions as well as on the Christian and empirical skeptics.[13]

James also developed some aspects of fideism that were original and unique. First, James's fideism juxtaposed the will and intellect, rather than faith and reason as traditional theorists had done for centuries in which, as McDermott captured it, "the will is 'prior' to the intellect."[14] Second, James argued that all belief must have some practical consequence, which made his fideism serve the interests of action, whereby coming to rational belief is determined by what action an individual takes based on it. For James, a fideistically justified form of belief was always action based in practical terms. Such a view was implicit in most forms of fideism, but James was explicit about this point. Like most of his doctrines, James did not invoke fideism consistently and did not develop it at one time or in one place but rather formulated it over time in a myriad of writings. One of the earliest instances appeared in 1875 when in reviewing P. G. Tait's *Unseen Universe* he offered the stronger version by associating a *duty* to believe with the practical difference in holding that belief.[15] But the main place James developed his fideism was in the first four essays of *The Will to Believe* (1897), each published at earlier dates, as a way to answer the central dilemma of belief, namely, what are we justified in believing when the evidence is insufficient?[16]

The thesis of the title essay was, as James put it, to establish a "justification of faith, a defense of our right to adopt a believing attitude in religious matters, in spite of the fact that our merely logical intellect may not have been coerced."[17] But the larger purpose was a justification of religious faith in the face of rising scientific determinism. James argued that in the case of a "forced option"—when all the facts were in but still did not point toward any definitive conclusion and where our belief directly affected our behavior—it was justified to defer to one's will, especially when all the known facts would never determine a definitive conclusion but people still needed to act. James developed the criteria individuals should use when forced to make a choice that carried real consequences for action *when all the facts were not known*. In cases where "no forced option" was present, that is, where a choice did not demand action that had real consequences, it was best that such decisions be left to science, such as whether or not there existed ether in the cosmos. Our daily action and behavior would not be changed by the truth or falsity of its existence. As James put it, "Let us agree, however, that wherever there is no forced option, the dispassionately judicial intellect [that is, the scientific mind] . . . , saving us as it does from dupery at any rate, ought to be our ideal."[18] But in cases where a fact would affect our behavior, where there was "forced option," then James claimed that "*our passional nature not only lawfully may, but must decide between propositions.*"[19] But by "passional nature" he did not mean a will toward absolute belief but rather "a will of complacence, assent, [and] encouragement, toward belief already there."[20] For James, then, the passional element of humans is their nonintellectual side where volitions, desires, opinions, and the "willing nature" reside.

Two significant cases of forced option were moral and religious ones, since these were matters where belief actually made a difference in life. In one of many key passages, he wrote,

> Since belief is measured by action, he who forbids us to believe religion to be true, necessarily forbids us to act as we should if we did believe it to be true. The whole defense of religious faith hinges upon action. If the action required or inspired by the religious hypothesis is in no way different from that dictated by the naturalistic hypothesis, then religious faith is a pure superfluity, better pruned away, and controversy about its legitimacy is a piece of idle trifling, unworthy of serious minds. I myself believe, of course, that the religious hypothesis gives to the world a greater expression which specifically determines our reactions, and makes them in a large part unlike what they might be on a purely naturalistic scheme of belief.[21]

In other words, James defended the importance of our passional nature in deciding matters of religious faith. Indeed, he even stated this fideistic sentiment in Pascalian terms by arguing "that not only as a matter of fact do we find our passional nature influencing us in our opinions, but that there are some options between opinions in which this influence must be regarded both as an inevitable and as a lawful determinant of our choice."[22]

At first blush James's fideism, especially in its strong form, appears to be an excuse to believe what one wants when the evidence is limited.[23] But this was not the case since James did not identify the will with desire. On the contrary, James thought the will provided an opening to rationality. James began developing this view as early as 1879 when he argued in "The Sentiment of Rationality" that no sound explanation could be offered for rationality that failed to account for the *feeling* of rationality. This "ultimate sense of logical fit"—when you *just know* that something is rational—James believed resided in the will, and its subjectivity was a central feature of James's philosophy.[24] The purpose of his essay was to answer the apparently straightforward question of what philosophers philosophize about. James had raised the issue as early as 1868 when he asserted in his notebook, "Philosophies owe their being to two impulses in the mind: (1) that after absolute intellectual unity or consistency; (2) that after an object we guarantee for our interests."[25] "The Sentiment of Rationality" was the maturation of these thoughts. As to the nature of the philosopher's inquiry, James answered, "They desire to attain a conception of the frame of things which shall on the whole be more rational than that somewhat chaotic view which every one by nature carries about with him under his hat." Anticipating the obvious questions as to how this rational conception is attained and kept separate from ignorance, he replied that the philosopher "recognize[s] its rationality as he recognizes everything else, by certain subjective marks with which it affects him. When he gets the marks, he may know that he has got the rationality."[26] What could such marks be? What were these feelings? "A strong feeling or ease, peace, rest, is one of them," James answered, adding, "The transition from a state of puzzle[ment] and perplexity to rational comprehension is full of relief and pleasure." When empiricism failed to deliver adequate knowledge, James argued, one turned to subjective experience. In short, the sentiment of rationality that supplemented scientifically gathered evidence emerged from the will exerting itself.[27]

The point of the "The Sentiment of Rationality," then, was to impose some order on the "fragmentary and chaotic" experiences of everyday life for which empiricism could not account. Feelings, James argued, help provide a sense of "ease, peace, and rest" when methodology fails.[28] But the argument was something more than that. It was also James's way of *redefining* rationality. He sought to analyze it as a psychological phenomenon part and parcel of our subjective mind. This did not mean James was defining rationality psychologically but rather arguing that rationality itself had psychological characteristics and that philosophers and the rest of us may have a certain "sentiment" once we recognize that this is the case. In other words, the essay represented James's attempt to develop both a psychology and a philosophy of rationality, or, in short, he was indicating there was a subjective element to rationality.[29]

Dismantling the traditional notion of rationality and replacing it with "living acts of reasoning" or "the full concrete act of thought," as James once called it, opened the discussion to asking whether philosophers have not, in the words of one astute James analyst, "overestimated intellectualist rationality to such an extent that they have distorted its relation to practical rationality and [thus] misunderstood its function as only one of the fundamental human drives to organize experience harmoniously."[30] In other words, has any philosophy ever provided a rational basis for itself? Could a rational framework be given for rationality? More critically, James's "craving for rationality" amounted to a precarious philosophical position since it perched itself, in the words of another perceptive James scholar, "between the Scylla of the appetite for certainty and the Charybdis of the evidence for uncertainty."[31] James's fideistic will, then, was the engine that drove his view that sentiment played a central role in rationality.

Whether radical or precarious (or both), James's theory of rationality was not a view from nowhere. Instead, it emerged partly from his attempt to solve long-standing debates in the history of philosophy between empiricists and rationalists, as well as between different kinds of empiricists, as to the nature of knowledge and its justification. This much is well known. But what has remained unknown until now is that it also developed from his immersion into psychical research, where he hoped to find those answers. James's numerous and variegated experiences with the investigation of psychic phenomena emerged at the intersection of his empiricism and fideism. Because of their mysterious nature, psychic phenomena demanded scientific inquiry. How better to unravel the extravagant claims that there existed phenomena that exceeded the bounds of the five senses and surpassed the known laws of nature than with the scientific method? Yet, because of the very definition of being "hidden," psychic phenomena also represented exactly the type of thing for which science could only explain so much. By its very nature, James found that empiricism fell short of a full explanation. For James, the recognition of this reality represented the perfect point at which the fideistic will should enter the justificatory process. Psychic phenomena, in other words, begged for the sentiment of rationality. How better to achieve that "logical sense of fit" than through studying the psychology of such occurrences? The subjective quality of psychic phenomena was thus an asset for psychical research in James's view; it was exactly the kind of fieldwork that could lend itself to James's reconstruction of rationality.

For James, then, psychical research was nothing if not simultaneously empirical and fideistic. In this broader epistemological sense, James's fideism consisted of two main parts. The first stipulated that when the intellect has done all that it can to understand the world via empiricism but still remains baffled, the human will must take control of the process of knowing. The second is that the will must also move to the forefront when the known evidence remains insufficient for effective theorizing, that is, when the five requirements of James's empirical methodology cannot be met. As Ralph Barton Perry nicely captured it, James's fideism concerned the "extra-theoretical motives ... [which] carry belief beyond the data of experience."[32] Or, as James himself put it, "I believe the only way to 'investigate' is to go in as [a] private individual, to satisfy one's *self*."[33] No sentiment better connected James's fideism and psychical research than this statement.

MENTAL MEDIUMS

To see for his own self, James began investigating mental mediums with abandon. In mental mediumship, individuals fell into a trance state during which an alter identity emerged in the form of a "control."[34] Trance mediumship, as it is often called, involved various "automatic" spoken and written acts to communicate, the former in a voice that was different in tone, style, and cadence from the medium's, the latter with chalk on slates, a lead pencil, or a planchette on a blank piece of paper (occasionally in conjunction with a Ouija board).[35] In one instance, James tried automatic writing with members of the Philosophical Club, from whom he might have been trying to raise funds for the ASPR, explaining to his wife they were "taking away six planchettes" upon leaving his Irving Street house (many regarded planchettes as mere toys, whereas James thought them useful tools).[36] In another case, James's friend Henry Hooper urged him to test a girl who had "lost her memory" from "trying planchette," a common complaint against remaining in the automatic state too long. But most of James's work with the planchette proved fruitless. Describing another sitting, he told Alice, "I'm just in from Charlestown where with Curtis, I have spent a psychical evening with his friends.... The girl tipped tables & wrote incoherent stuff with [a] planchette and pencil, whilst Curtis was controlled by the gloomy Beethoven [spirit] again and played a gruesome piece."[37]

As James noted, additional "automatic" behaviors included the playing of musical instruments.[38] One subject James investigated involved a girl from Beverly, Massachusetts, who while in her trance state played the piano automatically with superior skills compared with those in her regular waking state. She also spoke a foreign language that her control claimed was Spanish and that James realized was neither Portuguese nor Italian but did have "latinic intonations."³⁹ Mental mediums even produced historical writing. In one case, James learned that Thomas Spivey, an author and businessman, claimed to have produced several thousand manuscript pages and 30,000 illustrations contained in two books about the Roman senate! Spivey was sending them to James to evaluate and wanted his advice on where to publish them.⁴⁰ If James ever did reply, he might have advised him to consult Hudson Tuttle, an author who had published a collection of advice columns in the Chicago Spiritualist periodical *Progressive Thinker* and had turned them into a book called *Mediumship and Its Laws* (1900) that he had mailed to James for consideration.⁴¹

Mental mediumship was a boon for Spiritualists because automatism simultaneously removed some of the mysteriousness and unpredictability of the séance while generating copious instances of supposed communication with the "other world." In this way, automatism vastly simplified the séance while conferring more legitimacy on Spiritualism. Spiritualists thought automatism prophetic, and many Americans began to sit down and try automatic writing on their own. This egalitarian aspect made mental mediumship very popular with the general American public by the late nineteenth century, turning the once ritualistic séance into the informal practice of "sitting." Although no formal statistics have been gathered, James estimated one in twenty people, or 5 percent of the population, tried the planchette and/or Ouija boards.⁴² With a population of roughly 76 million in 1900, approximately 3.8 million people would have used them.⁴³ If James was even remotely accurate, the immense appeal of such toys and their psychic potential for so many Americans cannot be dismissed as a mere fad or the interest of a lunatic fringe, especially as it cut across race, class, and gender lines.⁴⁴

Trance mediumship was also a boon for psychical researchers. The increased number of "communications" immediately augmented their data pool. In one instance, James jocularly told his friend William Salter, "I heard the other night from a gentleman of exceptionally high standing the most wonderful medium story I ever heard. Its peculiarity was that this medium was a lady who knew nothing of spiritualism, but spontaneously . . . lost consciousness, and spoke exactly in the character of his departed wife a score of times."⁴⁵ Automatic productions also made the evaluation of data easier since it could be recorded by hand. Whereas the very validity of physical mediumship rested upon observation in the moment, which was fallible, mental mediumship afforded the examination of the written evidence after the sitting. This difference gave investigators a distinct advantage since they could qualitatively analyze the quantity of the information. In the case of automatic speech, psychical researchers often, though not always, hired a stenographer to provide a verbatim record so that independent parties could verify and evaluate the data after the fact in a more neutral environment. In other words, the reliance on immediate and direct observation became less important, while developing skillful examination of the evidence and more supple sophisticated interpretation of it became more so.

This fundamental change in the investigation of Spiritualism introduced a whole new dynamic into psychical research, making the young field an approximating science. Specifically, it meant psychical researchers would simultaneously have to be more diligent at gathering their data yet more flexible in forming their hypotheses. In one instance, James learned that Théodore Flournoy stumbled upon "a few good mediums in Geneva," one of whom was probably Hélène Smith, the subject of his book on mediumship, *From India to the Planet Mars*, which James admired.[46] In another instance, James told Flournoy that Charles Richet was studying an excellent medium in Paris "whom he hopes to subject to thorough observations and who is even better yet ... [and] in a good way to be considered serious."[47] This delicate balance between strict method and supple theorizing more closely approached the process of standard scientific practice in the natural sciences like physics than the investigations of physical mediumship could have ever hoped to achieve. In so doing, it provided psychical research with a modicum of legitimacy.

The outpouring of automatic phenomena made James a very busy psychical researcher. All kinds of individuals came or wrote to him professing their special ability. Some subjects barely got a hearing, such as Mrs. Williams and Mr. Wagnalls, while Mrs. Lord James was thought "worth looking into."[48] Several subjects in England whom F. W. H. Myers investigated included "Miss (Iris Jessica) Chaston," who produced "some good phenomena"; a "Miss Fyfe," who wanted to meet James on his next trip abroad; and Mrs. Raikes, from whom "good things were still coming."[49] And, of course, there was Mrs. Rosalie Thompson, Myers's star medium, with whom the Jameses and Myerses held numerous informal sittings at Richet's "chateau" at Carqueiranne in southern France in 1900, later corresponding about her abilities and about Myers's article on her in a special issue of the *Proceedings*.[50] James also corresponded with Richard Hodgson about Mrs. Thompson, with whom he had six sittings. Hodgson was more skeptical about her abilities and thought Myers might be her dupe, but James thought Hodgson was being a "bit too critical," adding, "I bet your impression of Mrs. T. is false, *in the main*," a view he shared with his wife.[51]

James considered others subjects whose cases he left open. One involved the "nondescript . . . girl at Hodgson's who gave 'impressions' of the most gelatinous sort" and described James's wife as "very cheerful & fond of society . . . , [and] a good woman . . . [who] meant well, but that we had had a quarrel this winter about this society business," which James told Alice that he would leave to her to decide whether the information was "insight, rubbish, or coincidence with certain germs of fact."[52] In another instance he told Alice he had spent a "rather tedious evening—2 very logy somnolent subjects. But at 1/2 past 10 one of them suddenly became a trance-medium of a rudimentary sort, and professed to be controlled by my father, etc. Perhaps more may come of it."[53] James thought another medium, Mrs. Smith, also seemed promising. He told Flournoy that "some of her phenomena grazed so closely upon the supernormal that one would like to see whether she ever does pass the barrier, as I believe it can be passed." He thus hoped "*someone* could continue work with Mrs. Smith," but after that work was conducted he changed his mind, telling Hodgson she "doesn't seem worth much."[54]

There was even a visit with a Spiritualist circle in Denver, Colorado, where James and Alice stopped on their way back from Stanford after the San Francisco earthquake in 1906 had cut short their term. Alice predicted the planned sitting would be an "interesting experience," but the leader of the group, "Dr." John Henry Gower, an English-born musician and mining engineer who had formed the group, which specialized in telekinesis (the supposed ability to move physical objects with the mind), was out of town when the Jameses arrived on 29 April.[55] So James spoke with the members who had been meeting for ten years but had not kept any written records. Based on the group's testimony, he found that "movements with contact were often inexplicable" and concluded that the evidence for table levitation was subjective but nonetheless "much impressed" him.[56] As he put it to a colleague back at Stanford, "This is the 'closest' *I* have ever come to that phenomenon."[57] That colleague urged James to also stop in Indianapolis to sit with Mrs. May Eliza Wright Sewall, an American educator and reformer. Professing mediumistic skills, she begged James to stop for a sitting, but Alice was not interested in the investigation, so the Jameses returned straight home. Still, James pledged to open a correspondence with her, writing, "The case baffles me entirely."[58] Such encounters indicate that from the mid-1880s onward, James investigated many mental mediums like these though mostly with limited results.

The ASPR's Committee on Mediumistic Phenomena, on which James sat, investigated an even larger number of subjects. In 1887 it issued the first of two reports. William Bullard, who chaired the committee, wrote the first one. After initial investigations, the committee noted that while it had found one medium "who has made a decidedly favorable impression on certain members," it was having trouble finding enough people with supposed mediumistic abilities to investigate.[59] By 1889, the second report, written by the new chair, Joseph Warren, revealed that little had changed in the intervening period except that one trance medium who had shown promise continued to impress the committee. Warren reported that eight to ten decent sittings had been conducted and concluded that if enough funds could be found, the committee was "of the opinion that an extension of the investigation would be very desirable."[60] James was of exactly the same opinion, since he was the first to find the promising medium Mrs. Leonora Piper.[61]

ONE WHITE CROW

Mrs. Piper was one of the most celebrated mediums in the history of Spiritualism. Born in Nashua, New Hampshire, and raised a devout Congregationalist in Methuen, Massachusetts, Leonora Evelina Simonds had several episodes during childhood involving, as one scholar put it, "the loss of consciousness and had vision-like experiences suggesting knowledge of distant events." Her first one occurred at age eight when Leonora had a premonition of the death of her "Aunt Sara," the date and times of which supposedly corresponded to the actual event. In 1881, at age twenty-two, Leonora married William Piper but in 1884 developed an ovarian tumor after being run into with an ice sled. On the recommendation of her father-in-law, an avowed Spiritualist, Leonora sought the services of J. R. Cocke, a blind medium and spiritual healer who advertised himself in the *Banner of Light*, Boston's leading Spiritualist newspaper, as an "unconscious entranced musical medium." "Doctor" Cocke automatically played great piano works (his control claimed to be none other than Johann Sebastian Bach) but mostly helped others develop their mediumistic talents.[62] Mrs. Piper soon began to fall into trances and write automatically, of which she later wrote serendipitously that "only by the merest chance did I discover that I possess a power wholly unexplained to myself and mystifying to my family and friends." For a short time, she worked as a professional medium in Boston, charging one dollar per person per sitting, producing automatic writing messages.[63]

James's relationship with Mrs. Piper began in the late summer or early fall of 1885 when his mother-in-law, Mrs. Gibbens, who had "discovered" her through the circle of servants shared by the Jameses and Pipers, introduced her to him. As the story goes, Leonora participated in a "mesmeric circle" on Beacon Hill. "I was then living in Boston," she professed, when "my maid . . . told a friend who was a servant in the household of Professor William James . . . that I went into 'queer sleeps,' in which I said 'many strange things.' Professor James recognized that I was what is called a psychic, and took steps to make my acquaintance."[64] Through the chain of servants who worked for the Piper family, for the James family's friends, and for the James family, the information of Mrs. Piper's special skills disseminated. Of their servant, Mary, Alta Piper—Mrs. Piper's daughter—wrote somewhat disparagingly, "My grandparents had at that time in their service an old Irish servant who had been with them for years and who, while good-natured, faithful, and utterly devoted to the family, [was] possessed with all the Celtic imagination and ingrained superstition of her race." To her sister, Bridget, Mary regaled the stories of the "queer doings of my young Mrs. Piper." Like Mary, Bridget also worked as a maid on "the hill." She was employed by the family upon whom Mrs. Gibbens frequently called. During one of her visits, Alta says that Mrs. Gibbens learned of Mrs. Piper and was so amazed with her abilities that she requested a sitting for her daughter, Alice (James's wife). The request was granted, and after both women had sat with Mrs. Piper they relayed their experiences to William, who was "so impressed by the marvelous character of the facts which they brought back" that he obtained his own sitting with her.[65]

That initial sitting led to a dozen more during the fall of 1885. His accounts of them reveal that James tried to take some precautions, such as avoiding asking leading questions and keeping his and others' identities from her by using aliases for various family members. At first, Mrs. Piper did not communicate anything he found useful, but gradually she made many hits and near hits on numerous pieces of information that piqued his curiosity. Mrs. Piper, he wrote, "can at will pass into a trance condition, in which she is 'controlled' by a power purporting to be the spirit of a French doctor, who serves as the intermediary between the sitter and deceased friends." Compared with physical mediums like Helen Berry, he found that Mrs. Piper was a "much simpler and more satisfactory case" and visited her a dozen times more in the winter of 1885–86. Based on these twenty-four sittings, James satisfied himself that he had isolated a genuine phenomenon. He also recognized he had but a few instances of it, which he noted "would of itself be an important result if it could be established and generalized, but the record is obviously too imperfect for confident conclusions to be drawn from it in any direction." James then recommended the ASPR begin studying her systematically under strict conditions and stipulated that "if a good trance-subject could be

MRS. LEONORA PIPER (1859–1950), the famous Boston Spiritualist medium, in a trance, ca. 1895. Photo by Mrs. Eveleen Myers. Her phenomena convinced James of Spiritualism's "dramatic possibility." *Henry James Papers, MS Am 1094, box 1, p. 20, by permission of the Houghton Library, Harvard University.*

obtained for the [American] society [for Psychical Research] at the outset of his or her career, and kept from doing miscellaneous work until patiently and thoroughly observed and experimented on, with stenographic reports of trance, and as much attention paid to failures and errors as to successes, I am disposed to think that the results would in any event be of scientific value." James's approach to mental mediumship, then, was to find reliable subjects such as Mrs. Piper for long-term scientific study. He concluded that "if, after studying them it [the ASPR] should reach favorable conclusions, it would do vastly more to make the vaguer testimony already extant influential with the society as a whole, than it could do by discussing such testimony now." Advocating empiricism over fideism, he added, "Only *then* can the volume of evidence already extant on the subject be taken into account."[66]

James also kept notes of other sitters' accounts with Mrs. Piper. In one instance, she supplied a Mr. A. Y. with information he believed could not have been known to the medium (though another was less satisfactory). In a second instance, a Mr. E. D. C. of Boston wrote to him to say his wife's cousin's widower had got "admirable tests." In a third case, the British clergyman Joseph Carpenter described a sitting that convinced him Mrs. Piper had extraordinary powers but could not venture to say what they were.[67] Carpenter remained intrigued, though, for nearly four years later he described another sitting in which he had been "much impressed with Hodgson [as an investigator]" and additionally could find "no deceit on the part of Mrs. Piper." Still, he had difficulty reconciling certain inconsistencies in her revelations and remained very "troubled about his own sitting. Why would his parents, for instance, who had died many years ago and given no sign of a desire to communicate, take advantage of an appointment with Mrs. Piper made by James on Carpenter's behalf?" Nonetheless, he believed Hodgson had discovered something original in her.[68] From all these sittings, James concluded that Mrs. Piper was not a fraud. However, although he had done the empirical work, he expressed his findings fideistically: "My own conviction is not evidence, but it seems fitting to record it. I am persuaded of the medium's honesty, and of the genuineness of her trance; and although at first disposed to think that the 'hits' she made were either lucky coincidences, or the result of knowledge on her part of who the sitter was and of his or her family affairs, I now believe her to be in possession of a power as yet unexplained."[69] Mrs. Piper, then, appeared to James to be a genuine subject capable of generating exactly the kind of facts that psychical researchers sought.

James did not sit with Mrs. Piper again for the next few years, but by the late 1880s she resumed an important role in his tertium quid approach to psychical research. Three cases stand out in this regard: those involving the deaths of Catherine Walsh, Baby Eliza, and Hannah Wild. The passing of Catherine Walsh, a little after midnight on 6 March 1889, whose correct date and time Mrs. Piper identified before James learned of it from a telegram, led to an encore sitting on 7 November 1889 in which "Aunt Kate" appeared as Mrs. Piper's control. Hodgson, who conducted the sitting, recorded her comments. They contained the usual cornucopia of mundane details regarding whether Hodgson had eaten fish for breakfast and whether it had been he or James who spilled the tea, as well as the usual assurances that she and others on the "other side" were well. "Aunt Kate" also complained of being cold in her left hand and made Mrs. Piper hold Hodgson's right hand in her right one. Hodgson found the results "the most striking personal thing," since he had dined on fish, though Miss E. R. Walsh testified in a letter that Aunt Kate's paralysis occurred on her right side, not her left. James did not participate in this particular sitting but read Hodgson's account shortly thereafter and noted that while most of the information amounted to "platitudes," he found the event "very interesting" since Mrs. Piper referred to information about Mrs. Walsh from three years prior that James believed only he knew about. In other words, Mrs. Piper seemed to know things in her trance state that she did not in her waking one, even though she did not always get the details exactly right.[70]

The Baby Eliza case referred to the daughter of William and Mary Salter who had died from diphtheria. The sitting included Eliza's physician and her parents; William MacKintire, a philosopher holding an appointment as a lecturer at the Society for Ethical Culture; and Mary Sherwin Gibbens, one of Alice Gibbens James's two sisters, as well as James and a stenographer. During the sitting, an identity emerged purporting to be "Baby Eliza," who seemed to know information that neither she (as a small child) nor Mrs. Piper (through conscious contact with the Salters) could have otherwise known, such as how she had caught diphtheria, which James later confirmed was correct. Most puzzling to everyone was the knife incident where "Baby Eliza" asked James to remove the contents from his pockets (a common practice in Spiritualism), in which she took a special interest. Afterward, the Salters and James discussed how Eliza had been drawn to James's knife right before she died (trying to open and close it). Afterward the group exchanged letters in which they tried to decide if Mrs. Piper had ever heard the story but agreed that it was unlikely. While Mrs. Salter's mother might have relayed the story, Mrs. Piper signed a sworn statement indicating she had not. They also agreed that while it was possible that either James or the Salters had relayed the story to her, neither recalled doing so. The only possibility was a comment Mrs. Salter made once to Mrs. Piper that "I thought I might get a word from Baby." James concluded there was something genuine to the claims of "Baby Eliza" but could not figure out how or why.[71]

The third case involved the Wild sisters, Elizabeth Wild Blodgett, the wife of Charles Blodgett, a physician in Holyoke, Massachusetts, and Hannah, who died on 28 July 1886. Upon learning of Hannah's imminent demise, the two sisters devised a test for the survival hypothesis in which Hannah left several sealed letters of whose contents only she knew. After she died, she would try to communicate their subject matter to Elizabeth in a séance. The letters were entrusted to James until such arrangements could be made, with James assuring Mrs. Blodgett that "your three most earnest and interesting letters are in my hands, together with [the portrait of] your sister's noble face & the lock of [her] hair."[72] As this case represented an ideal opportunity to test Mrs. Piper's abilities, the ASPR organized a sitting for Elizabeth upon Hannah's death in which Leonora used automatic writing to try to "reproduce" the letters. While she correctly identified Hannah as the author, Leonora's control failed to distinguish anything resembling the contents, prompting James to observe that "the two letters had nothing in common." With disappointing results, the ASPR arranged for two additional attempts, but Mrs. Piper failed to ascertain the contents on those occasions as well, though she did correctly identify some in subsequent sittings. These "hits" were of a trivial nature—she knew the location of a lost waistcoat and a misplaced bankbook; that James had killed a black and white cat with ether for an experiment; that letters had been sent to relatives containing contents of which no one outside the family knew; and of many events in the James family nursery—but they seemed correct and thus required an explanation besides fraud. Of them, James wrote fideistically that "insignificant as the things sound when read, the accumulation of a large number of them has an irresistible effect."[73] But he also thought the work had met his empirical standards, concluding in "A Record of Observations of Certain Phenomena of Trance" that "it would be hard to devise a better test than this."[74] James had been so concerned for the case to appear empirical that in telling Alice he had to "look up some Blodgett letters" for the publication of this article, he believed he had given the mistaken impression that Mrs. Piper had seen Hannah's sealed letters in advance and immediately asked Myers to clarify matters, to which Myers assured James he would "see that the correction is made *re* Blodgett."[75]

The Aunt Kate, Baby Eliza, and Hannah Wild cases were indicative of most sittings with Mrs. Piper and trance mediums more generally. Typically, the returning "spirit" was a recently deceased relative or friend, the kind of information revealed was trivial, and the number of hits was only sometimes or partially correct. Regarding her success rate, James explained to Mrs. Blodgett that Mrs. Piper was not accurate in every instance and that she "fails however with about 1/2 her sitters, or more." Still, he assured her that "I entirely believe in my medium."[76] Since 50 percent accuracy was a poor empirical showing, James may have been invoking his fideism and listening to his sentiment of rationality that told him Mrs. Piper's abilities rang true. But he may also have been unwilling to accept the evidence suggesting she did not possess them. The tension between these two possibilities indicates James was trying his damnedest to balance the incomplete evidence consistently and fairly in a young field with little recognized or accepted methods of engagement. Reviewing these cases reveals just how much difficulty he had being simultaneously objective and fair yet open-minded and flexible. In the end, James seems to have decided that a 50 percent success rate counted as a dramatic possibility of human nature. After all, even getting correct "hits" half of the time required an explanation.

The early evidence Mrs. Piper produced, then, was partial and incomplete. This fact prompted James to proclaim the phenomena "baffling" and to dub trance mediumship sittings a "queer business." But these dynamics did not dismay James as much as inform him of the uncertain nature of mental mediumship. The first lesson was that there would be no immediate answers. As he put it to Mrs. Blodgett, the evidence "is most irritating for all who seek a revelation." A tertium quid seeker, James was not among that crowd. Instead, he sought a continuum of facts that could answer the question he had raised way back in 1874, namely, "What *is* all this mediumship?" The problem, however, was that his empirical approach alone did not yield sufficient facts. Indeed, since "the admixture of knowledge & ignorance, and low human passions and superhuman powers is what makes the problem so fasc[ina]ting," James found himself on the horns of a dilemma: how to make sense of inconclusive results that were neither nothing nor something—a perfect storm for his tertium quid method of inquiry.[77]

James's solution to this predicament was to call for further testing. His initial thought was to use slate writing, but it never transpired. As James explained to Alice in his first recorded reference to Mrs. Piper, "[Minot Judson] Savage did not come to Mrs. Piper's and we did not try the slates."[78] Since Mrs. Piper was a trance medium, it is odd that James thought slates could be employed to gather valid data. This test, however, was to have occurred *before* James had exposed physical mediums like Hannah Ross. In fact, 1885 would have been exactly the right moment in James's development with testing mediums for him to have applied the sealed slate test, so there is nothing unusual at all about this, but it seems James did not attempt the slate test again or to have applied any other method indicative of physical mediumship.[79]

Another kind of test, though, did materialize. James anesthetized Leonora during her trance states. The goal was to see how they differed from hypnotic ones when mixed with some chemical influence. James discovered that mediums in trance states do not behave the same way as hypnotized persons do and that anesthesia had a peculiar effect on Mrs. Piper. On one occasion, he made a small incision in her wrist with his penknife to see how her trance state would affect blood flow. In Alta's words, "The most drastic experiments ever tried in those early days was when Prof. James . . . during a sitting at which Mrs. James was present, made a small incision in . . . [her] left wrist. During the trance state no notice was taken of this action and the wound did not bleed; but immediately upon awakening the wound bled freely."[80] From this procedure, James concluded that trance states not only were quite different from waking states but also forcefully exemplified the power of the mental world over the physical. Unless he had witnessed it for himself, he too would have been forced to admit that nature disallowed for such dramatic possibilities.

James's and the ASPR's positive accounts prompted the SPR to test Mrs. Piper in 1889–90.[81] Before she embarked for England, James wrote her a bon voyage letter wishing her success, expressing his desire that she remain unaffected by the testing, telling her, "I hope you will continue to be the same simple, unassuming Yankee girl that you are now."[82] Myers informed James of her progress and boasted of several additional cases: "We have also got a capital English case a la Piper—but don't know as yet whether it will develop."[83] Mrs. Piper's case certainly developed quite well because the SPR planned to devote a special issue of the *Proceedings* to her.[84] Myers, Hodgson, Oliver Lodge, and Walter Leaf each wrote lengthy reports, as did James, for which Myers thanked him and informed him that his study inspired Richet to participate as well.[85] When the first set of reports was near completion, Myers noted that "the Piper report—(very long—) [is] to come out about Nov., but we *must* have a full *medical* report from America,—field of vision & all the rest of it. If she keeps really *well*, we *hope* to invite her over here again."[86] That, however, would not be too soon, since the testing and trip had exhausted Mrs. Piper. Indeed, over time the sittings wore her down. "Mrs. P. who has been sitting almost every day since last Sept.," James told G. Stanley Hall, "has intimated that she is tired out, and must take a long vacation."[87]

By 1890, after five years of the ASPR and SPR studying Mrs. Piper, James offered some provisional conclusions. In a summary report, James found that she had not yielded the kind and number of facts he sought, but he also believed that ignoring the accumulated data was irresponsible. Facing inconclusivity, James turned to his own subjective experience.[88] One standout instance involved a weeklong stay at the James country house in Chocorua, New Hampshire, where Mrs. Piper hooked the "largest bass" that had ever been caught in Lake Chocorua.[89] These more intimate settings helped James "to know her personally better than ever before" and confirmed his "belief that she is an absolutely simple and genuine person." Instead of invoking empiricism, though, James argued fideistically that "no one when challenged, can give 'evidence' to others for such beliefs as this. Yet we all live from day to day, and practically *I should be willing now to stake as much money on Mrs. Piper's honesty as that of anyone I know, and am quite satisfied to leave my reputation for wisdom or folly, so far as human nature is concerned, to stand or fall by this declaration*" (emphasis added).[90] James's astounding announcement essentially declared Mrs. Piper a "dramatic possibility," but it also revealed two problems. First, by becoming friendly with her, he had forfeited objectivity. Such a situation was akin to Eusapia Palladino living with Myers during his investigation of her—a mistake for which James had gently, though properly, rebuked him. Second, since Leonora seemed honest and genuine, he believed he could forgo his own empirical maxims and instead invoked his fideistic will; there was just something about her that rang true to him. Clearly, though, this would not convince skeptics.

Both problems underscored what the ASPR's Committee on Mediumistic Phenomena had warned against, namely, eminent men of science (presumably including James) offering their integrity as proof of mediumistic phenomena might point toward belief, but it bore little relation to the nature of evidence. James's plea was thus insufficient proof. By contrast, the committee sought to remain "perfectly neutral."[91] Sill, James did not shun empiricism. At the end of his report, he repeated his view "that, taking everything that I know of Mrs. P[iper] into account, the result is to make me feel as absolutely certain as I am of any personal fact in the world that she knows things in her trances that she cannot possibly have heard in her waking state."[92] In other words, while the evidence had been empirically generated, a provisional belief that Mrs. Piper was genuine required a leap of faith. In 1892, James buttressed this view in "What Psychical Research Has Accomplished."[93] After discussing the work and purpose of psychical research, James speculated about Mrs. Piper's abilities by noting that the

SPR's and ASPR's long reports "tend to substantiate the claim that hypernormal intelligence may be displayed in the trance state," adding that their "observations," which he found to be "entirely conclusive," indicated that she "has shown in her trances a knowledge of personal affairs of living and dead people which it is impossible to suppose that she can have gained in any 'natural' way."[94] She had, then, some unexplained abilities. For the remainder of the decade, James continued this tertium quid approach.

Despite some setbacks and challenges, this was a productive period for the ASPR and SPR. With each new report many members increasingly thought the research on Mrs. Piper was finally producing something akin to empirical results. In one instance, James wrote to Hodgson, "I'm glad [to hear] Mrs. P[iper] is 'progressing.'"[95] As had been the case with the Eusapia investigation, Myers was the most enthusiastic about Mrs. Piper. Giddy with the news that Hodgson's ongoing work was providing exceptional data and bolstered by James's provisional conclusions, Myers gushed to James, "Mrs. Piper is all right—and the universe is all right—. . . and an eternity of happiness and glory awaits you—. . . and the dear spirits are hovering around us in the Summer land."[96] Ever the more balanced and cautious of the two, James replied, "Here [in America] nothing goes on but Mrs. Piper—toujours Piper!— [only] I wish we could unearth a little variety."[97] But Myers's zeal could not be dampened. To James he wrote, "Toujours Piper, indeed! . . . Has there ever been, in any truly historical age, such a ray of hope and glory thrown upon the world before? Let us preach Piper and the Resurrection, none making us afraid . . .—there still lies many a deed before you, ere you pass . . . [over to] the Summer Land!"[98] Myers had thus decided Mrs. Piper was genuine and that the evidence supported a belief in the survival hypothesis. But James had given Myers some hope for this view, writing, "Hodgson writes good accounts of the Piper sitting in N[ew] Y[ork]. I am curious to see him on his return."[99] In return, Myers agreed it was "quite good," certainly much better than the "Eusapia material." He was certainly convinced that Mrs. Piper was worthy of the amount of labor and money that had been put into her testing and that her case stood the chance of further improving, especially given Hodgson's skills and experience.[100] James and Myers agreed, then, that Mrs. Piper was progressing, but James preferred a tertium quid interpretation of its meaning. That is, despite his tendency to invoke fideistic logic when the evidence was incomplete, James's empiricism kept him from making the leap of faith that Myers did that Mrs. Piper's unexplained abilities were proof for the afterlife. Instead, he sighed, "If only we could get up here some variation upon Piper."[101]

Seeking that variation, James arranged for several colleagues and friends from Harvard and other universities to sit with Mrs. Piper at his Cambridge house in 1894.[102] Nathaniel Southgate Shaler, professor of geology, Charles Eliot Norton, professor of art history, and Wendell Barrett each sat at least one time. Initially, Mrs. Piper was reluctant to participate. James explained to Alice that he "found Hodgson waiting to see me because Mrs. P[iper] . . . said to day she wouldn't come for the sittings." So James arranged for "the Shalers [to] come tomorrow . . . , Friday P.M.," and Norton [on] Saturday morn[ing]."[103] James Mark Baldwin, an experimental psychologist at Princeton, also had a sitting with Mrs. Piper around this time of which James sought Baldwin's notes for his own records.[104] Lightning Witmer, an experimental psychologist, and William Romaine Newbold, an educator, both from the University of Pennsylvania, were also slated to sit with Mrs. Piper. Unfortunately, she developed a case of poison ivy and canceled the appointment, forcing the three to discuss her case at James's club (though Newbold eventually sat with her). But the chat piqued James. Witmer "is a conceited little ignoramus on the subject," he told Alice, "and I think I must make a resolution and keep it, not to be inveighed into any Piper conversations again, but refer people to what is printed or to Arlington Heights [where Mrs. Piper lived]."[105] Still, James resumed the arranged sittings once she had recovered. "The Shalers had a very decent success with Mrs. Piper this P.M.," he told Alice, referring to a case involving a concealed letter test between Mrs. Shaler and her recently deceased brother. The Shalers "agree that it is inexplicable" and want "certain facts verified." Moreover, Norton planned to resume his sitting "tomorrow A.M. So far, so good!"[106]

Mrs. Piper, however, was tiring. James confided to Alice that "Mrs. P[iper] says she won't sit again till next Fall," but James pushed her to sit with Norton before beginning her summer vacation, though not without protest.[107] "The poor little innocent woman," James sympathized, "has to stamp her foot and shake her head occasionally, to make [us] believe she has any individuality left. It does seem to me to be all smoothing out into a sheet of tissue paper. But she too is pure in heart—after all a good thing."[108] Mrs. Piper was enough of a "good thing" to sit with Norton and his daughter Sara a couple of times at a Saturday Club dinner. Hodgson was there as well and "was convinced of the genuineness of the performance, and of the inexplicability of certain things, though it was a distinctly poor sitting. The Shalers['] was much better."[109] Norton found the second sitting equally decent, but James disagreed. Apparently Mrs. Piper was so exhausted by that point that she "could hardly get entranced. . . . It is a pity—but N[orton] is already a *moral* convert, and this is all I care for," James related, adding, "There was no question as to Mrs. Piper's good faith."[110] The high volume of sittings sometimes created overlap, such as with the Salters and William Lambert Richardson, an obstetrician and SPR member who wanted to conduct his own tests. "I have written to Mrs. P[iper] about the Salters," James told Alice. "She is supposed not to sit till Richardson had had her ..., [but] is off in the country somewhere."[111]

Although the results were mixed, the Cambridge sittings inspired the SPR to consider having Mrs. Piper back to England and perhaps to devote more space in the *Proceedings* to her. A flurry of letters from Myers in 1894–95 revealed the topsy-turvy twist of events. Initially, he told James he wanted to test Mrs. Piper by sending some of his brother's hair (who had just died) but counseled against her coming to England for further testing until all the new material was printed.[112] It seems the initial results were negative, for Myers told James the "Piper matter seemed poor."[113] By the following year, though, Myers reported that the Piper material was now good and worthy of the amount of labor and money that had been put into it and that it could improve still further especially with Hodgson's skills and experience.[114] Apparently Hodgson, who was in England at this point, concurred, for Myers told James that he had been delighted with how Hodgson spoke of Mrs. Piper with an "air of unswaggering triumph" and urged James to continue testing her.[115] As before, he was eager for more results.[116]

In 1896, James presented those results in his SPR presidential address.[117] Like all speeches of its kind, it recounted the organization's annual accomplishments, although James took it upon himself to summarize in some detail its entire history, covering all the major topics and research tracts and offering some provisional conclusions. Of Mrs. Piper and trance mediumship, he had finally reached a state of belief, writing, "For me the thunderbolt *has* fallen." Using the "language of the professional logic-shop," James proclaimed, "A universal proposition can be made untrue by a particular instance. If you wish to upset the law that all crows are black, you mustn't seek to show that no crows are; it is enough if you prove one single crow to be white. My own white crow is Mrs. Piper."[118] Such a hyperbolic but heartfelt statement was neither an emotional outburst nor an epistemological evasion made in a moment of intellectual panic or scholarly self-doubt. On the contrary, it was indicative of James's fideism, especially the view that the personal and subjective quality of experience becomes part of the evidential trail and eventually of justification itself. As a rule, James invoked fideism when his two empirical criteria had been applied but had not rendered a satisfactory outcome. Fideism was unnecessary for drawing conclusions about physical mediums, for instance, since empirical investigation alone had rendered valid knowledge. But in the case of trance mediums, where the nature of the phenomenon was complicated and inconsistent, and the meaning of the communications incomplete and uncertain, the study of them proved exceedingly difficult to render just empirical conclusions. As some sort of opinion was required, James believed it necessary to invoke fideism on these occasions. This proved especially the case for Mrs. Piper on whom James staked his intellectual reputation. In particular, his claim that she amounted to a white crow indicated he believed in what might be called the dramatic possibilities of life, that is, that nature was not organized in rigid, closed, and static ways but rather was flexible, open, and dynamic in ways that allowed for the seemingly impossible.

SKINNING WHITE CROWS

Some intellectuals in James's broad milieu were not persuaded his fideism justified the dramatic possibility argument. Members of the ASPR, for instance, who were sympathetic to the phenomena warned against the "inherent tendency of the human race to delight in mystery," which it could be argued James was guilty of committing.[119] Not surprisingly, the critics of psychical research, of which there were several varieties, were highly dubious about Mrs. Piper in particular and quite dismissive of mediumship in general. Thomas Huxley, the English biologist and Darwin defender who expressed deep-seated contempt for Spiritualism, represented the first kind—those who refused to participate on principle. Upon being asked by the council of the Dialectical Society in the 1860s to investigate it, Huxley responded by saying that it would be a waste of time, that it was too much trouble and an annoyance, and that he took no interest in the subject. Despite admitting that he had only once before examined a case, he maintained, "The only good that I can see in a demonstration of the truth of 'Spiritualism' is to furnish an additional argument against suicide. Better to live a crossing-sweeper than die and be made to talk twaddle by a 'medium' hired at a guinea a *séance*."[120] James would have appreciated the dour English humor but still rejected Huxley's reasoning as overly bifurcated. Invoking his tertium quid approach, James wrote with his own biting wit,

> Obviously the mind of the excellent Huxley has here but two wholesouled categories, namely, revelation or imposture.... Sentimental reasons bar revelation out, for the messages, he thinks, are not romantic enough for that; fraud exists anyhow; therefore the whole

thing is nothing but imposture. The odd point is that so few of those who talk in this way realize that they and the spiritists are using the same major premise and differing only in the minor. The major premise is: "Any spirit-revelation must be romantic." The minor of the spiritist is: "This *is* romantic"; that of the Huxleyan is: "This is dingy twaddle."[121]

Still, James realized that support from the scientific community would greatly benefit psychical research, writing, "Professor Huxley's bare 'endorsement' of Mrs. Piper, *e.g.*, would be more effective than volumes of notes by such as I."[122]

Hugo Münsterberg, a brass instrument psychologist whom James had helped hire as his replacement to run the psychological laboratory at Harvard in 1892, also refused to participate on principle. Münsterberg detested the whole American fascination with Spiritualism, a position that frustrated James.[123] Indeed, Münsterberg argued it was a superstition and a low form of mysticism. Not be outdone by Huxley, he held the séance in special contempt, likening it to a mere "variety show" where a "pathological woman" talks about one's "personal secrets at the rate of twenty francs a sitting!" Such a thing was simply too undignified for a professional psychologist to attend.[124] James pleaded with Münsterberg to sit privately with Mrs. Piper, but Münsterberg refused on the ground that he would be duped because he was so easily "hypnotizable." When James pressed Münsterberg that he at least allow his wife to sit to "see what *she* gets," James told James Cattell that he replied, "'Oh no!—I should never suffer my wife to such a place.' I call that real sportsmanlike keenness for new phenomena!"[125]

Even more intransigent was Frederick William Seward, an American politician and diplomat. He claimed (according to Myers) that psychical researchers defrauded the public because they cheated in their "pretended scientific reports" from which they benefited financially.[126] James could suffer this kind of uninformed criticism from outsiders, but when Josiah Royce, his colleague and philosophical sparring partner, objected to participate on similar grounds, James exploded. "I lost my temper this A.M. over Royce's cool and indifferent refusal to waste an hour over Mrs. P[iper]," he confided to his wife, adding, "It is simply disgraceful to a man in his position, the more so that (I fancy) he doesn't feel sure, as poor Münsterberg does, that Hodgson, Myers and I are dupes. It is a poor world!"[127]

But Royce and Münsterberg had their supporters. E. B. Titchener, another brass instrument psychologist trained in the German experimental tradition working at Cornell, was also critical of psychical research. He offered an equal rights argument in their defense. Scolding James, he wrote,

> As to the attitude of Royce and Münsterberg, I think again that you may be a little unfair. At any rate, I should probably refuse myself to spend time of Mrs. Piper, on the ground that I saw my path clear before me for a long series of bits of work useful to science, and that the whole of my experience forbade me to expect such useful results from medium-sittings. I do not know the S. P. R publications as well as I know the Studien; but I have read a lot of papers, and have spent some (not very much) time upon similar enquiries. I get nothing; my intellect doesn't digest these things. [B]ut I am as keen for fair play as anybody,—meaning thereby that you have your right to fight for your side, and that I have an equal right to fight for mine.[128]

With regard to Mrs. Piper, then, the critics who never sat with her and refused to on principle maintained she only appeared to be a white crow when in reality she was black as coal. But such objections were mere dogma to James, who insisted on empiricism.

Of those whom James convinced to sit with her over the years, they got no "hits," were unconvinced by the evidence, or thought she was a fraud. At the center of these disagreements lay different interpretations of empiricism. Was it ever justified to deny a priori the existence of psychic forces or defensible to reject said phenomena as scientifically worthless without even considering the evidence? Many of James's colleagues thought it was since naturalism must account for everything in this world, but James thought this an overly narrow interpretation of empiricism. As such, James was forced to defend his work with her and by extension all mediumship as scientifically legitimate and capable of producing meaningful results. That defense involved several debates in which James invoked both fideism and empiricism whereby he developed his tertium quid approach to trance mediumship.

Decent results also evaded G. Stanley Hall, who sat with Mrs. Piper, James, and Hodgson in 1887 during a session that lasted almost until midnight. Hall claimed he "got nothing which struck him," which prompted James to confide to Alice that Hall was "the queerest mixture of bigness & pettiness I ever knew."[129] Similarly, the physicist John Trowbridge, who had been at one of the 1894 Cambridge sessions, had what James called a "miserable sitting," complaining of her "insane cunning and groping" for details (that is, she "fished" for information). Trowbridge did not conclude, however, that she was pretending to be entranced or cheating but did maintain there was nothing supernormal about the phenomena.¹³⁰ Likewise, Edmund Burke Delabarre, a psychologist at Brown University and a one-year replacement for Hugo Münsterberg at Harvard's psychology lab in 1897–98, recalled years later that when he had been James's graduate student in the late 1880s "I had one or two sittings with her, puzzling as to how she could possibly have been able to mention so many facts concerning my private life, but otherwise not remarkable except that she ventured some prophecies which never were fulfilled."¹³¹ Hall's, Trowbridge's, and Delabarre's results were not uncommon in the study of trance mediumship, but they did little to persuade men of science of the empirical value of such work. Even the ASPR's Committee on Mediumistic Phenomena agreed, noting that "the conditions under which the phenomena are offered for observation . . . precluded any satisfactory examination."¹³²

James's trouble with getting reputable men of science to consider the evidence for mediumship is best exemplified in his debate with James McKeen Cattell, an experimental psychologist at Columbia and an archenemy of psychical research. The debate, which occurred in the pages of *Psychological Review* and *Science*, of which Cattell was the editor, captured each man's view and especially highlighted James's tertium quid method of inquiry. It began with Cattell's review of James's 1896 SPR presidential address in which James likened the evidence for Mrs. Piper to a bundle of faggots, that is, while each stick may seem weak, taken together the whole was relatively strong. Cattell did not believe Mrs. Piper was a white crow and noted that James's reasoning could show just the opposite. "When we have an enormous number of cases, and cannot find among them all a single one that is quite conclusive," Cattell argued, "the very number of cases may be interpreted as an index of the weakness of the evidence. The discovery of a great many gray crows would not prove that any crows are white, rather the more crows we examine and find to be black or gray, the less expectation have we of finding one that is white." In other words, Cattell maintained the empirical evidence for Mrs. Piper was inductively quite weak and statistically the odds were against her being the exception. In addition, although James's defense of Mrs. Piper carried weight with the public, Cattell was not impressed. He noted that history was replete with great men who had lent their names to discredited causes such as astrology or simply had mistakenly observed the phenomenon the way geese can be taken for swans.¹³³

But there was no mistake for James. He believed Cattell had simply misunderstood the evidence and James's argument. "Our reports are not of gray crows," he replied. "At the very worst they are of white crows without the

JAMES MCKEEN CATTELL (1860–1944), undated. Cattell vigorously opposed psychical research and argued that James's invoking of Mrs. Piper's phenomena to support his belief in Spiritualism was nothing more than a weak inductive argument. *Historical Photograph Collection, series X, box 21, University Archives, Rare Book and Manuscript Library, Columbia University Library, Columbia University.*

skins brought home." By admitting Mrs. Piper was not through-and-through a white crow James appeared to be backpedaling, but he was actually invoking an empirical argument. Basing their difference in what he called the "logic of presumption," James stipulated that because of the delicate nature of the phenomena it was unrealistic to presume the evidence would be as "perfect" as in other sciences. Being reasonable was a good thing, but there was also "such a thing as being too fair-minded, so that one wades in a very bog of over-reasonableness. For, in point of fact, the concrete evidence for most of the 'psychic' phenomena under discussion is good enough to hang a man twenty times over."[134] In other words, James implicitly invoked his fideism by claiming the regular empirical norms do not always apply in psychical research and that therefore he was justified. At the same time, though, he was also arguing inductively by stating the empirical evidence was in fact good enough for belief in Mrs. Piper. In this way, he was not backsliding so much as trying to carve a third path between empiricism and fideism.

Their argument continued two years later in the pages of *Science*. The impetus was the publication of Hodgson's second article on Mrs. Piper in which Hodgson advanced the survival hypothesis. Cattell focused on the "trivial character of the evidence for the heterogeneous mass of material" but directed his main criticism at James for defending Mrs. Piper as a "white crow." Now Cattell appeared to backslide, for he noted that James's reputation did indeed merit others' consideration of the evidence. On the other hand, the evidence itself had not changed his mind. Casting the issue as one of fraud, he wrote, "The difficulty has been that proving innumerable mediums to be frauds does not disprove the possibility (though it greatly reduces the likelihood) of one medium being genuine. But here we have the 'white crow' selected by Professor James from all the piebald crows exhibited by the Society [for Psychical Research]." Although the gray crows had become piebald ones, Cattell continued to assert that one case was inductively weak and thereby the evidence in favor of Mrs. Piper was *not* empirically strong enough to hang a man many times over. To bolster his claim, he cited the concluding statement of the five "well-known men of science" who were at some of the 1894 Cambridge sittings (James Baldwin, John Trowbridge, Nathaniel Shaler, James Peirce, and Silas Mitchell) and who were highly skeptical of the evidence: "'Truly,' they wrote, 'we have piped unto you, but ye have not danced.'"[135]

Cattell's charges (and tone) infuriated James. He fired off to *Science* a long, highly critical, and contemptuous letter, taking Cattell to task for his fallacious reasoning and misrepresentation of Hodgson's data. After complaining how hard it was to get a hearing with most scientists, let alone a fair one, James laid into Cattell for not following the same rules of reason in heterodox science as he would for that of orthodoxy. "But in mere matters of superstition as a medium's trances," he wrote, "it [the scientific mind] feels so confident of impunity and indulgence whatever it may say, provided it be only contemptuous enough, that it fairly revels in the untrained barbarians' arsenal of logical weapons, including various sophisms in the books." James then invoked two instances of Cattell's fallacious reasoning. First, "Your own comments seem to me an excellent illustration of this fact. If one wishes to refute a man who asserts that some A's are B's, the ordinary rule of logic is that one must not show that some *other* A's are *not* B's—one must show him either that those first A's themselves are not B's, or else that no A possibly can be a B." Then he scolded Cattell like a mere schoolboy failing at elementary logic for invoking but five instances from Hodgson's five hundred sittings and for substituting the opinions of the "well-known men of science" for his own. Invoking this as a violation of the rule of reasoning he had recited, James went for the jugular. "If, my dear sir, you were teaching Logic to a class of students, should you, or should you not, consider this a good instance by which to illustrate the style of reasoning termed 'irrelevant conclusion,' or *ignoratio elenchi*, in the chapter on fallacies? I myself think it an extraordinarily perfect instance." Second, rubbing salt in the wound, James criticized Cattell for using only selected bits of information from those five sittings that seemed to undermine Mrs. Piper. Invoking a lawyerly tone, he reprimanded Cattell: "I am not sure that the logic books contain any technical name for the fallacy here, but in legal language, it is sometimes called *suppressio veri*, sometimes something still less polite." In other words, by taking some evidence out of context and misrepresenting it, James charged Cattell with suppressing or concealing the truth and even with lying. Driving the stake home, he added sarcastically, "I am sure that you have committed these fallacies with the best of scientific consciences," which James claimed that for orthodox science Cattell would not have done.[136]

James was technically correct if rather insolent about these two points, but he had not really refuted Cattell's inductive argument that a profundity of data showing crows were black and a paucity of data revealing white ones diminished the likelihood that there were any white crows. Seemingly aware that he and Cattell evaluated evidence according to different interpretations of empiricism—Cattell following strict empiricism, James preferring fideist empiricism—he returned to his claim that psychical research data and orthodox science data were not the same. Instead, he likened it to the comparison between the evidence for insanity versus mental health in which "the usual moral rules don't apply. Mediums are scientific outlaws, and their defendants are quasi-insane."[137] James's reply, however, was a form of special pleading; James claimed the scientific method would lead to psychical facts, but when the investigations failed to produce data that fell in line with the kind collected on natural phenomena, then he claimed it was not like such phenomena. Cattell could have made such a point but simply stated that he did not have the space to describe all the material from the six-hundred-page report and instead had tried to summarize the findings by invoking the opinion of the five "well-known men of science." Attempting to close the debate, he noted both he and James had had a chance to state their "individual opinion" but feared their "disagreement is hopeless." As a brass instrument psychologist devoted to making experimental psychology scientific, he was concerned that James's defense of Mrs. Piper and his work in psychical research more broadly was doing much harm to the field. "We all acknowledge his leadership," Cattell concluded, "but we cannot follow him into the quagmires."[138]

James, however, would not drop the matter, though he did make it private. Writing an angry letter, he rebuked Cattell. "I have read your brief retort and live. Your state of prejudice is so *absolute*, that quite naively and unconsciously you perpetrate acts of insolence quite as remarkable as your lapses of logic, as if I were some minor or child making a nuisance in the psychological neighborhood," which James again asserted Cattell would not do if this had been an orthodox scientific matter. He noted that he had fifteen years of experience with the "facts," while Cattell would not even look at them. He also did not "care personally a rap for the treatment. . . . As you smile indulgently at me, so I, dear Cattell, at you. He smiles best who smiles last, and my prophetic soul is in no doubt about that."[139] But James was not done smiling. Eight months later he wrote to Cattell about "*our* little tiff in Science . . . over Mrs. Piper" to point out that Cattell forgot to include Herbert Nichols on his list of reputable scientists whom James claimed "was flabbergasted at what he got" and to make his "rejoinder," namely, "that of 8 colleagues whom I invited to sit with Mrs. P[iper] gratis at my house 5 declined. . . . I used to think the story of the peripatetic astronomers who wouldn't look through Galileo's telescope at Jupiter's moons (preferring aloofness coupled with authoritativeness) was a fable, but the complexion of the time gives it proof."[140] It was one more way James pointed out the limits to Cattell's strict interpretation of empiricism and by implication the necessity of adopting a more fideistic approach.

Having smiled last, James felt free to joke with Cattell about the whole "débrouiller." Much later, after Cattell apparently made some benign comments about psychical research, James advised him to "continue along that line and you will be saved, [and] will very likely after 'passing away' become a 'cabinet control' and instruct the younger generation in spiritual things."[141] More seriously, though, the passage of time allowed him to credit Cattell for showing the limitations of James's argument, even if, according to James, James had been too hard on him. "Your allusion to the 'roughest thing' ever said to (or of) you [I don't recall what it was, but it was in the 'psychic' controversy of course] makes me wish to say to you how admirably good tempered, tactful, and neutral you have always seemed to me as an editor. Thinking as you do about the spook business, it has always filled me with admiration to see how freely you gave me my head."[142] The matter seems to have ended there with James feeling he had vindicated himself, Hodgson, and Mrs. Piper while taking Cattell to task for his lapses in logic and narrow-mindedness. On the other hand, his defense of the evidence had failed to persuade one of the psychologists who he knew needed convincing if psychical research was to gain any traction as a legitimate scientific field. The evidence was just not inductively good enough for men like Cattell, and invoking fideism in its place was not going to change that reality. James's tertium quid approach to trance mediumship, then, was not scientific enough for the tough-minded self.

For his part, Cattell, who thought James had been too hard on him, even though Cattell gave as good as he got, continued to maintain his skepticism. In 1902 he rebuked psychical researchers at the SPR for assuming that writers for the *Psychological Review* shared the point of view of the authors of the *Proceedings*, who would naturally be sympathetic to psychic phenomena: "The phenomena are apparently not such as can be treated by scientific methods, and each must form an individual opinion. The undersigned believes that the facts reported do not require or justify the assumption of the supernormal as a working hypothesis. Neither does he regard the phenomena as suited to scientific investigation until the possibility of fraud has been excluded."[143] Cattell thus retained his skepticism about Mrs. Piper and remained unconvinced by James's fideist-infused empiricist justification of her.

But James had a larger and much more serious problem than convincing others of the evidence or of his fideist empiricism. Lurking throughout all these sittings and criticisms of trance mediumship and Mrs. Piper was the worst possible charge, namely, that she was a fraud. Charles Loring Jackson was an ASPR member who resigned because others whispered as much. As James lamented to his wife, "I have been aimlessly busy to day, part of the time over the Piper sittings. Jackson refuses, regarding her, from Perry's account, to be an ingenious fraud."[144] Others drew that conclusion as well. After his sitting with Mrs. Piper, Silas Mitchell called the whole thing a "very stupid" fraud and expressed no desire to see her ever again. His explanation was that she was nothing more than a mind reader.[145] Perhaps the most vociferous critic was none other than Horace Howard Furness, James's partner in exposing Mrs. Ross and the Berry sisters. When Furness had first heard from James that his early tests had been fruitful, he was hopeful. But after sitting with her a few times, he quickly became disenchanted. Mrs. Piper, he lamented, "broke my heart—I think I've never had a séance since. She fell into line with all the rest. Ask a medium a question containing a probability and an improbability and just as sure as the Devil reigns in this world, she'll take the improbability. I should have had a lovely time with her, if there hadn't been a tinge of sadness which always creeps over you when you come face to face with deceit."[146]

James, of course, did not think she was deceitful. To prove to Furness that she was honest and her trances genuine, he wrote to George Fullerton, the secretary of the Seybert Commission, which Furness chaired, to request that it formally test Mrs. Piper. Fullerton replied in the negative but without providing a reason.[147] James's long response, mixing witticism with seriousness, sought an explanation.

> I need not say that Hodgson and I have been much disappointed at the reply of the Seybert Commission. Having irretrievably lost our tails ourselves we should naturally have been pleased at the reduction of such very foxy vulpines as you 'uns to the same status. . . . We however are philosophical enough . . . , and we understand the tremendous odds which such opinions as ours have to overcome, especially in the minds of men who have had so untoward a run of luck as you had in your investigations. We are therefore not so much chagrined or discouraged as disappointed. But in return for this benignant disposition on our part we should like to ask you a favor . . . , [that] you candidly set down in writing the veritable grounds of your refusal. In case Mrs. P[iper] and the likes of her ever did hereafter *prevail*, it might be an interesting document in the history of opinion concerning her case, and the difficulties that lay in our path.[148]

Fullerton, who had been to many of the "cabinet séances" with James and was sympathetic, informed James he would forward his note. But James's elegant plea did not move Furness. In a reply that was equally pithy and playful, he told James, "I should with alacrity mount a pillory request where you and Hodgson to your heart[']s content can pelt me with dead Phinuits [Mrs. Piper's control] and, between showers of pickled peppers, make the

Summerland shake with the homeric laughter of Piperian gods." Furness cited the lack of funds in the Seybert Commission's treasury, but the real reason was his lack of conviction. The sessions he and Mitchell had had with her, he added, "were such unalleviated, not to say, ridiculous, failures, that we cannot from our own personal experiences ask our fellow-members to interrupt their busy professional vocations with an avocation so barren of promise—as far as Spiritualism is concerned.... Thus I cannot see what immediate good can be gained by spending shekels on Mrs. Piper for that which is not genuine."[149] For Furness, then, Mrs. Piper represented not a dramatic possibility of human nature but merely high drama, and all that Fullerton could tell James in response was that he was "really sorry."[150] Several years later, James tried to persuade Furness again but to no avail. To Cattell he mentioned that despite the SPR's offer to cover the costs, the Seybert Commission had "declined to see Mrs. P[iper]."[151] *Falsus in uno, falsus in omnibus* meant James would never be able to persuade men like Jackson, Mitchell, and Furness—fideistically or empirically. For them, there was no tertium quid to mediumship.

Despite all the objections to Mrs. Piper and trance mediumship, psychical researchers maintained they had discovered a genuine phenomenon worthy of scientific explanation. In pursuit of answers, they began accumulating their long-sought-after data pool, which they hoped would yield enough valid evidence to support the survival hypothesis. Upon the completion of numerous sittings and tests with Mrs. Piper, James concluded she was not a fraud and the phenomena she produced in her trance states were genuine. From these two judgments, he advanced what he believed to be a sound conclusion about Mrs. Piper's abilities, namely, that natural forces, including those studied by scientific psychology, could not yet explain them. As such, he concluded that "the definite *philosophy of her trances* is yet to be found" (emphasis added).[152] Still, James was convinced that there was something there. Although not willing to go on record as to what it was, he decided she amounted to a unique case—a "white crow"—that represented the dramatic possibility that psychical phenomena might be real. James reached this conclusion through the empirical investigation of Mrs. Piper, but he justified his belief in these phenomena by invoking philosophical fideism, much as he had done to defend religious belief. In this way, James continued his quest for psychical facts through implementing his tertium quid method of inquiry. It was one that steered a balanced middle path between the tough-minded scientists and skeptics who were unconvinced by the evidence that trance mediums produced and the tender-minded Spiritualists and his colleagues at the SPR, including Hodgson, who believed that the soul survives bodily death.

III

THEORIZING PSYCHICAL RESEARCH

six

CONSCIOUSNESS BEYOND THE MARGIN

The relative empirical success of mediumistic investigations emboldened psychical researchers to expand their quest to theorizing psychic phenomena. Members of the Sidgwick Group sought to explain the nature of trance states in particular because in their view they provided the conduit of communication with souls from the "Summerland" that, in turn, could be used to support the survival thesis. Edmund Gurney and Frederic Myers reasoned that if they could offer a general theory of trance states, they could unlock the mystery to all psychic phenomena. Their approach intertwined natural phenomena of a psychological type with supernatural phenomena of a religious kind that invariably led them to the unconscious. A notoriously slippery term lacking precise meaning that had undergone immense change over several centuries, three general kinds of theories of unconsciousness had emerged by the late nineteenth century: idealist, physiological, and pathological. The German philosophers Johann Gottfried von Herder, Eduard von Hartmann, and Arthur Schopenhauer, who worked in the Kantian transcendental idealist tradition, hypostatized a universal unconscious. The British physiologists Henry Maudsley, William Carpenter, and Alexander Bain, who worked in the empirical tradition of biological materialism, reduced unconscious mental states to a physical cerebration of the brain. The French psychologists Charles Richet, Jean-Martin Charcot, and Pierre Janet, who worked with hysterics and insane patients at the Salpêtrière Hospital in Paris, argued unconsciousness was a pathological condition. In their own way, each of these schools of thought attempted to explain what William James famously called "consciousness beyond the margin."

While all three theories facilitated a general understanding of unconsciousness, that of the Salpêtrière psychologists influenced psychical researchers the most. After all, the unconscious mental states found in hysterical and insane patients bore a remarkable similarity to those found in hypnotic and mediumistic subjects. Recognizing the overlap, James invented the term "exceptional mental states" to cover both the pathological and nonpathological varieties of unconscious activity and devoted time and effort to expounding the former, including his 1896 Lowell Lectures on abnormal psychology that addressed topics like multiple personality, demoniacal possession, and witchcraft.[1] These lectures indicate that James believed unconsciousness manifested pathology, but it was his concurrent work in psychical research that revealed it was also nonpathological, propelling James to move beyond the French school. That is, because the Salpêtrière theory had limited itself to the abnormal population, it made unconsciousness a malady. By stark contrast, psychical researchers found that hypnotic subjects and trance mediums were part of a larger though not yet universal population of nonpathological subjects whose unconscious activity could not be reduced to mental disease or brain cerebration. Thus, Gurney's experiments on "hypnotic memory" with his personal secretary George Smith and his "Brighton Boys," Myers's speculations about the "personality" of Mrs. Rosalie Thompson, and James's study of "secondary selves" in the automatic writing of Mrs. Leonora Piper and other mediums revealed a plethora of unconscious identities that, while fragmented, incomplete, and often incoherent, were nonetheless real and, in turn, exposed the inherent limitations of the Salpêtrière approach.

The failure of the French school to account for the nature of trance states left an explanatory vacuum that psychical researchers thus tried to fill. Through a remarkable and sustained effort of cross-fertilization in the late 1880s and 1890s, James and Myers co-invented the "subliminal self" theory that argued trance states were but one form of unconscious mental life. While Myers found a continuum between consciousness and unconsciousness in which supra- and subliminal selves lurked above and below the threshold of consciousness, between which ordinary, waking consciousness was but one stage, James argued for a center-margin model in which multiple "hidden selves" hovered at the borders of a principal consciousness. James reached his view during the late 1880s while drafting key chapters of *The Principles of Psychology*, a text more famously known for his theory that consciousness is like a flowing and continuous stream but that also claimed consciousness can "split off in two parts." The apparent contradiction of these two positions, however, was actually an aberration, since James's evolving view that consciousness had to be expanded to include these secondary states developed coterminously with his study of trance states in mental mediums while drafting the *Principles*. Although James did not develop his version of the subliminal self into a robust theory of unconscious as Myers did with his notion of "human personality," it nonetheless became part of his ontology. As his first biographer captured it, "The idea of consciousness 'beyond the margin' or 'below the threshold' was a metaphysical hypothesis of the first importance."[2] In particular, James argued for something more than the individualist theory that made unconsciousness unique to each person but not yet for a universal theory that made unconsciousness common to the human psyche writ large. Set against the German idealist and British materialist theories, respectively, and influenced by but ultimately rejecting of the French pathological one, then, James's notion of consciousness beyond the margin constituted his tertium quid approach to the unconscious.

THE UNCLASSIFIED RESIDUUM

"'The great field of new discoveries,' said a friend to me [James] the other day, 'is always the Unclassified Residuum.'"[3] And indeed James's friend was correct. Until the early 1600s, theories of the unconscious lacked precision because unconsciousness was considered disconnected from and secondary to consciousness. With the emergence of René Descartes's theory of mind in the mid-seventeenth century, however, the search for a unified theory of mental processes began in earnest. Intellectuals of all kinds—theologians, natural philosophers, poets, novelists—pursued an understanding of hidden mental life, with many seeking to connect conscious awareness with unconscious activity. During the eighteenth century, this work primarily took the form of introspection, observation, and hypostatization. Jean-Jacques Rousseau, for instance, used the introspective method to explore his own fluctuating moods and attributed them to forces that he could not ascertain by using his conscious. The German philosopher Johann Gottfried von Herder postulated the existence of the unconscious as a way to explain the imagination, dreams, passion, and mental illness. His work provided an opening to the study of unconsciousness from Johann Wolfgang von Goethe and other romantics (the imagination and passion) to physiologists and neurologists (insanity) and eventually to Sigmund Freud and his intellectual descendants (dreams). In the late eighteenth and early nineteenth centuries, two main approaches to the unconscious emerged: the school of transcendental idealist philosophy, exemplified by the German thinkers Immanuel Kant, Georg

Wilhelm Friedrich Hegel, Johann Gottlieb Fichte, and Friedrich Schelling, and the more empirical branch of philosophy, exemplified by the British thinkers David Hume and John Stuart Mill. By the mid-nineteenth century, three strands of thinking about the unconscious had emerged: supernatural, natural, and the hypostatized unconscious mind. The first suggested that an unconscious will beyond the conscious one caused people to act and held that it belonged to an unseen world beyond the immediate one that science could not explain. The second invoked the existence of introspective unconscious mental states or even an unconscious mind as a separate entity and denied the role of conscious observation. The third postulated the full-blown existence of a rational unconscious mind in contradistinction to the rational conscious one of the Christian tradition, such as in Gottfried Wilhelm Leibniz's theory of the soul. By the mid- to late nineteenth century, German and English theories of the unconscious became more precise. The advance of new scientific discoveries and the improvements to modern scientific method, with its insistence on reliably gathered data, instrument measurement, verifiability, and hypothesis testing, all contributed to this development. The German thinkers Eduard von Hartmann, C. G. Carus, and Gustav Fechner each developed sophisticated theories of the unconscious, with von Hartmann offering the first modern survey of the concept in his *Philosophy of the Unconscious* (1869). Fechner argued the human mind was much like an iceberg; what we observed consciously was akin to the part that barely stuck up above the surface of awareness. That is, most of what existed remained unseen or "unconscious." Friedrich Nietzsche best captured the various German theories of the unconscious, writing, "Consciousness only touches the surface. . . . The real continuous process takes place below our consciousness." In England, a series of theories were advanced by different sorts of thinkers such as William Hamilton, who placed the emotions at the center of the unconscious, Henry Maudsley, who connected it with mental pathology, and philosophical materialists such as William Carpenter, who approached it from the point of view of physiology, offering his notion of "unconscious cerebration" or a supposed physical division in the brain.[4]

In France, two schools of psychology dominated the discussion of the unconscious. The Salpêtrière school argued the unconscious amounted to a pathological condition of the brain.[5] As early as 1875, Charles Richet, a physiologist and editor of the *Revue Scientifique*, published an article on the use of hypnosis to explore somnambulistic states and suggested that altered states were pathological. Due to this work, Jean-Martin Charcot, the French neurologist who had been charged with running a special ward at the

Salpêtrière Hospital in Paris, decided to pursue the use of hypnosis to explore abnormal mental states in hysteric and epileptic patients. From the latter the former group learned to imitate what Charcot dubbed the "convulsion crisis." Upon founding with Richet the Société de Psychologie Physiologique, Charcot began to incorporate more experimental psychology into the laboratory at the Salpêtrière. In 1880, he established a clinic for the treatment of nervous diseases, upon whose patients he and the other clinicians performed their experiments. At Richet's suggestion, Charcot presented his findings in a series of lectures at the Académie des Sciences in 1882, which James attended, greatly influencing his own view about pathology.[6] Richet followed this with the publication of a series of additional experiments conducted throughout the remainder of the decade.[7] Their work caught the attention of a young philosophy student named Pierre Janet, Paul Janet's nephew, who was casting about for a dissertation topic. Janet conducted his early research on the hypnotism of hysterical patients at the Salpêtrière in the 1880s, focusing on their more philosophical aspects. Janet's most important work, *De l'Automatisme psychologique*, a reworking and expansion of his articles on hypnotism and hysteria that he had published between 1886 and 1889 in *Revue Philosophique*, the leading French journal of philosophy, was published in 1889.[8] Similarly, Alfred Binet, a French physiologist, conducted his research on multiple personality there, culminating in his work *On Double Consciousness* in 1889.[9] In short, Richet, Charcot, Janet, and Binet had used hypnosis to access nonconscious mental states and argued they were pathological.

The Salpêtrière's main competitor was the Nancy school.[10] Located in the Lorraine province, it took its namesake from the town's hospital. The Nancy's two main innovators were Auguste Ambroise Liébeault and Hippolyte Bernheim. Liébeault was a country doctor who ran a small practice earning a tidy sum treating local farm peasants who suffered from a variety of afflictions such as rheumatism, arthritis, ulcers, and pulmonary tuberculosis. After he retired, Liébeault spent twenty years experimenting with hypnotism on this population. Although the medical establishment thought him something of quack for using hypnotism (mesmerism had fallen into serious disrepute between 1850 and 1860) and his colleagues thought him a fool (he charged no fee because he was gathering experimental data), Liébeault discovered that "magnetism" worked. In his eight-volume pioneering work on magnetic sleep, *Du Sommeil et des États analogues*, Liébeault argued the hypnotic state was identical with natural sleep and showed that hypnotism was due mostly to suggestion. In particular, he discovered the rapport of the hypnotizer was crucial to successfully hypnotizing a subject (though he later adopted the "magnetic fluid" theory, which located the healing power outside the hypnotizer, a position his own work, ironically, had discredited twenty years prior). Still, Liébeault was able to demonstrate that the unconscious was not solely pathological by showing hypnotism could be used on nonhysterical patients and that its effects were due mainly to suggestion and rapport.[11]

If Liébeault was the father of the Nancy school, then Hippolyte Bernheim, who discovered and made Liébeault's work known to the world, was its founder. Bernheim was not an experimental psychologist but a specialist in internal medicine. After Germany had annexed Strasbourg in 1871, he left his post at the university hospital but became the titular professor of internal medicine at the new university hospital in Nancy in 1879. Hearing rumors of Liébeault's spectacular success, he paid him a visit in 1882. After conducting his own experiments, Bernheim became convinced of Liébeault's theories and began making them known around the same time Charcot had published his findings. In a paper and subsequent textbook, Bernheim challenged the Salpêtrière's theory that nonconscious mental states were pathological and made plain Liébeault's arguments of twenty years prior: that not only could one use hypnotism to heal a variety of ailments, including nervous disorders, but, more important, that hypnotism applied to healthy individuals revealed the existence of nonconscious mental states.[12]

As debates between the two schools ensued, it became apparent that exceptional mental states were much more widespread throughout the human population than had been recognized. For instance, several psychical research organizations in modern Germany that were influenced by the Nancy school debated the nature of consciousness. These included the Psychologische Gesellschaft (Psychological Society) founded in Munich in 1886 by Albert von Schrenck-Notzing and Carl du Prel, and Gesellschaft für Psychologische Forschung (Society for Psychological Research), a splinter of the first organization, that was founded in Berlin in 1889 by Max Dessoir and Albert Möll. Richard von Krafft-Ebing also followed the Nancy school, while Dessoir's work, *Das Döppel-Ich* (1890), provided a useful illustration of all their views.[13] By the fin de siècle, it was clear the Nancy school and its offshoots in Imperial Germany had challenged the Salpêtrière's theory of unconsciousness by expanding the realm of pathological selves to include healthy ones.

Surprisingly, some prominent historians of psychiatry, who often reduce their study of unconsciousness to pathology, have missed this significant development. The classic case is Henri Ellenberger's *The Discovery of the Unconscious*, which considered all the theorizing of unconsciousness prior to 1900 a prelude to the coming showdown between Freud and Carl Jung. As such, while Ellenberger gave some attention to Myers and Gurney and noted how the advent of "spiritism in the nineteenth century resulted in the discovery of new approaches to the conscious mind, such as automatic writing," and led to the study of new conditions such as "automatic somnambulism" and "mediumistic trance," he mostly ignored the contributions of psychical researchers and thereby missed an opportunity to discuss the emerging and competing view of the unconscious as nonpathological. Since Freud was the ultimate winner for Ellenberger and Freud had pathologized unconsciousness, this is not surprising. But it was hardly the whole history of exceptional mental states.[14]

To begin with, the French and Germans were not the first to use hypnosis to explore unconsciousness. Franz Mesmer, the Viennese physician, created modern hypnotism in the eighteenth century, and many subsequent pioneers of the psyche throughout the European continent, Britain, and the United States in the eighteenth and early nineteenth centuries experimented with hypnotism's precursors—mesmerism, "animal magnetism," and "sleep" as well—either for their healing effects or as indicators of unconsciousness. For instance, the physician Arnold Wienholt in early modern Germany used animal magnetism to heal nervousness, while the philosopher Heinrich Werner tried to construct a rational foundation upon which all psychic-like phenomena, from animal magnetism to somnambulism, could rest.[15] In France, A. M. J. de Chastenet de Puységur (Mesmer's heir) and his intellectual compatriot, J. P. F. Deleuze, a naturalist, repopularized animal magnetism in the early nineteenth century.[16] Even Abbé J. C. de Faria, the Indo-Portuguese philosopher (he was born in Goa) who became for a time a professor at the lycée in Marseille, experimented with early forms of hypnotism.[17] In Great Britain, John Elliotson, the English physician and professor of medicine, demonstrated magnetic healing techniques to his students at University College Hospital in London, while James Esdaile, the Scottish surgeon and employee of the East India Company who was working at a small hospital in Hooghly, India (about twenty-five miles north of Calcutta), used hypnotism as an anesthetic for amputations.[18] The physician James Braid, a fellow Scot, had demonstrated in the early 1850s that the power of hypnotism lay in suggestion, not in some mysterious "magnetic fluid" lurking in the ether.[19] And in the United States, La Roy Sunderland, the one-time revivalist-preacher and reformer, postulated his concept of "pathetizing," having found similarities between the states of religious ecstasy and animal magnetism.[20] While all these men pioneered the developments in hypnotism over two centuries, their work represents but a fraction of that performed.[21]

THE HIDDEN SELF

In the late summer of 1890, James published an informative essay called "The Hidden Self."[22] Written for the educated public and the initiated intellectual, it summarized the competing theories of unconsciousness. It also introduced a rich cornucopia of new vocabulary into the American psychological vernacular having to do with nonconscious mental life including "secondary consciousness," "secondary self," "secondary personality," "submerged self," "under self," "submerged consciousness," and "sub-conscious self." Classifying all such nonconscious phenomena as belonging to the "unclassified residuum," James argued that human beings possess an unconscious mental life that is every bit as significant as our conscious one but quickly noted that the scientific orthodoxy would object to such claims. "No part of the unclassified residuum has usually been treated with more contemptuous scientific disregard," he wrote, "than the mass of phenomena generally called *mystical*. Physiology will have nothing to do with them. Orthodox psychology turns its back upon them. Medicine sweeps them out." Against such positions, James argued the unclassified residuum had to be studied scientifically. "Repugnant as the mystical style of philosophizing may be . . . ," he continued, "there is no sort of doubt that it goes with a gift for meeting with certain kinds of phenomenal experience. The writer has been forced in the past few years to this admission; and he now believes that he who will pay attention to facts of the sort dear to mystics, while reflecting upon them in academic-scientific ways, will be in the best possible position to help philosophy."[23] In other words, James used "The Hidden Self" essay as an empirical tool to defend his tertium quid theorizing of the unconscious.

"The Hidden Self" addressed two broad but related issues: the research showing the existence of the unconscious and the therapeutic benefits such research could incur. James professed the latter was more important to psychology and more relevant to him personally since he longed for an effective treatment of his neurasthenia. As Ralph Barton Perry captured it, psychical research for James offered "the possibility of a more kindly treatment of suffering humanity." That is, if scientists could understand abnormal states, they might know better how to treat those individuals in clinical settings. Since psychical research was associated with a number of mind cures, it might offer the possibility of relief from his own mental suffering.[24] Still, James devoted the majority of the essay to explaining new research and theories. First, James reviewed Pierre Janet's influential *De l'Automatisme psychologique* in which Janet had argued for the existence of a "field of consciousness," especially the *idée fixe subconsciente*, a term that has been oversimplified to mean "obsession" but more accurately refers to the notion that ideas out of reach of conscious awareness have a natural tendency toward mental action. James rehearsed how the history of French experimental psychology had helped discover the existence of and delineate some of the nature of the unconscious. In particular, James focused on Janet's famous case study "Léonie," whom Janet had claimed manifested the idée fixe. James related to the reader how Janet had effectively used the method of hypnosis to discover and reach her alternate selves ("Léonie 1 knows only herself; Léonie 2 of herself and of Léonie 1; Léonie 3 knows of herself and of both the others") and emphasized how important hypnosis had become as an acceptable method of medical treatment and research tool. James identified Gurney, Binet, and Bernheim as having succeeded in "*tapping* the submerged consciousness." However, while Janet's work impressed James, he noted that Janet's data set was far too small to support his claim that alternative personalities exist only in abnormal subjects. By contrast, James noted similar effects had been discovered in persons who were neither epileptic nor hysteric, which suggested healthy individuals also manifested unconscious states. James thus concluded there existed "different personages into which one human being may be split."[25]

James invoked Gurney's research on hypnotic memory to support his view. Gurney was "the first to discover, by means of automatic writing, that the secondary self is awake," he wrote. In particular, Gurney's work showed that persons who have been hypnotized would perform actions when awake that were "suggested" to them while they were "under."[26] For his part, Gurney was much more impressed with the results in Nancy than in Paris. Like the others in the Sidgwick Group, Gurney was familiar with the French experimental psychologists. Their oeuvre, and its ramifications, first came to his attention through one of the Society for Psychical Research's more minor figures, Arthur Myers (Frederic's brother), a physician interested in the etiology of nervousness. In 1881, Arthur met with Charcot and toured his new wing at the Salpêtrière. After the SPR formed in 1882, he convinced his brother and Gurney to return with him to France to learn more at the Salpêtrière and Nancy hospitals.[27] Noting a few good French experiments, he told James, "I have made great friends with Richet, who is *excellent* in every respect.... They have some good hypnotic work going on,—much better (as far as I know) than anything that has been done in Germany.... [But] I don't think the Salpêtrière goings on entirely satisfactory. They don't allow enough for suggestion."[28]

In 1883–84, Gurney decided to follow his suspicion that the key to understanding hypnosis and altered mental states lay in suggestion. Over the next four years he devised a series of ingenious experiments that ultimately helped demonstrate the existence of secondary consciousness in healthy subjects. The first type, for which Gurney used a planchette and automatic writing, was designed to test for the existence of the hypnotic state as distinct from regular, waking consciousness. After the subjects were hypnotized, they were given a command to write upon waking. Upon being woken from the hypnotic state they were asked to verbalize the command, but they could not do so, not even for a substantial monetary reward. However, when given a planchette, which was kept out of sight on the other side of a screen through which only their hands were allowed to pass, they could write out the command without difficulty, not even knowing what they were writing! Such recollection demonstrated to Gurney's satisfaction that there exists something beyond consciousness. He called it "hypnotic memory."[29]

Gurney then gleefully revealed his results to James. "I have been extremely busy during the last few weeks with some hypnotic experiments." He had also been "writing a paper for 'Mind' on that subject," working hard with Frederic Myers and Frank Podmore on his upcoming book (*Phantasms of the Living*), and "examining some 'mesmeric' claims" with Henry and Eleanor Sidgwick.[30]

James's reply to Gurney appears lost, but his opinion regarding the latter's plan to publish these results can be gleaned from Gurney's next dispatch. James was concerned that Gurney might be rushing to judgment, writing, "I am very glad that you were interested by the hypnotic business. The results are really wonderfully uniform, in my experience, & I hope they will be repeated. . . . I ENTIRELY agree with what you say as to the need of *caution*." But while Gurney's approach was more cautious in "The Problems of Hypnotism," he did not heed James's advice to hold off on publishing the results so quickly.[31]

The next year Gurney and Myers published two more articles on these early results. This time they were more guarded. "We were too confident & sweeping in our tone in some of our magazine articles," Gurney admitted of their efforts. "I think our case is really strong enough to show that the subject ought to be earnestly prosecuted, & it is a great mistake to discount the result by the slightest exaggeration of its strength. I feel that every sentence written on these matters ought to *reek* with candour."[32] After four months of additional experiments with hypnotic subjects, he admitted the unconscious perplexed him: "I am puzzled about the unconscious self. I don[']t think, properly speaking, *he* is a *self*. He is more like a broken dispersed reflection; & yet he has a certain odd coherence, too. But I feel myself being philosophically turned inside out, with all this *unconscious psychosis*." Such remarks echoed the Salpêtrière psychologists' conclusions and suggested Gurney might have been mistaken after all.[33] Nonetheless, Gurney continued to experiment with hypnotic subjects up to the time of his death in 1888, with each set of tests confirming his results that multiple states of hypnotic memory exist. "The real interest of these differences [between the hypnotist and subject, and from subject to subject]," he noted, "is in the wider general fact to which they point—the delicate and far-reaching susceptibility of hypnotic 'subjects' to unconscious education." Although the idea to use automatic writing as a way to test for the nature of hypnotic states and what they revealed about the unconscious had come from Pierre Janet, who had used it to experiment on hysterical patients, Gurney's experiments showed that such states existed in individuals other than the mentally disturbed, a result indicating exceptional mental states could not be explained entirely by invoking insanity.[34]

Gurney's work on hypnotic memory impressed Myers. He placed Gurney's work on a par with the "*savants*" of the French schools as well as with the pioneering work of Elliotson, Esdaile, and Braid. Myers pointed out that between 1883 and 1888 Gurney had "devised and carried through . . . a complex series of experiments, surpassed by no other hypnotist in exactness . . . , with a definite view to the investigation of two great problems which lie on the borderland between physiology and psychology."[35] In 1883, when Myers first took up the issue, he believed unconscious cerebration explained Gurney's phenomenon, but his own experiments with hypnotism in subsequent years suggested the presence of a "secondary intelligence" or a "double-personality" that had nothing to do with brain separation. Carefully following the logical impetus of Gurney's work, Myers wrote several essays devoted to exploring how subjects could recall memories from previous hypnotized sessions when rehypnotized. There had to be some receptacle for these memories, he realized, but what had impressed Myers so much was not the existence of these states in hysterics but their reality in healthy individuals who had been able to write automatically.[36]

Myers's early articles in turn impressed James. He told George Croom Robertson at *Mind*, "It seems to me that Myers' papers on Automatic writing show a scientific intellect of very high order."[37] He singled out Myers's discussion of "double personality" in particular and noted how Myers invoked in his readers a growing sense of the existence of unconscious activity not yet captured by psychologists. James expressed these sentiments to Myers in a long letter in which he thanked him for copies of his articles from *Contemporary Review* and the *Proceedings* and confessed that Myers's arguments had filled him with "a lively admiration of your power of disentangling obscure things by the method of series, and of gradual approach. I hope to Heaven you may go on as successfully to the end. What you have written seems to me to cast a new light on those cases of mania in which the person seems double or transformed. But how to conceive of this 'unconscious' other fellow in us, I confess I don't yet know."[38] Although Myers's language in these early articles was still oriented toward pathology, the notion of hidden mental states existing in healthy individuals was brewing. For instance, Myers peppered one article with key phrases like "beneath the level of our consciousness," "super-conscious," and "sub-conscious," concluding that "mind acts on mind otherwise than by the recognized organs of sense."[39]

Gurney's and Myers's work, then, was a significant breakthrough because it suggested that a significantly large number of persons possessed degrees of unconsciousness. Indeed, it is fair to state that although the publication of Janet's early articles preceded Gurney's initial papers by just a few months, Gurney and Myers made original contributions to hypnotism and to the study of the unconscious and that Gurney developed it concurrently but independently from that of the French schools. "I know for a fact," Myers claimed, "that Edmund Gurney's experiments were thought out, and in great part performed, before he so much as heard [of Janet's results]."[40] In short, their work on hypnotism indicated the existence of unconsciousness not just in abnormal subjects, as Janet and others had demonstrated, but in normal ones as well.[41] Summarizing the various theories of unconsciousness in "The Hidden Self," James highlighted a host of hidden selves hovering in both abnormal and normal subjects: "[It has been] a very great step to have ascertained that the secondary self, or selves," he concluded, "*coexist* with the primary one" (emphasis added). This view indicates that by 1890 James had reached the position that there exists something in our minds akin to what we now call the unconscious.[42]

"CONSCIOUSNESS SPLIT-OFF IN TWO PARTS"

But it was not just others' theories of unconsciousness that led James to postulate the existence of an unconscious self. In addition to the French schools of pathology and Gurney's experiments with hypnotic memory, James's own study of the trance states in mental mediums during the late 1880s provided a wellspring for his tertium quid theory of unconsciousness. This is evident in *The Principles of Psychology*, especially in chapters 6, 8, 9, 10, and 27, where James's discussions of consciousness included his emergent views about unconsciousness. For instance, in the famous chapter 9, "The Stream of Thought," James claimed consciousness (or thought) is like a stream that is unified but flowing and continuous: "Consciousness, then, does not appear to itself chopped up in bits. Such words as 'chain' or 'train' do not describe it fitly as it presents itself in the first instance. It is nothing jointed; it flows. A 'river' and a 'stream' are the two metaphors by which it is most naturally described. *In talking of it hereafter, let us call it the stream of thought, of consciousness, or of subjective life*" (emphasis in the original).[43] Here James parted ways with the British associationists such as John Locke, Hume, and Mill who held that consciousness begins with sensations and maintained that it was constant, stable, and static and that taken together its parts constituted a whole mind. That is, they argued the bits and pieces of mental life (sensations, thoughts, perceptions, and emotions) *associated* themselves into a unified conscious. For James, though, the associationists had unintentionally developed a severe metaphysical hangover because they could not explain *how* these seemingly disconnected fragments unified into a coherent whole. In sharp contrast, James argued consciousness begins with thought that is dynamic, plastic, and ever-changing; he thus held a radically reconceived notion of consciousness. Elsewhere in the chapter, however, James advanced another view that was in tension with the first in which he claimed that consciousness could divide into two or more parts—a partition in the stream, as it were. This raises the question of how unified consciousness was in James's own model. "Although unity is the rule of each man's consciousness," James wrote, "in some individuals, at least, thoughts may split away from the others and form separate selves." The "some individuals" James had in mind were trance-mediums such as Mrs. Piper who manifested mental activity so powerful that their "consciousness split-off in two parts."[44]

The significance of this very different notion of consciousness is easy to miss. Since James presented his book as a comprehensive account of modern experimental psychology that addressed a set of topics, themes, and theories in a logical format, it initially appears to make sense to read *The Principles of Psychology* from cover to cover. However, James did not write the chapters chronologically but rather haphazardly and even chaotically.[45] Thus if one reads the above-mentioned chapters in the order James drafted them, then the impact of his psychical research on his second view of consciousness becomes quite apparent. When James began to conceive the *Principles* in 1878, he believed like most of his contemporaries that the mind could *not* be divided into two seemingly unrelated components. As a young instructor of physiological psychology, he did believe, however, that the brain could in extreme cases separate physically into two parts, a view Carpenter coined as "unconscious cerebration." Carpenter was a British physiologist who argued in his book *Principles of Mental Physiology* (1874) that all the phenomena associated with the concept of "mind," including the trance states of mental mediums as well as hypnotic states, could be explained by nerve tissue, that is, that physical forces were the antecedents of all consciousness. Since strict physiological psychologists like Carpenter equated mental states with brain states, unconscious cerebration amounted to putting some mental states out of communication with others. In other words, it allowed for consciousness (considered as brain states) to separate into two distinct parts, which became "unconscious," that is, cerebrally unaware of each other. Although James appreciated the pedagogic function of Carpenter's book, he found nothing new in its central claims, noting that while anatomists and physiologists could describe basic nerve reflexes in simple organisms, they could not *explain* all brain states or consciousness.[46]

James composed chapter 9 from articles he had published in 1879 and 1884 in which he explained how consciousness could split off in two parts in other instances as well.[47] In the section "Five Characters in Thought," James cited three cases of trance mediumship and possession, each manifesting the existence of a secondary self. Although the appearance and disappearance of each self was "relatively abrupt" and the duration of the state quite brief (lasting from a few minutes to a few hours), James claimed such states were significant nonetheless. However rudimentary these other selves appeared to be, "the buried feelings and thoughts proved now to exist in hysterical anesthetics, [and] in recipients of post-hypnotic suggestion . . . , themselves . . . parts of *secondary personal selves*," James found to exist in trance subjects as well. "These selves," he explained, "are for the most part very stupid and contracted, and are cut off at ordinary times from communications with the regular and normal self of the individual; but still they form conscious unities, have continuous memories, speak, write, invent distinct names for themselves, or adopt names that are suggested."[48] On occasion, James noted mental mediums like Mrs. Piper were able to induce their own "spontaneous secondary self." He found this phenomenon crude but valid, exclaiming, "I am inclined to think that these (often deplorably unintelligent) rudimentary utterances are the work of an inferior fraction of the subject's own natural mind, set free from control by the rest, and working after a set pattern fixed by the prejudices of the social environment."[49]

But the connections did not end there. James realized pathological patients and trance mediums who manifested a secondary consciousness shared a set of behaviors in common with religious ecstatics, hallucinators, and visionaries as well as with practitioners of witchcraft, magic, and demonology. "In a spiritualistic community we get optimistic messages, whilst in an ignorant Catholic village the secondary personage calls itself by the name of a demon, and proffers blasphemies and obscenities, instead of telling us how happy it is in the summer-land," he observed. Nonetheless, each type manifested a secondary self and taken together indicated there existed a significant population substantially larger and more diverse than Janet's hysterics, leading James to wonder how widespread the phenomenon was. "How far this splitting up of the mind into separate consciousness may exist *in each one of us*," James pondered, "is a problem" (emphasis added). Even though the evidence to date had failed to yield useful answers, he did not dismiss the possibility. Rather, James suggested psychical research stood at the forefront of the frontier called the unconscious: "All these facts taken together form unquestionably the beginning of an inquiry which is destined to throw a new light into the very abysses of our nature."[50] James wrote a nearly identical line in his psychical research essay "Notes on Automatic Writing," which was published one year *before* this chapter was drafted and highlights one of the many instances of cross-fertilization between James's psychical research and scientific psychology.[51] It also suggests that James's psychical research confirmed his view that unconsciousness could be found in healthy human beings, not just the insane.

Chapters 6 and 8 in the *Principles* reveal another instance of James's evolving view of unconsciousness. In "The Mind-Stuff Theory," which was mostly drafted by December 1886,[52] James rehearsed ten common arguments in favor of unconscious cerebration, which he called "unconscious thought," and rejected each one. Here James did not dismiss the possibility of unconscious *mental* states in abnormal minds, only that a physical division in the brain caused them.[53] But in "The Relations of Minds to Other Things," which was not drafted until somewhere between late 1889 and early 1890,[54] James employed numerous terms to describe this division. To indicate consciousness, he used terms like "primary or normal consciousness," "upper self," and "normal self," while for unconsciousness, he wrote of the "secondary consciousness," "submerged consciousness," "sub-consciousness," "subconscious self," "secondary self" and "secondary personage." Of consciousness and unconsciousness, then, he called them the "two selves."[55] Sometime between the writing of chapters 6 and 8, then, James had come to realize consciousness could indeed split off into two or more parts. Similarly, in a section entitled "'Unconsciousness' in Hysterics," James discussed hypnotic and trance states and cited Janet's and Binet's work that demonstrated under hypnosis and anesthesia there exists a *"form of secondary consciousness* entirely cut off from the primary or normal one, but susceptible to being *tapped* and made to testify to its existence in various odd ways."[56] Since Janet and Binet were committed to the view that secondary consciousness could be found only in hysterics, James acquiesced in calling it an "abnormal self." For Janet, secondary consciousness "is only possible where there is abnormal weakness, and consequently a defect of unifying or coordinating power. An hysterical women abandons part of her consciousness because she is too weak nervously to hold it together. The abandoned part meanwhile may solidify into a secondary or sub-conscious self."[57] Of the psychopathology at the Salpêtrière, James concluded, "It must be admitted, therefore, that *in certain persons*, at least, *the total possible consciousness may be split into parts which co-exist but mutually ignore each other.*"[58]

Three years before drafting chapter 8 of the *Principles*, James had begun exploring this issue in his psychical research essay "Report of the Committee on Mediumistic Phenomena" (1886). While he did not use language like "split-off from consciousness" or "double consciousness," James maintained that Mrs. Piper's trance state differed significantly from both her hypnotic and waking ones, a fact suggesting the likelihood of hidden mental life differing from regular moments of waking consciousness.[59] James repeated this rather startling discovery in "The Relations of Minds to Other Things" in the *Principles*, noting that "a young woman who had been writing automatically" had become his and Richard Hodgson's best subject.[60] In a clear reference to Mrs. Piper, he added, "I myself am persuaded by abundant acquaintance with the trances of one medium that the 'control' may be altogether different from any *possible* waking self of the person.... I record my bare opinion here unsupported by the evidence, not of course, in order to convert anyone to my view, but because I am persuaded that a serious study of these trance-phenomena is one of the greatest needs of psychology."[61] For James, then, Mrs. Piper demonstrated that such alternate selves exist in nonhysterical subjects. Since the summary of that chapter's material was most likely extracted from his views in the article, his conclusion represented another instance of successful cross-fertilization between James's psychical research and his scientific psychology. As he had put it in "The Hidden Self," "There are trances which obey another type other than Janet's abnormal one," adding, "I know a non-hysterical woman who, in her trances, knows facts which altogether transcend her *possible* normal consciousness, facts about the lives of people whom she never saw or heard of before." Recognizing the controversial quality of this position, he explained, "I am well aware of all the liabilities to which this statement exposes me, and I make it deliberately, having practically no doubt whatever of its truth. My *own* impression is that the trance-condition is an immensely complex and fluctuating thing, into the understanding of which we have hardly begun to penetrate."[62]

Chapter 10 of the *Principles* further exemplifies James's emergent view of unconsciousness. In the section "Consciousness of Self," James argued the evidence indicating consciousness is like a stream extended to other selves. Noting the intricacy of the phenomena and the early state of the research, James identified several phases of mediumship in automatic writing. Between the lowest and highest levels "comes writing unconsciously," James found, "even whilst engaged in reading or talk. Inspirational speaking, playing on musical instruments, etc., also belong to the relatively lower phases of possession, in which the normal self is not excluded from conscious participation in the performance, though their initiative seems to come from elsewhere."[63] Realizing it would be "rash" to overstate the frequency of consciousness splitting off into two parts, he admitted such phenomena were not unique or even as rare as he initially supposed: "In view of the phenomena of thought-transference, mesmeric influence and spirit-control, which are being alleged nowadays on better authority than ever before . . . , the definitively closed nature of our personal consciousness is probably an average statistical resultant of many conditions."[64] Clearly James did not think trance states were abnormal or that pathology could explain Spiritualism. In fact, he concluded that cases like Mrs. Piper's demonstrated that consciousness could split off in two parts in normal, sane individuals.

> The subject during the secondary consciousness speaks, writes, or acts as if animated by a foreign person, and often names this foreign person and gives his history. In old times the foreign "control" was usually a demon . . . , [but in modern times] mediumistic possession in all its grades seems to form a perfectly natural special type of alternate personality, and susceptibility to it in some form is by no means an uncommon gift, in persons who have no other obvious nervous anomaly. . . . Whether all sub-conscious selves are peculiarly susceptible to a certain stratum of the *Zeitgeist*, and get their inspiration from it, I know not, but this is obviously the case with the secondary selves which become "developed" in spiritualist circles.[65]

James's realization did not lead him to conclude that unconsciousness was disconnected from consciousness, but it did reveal he believed there was more to consciousness beyond the margin than mere abnormality. Trace states, then, were clearly of the highest importance to James's evolving view of the unconscious.

Finally, evidence from chapter 27 of *The Principles of Psychology* indicates research other than that of the French schools influenced James's view of unconsciousness. In the section called "Hypnotism," James described how not only the French pathologists but also the British psychical researchers had discovered that hypnosis revealed the existence of unconscious activity. Throughout the chapter James discussed the history and contemporary knowledge of hypnotism, especially the work of Janet and Gurney. First, James covered the various techniques for hypnotizing subjects. Next, he reviewed and evaluated the three common explanations of the hypnotic state: animal magnetism, neurosis, and suggestion. He indicated how the first had been discarded in the absence of any evidence, while the second was limited because it reduced hypnotic states to pathology. James pointed out that suggestion had become an all-encompassing phrase invoked to explain hypnotic phenomena when in fact there were degrees and limitations to it.[66] Since the chapter on hypnotism occurred second-to-last in the *Principles*, it is often overlooked or merely assumed less relevant than others. However, as with chapters 6, 8, and 9, James wrote this one several years before finishing the *Principles* in 1890, completing various drafts between the spring of 1887 and November 1888.[67] Indeed, even before James drafted this chapter, he had learned of the central role of hypnotism in pointing up exceptional mental states during the mid-1880s. Although he rehashed Janet's abnormal psychology in this chapter, James devoted the majority of his space to examining the different symptoms of the trance such as amnesia, suggestibility, effects on voluntary muscles, and hallucinations. He focused in particular on Gurney's new and revolutionary notion of "post-hypnotic memory." As James composed this chapter, a wider notion of unconsciousness was dawning on him. In short, when James began writing chapter 6 of the *Principles* in 1886, he did not believe in the unconscious in any form, but by 1889–90, after having composed chapters 8, 9, and 27, he accepted the unconscious to a degree, namely, that consciousness can split off in two parts in healthy and normal persons.

Mrs. Piper was not the only case that convinced James. Indeed, James actively investigated, tested, read up on, wrote letters about, or in some way passed intellectual judgment on numerous trance mediums into the new century. Some of James's other subjects were his students, family, friends, and relatives, while others were individuals Hodgson had located through newspaper advertisements. Since James used a single letter to conceal the subjects' identities and protect their privacy ("Mr. C.," "Miss D.," and "Mrs. S.," or even just "a lady" or "a gentleman"), their identities are unknown. Many of these subjects did not yield the type of data James had hoped for, but some did.[68] As he explained to his wife, Alice, once, he had gone to "and interview[ed] with an automatic writer—very good."[69]

William T. Smith, John N. Arnold, and C. H. Perkins were three of his best subjects whom he did identify. Smith was a healthy twenty-one-year-old Massachusetts Institute of Technology student. Upon falling into a trance, he would begin to write automatically (sometimes in Greek) with a planchette or an ordinary pencil, exhibiting some skill with both his right and left hands. James asked him questions about his day and what he was currently thinking. To test for the genuineness of Smith's trance state, when one hand would begin to write, James pricked it gently with a small pin, followed by the hand not writing. While the first one showed no reaction, the latter flinched, which suggested the possibility of two different sets of mental states at work in the same psyche and thus some genuineness of the trance. James later confirmed this by pricking Mrs. Thompson (Myers's medium), informing a colleague that although the result "tallies with the demeanor of [Théodore] Flournoy's case" for additional confirmation, "our conception of 'trance' is anything but definite, and I know of no test of genuineness."[70] Despite such positive affirmation, James's view that prick tests were inconclusive, that no test could be, and that the investigator was thereby forced to rely on impression seemed to be guided by his tertium quid.

Additional sittings with Smith and other automatic writing mediums verify his third way. Beginning in January 1888, James and Hodgson conducted multiple sessions with Smith. One of these occurred in conjunction with James's brother Robertson in Concord, Massachusetts, where both Smith and Robertson then resided. To Alice, he explained he was to spend an evening of "planchette writing" with the two men. Two days later, he described that sitting to Alice, writing, "I am just in from Concord where I passed the night, at Bob's house. The planchette exp'ts were at a pretty new house on a hill top with an exquisite moonlight view over a frozen river & fields, but young Smith did nothing more wonderful than I had seen him do before at Hodgson's [apartment in Boston]." Nonetheless, these experiments suggested to James that Smith might possess telepathic and clairvoyant abilities.[71] Similarly, in late October of 1889 James tested John N. Arnold, a clerk from Providence, Rhode Island. In his trance state, Arnold used a pencil to write automatically on an oversized foolscap, on which he scribbled copious lines, squiggles, and words, including the name "Lydia" (his sister-in-law's name). He also wrote the sentence "I[']ve met you before, Robert Hare," as well as the word "Onset." Two summers prior to this session, Arnold had met the son of Judge Hare, whose first name may have been Robert. This experiment seemed very inconclusive to James, but there were many others that may have yielded much more significant results. Upon going through James's papers after he died, his son Henry III wrote a note saying, "This [the foolscap] is an example of many, many documents & papers that have been destroyed. W. J. really did a great deal of work on such things at one time."[72]

Finally, James tested C. H. Perkins in 1903–4. Perkins was a fifty-year-old married man, respected in his community. He had made his living as a bookkeeper until he injured his back in an elevator accident in 1901. During his recovery, Perkins noticed nervousness and twitching in his hands, which led to discovering his ability for automatic drawing and writing. After meeting through a hypnotist they both knew, Perkins described to James how he discovered his ability, the type of drawings he made—mostly primitive figures with sticklike or potato-shaped bodies with ancient looking faces—and the progress he made over three months. He also noted how his "power" had overtaken him, that he was not consciously moving or directing his hand, and how the process frequently caused him to fall into a hypnotic-like sleep.[73] After James read over his case, he forwarded it with some letters to James Cattell for publication. "I don't know whether this kind of case is in the line of the Pop[ular] Sci[ence Monthly]," he wondered, but "it is a rather odd one from the monotony and idiosyncrasy of the work done. The writer . . . wrote it out exclusively at my suggestion, and I have patched together in the first part of the narrative data communicated to me in successive letters. Send the whole business back to me if you can't use it, and, if you can, send back the drawings which you don't choose to print."[74] Cattell responded that he would publish the case and asked of Perkins's expectation for remuneration, to which James replied, "I never thought of hinting at any special payment for him," indicating that while he took psychical research seriously, he treated it equally with his other endeavors. "Pay whatever usual price the magazine would pay for that much of a contribution."[75]

James learned several important details from investigating automatic writing and drawing mediums. First, the writer tended to become drowsy and drift into a form of sleep similar to a trance state. Second, the writing arm showed involuntary spasms at regular intervals before the writing began. Third, it also usually became anesthetic during a session (the arm was immune to gentle pinpricking). Fourth, the execution of the writing manifested what James called *"freakiness,"* meaning mirror-script, spelling backwards, writing the last letter of each word first, writing from right to left, bottom to top, or from the bottom right-hand corner of the page to the top left-hand corner, and so forth. Finally, James noticed that two persons could often successfully write (with a planchette) while neither individual could do so alone.[76]

James offered a new and somewhat controversial explanation for these varied phenomena, but not without first noting in his usual cautious manner that these cases had limitations. For example, he suggested that while Smith might have demonstrated thought-transference or clairvoyance, the usual problems developed to prevent James from verifying them to his satisfaction: there existed too little data, some data was skewed, some instances involved likely coincidence or even fraud, and some cases lacked verbatim stenographic reports. Still, these cases indicated to James that there must be hidden mental activity occurring in the human psyche—more of a "something," as he called it (states, entities, action, processes)—than that reserved for regular waking moments of consciousness. In fact, he concluded that these cases showed consciousness can divide, writing, "What we have [is] the consciousness of a subject split into two parts." The one part, exemplified by the writing hand, which he called the "automatic consciousness," seemed to operate through suggestion, while the other nonwriting hand, which he dubbed the "mouth-consciousness," did not. Both were ignorant of the other during the same activity when both consciousnesses were "in communication with the ear," that is, subject to audio stimulation.[77] Moreover, James noticed there was a "foreignness in the personality," by which he meant each of the two split-off parts possessed different behavioral attributes. While the "lower" consciousness seemed less responsive to outside stimuli, the "upper consciousness seems to cooperate in these cases." James posited that the "lower form" corresponded with demonic possession, while the "higher one" correlated with spiritual communication, which he supposed might come from the "summer-land."[78] That James used the unfortunate terms "lower" and "higher" indicates the strong influence that rigid Victorian dichotomies still had on his epistemological framework by the late nineteenth century. That he also correlated the "upper" with "good" and the "lower" with "evil" further indicates the presence of puritanical moralizing lingering in his thought. Still, suggesting demonic possession posed a danger to the health of the human psyche while simultaneously maintaining spirit-communication was enlightening even though it indicated James was not just studying these psychic phenomena but also passing ethical judgment upon them as his father had before.

Certainly he expressed more sympathy with the latter than the former. This is evidenced by the fact that James sometimes believed consciousness split off in two parts amounted to nothing more than pathology, a "dissociation of the consciousness into mutually exclusive parts," as he put it.[79] Nonetheless, James's experiments with automatic writers were highly significant because they opened up his thinking about the unconscious. Consciousness splitting "is evidently a phenomenon destined," he claimed, "to cast a light into the abysses of Psychology." Still, he noted cautiously, "the whole subject is at present a perfect puzzle on the theoretic side."[80]

By 1904, James had spent two decades studying automatic writing and had conducted enough experiments to be able to classify the phenomena into two types. The first kind exhibited muscle movement without deliberate intention or awareness, while the second was a form of "subconscious action of intelligence."[81] Although there were some problems with the research, James argued consistency was required, not just for one subject but between different subjects in which repeatability and verifiability were demonstrated. "The great desideratum is to get cases which can be examined continuously," he wrote. Still, for James, these cases met enough of his empiricist demands that he believed he could offer a valid if provisional conclusion, namely, that the "boundaries of individuality" were fluid.[82] James first developed this view in his psychical research essays from the mid-1880s, elaborated it in key chapters in *The Principles of Psychology* during the late 1880s, and expanded it in additional psychical research essays thereafter. From studying automatic writing, then, James discovered some surprising feats. It was, he stated, "unquestionably a field from which a rich harvest of instruction may be hoped."[83]

THE SUBLIMINAL SELF

James's emerging ontology of consciousness revealed the pressing need for a complex and dynamic model of the human psyche. In 1892, just two years after the publication of the *Principles* and "A Record of Observations of Certain Phenomena of Trance," James began to develop it. In "What Psychical Research Has Accomplished," James continued to explore the nature of Mrs. Piper's abilities and argued that trance states in mental mediums demonstrated the existence of "extra-consciousness," a phrase he had first used in the *Principles*. As he proceeded through the essay, he widened that notion to stipulate that *all* mental life belonged to the "strata of consciousness." He also argued for the "simultaneous existence of two *different* strata of consciousness, ignorant of each other, in the same person" (emphasis added).

Significantly, James invented or applied several new theoretical terms to delineate these strata, including "below the threshold," "above the threshold," "subconscious mental operations," and, most famously, "beyond the margin." Most crucially, James depicted the unconscious as a noun rather than as an adjective, that is, as an entity rather than a series of descriptive mental states.[84] As such, any new theory would have to move beyond the bifurcated upstairs-downstairs model of the conscious and unconscious that he had presented in the *Principles* and capture both regular waking states and the entire panoply of hidden mental life. The new model to emerge from "consciousness split-off in two parts" was that of the "subliminal self." As James put it, "We all have potentially a 'subliminal self,' which may make at any time irruption into our ordinary lives. In its lowest phases it is only the depository of our forgotten memories; in its highest, we don't know what it is at all. . . . Whatever it is, it is subconscious."[85] This statement reveals that James was moving beyond a theory of individual unconsciousness but had not embraced a universal one. Since he developed it through the study of trance states, it is fair to claim the "subliminal self" theory emerged more from American and British psychical research than from German physiology or French pathology.

James was not the first psychical researcher to advance a new theory of mind. Frederic Myers used the phrase "beneath the level of our consciousness" as early as 1884 and in a series of essays written between 1892 and 1895 when he developed his theory of the subliminal self.[86] These early articles became the theoretical basis for his most important book, *Human Personality and Its Survival of Bodily Death*, a seven-hundred-page work in two volumes published posthumously in 1903.[87] It examined psychical research topics such as degeneration of personality, genius, sleep, hypnotism, sensory automatism, phantasms of the dead, motor automatism, trance, possession, and ecstasy to advance a theory of the entire human psyche. The grand theme guiding Myers's life was whether or not mankind has an immortal soul—does his "personality," as he called it, survive bodily death?—and the purpose of *Human Personality* was to advance a thoroughly and carefully investigated answer to this question. Psychical research constituted Myers's means while psychic phenomena occurring in Spiritualist mediums made up his subject matter. Ultimately, Myers sought to reconcile "Science" and "Religion" by using modern scientific methods to confirm theological speculations regarding the immortality of the soul. It was a project many intellectuals, not just psychical researchers, would attempt during the half century stretching from the publication of Charles Darwin's *On the Origin of Species* in 1859 to the onset of World War I in 1914.[88]

Myers stipulated that the first step toward developing a theory of personality was to acknowledge that psychical research had now demonstrated beyond a reasonable doubt the existence of hidden mental states in healthy human psyches. "Each of us is in reality an abiding psychical entity far more extensive than he knows—an individuality which can never express itself completely through any corporeal manifestation. The Self manifests itself through the organism; but there is always some part of the Self unmanifested; and always ... some power of organic expression in abeyance or in reserve."[89] This much was accepted by French pathologists and to a degree by German physiologists, as well as by James, who was so impressed with this passage that he quoted it in "What Psychical Research Has Accomplished."[90] Myers, however, soon discovered that this "reserve" was neither abnormal nor a function of a divided brain but rather a function of healthy minds. James knew this much as well. Flattering Myers, he wrote that he was "delighted to see your proof on Sensory automatism [in the *Proceedings*]."[91]

Myers's positions beyond this first one, though, were solely his own. In a second and more radical step, Myers argued that regular moments of consciousness constituted but a *mere fraction* of all mental life.

> All this psychical action, I hold is conscious; all is included in an actual or potential memory below the threshold of our habitual consciousness. For all which lies below that threshold *subliminal* seems the fittest word. "Unconscious," or even "subconscious," would be directly misleading; and to speak ... of the *secondary* self may give the impression either that there cannot be more selves than two, or that the *supraliminal* self, the self above the threshold,—the *empirical* self, the self of common experience—is in some way superior to other possible selves.... I hold ... that this subliminal consciousness and subliminal memory may embrace a far wider range both of physiological and of psychical activity than is open to our supraliminal consciousness, [and] to our supraliminal memory. The spectrum of consciousness, if I may so call it, is the subliminal self indefinitely extended at both ends.[92]

For Myers, then, the "Self" should be conceived along a continuous horizontal spectrum, not as an upstairs-downstairs house, with its implied hierarchy of primary and secondary status, as if unconsciousness were somehow inferior to consciousness. Instead, Myers offered a new model that stipulated a vast continuum spreading democratically along an east-west axis to capture all mental life—physiological, psychical, and spiritual. Thus, for Myers, the regular "Conscious Self" constituted but one "part" of our mind, whereas there existed a whole other realm of mental activity that psychical researchers were just beginning to understand.

Like many social scientists during the late nineteenth century, Myers turned to metaphors from the natural sciences to explain his psychological theory. Unknown and unobservable phenomena could be illuminated by invoking the known and observable kind, even if Myers did not understand that this act changed one's conception of both.[93] He was particularly fond of invoking the color spectrum of light, likening the mind to the entire band of color, some of which, he reminded his readers, is visible to the naked eye, some of which is not. Myers compared the conscious self to the visible part of the solar spectrum and the subliminal "parts" to the red and violet ends, that is, those not directly observable but known to exist.[94] But it was James who best captured Myers's spectrum: "The ordinary consciousness Mr. Myers likens to the visible part of the solar spectrum; the total consciousness is like that spectrum prolonged by the inclusion of the ultra-red and ultra-violet rays. In the psychic spectrum the 'ultra' parts may embrace a far wider range, both of physiological and of psychical activity, than is open to our ordinary consciousness and memory. At the lower end we have the *physiological* extension, mind-cures, 'stigmatization' of ecstatics, etc.; in the upper, the hyper-normal cognitions of the medium-trance."[95] James explained that for Myers a person might have any number of varied experiences in any of these states across the spectrum. As James understood the theory, ordinary conscious experiences were like those of the visible parts of the solar spectrum, while "beyond the margin" experiences were like those of the nonvisible parts. They existed, but they were difficult to access. To do so, one had to probe for them. Hypnotism was one method, automatic writing another. Since mental mediums were effective at both, they were useful subjects for exploring the nature of the subliminal self.

Myers derived his argument for the existence of these unobservable portions of the spectrum of the Self from two sources: British psychical research and French experimental psychology. He cited the data gathered from twenty years of work by the SPR (mostly) on hypnotism, particularly that of Gurney (and himself and Podmore) as advanced in *Phantasms of the Living* (1886), which he believed had demonstrated the truth of telepathy, but also in subsequent work with Spiritualist mediums such as William Stainton Moses, Daniel Dunglas Home, and Mrs. Piper. While Myers devoted a fair amount of space in *Human Personality* to discussing and expounding upon the work of French experimental psychology, he realized, as James had, that theirs was but a step in a much longer staircase toward a more robust theory of mind. Throughout the book Myers referred frequently to Mrs. Piper, devoting a section to her in chapter 9 called "Trance, Possession, and Ecstasy."[96] Essentially it recounted some basic background information about her and her trances, including three of her five stages, as well as James's and Hodgson's work with her over the years. Indeed, Myers provided one of the best analyses of her that exists in the annals of psychical research:

> She presents an instance of automatism of the extreme type where the "possession" is not merely local or partial, but affects, so to say, the whole psychical area,—where the subliminal self is for a time completely displaced, and the whole personality appears to suffer intermittent change. In other words, she passes into a trance, during which her organs of speech or writing are "controlled" by other personalities than the normal waking one. Occasionally, either just before or just after the trance, the subliminal self appears to take some control of the organism for a brief interval; but with this exception the personalities that speak or write during her trance claim to be discarnate.[97]

For Myers, then, trance states indicated the existence and even priority of subliminal mental life.

Myers found the subliminal consciousness particularly fascinating because that portion of the spectrum seemed to contain a rich and significant amount of mental activity, including, but not limited to, trance states, hypnotic states, and those related to "sleep" (natural or somnambulistic). Myers stipulated the subliminal consciousness communicated with the regular conscious self through what he called "subliminal uprushes." These could emerge in any number of forms, including sensory or auditory hallucinations ("automatisms"), and be expressed in writing or speech ("automatic writing" for a medium of the possessed agent, verbal patterns for the hypnotized). Myers postulated the subliminal self stored memories, activated dreams, and was the wellspring of the imagination.[98] Subliminal consciousness for Myers was close to but not the same thing as the sub- or unconscious. As such, he was careful to avoid using these words because of their association with pathology and unconscious cerebration. However, while Myers did not conceive of the mind as a thing comprising two parts, at times he succumbed to such dichotomies, especially in stipulating a realm "above" and "below" a threshold to regular consciousness in which further realms of mental activity heretofore not understood by science lay. The upper realm he called the "supraliminal" ("above the threshold") and the lower one the "subliminal" ("below the threshold"). He argued the two taken together—supra- and subliminal consciousness—constituted a complete "Self" or "Personality." Still, for Myers, mind was much more dynamic than psychology or philosophy had yet discovered.[99]

Subliminal consciousness, then, occupied a very rich if crowded segment of the mental spectrum. Since so much key information and various abilities of the human personality resided there, Myers argued, it must constitute a central feature of the mind, perhaps even be its command center. Given that, it seemed that subliminal consciousness might hold more to understanding the self than regular waking consciousness. This conclusion amounted to a very heterodox if not heretical theory of mind, at least from the point of view of British empiricism (ironically, one of the traditions Myers relied on), since it turned on its conceptual head the ontological status of consciousness and unconsciousness. In one fell swoop Myers abandoned notions like "unconscious cerebration," "pathological selves," "consciousness split-off in two parts," "double personality," and even "subconscious" and "unconscious" and in their place substituted not just a second set of states or a second entity to be contrasted with regular consciousness, as all the attempts to map the human psyche had done prior to Myers's theory, but *an entirely new model of the human self*. As Myers put it, "'The Subliminal Self' is a name for an aggregate of potential personalities, with imperfectly known capacities of perception and action, but none of them identical with the assumed individuality beneath them or entitled to share in any of kind of 'imperturbability, indisceptability, incorruptibility,' which the philosopher may ascribe to an incorporeal soul."[100] "Personality" or "Self" thus became the dominant notion for Myers; it was not only broad enough to capture consciousness, subconsciousness, and unconsciousness and all of their derivatives but also elastic enough to allow for additional mental furniture. On his way to trying to prove immortality in *Human Personality*, then, Myers advanced an original and powerful theory of mind.

Although Myers developed his theory of the subliminal self more extensively than did James, it was actually a joint invention. After all, the two men had been corresponding and had read thoroughly each other's work for seven years by that point. Myers's preoccupation with unraveling the complex nature of the human psyche indicates his debt to James.

> I suggest, then, that the stream of consciousness in which we habitually live is not the only consciousness which exists in connection

with our organism. Our habitual or empirical consciousness may consist of a mere selection from a multitude of thoughts and sensations, of which some at least are equally conscious with those that we empirically know. I accord no primacy to my ordinary waking self. . . . It is perfectly possible that other thoughts, feelings, and memories, wither isolated or in continuous connections, may now be actively conscious . . . "within me." . . . I may assume these various personalities under one single consciousness, in which ultimate and complete consciousness the empirical consciousness[,] which at this moment directs my hand[,] may be *only one element out of many*.[101] (emphasis added)

For Myers, then, James's stream of consciousness opened the door to the great reservoir of human personality. By turn, Myers's theory impressed James so much that he claimed the challenge of determining the nature of the subliminal consciousness would be known henceforth as the *"problem of Myers."*[102]

In reality, several psychical researchers had contributed to the "problem of Myers." Myers dedicated *Human Personality* to Gurney and Sidgwick because it built on their work, while Hodgson edited it for posthumous publication in 1901. And Myers stated that central members of the Sidgwick Group had made his work possible.[103] It seems he meant James since *The Principles of Psychology* and his essays in psychical research permeate *Human Personality*.[104] Nowhere was this more apparent than in Myers's reliance on metaphors, such as his appeal to flowing water to describe subliminal consciousness just as James had done to depict ordinary consciousness. "There seem to be subliminal tendencies sitting steadily in certain obscure directions," Myers wrote, "bearing as little relation to the individual characteristics of the person to the deep of whose being we have somehow penetrated as profound ocean-currents bear to waves and winds on the surface of the sea."[105] Myers also deferred to James's views on eight occasions throughout *Human Personality*.[106] In one he cited a passage from the *Principles*: "One curious thing about trance utterances is their general similarity in different individuals. . . . It seems exactly as if one author composed more than half of the trance messages, no matter by whom they are uttered. Whether all sub-conscious selves are peculiarly susceptible to a certain stratum of the *Zeitgeist*, and get their inspiration from it, I know not."[107] Such passages revolved around a mutually emergent understanding of the nature of the trance state and indicate a rich cross-fertilization of data.

Ever modest, James understood Myers had paved the way forward. For despite Myers's lack of formal training, James believed Myers's theory would shape the future of all psychology. "Myers'[s] great principle of research," James wrote admiringly and without hyperbole, "was that in order to understand any one species of fact we ought to have all the species of the same general class of fact before us.... Through him [Myers] *for the first time*, psychologists are in possession of their full material, and mental phenomena are set down in an adequate inventory" (emphasis added). Of course, James realized scientific research did not occur in a vacuum and that Myers's work had been supported by his research and that of others, especially Janet's and Gurney's experiments: "Without the simultaneous work on hypnotism and hysteria begun by others, he could not have pushed his own work so far. But he is so far the only generalizer of the problem and the only user of all the methods. These are so many ways of putting the Subliminal [Self] on tap." In fact, as James had discovered through his own research on Mrs. Piper's trance states, there existed numerous ways to access the subliminal self.[108]

James recognized the major merit of Myers's theory was its ability to unify the seemingly disparate psychic phenomena into one system. "One cannot help admiring," James wrote, "the great originality with which Myers wove such an extraordinarily detached and discontinuous series of phenomena together. Unconscious cerebration, dreams, hypnotism, hysteria, inspirations of genius, the willing-game, planchette, crystal-gazing, hallucinatory voices, apparitions of the dying, medium-trances, demonical possession, clairvoyance, thought-transference—even ghosts.... Yet Myers ... made a system of them."[109] To make a universal system out of psychic phenomena had been the central goal of the Sidgwick Group since the 1870s when Sidgwick, Myers, and Gurney had first begun investigating physical mediums and mesmeric healers. To incorporate that system into scientific psychology and to establish a new theory of mind warranted the gratitude Myers received from his colleagues. "Myers's resourceful intellect has certainly done a service to psychology," James wrote after Myers had passed away. "He will always be remembered in psychology as the pioneer who staked out a vast tract of mental wilderness and planted the flag of genuine science upon it."[110]

While James believed Myers had provided an impressive new theory of consciousness beyond the margin, he did not think it unassailable. In fact, of all the reviews of *Human Personality*, James's was one of the most critical, albeit in a typically Jamesian sort of way. That is, while James did not believe Myers had advanced sound and compelling arguments configuring the exact nature of the subliminal self, he did think Myers had succeeded at initiating a new terrain and a new vocabulary upon which to debate it. To James, the latter amounted to a substantial accomplishment, but the former demanded his critique despite his protestations otherwise.[111] The review focused on the essential features of Myers's theory, which he called a "vast synthesis, but a coherent one, not withstanding the vagueness of some of the terms that figure in it." James agreed Myers had demonstrated that subliminal consciousness was "an actuality" and that it was rightly contrasted with "ordinary consciousness." He likewise agreed Myers had shown psychic phenomena are in fact "natural kinds of phenomena which ought, just like other natural events, to be followed up by scientific curiosity." James pointed out that each of these accomplishments was new to psychology at the turn of the twentieth century and thus was to Myers's credit.[112] The real issue, then, was not whether such phenomena existed but how widespread they were. Neurologists and their ilk tended to see things such as trance mediums and double personalities as regressive qualities in human nature, or what James stipulated they would call "pathological freaks of idiosyncrasy." By contrast, Myers thought such phenomena were "evolutive," that is, "germs of something not yet evolved," to be found (potentially) throughout humanity. Myers believed that the widespread occurrence of such phenomena indicated the existence of the subliminal self and associated it with the "evolutive" rather than "dissolutive" elements of the human psyche. James noted this was less an argument proved than a position staked out, but he allowed Myers this much even as a "conservative critic" would be less lenient.[113]

James's main objection to *Human Personality* was with Myers's attempt to demonstrate the immortality of the soul, which James found highly problematic. After establishing the existence of subliminal consciousness and suggesting it typified the more evolutive elements of our nature, Myers associated it with not only supernormal phenomena (phantasms, trance states, and the like) but also supernatural entities such as spirits. Indeed, Myers maintained this world and the "world of spirits" were one and the same and that the totality of these spirits constituted what Myers called "The Absolute Soul of the World." The problem, however, was that these claims were stipulated, not argued for, and required from the reader several gigantic leaps of faith. Phrases like "The Absolute Soul of the World" litter *Human Personality* and exemplify Myers's penchant for theology. They also tended to draw the ire of Myers's foes, who attacked him for lacking formal scientific training, exhibiting a lyrical style of prose, and showing an "emotional interest in immortality." By contrast, James believed the tripartite accusation leveled against Myers was unjust and contended that if one read the work carefully, Myers's scientific ability was admirably demonstrated; the poetic style was distracting at times but beside the point.[114]

The conservative critics James had in mind were George Frederick Stout, a British philosopher who served as editor of *Mind* from 1892 onward, and William McDougall, a pathologist and author of *Outline of Abnormal Psychology* (1926). To defend against the notion of Myers's subliminal consciousness without resorting to the materialist notion of unconscious cerebration, Stout and McDougall had to support the spirit hypothesis in their reviews. On the hilarity of this point, James wrote to Hodgson, "Have you read Stout's review of Myers in the Hibbert Journal? & W[illiam] McDougall's in Mind? Both deny that he [Myers] has proved the existence of a subliminal [consciousness] except as an (exceptionally existing) receptacle of lapsed supraliminal memorys [*sic*]. It would give Myers a second immortality to read their declarations of preference for the spirit hypothesis. To have scientists fall back on spirits to defend themselves against Myers's subliminal [consciousness] is truly a delicious irony of fate!"[115] Andrew Lang, the Scots author whose passion for folklore brought him in contact with psychical research, was less amused. These critics "entirely confine themselves to his *theory*, which practically is neither here nor there," he complained to James. "His facts are the radium of human nature, so to speak, and these official persons do not look at them."[116] But Stout's and McDougall's critiques were not without merit. First, Myers's empirical evidence was too weak to argue that all humans possess a subliminal consciousness, and second, even if the data were decent, there was far too little of it to support Myers's heavy-handed generalization that the existence of subliminal consciousness proved immortality of the soul. In short, the critics claimed that Myers's data was bad and that his theory rested on a weak inductive argument.[117]

Although James would have liked to have been convinced by Myers's arguments, he found himself agreeing with both points, writing, "The types of cases he uses as stepping-stones are some of them, at present, either in quality or quantity, decidedly weak supports," and "He may extend the subliminal too far when he supposes that all of us possess it." But James was quick to note that the critics who pointed out the first objection failed to consider the widespread practice of mental mediumship and automatic writing. This suggested strongly the data pool was actually much larger than the critics had supposed. Certainly James thought so. His research with Mrs. Piper had convinced him of this point. In fact, James noted that while Myers mostly relied on the tools of hypnotism to point up the reality of veridical phantasms, possession, various elements of "sleep," and telekinesis, it was the data generated by trance mediums that Myers found the most compelling. That Myers died before he could assess the value of the total body of such evidence for spirit-return, James proclaimed, should not be held against him.[118]

In addition to the scientific and logical problems, there existed a conceptual one. James believed Myers's correlation of the subliminal self with the evolutive quality of human nature was confused. Referring to Myers's insistence that the subliminal contains both progressive *and* regressive elements, he queried, "Are there three zones of subliminal life, of which the inner most is *dissolutive*, the middle one *superior* (the zone of genius, telepathy, etc.), and the outer most *supreme* and receptive directly of the impact of the spirit-world? Or is the subliminal superior throughout when considered in itself?" That is, how could the existence of pathological secondary selves found in hysterics and epileptics be developmental? Indeed, how could any phenomenon be simultaneously dissolutive and evolutive? Since Myers had argued that subliminal consciousness accounted for *both* hypnotic states in hysterics (dissolutive) and trance states in mental mediums (evolutive), it appeared he had assigned far too much explanatory power to this idea. As James pointed out, the subliminal self could not be all this encompassing; there must be some kind of conceptual mistake.[119] Myers seemed either unaware of such murkiness or did not want to admit it, since in his view what psychic phenomena yielded was proof for the survival of the soul. For Spiritualists this was axiomatic, but for scientific psychologists it begged empirical proof. Of course Myers *had* tried to show in *Human Personality* that the principles of modern science had grounded this position, and James would have liked to believe that, but he recognized Myers had fallen several steps short. Since Myers already believed in human immortality, scientific investigation was not actually proving it but merely affirming it. That is, Myers's theory was revelation, not innovation, or in less charitable terms theology masquerading as science. Despite this and other shortcomings, James concluded that *Human Personality* constituted a "worthy monument to his memory" and that "the subliminal region, as Myers conceived it, will remain a *vera causa* in psychology."[120]

Upon completing his review, James confided to F. C. S. Schiller that the experience had raised his opinion of Myers but not of the system itself: "The piles driven into the quicksand are too few for such a structure." On the other hand, he found the book "essential as a preliminary attempt at methodizing." James also continued to believe that *Human Personality* would "doubtless keep a very honourable place in history."[121] Schiller, who also wrote a review, agreed with James's mixed assessment. He found "plenty of weak spots" and intensely "dislike[d] his rhetoric" because it failed to somehow "ring true," but "the bigness & coherence of the idea" for systematizing all mental life as a personality "impressed" him.[122] Schiller and James, then, agreed that Myers's book had made an original and significant contribution to theories of the unconscious, even if it had not been entirely convincing.

Théodore Flournoy, who was working out his own theory of unconsciousness, also wrote a review of *Human Personality*. It echoed James's and Schiller's mixed conclusion, even if Flournoy (according to James) provided a more sympathetic defense of the system.[123] Attempting a rebalance indicative of his tertium quid approach, James confessed to Flournoy, "The fact is such a book need not be *criticized* at all at present. It is obviously too soon for it to be either refuted or established by mere criticism. It is a hypothetical construction of genius which must be kept hanging up, as it were, for new observations to be referred to. As the years accumulate these in a more favorable or in a more unfavorable sense, it will tend to stant [sic] or fall."[124] Reassuring himself, the next day he wrote Schiller nearly identical lines.[125] Still, he could not fully endorse Myers. "Reading the volumes has given me a higher opinion than ever of Myers's constructive gifts," he told Flournoy, "but on the whole a lower opinion of the objective solidity of the system. So many of the facts which form the pillars are still dubious."[126] And yet, on several occasions, James predicted that *Human Personality* would be "epoch-making" and "count in history as the first decisive footmark made on a new pathway of science," a conclusion Oliver Lodge shared too.[127] He even went so far as to proclaim that "I seriously believe that the general problem of the subliminal, as Myers propounds it, promises to be one of the *great* problems, possible [sic] even the greatest problem, of psychology."[128] To a family friend he added, "Fifty or a hundred years hence, people will know better than now whether his instinct for truth was a sound one; and perhaps will then pat me on the back for backing him."[129] But James turned out to be dead wrong. Myers's theory was quickly forgotten and his book relegated to history's dustbin, while Freud's theory of unconsciousness in *The Interpretation of Dreams* (1899), and those of his intellectual descendants, dominated introspective psychology for the first half of the twentieth century.[130]

The foregoing suggests Myers might be considered a third way thinker. One recent Myers scholar, Emily Williams Kelly, makes this case. She maintains Myers (and Gurney) absorbed the tertium quid approach from John Stuart Mill, whose attempt to find moderate middles between two extremes in any given debate washed off on the Cambridge intellectuals during the 1860s. In particular, she argues Myers's subliminal self theory was designed to "resolve the apparent conflict between the old concept of mind as a unity [that is, Cartesianism] and the new concept of mind as a multiplicity [that is, British associationism], and affirm that both views are in fact correct, although incomplete." Kelly holds that once Myers's arcane vocabulary is worked out consistently—"*Individuality*, or *Self*," referred to "'the underlying psychological unity . . . existing beneath all our phenomenal manifestations,'" while "*personality*, or *self*," pointed up "those 'more external and transitory'" mental states "formed from 'elements of our being'"—Myers's views on the two levels of the human psyche can be properly understood. Myers, she concludes, found a "synthesis" of the two levels to offer a whole he called the "'perdurable unity'" of being, adding, "There may in fact be an underlying unity to human personality."[131]

There are two shortcomings to this interpretation that suggest an overly sympathetic reading of Myers. First, Myers's frequent interchanging of the terms "Individuality" and "Self" with "personality" and "self," respectively, suggests not a lamentable inconsistency that when properly untangled can be made to work, as Kelly maintains, but rather a profound confusion as to what Myers really meant. Just because he frequently claimed there existed a "perdurable unity" did not mean he could in any clear and consistent manner show how these four terms established its coherent reality. As James himself had indicated, the whole system did not add up at the end of the day. Second, and more problematic, is the undeniable fact that Myers's so-called perdurable unity was driven by his predetermined belief in the afterlife; he sought to find an all-encompassing theory of human personality precisely because of that belief. For this reason there is no feasible way to uncouple Myers's supernaturalism from his naturalism. Thus, while Myers had a theory of mind, it was unconducive to the empiricism and open-minded approach found in James's tertium quid. As such, it is difficult to make Myers unproblematically into a third way thinker, at least of a Jamesian sort.

Nonetheless, there is some textual evidence indicating James thought Myers was *trying* to establish a third way. One instance is a review of two books James wrote for the American Society of Psychical Research, Andrew Lang's *Cock Lane and Common-Sense* (1894), a broad historical account of all the various types of occult phenomena since the rise of ancient civilizations, which Lang argued were best explained by superstitious folklore that had been appealed to, reinforced, and copied over time by acts of fraud, and Carl du Prel's *Die Entdeckung der Seele durch die Geheimwissenshaften* (1894), which argued occult phenomena arose from part of our soul that, unlike our conscious intelligence, was not aware of it and that this part of our hidden soul (as well as our ego) was dependent on one Kantian Transcendental Subject not ultimately knowable by us. James found Lang's argument unconvincing because Lang failed to offer an alternative explanation for occult phenomena and du Prel's equally so because it took as a matter of faith the existence of occult phenomena without investigation. One was too skeptical while the other was too credulous. As such, James concluded, "Between Mr. Lang's facility in leaving things unsettled, and Baron du Prel's facility in concluding them, *it seems as if a better path might be found*. Might not the earnest temper of science be combined somewhere with du Prel's learning and the power of doubt of Lang? So far Mr. Myers's papers on the 'Subliminal Self' seem to have kept nearest to this ideal" (emphasis added).[132]

For his part, unencumbered by Myers's commitment to a belief in the afterlife, James had tried to steer a middle path between two sets of competing theories of the unconscious. On the one hand, although clearly influenced during the 1870s and 1880s by British materialists such as Maudsley, Bain, and Carpenter and by French pathologists such as Richet, Charcot, and Janet, both groups of which had made unconsciousness unique to individuals, James moved beyond these theories because of their tendency to reduce unconsciousness to either brain cerebration or abnormal selves indicative of hysterical and insane patients, respectively. With the publication of *The Principles of Psychology* in 1890 as well as several psychical research essays written between 1886 and 1904, James argued there were simply far too many kinds of hidden selves that split off from regular consciousness to be accounted for in these ways. On the other hand, James rejected the universal theories of unconsciousness represented by the German idealist philosophers such as Herder, von Hartmann, and Schopenhauer, who hypostatized the universal unconscious, and especially by Freud, all of which he found overly systematic and far too rigid to account for the idiosyncrasies of various human psyches. Instead, while never fully developing his own theory of unconsciousness, James preferred his interpretation of "the subliminal self" that he found existed in more than a few individuals—pathological and nonpathological alike—but was not yet prepared to argue for a universal theory of unconsciousness; exceptional mental states were exceptional for a reason. Myers, it seems, had gone too far. As James put it years later, "The name 'subliminal self' is a sort of blanket-title for a region for which there is no typographical survey, but through it as an intermediary the diesseits [this world] and jenseits [the hereafter] *may* be united in ways which at present we can't even guess."[133] In this way, James's psychical research on the trance states of mental mediums invoked his tertium quid, which, in turn, led him to advance a theory of consciousness beyond the margin.

Since several James scholars have reduced James's consciousness beyond the margin to abnormal psychology, they have missed this crucial development in his thought and thus failed to realize the key role that psychical research played in shaping James's theory of the unconscious. For instance, Ralph Barton Perry, while usually a reliable barometer, offered French pathology as the primary reason for James's interest in exceptional mental states. He contended James's medical training and his own personal experiences with depression "drew him in the direction of the French school of Charcot. . . . There was no sharp dividing line between psychopathology, so considered, and psychical research. They both belonged broadly to the field of abnormal mentality, and constituted a part of what James regarded as the domain of psychology." As such, Perry argued James's treatment of exceptional mental states in the *Principles* gave him "a place in the development of abnormal psychology and psychopathology."[134]

Gerald Myers reinforced this argument, writing, "James was drawn to the notion of the subconscious . . . because it fitted neatly with important events in his life, regenerative experiences in which a sudden, surprising resurgence of energy occurred in the midst of a pathological apathy." In particular, Myers noted that "James was impressed by the evidence from pathology for the existence of unconscious states; he cited the works of Hippolyte Bernheim, Alfred Binet, Edmund Gurney, and Jules and Pierre Janet on the unconscious perception found in hysterics." Referring to James's adoption of a personalized unconsciousness, Myers added that "James believed that it was confirmed by the work on multiple personality in abnormal psychology and the study of mediumship in psychical research." From this, Myers concluded, "there is no system of the unconscious in James as there is in Freud."[135]

Finally, Eugene Taylor went so far as to claim James offered a "psychology of the subconscious *unique* to each individual" (emphasis added) and that while James's interest in abnormal psychology unified the disparate schools of psychology in the 1890s, he did not make the great leap to positing the universal existence of an unconscious entity. Instead, James embraced neither an unconscious entity nor unconscious states but rather advanced the view there were multiple and divided states of consciousness, only some disparately aware of the other. In particular, Taylor showed how James was arguing against both German idealists and British materialists and claimed James rejected these two extremes because a third and more plausible view emerged, namely, the idea of "dissociated" or "abnormal" consciousness, as put forth by French pathology: "There are only multiple states of consciousness [for James], each aware or unaware to some degree of the others.

Actually, it was an idea that James only half-acknowledged in *The Principles* and did not develop more fully until after 1890."[136]

As this chapter indicates, there is much to the received view regarding the influence of French pathology on James's assessment of abnormal exceptional mental states. However, by overemphasizing it, this interpretation bypasses the crucial role that psychical research played in James's theorizing about unconsciousness. Moreover, since James developed a fairly sophisticated view of consciousness split off in two parts before, during, and after the writing of *The Principles of Psychology*, it underplays both points and inadvertently misleads readers into thinking James's primary interest was psychopathology when in fact his psychical research was equally if not more so. When James's views of pathological and nonpathological unconsciousness are evaluated together, it becomes clear that James found evidence in psychical research to support something more than an individualist theory of the unconscious but not quite a universal one. Such a position reveals James's tertium quid approach to the "unclassified residuum."

seven

THE UNSEEN WORLD

Whatever the shortcomings of the subliminal self theory, researchers at the Society for Psychical Research believed it adequately explained the nature of trance states in Spiritualist mediums. Steeped in the thorny debates about the nature of the unconscious, the Sidgwick Group maintained that the theory showed communication with the dead was possible. Such a possibility brought the SPR full circle to its original mission to provide scientific evidence for immortality. Believing it was on the verge of such proof at the dawn of the new century, the Sidgwick Group turned its focus to theorizing the afterlife. This priority intensified with the deaths of pivotal SPR members Edmund Gurney (1888), Henry Sidgwick (1900), F. W. H. Myers (1901), and Richard Hodgson (1905). Their deaths could easily have justified William James's ending his commitment to psychical research, but instead they bolstered it, inspiring him to explore the possibility of their souls surviving as he continued to write prolifically about psychical research. More exactly, the supposed spirit-returns of Gurney, Sidgwick, Myers, and Hodgson motivated James to forge an original theory of immortality. Since the Sidgwick Group had always been interested in "communications" from associates and family members who had passed on to the "other world," it was predictable that SPR members would try contact the living upon their own deaths. The SPR even codified this process with Oliver Lodge writing that it was "determined to make the working hypothesis that deceased members of the S.P.R. may conceivably have something to do with the messages."[1] As more and more of the first generation of transatlantic psychical researchers passed away, the remaining members increasingly committed themselves to contacting recently departed colleagues. In so doing, they made the survival thesis central to psychical research.

James was no exception. When he was nearing the completion of *The Principles of Psychology*, he told a friend, "I believe myself that the 'unseen world' is now the next thing in order to investigate."[2] Referring to the spiritual world in general and to immortality in particular, James was invoking the perennial question of what happens to the soul upon bodily death. From that point onward, immortality occupied his attention. In this way, James's desire to explain the deaths of his psychical brethren drove his theory of the survival thesis. But what did the "unseen world" mean for James? In contrast to members of the Sidgwick Group, who as Anglicans in spiritual crisis had turned to psychical research to prove the immortal soul doctrine, James approached immortality neither as a moral nor as a theological issue but rather as an epistemological and metaphysical one. Moreover, instead of assuming the existence of the soul, as most theorists had, James rejected that notion and instead asked what happened to consciousness.[3] Because he recognized that the laws of physics dictated that consciousness as a form of energy must go somewhere upon bodily death, he theorized it did not die off but instead melded organically with all previous consciousness that was stored over time in the cosmos. He suggested this mishmash of leftover consciousness floated in what he called the "Mother Sea of consciousness" and argued it was not the soul that survives bodily death and ascends to heaven to live on eternally but rather bits and pieces of consciousness. Essentially a pre-Jungian theory of an ur-consciousness, James invoked multiple wills to explain what he called the "sublime reservoir." It was a brand-new hypothesis.

James developed this theory of immortality over a twenty-year period, from 1890 to 1909. It emerged in his psychical research essay "A Record of Observations of Certain Phenomena of Trance" (1890), where James first mentioned the notion of a "cosmic reservoir"; in an especially revealing letter to the psychologist G. Stanley Hall in 1894 that asserted Mrs. Leonora Piper tapped the "subliminal reservoir" of consciousness; and in a review of Hodgson's lengthy article on the nature of Mrs. Piper's trance state in 1898 that sympathized with Hodgson's support for the survival hypothesis. The most important writing, though, was his "Report on Mrs. Piper's Hodgson-Control" (1909), a lengthy essay that recounted and analyzed various sittings with the medium, indicating the possibility that an identity purporting to be Hodgson was communicating from "beyond the veil." James had worked out two key elements of this emergent theory in the Ingersoll and Gifford Lectures subsequently published as *Human Immortality* (1898) and *The Varieties of Religious Experience* (1902), respectively. In the first, he analyzed immortality in the context of the debates about the brain's functional relation to consciousness, and in the second he discussed it in relation to religious belief and mystical experience. Finally, James built the cosmological platform for the theory in his Hibbert Lectures at Oxford, published as *A Pluralistic Universe* (1909), in which he invoked Gustav Fechner's earth soul theory, or the view that all living things have a soul that eventually unites with the ultimate soul—God. However, while James retained the earth soul theory's cosmology for its support of his pluralism (the view that the universe is many), he rejected its theological rudiments because of its monism (the view that the universe is one) and thus did not commit himself logically to a belief in God.

All of these writings reveal that James's sublime reservoir theory attempted to explain more than just spirit-return. It was also designed to combat two responses to the classical mind-body problem that had captured James's attention since the 1860s. The first was the materialist theory of mind, represented by two related but distinct groups: the eighteenth- and nineteenth-century French and German "medical materialists" such as Julien Offray de La Mettrie, Pierre-Jean-George Cabanis, Paul-Henri Dietrich (Baron d'Holbach), and Friedrich Karl Christian Ludwig Büchner who interpreted the mind-body problem through a physiological lens to argue collectively that mental states (mind) are essentially physical manifestations in the brain, and the British physiologists Henry Maudsley, William B. Carpenter, and Alexander Bain, who reduced consciousness to brain states and argued consciousness dies off when the body does. The totality of these two theories denied the immortality thesis of the soul and the extension of consciousness beyond brain death. At the other end of the immortality spectrum, which James's theory was also designed to rebut, were adherents of the Platonic-Cartesian theory of dualism, including most Christians, Spiritualists, and the Sidgwick Group. This second cluster stipulated that mental life (mind, soul) was essentially noncorporeal and ontologically distinct from and prior to corporeal matter (body, brain) and argued that the mind (or soul) ascended to the afterlife upon bodily death, thus affirming immortality.

James rejected the intellectual framework of both camps. He argued against the classical mind-body dualism because the materialist theory was reductionist while the immortal soul doctrine espoused absolute idealism. James opposed both camps because they were instances of monism, which violated his pluralism, the linchpin of his metaphysics. For James, the former school too quickly denied the immortality thesis, while the latter one too easily accepted it. This configuration recalled James's tough- and tender-minded intellectual taxonomy, and once again he rejected it as too bifurcated and unable to capture the complexities of the universe. Instead, James offered a third hypothesis. He construed consciousness supernaturally but used naturalistic terms, creating what his first biographer called a "piecemeal supernaturalism." The advantage of this approach was that it accounted for the idiosyncratic nature of séance "communications" because it did not designate them solely as phenomena of the medium's psychology or as evidence that the soul survives bodily death, while at the same time it postulated them as something in between—part psychological and part metaphysical. In this way, James's psychical research facilitated his theory of immortality. As that same biographer argued, it "afforded an experimental approach to religion . . . [by providing] scientific support for a supernaturalistic faith."[4] In short, James's sublime reservoir theory of immortality also manifested his tertium quid.

IMMORTALITY

Immortality became the final focus of James's psychical research. But what did James and his colleagues mean by the term, what kinds of evidence did they think would support the survival thesis, and how should they theorize it? Three prominent doctrines of immortality circulated widely throughout Western Christianity when psychical researchers adopted the topic in the late nineteenth century: the immortal soul doctrine, which holds there exists a corporeal body and an incorporeal soul and that the latter is the essential part of the person that lives forever; the reconstitution doctrine (of which resurrection is a version), which holds that God literally reconstitutes the person after bodily death; and the shadow-man doctrine, which holds that there is a shadow person lurking invisibly in the physical body who departs after bodily death.[5] While some Spiritualists opted for the third view, the first had the most philosophical and theological traction for Anglicans, especially given that most modern Christians denied that mere mortals were reconstituted. Many theorists advanced versions of the immortal soul doctrine over the millennia, but Plato's and Descartes's versions captured it most robustly. Typifying this broad dualistic tradition, Descartes argued there are two kinds of matter, physical and mental (or mind and matter), and that humans are reducible to the mental, that the mind is a substance whose primary purpose is to think, and that this mind or soul survives bodily death. "Our soul," he stipulated, "is in its nature entirely independent of the body, and in consequence . . . it is not liable to die with it . . . [such that] we are naturally inclined to judge that it is immortal."[6]

Spirit-Return

The Sidgwick Group adhered to the Platonic-Cartesian immortal soul thesis. They believed that in addition to being consistent with Broad Church doctrine, which eased them as Anglicans, it lent itself to scientific testing. However, the Platonic-Cartesian framework led members of the group to engage in circular reasoning. In their attempt to use mediumistic evidence to prove immortality, they in fact assumed immortality to exist in the first place. Anthony Flew captured this fallacy best, writing, "It is only insofar as a person is essentially incorporeal that it can even make sense to suggest that someone years ago dead, buried, and dissolved is even now communicating with us through a medium."[7] Seemingly unaware of or indifferent to such circular reasoning, the SPR tried to demonstrate spirit-return empirically in the form of three communication tests—clairvoyance, sealed letters, and cross-correspondence—and thus prove immortality. The clairvoyance test involved a psychical researcher asking the control identity to name some predetermined set of numbers, letters, or symbols hidden from view. But the quality of the evidence for clairvoyance with the controls was quite poor. For instance, after Lodge employed a children's box full of cards with alphabet letters (L, K, Q, U, C, N), "Gurney" could not identify even one and Lodge concluded the test "entirely failed."[8]

Sealed letters were also used as a form of verification. Psychical researchers left one or more letters before they died. After each passed away, the contents were compared with "communications" through a medium and examined for accuracy. If there was some content overlap, then the "communication" was considered evidential support for the belief in immortality. These letters were very precious because so few had been written and preserved. As Lodge reminded James, "With regard to your sealed envelope, I trust that you will by no means open it unless specially and very formally requested to do so, or of course unless you make up your mind in the same sort of way. These envelopes are scarce: it is indeed the only one I know of except my own."[9] Of course, if anyone could have been entrusted with these prized possessions, it was James. He once reassured Mary Robbins Hillard, an American educator and SPR member from Waterbury, Connecticut, who had entrusted him with just such a letter, that he had firmly in his keep her "two messages locked up, and have notified Miss [Alice] Johnson & Hyslop to be on the lookout for them at their respective 'lights.'" He added in his postscript that he had a sealed envelope from Hodgson too.[10]

Gurney did not leave a sealed letter, but Sidgwick and Myers did—the former in 1900 and the latter in 1890. The SPR treated both like religious artifacts. Of Myers's letter, Lodge explained to James, "I propose to make a ceremony of it, and to take it up to London for the purpose. It has been in a bank for some years. I should think he gave it [to] me about 1890, much the same as yours. The date is of course on it, but I have not seen it for a long time."[11] According to Sidgwick's biographer, the SPR tested both letters over eight years, but all efforts failed.[12] As Eleanor Sidgwick put it to James, "The result was blank..., [and] there is no evidence of any attempt to communicate the contents of either envelope."[13] Eleanor never put much stock in sealed letter tests, since she claimed that she would never have remembered posthumously what she put in her own letter,[14] but such ex post facto rationalization belied the purpose of writing such letters and the seriousness of the SPR in testing them. Had the results been positive, she and the SPR most assuredly would have trumpeted them as verification of the soul's survival.

The third and most poignant form of verification was the cross-correspondence test. It was also the most complex. Beginning with Myers's death in 1901, multiple SPR mediums began receiving apparently similar messages from Myers and other identities purporting to be the surviving souls of departed SPR members. The SPR thought the information might be verified by using two different mediums with two different sets of sitters in two different séances held at two different times in two different locations. For instance, Eleanor Sidgwick in the United Kingdom might receive a message through one entranced medium from a control identity purporting to be a deceased spirit of a psychical researcher (for example, her husband), which might be mimicked in some way through a second entranced medium in a sitting with James in the United States. If the messages overlapped, then cross-correspondence was considered to have occurred. This method did not necessarily rule out the possibility that the information had been stored in the medium's subliminal self, but it did seem to rule out fraud since one medium could not know what information was coming through the other medium. Some sitters were deliberately kept out of the cross-correspondence sittings to avoid overcomplicating them or introducing additional bias. As James explained it, "All 'stray' sitters will be excluded, as was the case in London."[15] The SPR increasingly believed this method was the most evidential in proving the spirit incarnate, and it dominated the SPR's testing for nearly a quarter of a century, from around 1900 through the early 1920s.

A particularly poignant case involving James occurred in 1906–7 with the appearance of the Hodgson-control. J. G. Piddington headed the study, and the SPR devoted a special issue of the *Proceedings* to his report.[16] The project also bonded James with Piddington in the ways that he had with the core members of the Sidgwick Group years before. "Piddington is a splendid fellow," he told his son, and "he, George dorr [sic] & I are a trio of friends for life."[17] The study used two mediums: Mrs. Margaret de Gaudrion Merrifield Verrall, a lecturer in classics at Newnham College, where Mrs. Sidgwick was principal and the likely source of her connection to the SPR, and Mrs. Piper, through whom the Hodgson-control first appeared shortly after Hodgson's death in 1905 and who was subsequently sent to the SPR offices in England from November 1906 to June 1907 for the explicit purpose of cross-correspondence testing, where she also received messages from the Hodgson-control.[18] Piddington looked for overlap and argued that chance could not account for the coincidences of expression in seventy-four instances, a result that impressed some. James, for instance, told his wife, Alice, "Stickney thinks Mrs. P. an *essential* truth teller, though an embroiderer . . . [but] believes she has good antecedents."[19] Eleanor Sidgwick, who had much to gain from these tests if one of the control identities turned out to be the surviving soul of her husband, also found these results encouraging. To James she mailed copies of transcripts of the sittings with Mrs. Verrall regarding Hodgson's sealed letter.[20] Two years later, after the sealed letter test for her husband had failed, she wrote to James more hopefully about Piddington, finding "striking correspondences" between his sittings with Mrs. Verrall in England and George Dorr's sittings with Mrs. Piper in Boston.[21] James participated in the latter, explaining to Eleanor that

> I saw the Piper family yesterday, in good health and spirits, and excellently pleased with England and their treatment there. . . . I had a sitting, along with Mrs. Ledyard, and entrusted three messages to "Hodgson," as follows:
>
> (1) To Mrs. Verrall he was to dictate "*Statue of Liberty.*"
> (2) To Mrs. Flemming, "*Rose-bush.*"
> (3) To Mrs. Raikes "*The World is yellow.*"[22]

Eleanor then held a sitting with Mrs. Verrall during which "Hodgson" appeared and confirmed he had left a letter with James, the contents of which he hoped to reveal once he "passed over." But, as Eleanor explained to James in a lengthy letter that included copies of the relevant dialogue, neither the content of Hodgson's sealed letter nor James's three-point message was accurately relayed, indicating that no cross-correspondence had occurred.[23]

The cross-correspondence tests initially impressed James. In one instance he told F. C. S. Schiller that Hodgson might "still be energizing somewhere— it's not a case of '*requiescat* [a prayer for the reposed dead].'"[24] He also made similar comments to his close friend Thomas Perry, the American literary scholar, writing, "(So funny is the structure of the Universe that) he seems to be showing his usual energy at the other end of the line."[25] A sitting that James and his wife had with Mrs. Minnie Meserve Soule, a trance medium residing in Somerville, Massachusetts, suggested as much.[26] James described to James Hyslop that at a prior sitting with Mrs. Piper, the Hodgson-control had announced it had a new way of "establishing" its identity. "Hodgson" would send a word (*"bellum"*) to Hyslop in a sitting with another medium, Mrs. Soule. However, "Hodgson" had not been able to get through, so James and his wife had a sitting with Mrs. Soule at which "the Piper group was announced." The only problem was that "Hodgson" could not bring forth the message, only something "impersonal," but alluded to his attempt to contact Hyslop in this way. The Hodgson-control, however, was able to recognize James, calling him by his full name even though he had never seen Mrs. Soule before despite his wife having had a sitting with her ten years prior.[27]

As for the validity of cross-correspondence, James had faith in the SPR to keep the testing scientific. He assured Henry Bowditch that Mrs. Sidgwick was quite able, that the SPR had kept Mrs. Piper focused, and that no outside sitters had been allowed.[28] Indeed, after consulting with Eleanor, Lodge, Piddington, and Miss Johnson, he encouraged Mrs. Piper to give sittings along "evidential lines" and not give "advice sittings."[29] For his own part, James found the work very good, telling a friend who shared his interest in psychical research that when he visited Piddington in England, his "lap [was] full of Pid's proofs of the Piper-Verrall work of last winter." They were "excellent proofs of cross-correspondence, so far as I have read the stuff," adding for good measure, "They are a [*sic*] expert lot over here."[30] James repeated this positive assessment to Flournoy the following month, writing, "I have just read Miss Johnson's report in the last S.P.R. *Proceedings* and have a good bit of the proofs of Piddington[']s on cross-correspondence between Mrs. Piper[,] Mrs. Verrall, and Mrs. Holland, which is to appear in the next number. You will be much interested. . . . It seems to me that these reports open a new chapter in the history of automatism; and Piddington's and Johnson's ability is of the highest order."[31]

However, as had so often been the case with James's psychical research, once he had read the reports more carefully and reexamined the results, he retreated from his initial rosy view. He began in his usual empirical way by wondering whether better evidence would be forthcoming. James was particularly interested in a sitting in which the Myers-control supposedly communicated a message to Piddington in a dream (one of the seventy-four supposed confirming instances). He speculated that a medium's trance and deep sleep states might not be so distinct and asked whether all people might be mediums in sleep. Should not the SPR be studying dreams as well as trance states? He also recommended that visual tests be tried since the mediums showed auditory sensory abilities. Finally, he suggested experiments be conducted on "entranced ears," not just on the eyes.[32] In other words, Piddington's report opened up more questions than it had answered.

While James eventually presented these concerns to Piddington, he initially showered him with praise, noting he had read "every word" of the report, saying how much it impressed him. He also stated that Piddington was a philological genius, since he had so carefully identified and deciphered all the utterances in the way a philologist would of an unknown language. But while James was "of course convinced that *some of the cross-correspondence points* are real," he remained doubtful about their totality. He was especially concerned about the quality of the evidence and the extremely opaque methods that Piddington had used to substantiate the phenomenon. The "common critics," who would not follow all the complexities, "will say that the thing is getting too finespun to follow, and that if *such* proofs have to be worked the 'spirits' are of too vapory a consistency to be attended to any longer." As such, James wished that the evidence was "more *crass* and less elusive." Indeed, James thought in two cases the Myers control material "shimmers to me on the brink of improbability," concluding that the claims about the reality of cross-correspondence was much like the theory that Francis Bacon was really Shakespeare: not provable but unconvincing.[33]

Mrs. Piper's Hodgson-Control

Unsatisfied with the evidence for spirit-return that others had generated, James conducted his own investigation. In so doing, his role in the spirit-return phenomenon shifted from commentator and analyst to experimentalist and theorist. The result was his "Report on Mrs. Piper's Hodgson-Control," an account of more than two hundred pages written and published in two parts for the 1909 edition of the *Proceedings*, the first of which was read aloud by Piddington at the general meeting of the SPR in London on 28 January 1909.[34]

It was his longest and most sophisticated psychical research essay, taking four years to complete.[35] The reasons for its delay are crucial to understanding its relationship with James's philosophy because the venture came at a very inopportune time. As is well known, the last half decade of James's life was his most prolific as a philosopher; he was absorbed in writing and delivering many or all of the essays and lectures that became *Pragmatism* (1907), *The Meaning of Truth* (1909), *A Pluralistic Universe* (1909), *Some Problems of Philosophy* (1911), and *Essays in Radical Empiricism* (1912), the last two published posthumously, as well as his most important political essay, "The Moral Equivalent of War" (1910).[36] That James did not decline taking on the Hodgson-control project, despite being at his intellectual pinnacle and having obvious justification and inclination to do so, reiterates his loyalty to Hodgson and the SPR and indicates the centrality of psychical research in James's thought. Some philosophers may cringe, but there is no denying the historical fact that while James was writing up his best philosophy, he was also working out his best psychical research. And the two, it can be demonstrated, shared some substantial overlapping content.

Hodgson's first purported message came just eight days after his death on 20 December 1905, when "Rector," then Mrs. Piper's primary control, wrote through Mrs. Piper's entranced hand "HODGSON."[37] Shortly thereafter, "Hodgson" took over as Mrs. Piper's primary control, a phase which lasted six years, until 1911.[38] During that period, but especially between 28 December 1905 and 1 January 1908, "Hodgson" appeared dozens of times and gave many answers to numerous questions posed by many psychical researchers (James, Hyslop, Piddington, Dorr, William Newbold, and James Jackson Putnam), James family members (Alice and William Jr.), several sympathetic women who had known Hodgson (Mrs. Theodate Pope and Miss Hillard), and a few others to whom James gave aliases ("Mrs. Lyman" and "Miss Bergman"). The work then continued intermittently through December 1908, during which time James held multiple sittings with numerous trusted friends and strangers alike in which the Hodgson-control appeared. Most were held at George Dorr's house in Boston, and James attended and participated in many of these. All had mixed results. For instance, James told his wife that Mrs. Ledyard was going to have another sitting after her first one at which "Hodgson" appeared "in much better shape than before, and has much advice to give."[39] Similarly, he told Thomas Perry that at Dorr's he saw the entire Piper family, who had apparently enjoyed their trip to England where the SPR had treated them well. He noted that "Hodgson" had a message for Thomas regarding whether he or his wife remembered an appointment with "George" Pellew.[40]

James also used data that other psychical researchers had collected from sittings with Mrs. Piper in which the Hodgson-control appeared. James found Hyslop's accounts quite useful but vehemently opposed Hyslop's idea to publish his own "special report." Instead, James felt it best to present all the material in one place in to order to make the strongest argument, which is what his report was going to be, and to avoid presenting material in piecemeal fashion where it could be attacked, which is what he charged that Hugo Münsterberg had done with some of Hyslop's other articles.[41] He also wanted to contain to the SPR the knowledge of the report and any views attached to it. Thus, James told Isaac Kauffman Funk, an independent psychical researcher, that he had not seen any of the interviews and had not spoken to reporters about this matter, and when a student asked him about the "Hodgson manifestations" he replied simply that spirit-return had not been proven.[42]

All in all, James collated sixty-nine sittings and condensed them to eleven thematic episodes for coherence. He noted that these amounted to only one-sixth of the records but were representative of the best, middling, and worst cases. Each involved "testing" the Hodgson-control by asking it about episodes and quotations that only it and the sitter knew, such as the whereabouts of a peculiar ring Hodgson wore but went missing after his death, the source of a poem his "spirit" composed during a sitting, the many extracurricular events that occurred when Hodgson had visited George Dorr at "Oldfarm" in Bar Harbor, Maine, and even Hodgson's marriage proposal to a young woman that he had kept secret over the years.

While collecting data for the report, James was asked what he thought the likely outcome would be, but he wisely declined to go on record with a final opinion before all the evidence was in. For instance, he told Piddington the report "will be without a decided conclusion—what *it* means will depend on what all the other records mean." But he was willing to speculate, for he added, "They doubtless make more unequivocally for spirits than does this."[43] However, James told his second son that "R[ichard] H[odgson] comes with an extraordinary dramatic verisimilitude, but when you come to ask if the signs of his being really there are *unmistakeable*, the affirmative answer *bleibt aus* [is absent/not present]."[44] He likewise informed his youngest son that he planned to conclude the report against Hodgson's presence being real but then three weeks later told him, "I ought to finish up my Hodgson report which . . . admits of no sharp conclusions."[45] Such apparent inconsistency was in fact just James's empiricism at work. While the evidence impressed him at times, it did not at others. Metaphysical reality and its epistemological truth was a fluid process, and his final opinion would have to wait. Since the evidence was inconclusive, the rational decision would be to not make any affirmative statements one way or the other. As he confided to William Jr., "It almost sickens me to think that the final verdict once more is like[ly] to be 'baffling,'" which was the exact comment he made to Schiller: "*Not convincing, to me: but baffling exceedingly.*"[46] Once again James's reasoning typified his tertium quid approach to psychical research.

The purpose of the report was to determine the nature of the control-identity claiming to be Richard Hodgson (or by extension any such "spirit"). The primary question James tried to answer was, "*Are there any unmistakable indications in the messages in question that something we may call the 'spirit' of Hodgson was probably really there?*"[47] Or, as he put it elsewhere in the report, "What I am sifting these records for is independent evidence of such return."[48] The strategy James used to answer this question was to compare the spirit-return hypothesis against seven other possible explanations:

(1) Lucky chance-hits.
(2) Common Gossip.
(3) Indications unwarily furnished by the sitters.
(4) Information received from R. H. during his lifetime, by the waking Mrs. P. and stored up, either supraliminally or subliminally, in her memory.
(5) Information received from the living R. H., or others, at sittings, and kept in Mrs. Piper's trance-memory, but out of reach of her waking consciousness.
(6) "Telepathy," *i.e.* the tapping of the sitter's mind, or that of some distant living person, in an inexplicable way.
(7) Access to some cosmic reservoir, where the memory of all mundane facts is stored and grouped around personal centres of association.[49]

The first five were naturalistic explanations and the last two supernatural, or "mystical," as James inexactly put it.[50] James stipulated reasonably that only if the first five were made improbable could the latter two be considered. In the introduction to part 1 of the report, James maintained that the first three possibilities could not explain the phenomena in most instances; there were too many controls against them. For the fourth and fifth explanations, he admitted that Mrs. Piper did manifest a secondary personality at times—he believed the "Imperator Band" and "Rector," two of her control-identities, were her own "dream creations"—but he thought that in other cases this pathological explanation could not account for the phenomenon.⁵¹ He also admitted periodically in the report that Mrs. Piper's subliminal self might explain it. For these two explanations (#4 and #5), James understood that because Hodgson and Mrs. Piper had worked so closely for so long, those two possibilities presented the most a priori likely explanation. For instance, he once told an Italian psychical researcher that "in certain individuals the intuitions become very marked—I think these individuals ('mediums') are a discontinuous psychological variety, but the intuitions even here are not systematized—they are mere gleams and flashes, and immediately get absorbed into the mass of fictitious personation and repetition that constitute the basis of the medium's subliminal mentality."⁵² Nonetheless, James argued the fourth and fifth explanations were in fact the *least* likely because Hodgson had been especially careful not to talk shop with Mrs. Piper when she was not entranced and controlled what others said when she was. That being the case, he still believed Mrs. Piper's abilities were, at minimum, "supernormal . . . unquestionably."⁵³ While James sometimes found that one of the natural explanations could account for the supposed communications, there were too many other instances where they could not. He thus dismissed the naturalistic hypothesis for those cases. As such, the primary focus of the report compared and contrasted the "telepathy-theory" (#6) and the "cosmic-reservoir theory" (#7) against the spirit-return hypothesis.⁵⁴ Justifying this approach, he told a friend, "I have taken the rigorous method of denying a spirit where any other explanation was morally and fisically [*sic*] *possible*."⁵⁵ In other words, James was primarily interested in the supernormal and supernatural explanations, and most of the report was devoted to analyzing which of those two best explained Mrs. Piper's Hodgson-control.

Like so much of his psychical research writing, then, the Hodgson-control report was an exercise in asking the reader to at least consider spectacular but highly unlikely outcomes. Throughout the report, James frequently resorted to one of his favorite kinds of argument, invoking his "dramatic impression" or pointing out the "dramatic possibility" and even "dramatic probability" left on him by the sum total of the data. Although he admitted the evidence was weak in places and even presented cases where it was so, he considered the sum total to be persuasive. Taken together, James wrote, the cases "produce a cumulative effect on the mind . . . [in which conviction] grows first possible, then plausible, then natural, and finally probable in a high degree."⁵⁶ In a letter to a friend, he described his personal opinion this way: "My own feeling of the 'dramatic probabilities' makes pretty strongly for *something that represents* the living R[ichard] H[odgson] being active in the results—tho I'm sure that the phenomenon is so complex, that we can't guess what that something may be like."[57] Such argumentation recalled his debates with James Cattell over Mrs. Piper in which James invoked the bundle of sticks metaphor—individual weak sticks together make a strong bunch—and once again revealed James's fideism and penchant for embracing weak inductive arguments or what he dubbed the "mere logic of presumption."[58]

Unfortunately for James, his argument suffered on several fronts. First, it made probability invalidly, if inadvertently, an aspect of the belief rather than of the phenomenon. Second, it cut sharply against the grain of both the logic and the history of scientific reasoning. For instance, the principle of Ockham's razor maintains that when you have two competing theories consistent with the data, the simpler of the two is preferred, which would favor the naturalistic explanations (#4 or #5) instead of the supernormal and supernatural ones (#6 and #7 and the spirit hypothesis). Fortunately, James anticipated this objection:

> The common-sense rule of presumption in scientific logic is never to assume an unknown agent where there is a known one, and never to choose a rarer cause for a phenomenon when a commoner one will account for it. The usual is always the more probable, and exceptional principles should be invoked only when the use of ordinary ones is impossible.... Our rule of presumption should lead us then to deny spirits and to explain the Piper-phenomena by a mixture of fraud, subconscious personation, lucky accident, and telepathy, whenever such an explanation remains possible.

But James had an answer in the form of the exception to the rule: "As soon, therefore, as we drop our routine rule of presumption, and ask straight for truth, and nothing but truth, we find that *the whole question is as to whether the exceptional case confronts us.*" For James, the spirit hypothesis was compatible with the exceptional model even if "spirit-return was not proved by the Hodgson-control material."[59] James's reply to Ockham's razor, however, was problematic since it tried to isolate data points into two categories, the routine and exceptional, and then sought a theory to explain the latter when what scientists in fact do is pose hypotheses to explain all data points while using the outlying cases as indicators of the hypotheses' limits. James, it seems, had it exactly backwards. Weak reasoning or not, the "dramatic possibility" argument formed the base for his report as it had been to his approach to psychical phenomena all along.

The Hodgson-control report was James's most important essay in psychical research. This was not because of the evidence it contained, which James admitted was weak, or because of the methodology, which he realized was shoddy, or even because of his argument for spirit-return, which cut against the logic of scientific reasoning. On the contrary, the report was significant for its original theory of immortality. It advanced three stipulations—that the will is fragmented and multiple (not unified or singular), that the brain transmits rather than produces consciousness, and that energy transfers from the earthy realm to the cosmological one.

The Will and Immortality

Using his "dramatic possibility" framework, James looked for the common denominator of the supernormal and supernatural explanations. He found a desire to communicate, which meant invoking the notion of the will. "The active cause of the communications," he wrote, "is on any hypothesis [that is, #4, #5, #6, #7, and spirit-return] a will of some kind, be it the will of R[ichard] H[odgson]'s spirit [that is, spirit-return], of lower supernatural intelligences [#7], or of Mrs. Piper's subliminal [self] [#6]. . . . [There is] a will to say something which the machinery fails to bring through."[60] James also realized the previous attempts to explain the phenomenon had failed because they assumed only one will—namely, a soul—trying to communicate from the "other world." But this was too bifurcated for James's tertium quid approach. Instead, James postulated there were two wills at work: the will to personate and the will to communicate. The former involved some kind of identity in the medium (for example, Mrs. Piper) trying to communicate—the information stored up either in her subliminal memory or in her trance memory or both (#4 and #5). A subspecies of this kind of will was what James called the "will-to-deceive," since there were too many sittings in which this identity often tried to fool the sitters by deliberately providing false information. This could be a medium's secondary personality created in her dream-life (that is, that did not correspond to external reality) and thus indicated a kind of pathology. As James put it, "That a 'will to personate' is a factor in the Piper-phenomenon I fully believe, and I believe with unshakeable firmness that this will is able to draw on supernormal sources of information. It can 'tap,' possibly the sitter's memories, possibly those of distant human beings, possibly some cosmic reservoir in which the memories of earth are stored, whether in the shape of 'spirits' or not."[61] Whether healthy or pathological, though, the will to personate existed in the medium (mind, brain), not out there in the universe. It was clearly a *psychological* phenomenon and thus belonged to the naturalistic set of explanations. James well understood this and had offered his subliminal self theory to explain it.

James, however, believed that telepathy between the sitter and the medium could not fully explain the phenomenon: "If this will [to personate] were the only will concerned in the performance, the phenomenon would be humbug pure and simple, and the minds tapped telepathically in it would play an entirely passive role—that is, the telepathic data would be fished out by the personating will, not forced upon it by desires to communicate, acting externally to itself."[62] As such, James postulated that a medium's will was not the only active one during any given "communication." There had to be an *additional* will present in the séance, or what he called a "will-to-communicate." This will, in stark contrast to the will to personate, was clearly *metaphysical* in that it existed outside of a medium (mind, brain), to which James hypostatized an ontological status. As James put it, it was "possible to complicate the hypothesis. Extraneous 'wills to communicate' may contribute to the results as well as a 'will to personate,' and the two kinds of will[s] may be distinct in entity, though capable of helping each other out. The will to communicate ... would be, on the *prima facie* view of it, the will of Hodgson's [or any deceased person's] surviving spirit."[63] In other words, James argued that "Hodgson's spirit" was a will communicating through Mrs. Piper from the sublime reservoir of such wills. James thus believed there were at least two basic kinds of wills at work in the phenomenon.

In addition, James identified two subtypes of this second, metaphysical will: "permanent" and "improvised." "The question then presents itself," he asked, "in what shape is it most reasonable to suppose the will thus postulated is actually there?" Invoking "pneumatological possibilities," as he was wont to do, James answered, "The will to communicate may come either from permanent entities, or from an entity that arises for the occasion." An example of the former would be "R. H.'s spirit." So, too, would "inferior parasitic spirits" such as demons and the like. James seemed to be implying these were supernatural. If so, it supported the survival hypothesis, since if the entity trying to communicate through Mrs. Piper really was Hodgson's spirit, it would have meant his soul survived bodily death. Of permanent wills to communicate, James wrote, "There is no *a priori* reason why human spirits and other spiritual beings might not either co-operate at the same time in the same phenomenon, or alternately produce different manifestations."[64]

The improvised will to communicate was more complicated. To explain it, James turned to how memory functions. While alive we carry our memories in the brain, but when the body dies and the brain stops working, he asked, what happens to them? James postulated they leave traces in the universe and that upon physical death all the traces of one human life enter the universe and mingle with all the other ones in a vast cosmological stew. James called this the "cosmic reservoir." As such, he wrote, "An improvised will might be a limited process of consciousness arising in the cosmic reservoir of earth's memories."[65] To illuminate the cosmic reservoir idea, James offered the analogy of the same room in which different people over time breathe and have conversations and likened the communication to "Marconi-stations" or wireless telegraphy in which different signals use the same wire and broadcasting and receiving stations to communicate information (mediums were akin to stations). James theorized that when Hodgson died, his traces would have entered the reservoir and his will would be attempting to communicate, but since it was all a great hodgepodge, the messages came through as disorganized, piecemeal, often nonsensically, and even wrong.[66] James intuited this idea from the very beginning, explaining to his brother that "the Hodgson control is panning out extremely plausibly—something occurred yesterday regarding an old conversation between H[odgson] & me, that brings the notion of his ghost being there closer to me than I have ever felt it before."[67]

Still, how did the "traces" of Hodgson find familiar persons in séances, or, using the radio analogy, how did they find the same wave frequency? After all, because the radio spectrum is rather broad, the odds would be quite low for the presumed billions or even trillions of traces of consciousness floating in the cosmic reservoir to find the sitters of their beloved ones in the earthly realm. To explain the attraction, James invoked the Spiritualist's notion of psychometry, or detecting the history and nature of an object through holding it.[68] For instance, when individuals sat with a medium, they supposedly left "traces" of having been there— such as their interactions with the live Hodgson over the years—which were stored as memories in a medium's subliminal self. Those memories then attracted Hodgson's "traces" from the sublime reservoir, which the medium "tapped" while in a trance state. Spiritualists called this process "influence." In the radio analogy, it amounted to finding a clear frequency through fine-tuning. As James described it, "If, now, the *rest of the system of physical traces* left behind by Hodgson's acts were by some sort of mutual induction throughout its extent, thrown into gear and made to vibrate all at once, by the presence of such human bodies to the medium, we should have a Hodgson-system active in the cosmos again, and the 'conscious aspect' of this vibrating system might be Hodgson's spirit redivivus, and recollecting and willing in a certain momentary way."[69] Reaching the limit of his radio analogy, James resorted to two favorite analogies from physics as familiar to early twentieth-century scientists as Marconi stations (especially Lodge, who helped pioneer radiometry): light and celestial bodies.

> A natural way of representing the process [of interacting wills] would be to suppose the spirit to have found that by pressing, so to speak, against "the light," it can make fragmentary gleams and flashes of what it wishes to say.... The two wills might strike up a sort of partnership and stir each other up. It might even be that the "will to personate" would be inert unless it were aroused to activity by the other will. We might imagine the relation to be analogous to that of two physical bodies, from neither of which, when alone, mechanical, thermal, or electrical effects can proceed, but if the other body be present, and show a difference of "potential," action starts up and goes on apace.[70]

The basic point to James's insight was that multiple wills were required to explain the phenomenon of supposed spirit communication. This was a new contribution to both will and immortality theory that James had reached entirely through psychical research.

The advantages to James's multiple will theory were obvious. First, it accounted for the messiness of mediumship, especially the often confused, garbled, and weak quality of the purported messages from the "other world," which both the naturalistic and spirit-return hypotheses could not explain adequately. Second, it squared with the law of conservation of energy, which was very important since James believed psychic phenomena was part of the natural world and thereby subject to the laws of nature. Third, it revealed why mediums often behaved in seemingly odd ways in trying to personate the will to communicate, which was the basis for the charge of fraud, a position James had tried hard his whole career to disabuse his critics of and for which he could now provide an explanation that was not ad hoc.

The disadvantages to the theory, however, were equally obvious. First, James's "dramatic possibility" reasoning violated the principle of Ockham's razor. By invoking additional "entities," James unnecessarily complicated both theories of the will and the cosmos and in so doing ran afoul of Western philosophical and scientific traditions. Second, the explanation was confused, or at least not well developed. Was it a metaphysical theory about the cosmos or an epistemological one about consciousness?[71] James seemed to be offering it as both due to his firm opposition to monism and commitment to pluralism. But the lack of a scientific explanation of what held all these wills together made that commitment appear more ideological than philosophical, which violated tertium quid thinking. Third, the theory was counterintuitive. The notion that consciousness survives human death, floats in the form of traces throughout the cosmos, and communicates with the consciousness of living people through a medium's subliminal self asks people to believe more things contrary to the naturalistic thesis than does the spirit-hypothesis. As such, a critic could rightly contend that while James's will theory cleared up many of the mysteries surrounding mediumship, it offered still more in the process.

These problems should have given James much pause. They did not for two related reasons, one having to do with his personal psychology and the other with the phenomena. James had not accepted the spirit-hypothesis because the complexity of events prohibited it. Elaborating his state of mind to a friend, James agreed that "the spirit-theory is undoubtedly not only the most natural, but the simplest, and I have great respect for Hodgson's and Hyslop's arguments when they adopt it. At the same time, the electric current called *belief* has not yet closed in my mind. Whatever the explanation be, trance-mediumship is an excessively *complex* phenomenon, in which many concurrent factors are engaged. That is why interpretation is so hard."[72] Not surprisingly, once James finally did offer his belief, it was pregnant with likelihoods and replete with caveats. Maintaining he did not have to explain everything, he concluded the report in this way:

> It is enough to indicate these various possibilities, which a serious student of this part of nature has to weigh altogether, and between which his decision must fall. His vote will always be cast (if ever it be cast) by the sense of dramatic probabilities of nature which the sum total of his experience has begotten in him. *I myself feel as if an external will to communicate were probably there*, that is, I find myself doubting, in consequence of my whole acquaintance with that sphere of phenomena, that Mrs. Piper's dream-life, even if equipped with "telepathic" powers, accounts for all the results found. But if asked whether the will to communicate be Hodgson's or be some mere spirit-counterfeit of Hodgson, I remain uncertain and await more facts, facts which may not point clearly to a conclusion for fifty or a hundred years.[73]

James's open-ended resolution was simultaneously exciting for Spiritualists and disappointing for skeptics. On the one hand, it indicated he believed there *could* be some truth to the spirit-hypothesis—that spirits from the "other world" can and do communicate with those of the living through the trances of a Spiritualist medium like Mrs. Piper. However provisionally, James developed the view that there must be an external will to communicate—not an earthly one but a supernatural one. On the other hand, he left undecided whether or not that will was Hodgson's (and by extension any deceased person's) and whether or not people could ever know whose spirit was trying to communicate with them. In this regard, James's multiple will theory amounted to a modified version of the spirit hypothesis. Lodge, whose report on the Gurney-control contained a section on the Myers- and Hodgson-controls, agreed.[74] Upon reading it, James responded favorably, "I find it charmingly done, for *frankness* & unpretending sincerity ..., [and] I think the whole article entirely conclusive—to *every* reader, I should think—of supra-normality, and dramatically very suggestive of spirit-presence."[75] Thus, although James did not believe that Hodgson's surviving energy was identical to Hodgson's soul, the thesis did stipulate that *something* had outlasted Hodgson's material presence on earth. Since James's thesis invoked the ontological existence of nonmaterial entities, this was essentially a theory of supernaturalism.[76] This position was as close as James would ever get to the Sidgwick Group's belief in immortality.

More important, since James's multiple will theory invoked his plea for more facts that might or might not affect the truth of the matter in the long run, it exemplified his pragmatic empiricism. Indeed, the facts would have to improve over time in further studies for James to experience the "electric current called belief," because the Hodgson-control case had not yet provided it. James made this clear in the five conclusions to part 1 of the report. First, Mrs. Piper's Hodgson-control was "an exceptionally bad one for testing spirit-return." Second, the data did not offer a "knock-down proof for the return of Hodgson's spirit," even if, third, the phenomena were compatible with the spirit-return hypothesis. Fourth, the case by itself, while baffling, could not be evaluated on its own but instead "belongs with the whole residual mass of Piper-phenomena." Finally, James was willing to reverse his "negative conclusions of this limited report" as new data became available. He then made his familiar plea for making "more and more observations" until "we have the facts in sufficient number.... We can therefore well afford to play a waiting game."[77] In the meantime, the most he would permit of himself was to speculate on the likelihood of supernormal and supernatural explanations. "Mrs. Piper has supernormal knowledge in her trances," he stated with conviction, "but whether it comes from 'tapping the minds' of living people, or from some common cosmic reservoir of memories, or from surviving 'spirits' of the departed, is a question impossible for *me* to answer just now to my own satisfaction."[78]

James's ambivalence initially reflected a bewilderment common throughout the report. As with most of his psychical research analyses, James found the phenomenon "baffling" in nature. Upon closer examination, however, his conclusion was one of compatibility. That is, James tried to balance between a fideist and strictly empiricist interpretation by arguing that both natural and supernatural explanations were *compatible* with the evidence. Since James realized that compatibility was not the same as causality, he argued the final outcome depended on the type of personality assessing the case. Invoking one of the cases in which a supposed spirit returned to complain about a missing ring, James explained,

> If you are willing beforehand to allow that a half-awakened spirit may come and mix its imperfect memories with the habits of the trance-automatism, and you apperceive the message sympathetically, what you get is entirely congenial with your hypothesis. But if you insist that nothing but knock-down evidence for the spirits shall be counted, then, since what comes is also compatible with natural causes, your hardness of heart remains unbroken, and you continue to explain things by automatic personation and accidental coincidence, with perhaps a dash of thought-transference thrown in.[79]

James's reasoning recalls his tender- and tough-minded dichotomy. The truth of the matter depended pragmatically and empirically on whether better facts could be discovered as new data rolled in over time. In this way, James sought an alternative to the natural and supernatural explanations of mediumship that simultaneously remained consistent with his metaphysical pluralism, epistemological pragmatism, and empirical views about consciousness, thus making the multiple will thesis an instance of his tertium quid.

Consciousness and Immortality

For all of its uniqueness, James's sublime reservoir theory was not a view from nowhere. Its intellectual roots can be traced to his psychical research and scientific psychology of the 1890s, when James developed the psychological dimension of the theory in conjunction with the subliminal self, and to his metaphysical writings of the first decade of the 1900s, when he created the cosmological components in relation to his pluralism. In addition to explaining spirit-return, then, James more broadly developed his theory of immortality in the respective contexts of the psychological debates about the nature of the brain and consciousness and of the metaphysical ones about the nature of the cosmos.

The psychological component to the sublime reservoir theory—in particular the use of the term "conscious" in James's phrase "sublime *conscious* reservoir"—first emerged in 1890 with the publication not of *The Principles of Psychology*, as one might expect, but of "A Record of Observations of Certain Phenomena of Trance," where James used the term "reservoir" psychologically in the context of the subliminal self. Referring to Mrs. Piper's possible telepathic ability, James maintained that "it is certainly not that of the sitter's *conscious* thought. It is rather the reservoir of his potential knowledge which is tapped; and not always *that*, but the knowledge of some distant living person."[80] James invoked this idea four years later in 1894 while attempting to ease G. Stanley Hall's skepticism of Mrs. Piper's supposed supernormal abilities. "She has little or no 'clairvoyant' power, and so far as her achievements can be explained by mind reading, it is the subliminal reser[v]oir that she gets at, and not the momentary consciousness of the sitter," he wrote. "The only way to take her is on her own ground." Citing her high levels of success, James recommended Hall try psychometry: "Sit and see what names and facts the 'aura of your person' suggest to her; or bring an object closely associated with some other person (recently dead if possible), give it to her to handle and see what it brings out."[81] Finally, in a lengthy review of Richard Hodgson's 1898 essay on Mrs. Piper, James again analyzed her supposed supernormal abilities in relation to the sublime reservoir: "Mrs. Piper's trance memory is no ordinary human memory; and we have to explain its singular perfection either as the natural endowment of her solitary subliminal self, or as a collection of distinct memory-systems, each with a communicating 'spirit,' as its vehicle." After invoking the importance of her subliminal self in relation to trance communication, he elaborated the "floating mind-stuff in the world, infra-human, yet possessed of fragmentary gleams of superhuman cognition, unable to gather itself together except by taking advantage of the trance states of some existing human organism."[82] The emphasis of the terms "conscious," "subliminal," and "reservoir" reveals that throughout the 1890s James not only conceptualized the phenomenon in *psychological* terms but also used psychical research to develop the framework of the sublime reservoir thesis.

However, the particular use of these terms also reveal that James was not yet thinking about the sublime reservoir theory in metaphysical terms. That move—the use of the term "cosmic" in James's phrase "sublime *cosmic* reservoir"—first emerged in James's 1897 Ingersoll lectures on human immortality subsequently published as *Human Immortality: Two Supposed Objections to the Doctrine* in 1898.[83] As the subtitle indicates, the main point of the lectures was to rebut two common arguments against the immortality thesis: the materialist argument and the overcrowded heaven argument (only the first is relevant to the sublime reservoir theory). One common definition of materialism holds that "matter is fundamental and that whatever else exists is dependent on matter; in its most extreme form materialism is the view that whatever exists is physical. In this view, all mental events are in some way synonymous with or dependent on physical events."[84] The materialist argument against immortality in particular holds that the immortality thesis is wrong because if it were right, noncorporeal thought (mind, soul, consciousness) would have to survive bodily death, in this case that of the brain. But because thought is dependent on the brain, thought cannot survive the brain's death. In James's words, materialism argues that *"thought is a function of the brain,"* which he dubbed the "psycho-physiological formula" (P-P).[85]

French and German physiologists since the eighteenth century had developed this then-radical view. For instance, Julien Offray de La Mettrie argued in *L'Homme machine* (1748) that man was like a "self-moving machine," pointing to all the commonsense evidence of the effects of bodily needs on mental activity. Jean Cabanis, who took Mettrie's radical view one step further, drew a direct analogy between the brain and the digestive system. He argued in *Rapport du physique et du moral de l'homme* (1802) that the brain was an organ that secreted thoughts just the way the liver secretes bile, thus making mental events products of physical brain activity. And Baron d'Holbach (Paul-Henri Dietrich) argued in *Système de la nature* (1770), known as the "Bible of all materialism," that there exists nothing outside of physical nature. He postulated that all mental events such as ideas, thoughts, and feelings were by definition physical ones, and only mechanical causes could explain their motion. These arguments were brought together in the nineteenth century by Ludwig Büchner. Büchner was the first to generalize these experimental findings, arguing in *Kraft und Stoff* (1855) the view that there is no force without matter and vice versa had been proved a posteriori. But, as one scholar explained, it was Darwin's *On the Origin of Species* (1859) and *Descent of Man* (1871) and Huxley's *Man's Place in Nature* (1863) that "provided a plausible, empirically grounded case for two of the main planks of materialism, the claim that the organization of living things into forms admirably suited for survival and reproduction admits of explanation without appeal to immanent or transcendent purposes and the claim that man is a part and product of the natural world," a view that ever since has provided the basis for modern materialism.[86]

James opposed materialism in all its guises. He opposed metaphysical materialism because it was a monist theory, and monism violated his pluralism. He opposed the medical materialism of the physiologists, whom he cited at length in *Human Immortality*, because he thought the P-P axiom failed to prove materialism and thereby to negate the immortality thesis. Instead, he asked whether believing that axiom "logically compels us to disbelieve immortality" and answered it did not.[87] The problem, he explained, was that the P-P axiom relied on a particular theory of brain function known as the "theory of production," which held that the brain's function was to produce consciousness. James was also critical of the "theory of combination," or the view that consciousness is the by-product or "mind stuff" left over from the complex process of a stream of nerve messages in the brain, but he did not address it in these lectures since he had argued against it in chapter 6 of the *Principles*.[88] Also known as the mind stuff theory, it was defended most ably by William Clifford, who held it to be logically incompatible with individual immortality. Because James opposed it, it is reasonable to suggest that James was thinking about defending the immortality thesis in the form of consciousness surviving bodily death, even though he did not describe it as a sublime conscious reservoir, which he had left for his psychical research.[89]

By contrast, James argued in favor of the "theory of separation" of brain states. It allowed for both physical and mental events to coexist and thus did not make the latter dependent on the former. In this view, the brain-function theory of consciousness could be "compatible" with theories of immortality, though it was not an argument in favor of them or of dualism. Given the separation of brain states from thought itself, James argued in favor of one version of separation known as the "transmission theory," which held that the brain's function was to strain or siphon consciousness. Thus, unlike the production theory, which stipulated that consciousness would cease when the body died, the transmission theory held that if the brain transmitted already existing consciousness, then upon bodily death it was logically possible for consciousness to continue. James advocated this latter interpretation for a number of reasons, not least of which was its compatibility with immortality in the form of surviving consciousness but not a mind or soul per se.[90] In fact, James had dispensed with the concept of the soul as early as 1890. In a section of the *Principles* he called "The Substantialist Theory of the Soul," James argued the term lacked all psychological usefulness and was thus superfluous to understanding conscious experience empirically. While he recognized the substantialist theory of the soul had held wide appeal from Plato and Aristotle through John Locke and Immanuel Kant, he argued that advances in brain science since the eighteenth century had rendered that theory outdated. Any attempt to invoke the soul, James argued, simply added nothing more and only complicated what his notion of conscious experience could explain by itself. "The Soul-theory," he concluded, "is a complete superfluity."[91] This position was as close as James would ever get to the medical materialists.

James's brain transmission theory had roots in two philosophers: Schiller and Kant. Amid conceptualizing his arguments for the Ingersoll Lectures, James told Schiller of his plans to use the theory and inquired about its origins: "I write to you ... for the practical purpose of asking you what *history* ... the idea may have which propound in [your] R[iddles] of the S[phinx] of the brain acting not as producer of consciousness but as sifter, limiter, and individualizer thereof." James also mentioned Kant, who, in *Critique of Pure Reason*,

> expresses the hypothesis very clearly, but gives no reference to the previous opinion. For several years past I have defended the view to my students, and was accordingly pleased to find it in your book, and last year [1896] in Kant. I supposed myself to have had the tho't spontaneously, but it may have been sown in my mind by K[ant] years ago, & then become "subliminal." Do you know any forerunners? If, *without research*, you can merely name them, I shall be obliged, for I am going publicly to make use of the idea and want to appear "posted."[92]

Schiller wrote *Riddles of the Sphinx* (1891) to resolve many of the classic conundrums in the history of philosophy. In *Human Immortality* James cited the chapter "Matter and Force" where Schiller argued matter was ultimately spiritual and thereby denied the theory of materialism. One sentence especially supports James's brain transmission theory: "Matter is not that which *produces* consciousness, but that which limits it and confines its intensity within certain limits: material organization does not construct consciousness out of arrangement of atoms, but contracts its manifestation within the sphere which it permits."[93] Likewise, a quotation in Kant's *Critique of Pure Reason* also supported the theory: "Thus regarded, the body would not be the cause of thought, but merely a restrictive condition of it, and therefore, while indeed furthering the sensible and animal life, it would because of this very fact have to be considered a hindrance to the pure and spiritual life. The dependence of the animal and sensible upon the bodily constitution would then in nowise prove the dependence of our entire life upon the state of our organs."[94] Having found his textual support, then, James told Schiller he had settled on this theory, adding, "I treat the matter very inferiorly to you, but use your conception of the brain as a sifting agency, which explains my question in the [first] letter."[95]

If Schiller and Kant provided the intellectual roots for James's brain transmission theory in *Human Immortality*, his sister's pending death provided the occasion to connect it with his sublime reservoir theory. As early as 1891, James confessed to Alice, "These inhibitions, these split-up selves, all these new facts that are gradually coming to light about our organization [the SPR], these enlargements of the self in trance, etc., are bringing me to turn for light in the direction of all sorts of despised spiritualistic and unscientific ideas." This was a clear reference to the psychological component of the sublime reservoir theory within the context of his arguments in the *Principles* and in "A Record of Observations of Certain Phenomena of Trance." But James added the metaphysical explanation too. "And what a queer contradiction comes to the ordinary scientific argument against immortality (based on body being mind's condition and mind going *out* when body is gone)," he wrote, "when one must believe . . . that some infernality in the body *prevents* really existing parts of the mind from coming to their effective rights at all, suppresses them, and blots them out from participation in this world's experiences, although they are *there* all the time." Trying to persuade Alice of his theory, he continued, "When that which is *you* passes out of the body, I am sure that there will be an explosion of liberated force and life till then eclipsed and kept down. I can hardly imagine *your* transition without a great oscillation of both 'worlds' as they regain their new equilibrium after the change! Everyone will feel the shock, but you yourself will be more surprised than anybody else."[96]

William's intellectualizing of his sister's imminent death may appear insensitive or even a form of denial, but Alice's reply indicates just the opposite. Ever the realist, Alice told William, "Of course I could have wanted nothing else and should have felt, notwithstanding my 'unsentimentality[,]' very much wounded & *incomprise* [misunderstood] had you walked round and not up to my demise." Indeed, her reply attempted to make his theory of immortality hers. "Your philosophy of the transition is entirely mine," she claimed, "and at this remoteness I will venture upon the impertinence of congratulating you upon having arrived 'at nearly fifty' at the point at which I started at fifteen! 'Twas always thus of old, but in time you usually, as now, caught up."[97] Despite Alice's deliberate use of the French term for being misunderstood as a way to emphasize her seriousness, it is possible to read such competitive jousting—a hallmark of their lifelong relationship—as an indication of Alice's fury at William for not being warm without sentimentalizing. Either way, although James used the language of "mind" (not "soul" or even "consciousness"), his concern with immortality was unambiguous.

The problem for James, however, was that his argument in defense of survival was atrociously bad; it is circular because it assumes a noncorporeal mind exists in the first place and essentialist because it assumes that noncorporeal mind enjoys a superior ontological status to that of the material brain. But it is an excellent piece of historical evidence confirming the view that James sought a theory of immortality via surviving consciousness as early as 1891 and reveals his sister's pending death was as much a source of his brain transmission theory as Schiller or Kant had been.

It was in these contexts of working out the brain transmission theory during the 1890s that we find James simultaneously advancing the sublime reservoir theory through his psychical research. In three distinct places in *Human Immortality*, he defended his brain transmission theory on the ground that it could explain psychical phenomena. "The transmission-theory," he maintained, "puts itself in touch with a whole class of experiences that are with difficulty explained by the production theory. I refer to those obscure and exceptional phenomena reported at all times throughout human history, which the 'psychical researchers' . . . are doing so much to rehabilitate." Once again, James invoked Mrs. Piper's abilities to exemplify his point: "A medium . . . will show knowledge of his sitter's private affairs which it seems impossible he should have acquired through sight or hearing." He also invoked phantasms, continuing, "Or you will have an apparition of some one who is now dying hundreds of miles away. On the production-theory one does not see from what sensations such odd bits of knowledge are produced. On the transmission-theory, they don't have to be 'produced,'—they exist ready-made in the transcendental world, and all that is needed is an abnormal lowering of the brain-threshold to let them through." James concluded of these psychical phenomena that we need not deny the reality of brain states; rather, "We need only suppose the continuity of our consciousness with a mother-sea, to allow for exceptional waves occasionally pouring over the dam."[98] Such examples, which include one of the earliest uses of the phrase "Mother Sea," show that the origins of James's brain transmission theory were developed in tandem with his psychical research.[99]

James's brain transmission theory garnered positive reaction from some philosophers. Shadworth Hodgson, for instance, found it compelling: "Your theory of 'transmission' is beautifully congruent with my view of the brain as the real condition (not cause) of consciousness."[100] George

Howison approved of it and also found additional problems with materialism and the production theory of the brain, writing, "I think it shows the unsatisfactory limitations of empirical philosophy in a way that the human spirit interested in the question of immortality cannot be satisfied with."[101] And William Kennedy, the literary critic, praised the theory for following Whitman's, whom Kennedy admired, writing in a review that it "shows the influence of Walt Whitman's cosmic mind upon this his admiring pupil, not only in its superb breadth of sympathy, but in some special treatments of the topic of immortality."[102] James replied he had stipulated that even though the transmission theory was consistent with the transcendental mind, it was not dependent on it: "I say in a note that the 'mother sea' need not be monistically or 'transcendental-absolutely' determined. . . . I am against *monistic transcendental idealism*."[103]

There were, however, shortcomings to James's brain transmission theory. Several philosophers and psychologists argued it was not really a theory of immortality, and even if it was one it was not fully developed or individualistic enough. Schiller, for instance, thought the transmission theory offered too little to be of any value. On this point he told James to wait for his reviews in *Nation* and *Mind*.[104] James Ward thought it was useful but maintained the notion that consciousness surviving bodily death was not a theory of immortality but something else. "The only immortality I can think of," he told James, "is not 'remerging in the general Soul' but an abiding consciousness of being an abiding idea there in place of sinking into the Divine. This may be eternal life but it is not immortality."[105] Because of this problem, James's theory would not satisfy most people who wanted something more personal. James offered a reply of sorts in a letter to Flournoy, who had also been critical. "If you had the slightest spark of scientific imagination," James needled, "you would see that the mother-sea is of a glutinous consistency." Likening his view of immortality to that of "'the white radiance of eternity,'" a reference to Percy Bysshe Shelley's *Adonais*, James explained that when Mrs. Piper "strains off portions of her being through the dome of many-colored glass, they stick so tenaciously that she must shake herself hard to get rid of them."[106] But this was just too metaphorical, vague, and undeveloped to satisfy his critics. Charles Strong, for instance, could agree with James that the production theory of the brain was mistaken but pointed out that James's transmission theory made "no attempt to construe the connection between the sea of consciousness & the finite rills. The conception remains in the state of a poetic fancy." Emphasizing his point, he quoted a few lines from George Santayana's sonnet on the soul's immortality, which he found to be far more eloquent.[107]

James Ward agreed. "The question," he told James, "what is the relation of the 'white radiance' or, may be, its source, 'the super-solar blaze' to the subjects that receive it as a kaleidoscopic show—this, the main point as it seems to me—does not come clearly to the fore."[108] Like Strong, Ward did not see a full-blown theory of immortality but a surfeit of poetic sentiment—beautiful, perhaps, but not convincing.

James answered this objection by offering his "checkbook stub" metaphor. Explaining how personal memory was maintained after bodily death, he told Flournoy, "Then, as there is no action without reaction, the shake is felt by both members, and remains registered in the mother-sea, like a 'stub' in a check book, preserving memory of the transaction. These stubs form the basis of the immortal account, which we begin when the prismatic dome is shattered."[109] James repeated this explanation to Ward as well, writing, "The individual's consciousness may survive the brain, for in the Mother Sea the scars of cerebral operations may remain as records of the transactions, like stubs in a check book, and form the basis of an externally remembered account."[110] This elucidation may have satisfied some, but the critics maintained that James's theory was still not individualistic enough. That is, it failed to explain how the bits of Hodgson's consciousness actually connected up with the traces of "Hodgson" in the mother sea of consciousness rather than getting lost amid all the others. How was personal identity ensured in the cosmos? Without such a direct connection, it was unclear any individual's consciousness survived intact, and most people required a guarantee of the survival of their own unique identity to call this immortality. As Howison put it to James, "The one weak point in your exposition . . . is your failure to connect your argument *securely* with the possibility of *individual* immortality. . . . You do not make the possible 'many minds behind the scenes' identical with *our* minds. . . . But if these transcendent minds are not *ours*, of what earthly avail is their survival of the death of the brain to us? *Some* things," he added, may live on, but "what is that to us?"[111]

James answered this final objection to his brain transmission theory by making clear that he did not have a problem with correlating the traces of surviving consciousness with an individual personal identity. Elaborating his position, he told Ward, "I should have said more explicitly that there is no objection to considering the Mother Sea in as individualistic a form as you like. We should then . . . be filtered into this world's experiences, and then be re-united to our deeper truer selves."[112] And to Howison he confessed, "I never caught, till I read it, the idea that my supposition about the brain could be worked by the ordinary spiritualistic philosophy by simply making the 'mother sea' consist of the collection of individual spirits, each in a completer and truer form than what filters through into this phenomenal life."[113] Referring to Howison's specific suggestion, he added, "I wish I had tho't of that." Indeed, James thought the point valid enough to incorporate it into the preface to the second edition of *Human Immortality*.[114] He was not willing, however, to make spirits into an organized hierarchal system. For instance, of Wincenty Lutoslawski's theory of immortality, he wrote, "The universe is a great hierarchic system of such individual souls," a view he thought utopian and romantic even if it simultaneously opposed materialism and idealism while being a version of pluralism. For James, spirits and souls could not be "ultimate and irreducible facts" or what Lutoslawski called "substances."[115] Such a view was too essentialized and violated both his empirical pragmatism and his metaphysical pluralism. Thus, while James was willing to allow for the possibility that surviving bits of consciousness could be equated with individuals, he was not willing to make them fundamentally irreducible facts of consciousness in the cosmos. As he put it to Schiller in a discussion about ghosts that equally applied to souls, "I don't see why some things should not permanently be only halfway in the Cosmos."[116] Such a view spoke loudly of his tertium quid approach.

Cosmology and Immortality

The language contained in *Human Immortality*—the "Mother Sea of consciousness," "a collection of distinct memory-systems," "floating mind-stuff in the world," and "the stub in a check book"—reveals James was moving toward a view that the survival of consciousness beyond bodily death was metaphysical and thereby shows that the sublime reservoir theory was not only psychological but increasingly philosophical. He did not yet have, however, an account of the "Mother Sea" or what might be thought of as an ur-consciousness of the universe. For that he needed a cosmological theory, which James found in Gustav Fechner, a German psychologist, physicist, and professor at the University of Leipzig. Fechner began his career in the 1830s conducting groundbreaking work in the physics of electricity and perception until some experiments with afterimages in 1838–39 involving staring at the sun for too long blinded him for three years and led to a nervous breakdown and his subsequent reclusion. During that time, Fechner's faith sustained him, and he turned to more metaphysical issues, especially the question of survival, and set about to refute materialism. Miraculously, Fechner recovered and returned to the same university as a professor of philosophy in 1848, where he did his most well known work in psychophysics, including the idea of a conscious "threshold"—the same notion James had advanced in *The Principles of Psychology* and *Human Immortality* in support of his subliminal self theory. In *Zend-Avesta* (1851), Fechner sought to show there was a God and argued the entire universe is spiritual, with the physical or material universe being an extension of it. Atoms, for instance, he considered forces of energy, not physical entities in and of themselves. Consciousness, too, was a center of energy. Indeed, for Fechner, all living things were conscious and thus manifestations of energy. But Fechner's vision was much bigger than earthly panpsychism. The earth, moon, sun, stars, solar system, galaxy—the entire universe—possessed consciousness progressively all the way up to God. Fechner dubbed the belief that all things have consciousness "daylight," whereas the belief that they do not he called the "night view."[117] Fechner's argument for immortality was based in particular on the claim that conscious experience does not die out when the brain does but rather lives on in the form of memories that conjoin with others' memories in the collective consciousness of the universe, including, ultimately, with God. Thus, mind outlives the body; the soul survives death.[118]

Although it was monistic, James found Fechner's cosmology a useful springboard for his sublime reservoir theory. He elucidated Fechner's metaphysics on several occasions during the first decade of the 1900s. The first was in his introduction to the 1904 English translation of Fechner's book *Das Büchlein vom Leben nach dem Tode* (1836).[119] There, James recounted Fechner's panpsychism and "daylight" versus "night view" theories, as well as Fechner's theory of immortality known as the earth-soul theory. James explained how for Fechner the sum total of brain consciousness worked: "Now, impressed on the whole earth-mind as memories, they lead the life of ideas there, and realize themselves no longer in isolation, but along with all the similar vestiges left by other human lives, entering with these into new combinations, affected anew by experiences of the living, and affecting the living in their turn, enjoying, in short, that 'third stage' of existence." The end result of this process culminated in God for Fechner, or what James called "the totalized consciousness of the whole universe." In a dramatic impression moment, James allowed for that possibility, but he did not invoke it and argued he was not forced logically to accept a monistic God in support of his sublime reservoir theory. He simply needed cosmological support for the view that memory survives in the form of consciousness in the universe which, he maintained, Fechner's earth-soul theory provided in its minimalist version.[120]

Fechner's influence on James's theory of immortality is most apparent in "Concerning Fechner," "The Continuity of Experience," and "Conclusions," three of eight lectures James gave at Oxford in May 1908 as the "Hibbert Lectures at Manchester College on the Present Situation in Philosophy." They were published as *A Pluralistic Universe* and written while James was conducting the research for his Hodgson-control report.[121] There, and to his listeners at Oxford, James introduced Fechner's pantheism, panpsychism, and theory of immortality as a bulwark against monistic theories, especially Hegel's idealism, Josiah Royce's Absolute, and F. H. Bradley's neo-Hegelian idealism (Bradley was in the audience at Oxford). He admitted Fechner's earth-soul theory was monistic but noted his strategy was to "thicken up" the metaphysical possibilities to make room for his pluralism. As such, he invoked one of Fechner's insights, namely, the *"assumption that conscious experiences freely compound and separate themselves."*[122]

This key idea influenced James's evolving thinking about immortality. For instance, in "Concerning Fechner," James elaborated Fechner's theory at length:

> Fechner likens our individual persons on the earth unto so many sense-organs of the earth's soul. We add to its perceptive life so long as our own life lasts. It absorbs our perceptions, just as they occur, into its larger sphere of knowledge, and combines them with the other data there. When one of us dies, it is as if an eye of the world were closed, for all *perceptive* contributions from that particular quarter cease. But the memories and conceptual relations that have spun themselves round the perceptions of that person remain in the larger earth-life as distinct as ever, and form new relations and grow and develope [sic] throughout all the future, in the same way in which our own distinct objects of thought, once stored in memory, form new relations and develope [sic] throughout our whole finite life. This is Fechner's theory of immortality.[123]

James might as well have said, "This is my theory of immortality," since it was the conceptual basis for his sublime reservoir idea. Not coincidentally, he made remarkably similar comments at the end of the Hodgson report, where he hypostatized Hodgson's consciousness leaving traces on the material universe. James explained how this process worked by personalizing it: "During your life the traces are mainly in your brain; but after your death, since your brain is gone, they exist in the shape of all the records of your actions which the outer world stores up as the effects, immediate or remote, thereof, the cosmos being in some degree, however slight, made structurally different by every act of ours that takes place in it."[124]

Invoking Fechner's earth-soul theory, however, was unlikely to have convinced the skeptic. Much like the critics of James's brain transmission theory, a listener in the audience at Oxford might have well asked what guaranteed the survival of one's individual identity. James thought Fechner could explain it and answered at length:

> We rise upon the earth as wavelets rise upon the ocean. We grow out of her soil as leaves grow from a tree. The wavelets catch the sunbeams separately, [and] the leaves stir when the branches do not move. They realize their own events apart, just as in our own consciousness, when anything becomes emphatic, the background fades from observation. Yet the event works back upon the background, as the wavelet works upon the waves, or as the leaf's movements work upon the sap inside the branch. The whole sea and the whole tree are registers of what has happened, and are different for the wave's and the leaf's action having occurred. A grafted twig may modify its scion to the roots:—so [too] our outlived private experiences, impressed on the whole earth-mind as memories, lead the immortal life of ideas there, and become parts of the great system, fully distinguished from one another, just as we ourselves when alive were distinct, realizing themselves no longer isolatedly, but along with one another as so many partial systems, entering thus into new combinations, being affected by the perceptive experiences of those living then, and affecting the living in their turn—altho they are so seldom recognized by living men to do so.[125]

In other words, for Fechner personal identity survived bodily death in the form of memory and joined in the cosmos much like the way parts of nature survived by joining the greater whole. Similarly, for James, personal identity survived bodily death as traces of consciousness mingling with other such traces in the mother sea of consciousness like stubs in a checkbook. But the critic may well have just concluded Fechner's nature metaphor was no more helpful than James's accounting one. The question remained: what was to guarantee the survival of one's self as a whole self? After all, as Ward had pointed out years before, traces of selves floating in the cosmos hardly seemed like a theory of immortality worth embracing. Since neither Fechner nor James had a good answer to this criticism, there seemed little reason to abandon monism or even materialism. James's appeal to Fechner's earth-soul theory, much less to his pantheism and panpsychism, to support his pluralism would have likely fallen on stubborn Oxfordian ears.

But James clearly found Fechner's theory of immortality necessary. Invoking Fechner at the end of "The Continuity of Experience," James explained, "I find in some of these abnormal or supernormal facts the strongest suggestions in favor of a superior co-consciousness being possible. I doubt whether we shall ever understand some of them without using the very letter of Fechner's conception of a great reservoir in which the memories of earth's inhabitants are pooled and preserved, and from which, when the threshold lowers or the valve opens, information ordinarily shut out leaks into the mind of exceptional individuals [that is, mediums] among us." Noting that such "regions of inquiry are perhaps too spook-haunted to interest an academic audience," James invoked more mainstream religious experiences, claiming they were real and pointed "with reasonable probability to the continuity of our consciousness with a wider spiritual environment."[126] That James offered mediumship to support the existence of co-consciousness against monistic theories and in favor of pluralism in the context of Fechner's theory of immortality reveals the strong relationship between his metaphysics in *A Pluralistic Universe* and his psychical research in "Report on Mrs. Piper's Hodgson-Control." The textual connection is amplified in "Conclusions," where once again James expostulated at length:

> The drift of all the evidence we have seems to me to sweep us very strongly towards the belief in some form of superhuman life with which we may, unknown to ourselves, be co-conscious. We may be in the universe as dogs and cats are in our libraries, seeing the books and hearing the conversation, but having no inkling of the meaning of it all.... The analogies with ordinary psychology, with certain facts of pathology, with those of psychical research, so called, and with those of religious experience, establish, when taken together, a decidedly *formidable* probability in favor of a general view of the world almost identical with Fechner's. The outlines of the superhuman consciousness thus made probable must remain, however, very vague, and the number of functionally distinct "selves" it comports and carries has to be left entirely problematic.[127]

In short, James argued that the preponderance of evidence made it probable that Fechner's worldview was likely the correct one, even if he could not fully commit himself to it.

Despite going far out on that limb in support of Fechner, James was more cautious with his own theory of immortality. He noted he neither had an answer for the individualistic critique nor could say with confidence that an ur-consciousness existed. The most he could say in keeping with his pragmatic empiricism was that it was likely the evidence in the long run would demonstrate it. He also noted that a superhuman consciousness could be polytheistic or monotheistic, with Fechner's earth-soul theory tending toward the latter, but that his pluralistic theory of immortality did not require one to accept Fechner. "The only way of escape, I say, from all this is to be frankly pluralistic and assume that the superhuman consciousness, however vast it may be, has itself an external environment, and consequently is finite."[128] James reached precisely this conclusion in his Hodgson-control report at roughly the same time in 1909. In it he left unresolved the exact nature of the identity purporting to be Hodgson, thereby not solving the individualistic critique, but he did advance a theory of immortality that, given the right empirical conditions, might one day explain it. In this way, he linked his psychical research and his metaphysics.

Despite James's numerous attempts in the Hibbert Lectures to distinguish his theory of immortality as pluralistic from Fechner's monistic one, even while appealing to Fechner's earth-soul theory in support of his sublime reservoir thesis, one James scholar has argued that the sublime reservoir theory was monistic. Julius Bixler claimed that James's invoking a "confluent consciousness" shared much in common with the Absolute. James's use of the phrases "the mother-sea," "fountain-head," and "cosmic reservoir of memories" was proof. As such, Bixler wrote, "the great central consciousness seems to be similar to if not identical with the world-consciousness or cosmic consciousness to which James often alludes," and "the other interest" (psychical research) that "occupied his mind for a considerable period of time" was "the possibility of the existence of a spiritual environment of consciousness connecting all individual lives in one great cosmic continuum." Bixler thereby maintained that James's interest in psychical phenomena was related to his interest in religious experience and "not finally suggestive as to immortality." Offering James's defense of Mrs. Piper in particular, Bixler concluded, "It is impossible not to feel that James rejected immortality suggested by psychical research partly because it did not satisfy his sense for the religiously appropriate."[129]

As this chapter amply demonstrates, though, both of Bixler's claims are highly implausible. First, James's psychical research was the fountainhead of his theory of immortality, whereas lived religious experience played but a tertiary role in his interest in immortality and in his conceptualization of the theory. Second, James's sublime reservoir theory of immortality was not monistic but pluralistic. While James certainly did not have an answer to the individualistic critique, the mother sea of consciousness concept did not logically imply monism. After all, James emphasized traces of surviving consciousness floating in the sea, not that they were unified within that sea or were the same thing as the sea, a notable point of departure from Fechner's earth-soul theory. Unless the sea was the monistic entity akin to Fechner's God, which the above shows that James most certainly did not believe, then it is mistaken to characterize James's sublime reservoir theory of immortality as monistic. Bixler's problematic interpretation thus lay in not examining James's psychical research writings, especially the Hodgson-control report.

A fairer critique would be to argue, as James's contemporaries did, that the theory was not fully developed. Lloyd Morris later made this point. Unlike Bixler, Morris did not think James flirted with the Absolute but did reach something like the sublime reservoir theory. Regarding some ultimate power, he wrote, "The power might conceivably be only a larger and more godlike self, or which the finite self would then be only a 'mutilated expression'; and the universe might conceivably be a polytheism—a collection of such selves, of different degrees of inclusiveness, with no absolute unity in it realized at all."[130] For Morris, then, James's mother sea of consciousness was clearly pluralistic, though like Bixler he, too, seemed unaware of the significant role psychical research played in James's theory of immortality.

The best discussion of this topic to date is that of G. William Barnard. Barnard correctly located one of the origins of James's sublime conscious reservoir notion in Fechner's concept of the threshold of consciousness to defend the transmission theory of consciousness. He also pointed to the James-Myers theory of the subliminal self to explain how and where mystical and psychic experiences occur and especially to Fechner's earth-soul theory to hypothesize how consciousness might survive bodily death.[131] Barnard's discussion of all three points is lucid, balanced, and compelling. However, Bixler's primary aim was to show how all three illuminate James's theories of mysticism via the theory of compounding of consciousness. But those theories were expressed through and were a result of James's psychical research. The two interpretations are not incompatible, but whereas Barnard maintained James's psychological and philosophical doctrines informed James's thinking about mysticism, this chapter argues James's psychical research informed his psychology and philosophy to show it was central and typical of James's life and thought, a point Barnard could not make about James's interest in mysticism, which was of the whole but far less significant than psychical research.

The foregoing reveals that William James had a theory of immortality—the sublime reservoir thesis. It comprised three parts: the will, the brain transmission theory, and a pluralistic cosmos. For James, consciousness, not the soul, survived bodily death. Its form was a fragmented memory manifested as a will to communicate. This will was ostensibly individualistic but not finally atomistic since it melded with all other such wills, each manifesting their own fragmented memories, in the great sea of consciousness to form one large ur-consciousness. This consciousness was not God for James, as it was for Fechner, but a not-yet-understood metaphysical aspect of ultimate reality. Like his theory of the subliminal self, which was intricately connected with his view of immortality, James did not state the sublime reservoir thesis in one place. Rather, he developed it gradually over two decades, from 1890 to 1909, in his writings on scientific psychology, religion, and especially psychical research. In particular, James advanced different aspects of the theory in *The Principles of Psychology*, where James rejected the concept of the soul, in *Human Immortality*, where James adopted the brain transmission theory, and in *The Varieties of Religious Experience*, where James stipulated the subliminal self was the conduit to the sublime reservoir.

But it was in his psychical research essays such as "A Record of Observations of Certain Phenomena of Trance" that James first conceived the language and germinated the seed of the thesis, and especially in "Report on Mrs. Piper's Hodgson-Control," in which James carefully worked out the multiple wills and pluralistic elements of the thesis, the latter simultaneously advanced in his metaphysical work *A Pluralistic Universe*. Part psychological and part metaphysical, then, the sublime reservoir theory was neither purely naturalistic nor entirely supernatural but rather something in between. Such a view agreed with his psychical brethren at the SPR who believed something survived bodily death, even to the point of a certain individualistic something, but stopped short of essentializing that something or equivocating it with the soul. In that sense, it agreed with the medical materialists that the soul was no longer a useful concept and that all conceptualization of consciousness must be centered on the brain but disagreed with them that consciousness ceases when the brain dies. As such, neither adherents of the Platonic-Cartesian theory of dualism, which supported the immortal soul doctrine so cherished by most Christians, Spiritualists, and especially the Sidgwick Group, nor advocates of the material view of the brain, which supported the brain production thesis held by most medical materialists and physiological psychologists, nor even devotees of idealism such as Royce and Bradley, who advanced monistic theories of the cosmos, satisfied James's thinking about immortality.

By contrast, James's sublime reservoir thesis was a new kind of theory about the possibility of a future life. It was strictly empirical, since it theorized based on observed facts and their logical inference, and broadly pragmatic, since it stipulated the theory's intellectual usefulness would be revised, confirmed, or discarded in the long run as new facts emerged from the investigation of the "unseen world." In this way, James's sublime reservoir theory of immortality became the final instance of his tertium quid intellectual disposition.

Conclusion

TERTIUM QUID REDUX

Two months before he died in August 1910, William James told Henry Adams that he was "an old man soon about to meet his maker."[1] Even before his prophecy, James began finishing his major philosophical writings *A Pluralistic Universe* and *The Meaning of Truth*. He also began wrapping up his psychical research, telling the novelist Hamlin Garland that he had had "no direct contact with mediums for many years.... Practically, I am quite out of it. Haven't the time or the energy!"[2] Like many such statements, however, James was being cagey, revealing his desire to distance himself from the subject while being profoundly unable to walk away from it. In fact, James engaged psychical research tenaciously during his final years. He remained focused on Mrs. Leonora Piper, helping the Society for Psychical Research secure control of its research on her, overseeing the discussion regarding her future, and facilitating a major new test of her. He also supported studies of other mental mediums. Quite surprisingly, James resumed his study of Eusapia Palladino and sat with a table-levitating group in Bar Harbor, Maine, and with several physical mediums in New York City. James also continued to nurture his friendships with colleagues on both sides of the Atlantic, such as George Dorr and J. G. Piddington, as well as established a new one with Hereward Carrington. He likewise continued to encourage several family members and close friends to explore their psychic abilities, and he sustained his debates with the critics of psychical research, such as the authors of a Columbia University report who, after testing Eusapia, concluded she cheated. Most significantly, James wrote his last popular psychical research essay summarizing his final opinions. All in all, James not only was far from "out of it" but also was actively engaged in psychical research up to the very end of his life.

James's primary role with mental mediums during his final years focused on Mrs. Piper. Since Richard Hodgson had been her main handler for nearly two decades, his death in 1905 prompted questions about her future as well as about the rightful ownership of Hodgson's massive tome of unpublished research on her. James Hyslop, the president of the newly re-formed American Society of Psychical Research who was looking to expand his organization's reach and influence, laid claim to Mrs. Piper and Hodgson's research.³ The SPR leaders strenuously opposed this plan. They argued that since the work had been carried out under the SPR's auspices and since Hodgson had been its officer, ownership of the material and control of Mrs. Piper belonged to the SPR.⁴ They were also concerned that the private correspondence scattered amid Hodgson's rooms, which had served as the ASPR office for all those years, might contain compromising information about F. W. H. Myers's affairs that, if made public, might sully his reputation. As such, Oliver Lodge instructed James, "Don't let it get out of your control."⁵ James agreed with his SPR colleagues that Hyslop had far overstepped his jurisdiction, telling Isaac Funk, whom Hyslop had enlisted as an envoy to persuade James of his plan, that "if the Branch remains alive, the Council will publish; if it dissolves, the records revert to the parent Society. This is the legal view."⁶ In fact, the last act the ASPR took before disbanding itself was to ask the SPR to send Piddington to the United States "to débrouiller the whole mass of papers left in R. H.'s rooms."⁷

Typically, James grew weary with the issue and relegated control to George Dorr and to his wife, Alice, whom he noted had had "much trouble and [been at] logger-heads . . . over S.P.R. affairs (as my lieutenant) on account of Hodgson's death."⁸ But the dogged Hyslop did not relent, and matters worsened, prompting James to complain to Alice that all "these jealousies around Mrs. P. are deplorable."⁹ Eventually, though, James, who had distanced himself because of his severe dislike of Hyslop and his popularization of mediumship, convinced Hyslop to give up the matter, and the SPR prevailed. With Hodgson's research and private papers went Mrs. Piper to England in 1906–7, and so too her management. Piddington, another SPR leader whom James had befriended, became her primary handler, while Alice Johnson, the SPR's secretary who came with Piddington to the United States to fetch Mrs. Piper and the Hodgson material, stayed at his house.¹⁰ Such hospitality typified James's loyalty to the SPR. Ironically, and perhaps a little cruelly, his loyalty did not extend to Mrs. Piper. When asked to contribute funds for her future security, he declared that he was unwilling "to take any active or financial responsibility whatever," adding "Years ago I foresaw the problem of her future looming ahead and have consistently avoided incurring responsibility."[11] Given his decades-long support of Mrs. Piper, this seems unexplainable, yet even as James distanced himself from his "white crow," he continued to arrange sittings for his wife, daughter, son, and close friends and sat with her for the last time in May 1909.[12] He also wanted to resume work on the "psychic synthesis" problem, but his poor health prevented him from "taking up any active work in psychics."[13] Instead, he rallied support for Julian Ochorowicz's "Polish medium" and a new but unidentified SPR automatic writing subject "of great importance."[14]

Finally, James supported G. Stanley Hall's plan to test Mrs. Piper.—against Lodge's wishes.[15] James reasoned that Hall's tests would provide an opening to resume the debate over her value to scientific psychology, explaining to Dorr that "the only real question at stake is as to Mrs. Piper's *supernormal knowledge*."[16] James told Hall to look for his upcoming report on Mrs. Piper, to which Hall replied he was "glad" to learn of it and that his own tests would reveal a "new phase of the Piper problem."[17] Hall published the results in a book called *Studies in Spiritism*, written by his assistant Amy Tanner.[18] Contrary to James's expectations, the results did not reveal a "new phase," because Hall simply advanced a version of the pathological explanation of Mrs. Piper. The Hodgson-control was, Hall concluded, nothing more than a "parasitic secondary personality."[19] James passed away before the book was published, so he was unable to respond, although during the testing phase Hall informed James of his ability to trick the Hodgson-control into lying, which James acknowledged was "interesting psychologically."[20] Some commentators believe *Studies in Spiritism* was the deathblow to James's defense of Mrs. Piper. One even wrote that the book led to a "devastating outcome."[21] This claim, however, does not prove Hall's argument; it merely reasserts it. By contrast, as argued herein, James possessed a sufficient argument in the form of a tertium quid to rebut Hall. Given James's long-term opposition to Hall, it seems highly likely he would have made it had he lived long enough. Moreover, Hyslop found multiple factual discrepancies in *Studies in Spiritism*.[22] However, the occurrence of James's death before the debate could play out precludes final judgment on this matter.

James's defense of Mrs. Piper and mental mediumship during his final years was highly predictable, but his rekindled interest in physical mediumship, especially his defense of Eusapia Palladino, was quite shocking.[23] Sparked by a new round of testing led by well-known scientists in France, Italy, and Britain, Eusapia enjoyed a brief renaissance from 1905 to 1910, which James dubbed the "Eusapia boom."[24] Amazingly, James's reading of the European reports prompted him to revisit the "human rat hole" of physical mediumship and to make numerous dodgy statements in defense of Eusapia. For instance, he told various friends that he thought Enrico Morselli's book would "settle" the scandalous "condition of opinion as regards 'physical mediumship,'" that he "rejoice[d] in the triumph of Eusapia," that Eusapia had been "vindicate[ed]," that "physical phenomena also seem to be entering upon a new phase in their history," and that "public opinion" would finally catch up to the new reality.[25] He emphasized that Marie and Pierre Curie's "very masterly" report on her "makes ordinary observation seem like child's play," that "no one who has seen much of Eusapia of late preserves any doubts about her genuineness," and that "Hodgson was evidently premature in his condemnation of E. P."[26] He concluded that "judging by ... [*Annales des Sciences Psychiques*] the proof seems overwhelming," that "after Courtier's report on Eusapia, I don't think any [further] 'investigation' here will be worth much 'scientifically,'" that he "always suspected that she would turn out good," and that the tests "cast retrospective credit on [William] Crooke's [*sic*] ancient testimony."[27] Finally, he proclaimed with uncharacteristic certainty, "I feel morally convinced[,] that is I would *bet* heavily—that the future will corroborate all this 'teleplasty' ... as a field of real experience surrounding the acknowledged order of nature and of tremendous cosmic import, whatever the import may be."[28] Despite the use of the term "bet," however, James's position was unpragmatic, and his use of absolutist language was atypical. It was one of the very few times he betrayed his tertium quid method of inquiry in favor of a dogmatic one. These statements were equally unwise since their substance was later proven false, revealing just how foolish he had been in defending them. They also reveal how difficult it had been for James to defend his tertium quid approach over the decades. As he confessed to Eleanor Sidgwick, "It has been an enormous relief to my mind to quit the balancing attitude which I have voluntarily maintained for 15 years, and come to a stable belief in the matter."[29] In fact, as this book has shown, James had embraced the third way throughout much of his lifetime.

The perils of abandoning his tertium quid for temporary psychological relief manifested themselves in James's misguided, if well-intentioned, support for Hereward Carrington, Eusapia's primary backer in England and the United States. An upcoming second- generation psychical researcher who went on to a distinguished career in the field, Carrington convinced the SPR council to reopen Eusapia's file for new rounds of testing in 1908.[30] Subsequent testing in 1909, which James closely followed, led Carrington to argue that while Eusapia cheated on some occasions, she produced decent

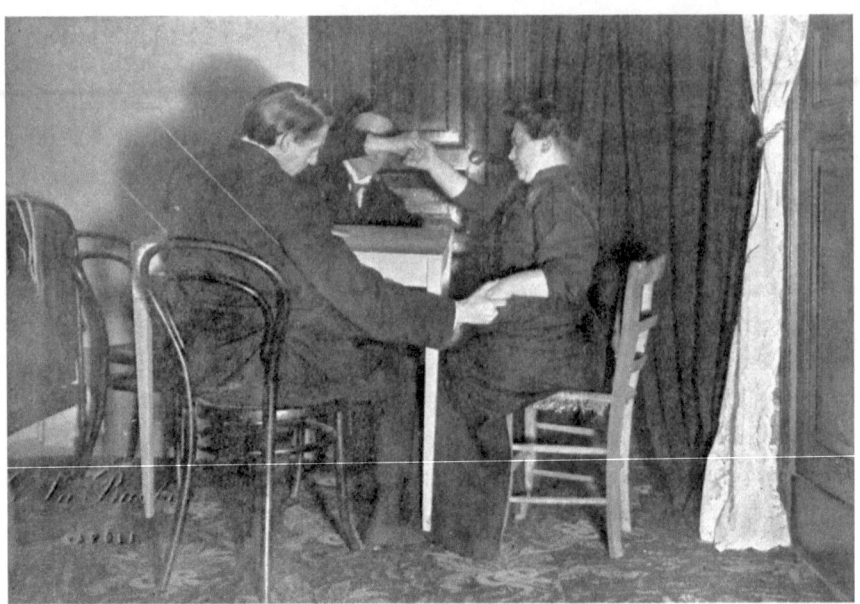

HEREWARD CARRINGTON (1880–1958) and EUSAPIA PALLADINO (1854–1918), ca. 1908–1909. Sittings like these persuaded James late in his life to reconsider the evidence for physical mediumship. *Hereward Carrington,* Eusapia Palladino and Her Phenomena *(New York: B. W. Dodge, 1909).*

phenomena on others requiring explanation.[31] James had reached this conclusion many years prior, so it made the two men natural allies. Indeed, when the two first met in New York City in 1907, Carrington impressed James as "tip-top: 28 years old, slender, neutral socially, an intellect primarily . . . for professional purposes, [and] . . . fair minded."[32] James subsequently befriended him much as he had the members of the Sidgwick Group, and for a brief time the two men worked in tandem in their support of Eusapia. In 1909, for instance, Carrington gave a speech at the Twentieth Century Club in Boston that invoked James's defense of Eusapia, while James, who introduced Carrington, vouched for his expertise and praised him for understanding her case.[33]

With SPR approval and James's support, Carrington subsequently organized two Eusapia tours in the United States. The first occurred in the fall of 1908, when she held sittings with a number of interested parties such as Hugo Münsterberg at Harvard, a brass instrument psychologist skeptical of psychic phenomena and critical of James's psychical research, and the second in the winter of 1909–10, when James sat with her and experienced a queer "twisting of my chair."[34] William Pepperell Montague, a professor in the Department of Philosophy and Psychology at Columbia University, had a sitting, too. Montague observed "good levitations," floating furniture, and a spectral hand but also a great deal of what he took to be cheating. More important, he noted the unscientific character of these sittings, since Carrington had "made a miserable mistake in not seggregating [sic] the incidental spiritists and others who support the show from the scientists who are investigating it," and vowed to conduct his own investigation.[35]

So, in January 1910, Montague and a team of investigators tested Eusapia at Columbia's physical laboratory.[36] Ever in search of support from orthodox scientists, James endorsed the tests and persuaded Carrington to allow them because the question of Eusapia's validity had to be determined by "authority, as in all science."[37] James thought the American tests would verify the French, Italian, and British results, although he cautioned the researchers against trying to prove too much.[38] But the Columbia team, whose report was published in *Science* magazine, not only found a lack of evidence supporting supernormal phenomena but also offered massive evidence of fraud even while admitting that the difficulties in meeting the standards of rigorous scientific method had somewhat limited their testing.[39]

The report's damning conclusion threw Carrington on the defensive. He wanted to conduct a new round of tests to rebut the Columbia results, but James counseled him to relent: "Don't get your 'back up' and your teeth set to ram the thing by more 'evidence' down reluctant throats—you can't do it—*no* evidence will suffice after what they have seen; and Eusapia deserves it all! Her methods are too detestable for nomenclature! You are a serious student; leave your reputation in the hands of history, and pass on to more deserving subjects.... [It is] the dignified course." He also added a statement suggesting he had been mistaken as well. The Columbia report "proved fraud to be much more continuous and ubiquitous than you [or I] had supposed.... The case is too mixed for truth to be thrashed out ever on purely evidential lines.... Eusapia, if *true*, deserves to have it *never known*, for her essential mendacity, and you, of clear-seeing in her case, must wait for the retrospective corroboration to be cast on her and you by possible future cases."[40]

But Carrington was not persuaded and instead took his case to the court of public opinion. He found three sympathizers (Howard Thurston, a professional magician; Joseph F. Rinn, the secretary of the Metropolitan Psychical Society; and Rinn's lackey, W. S. Davis, "Spruce St. printer") who made public offers of $1,000 to anyone who could prove her a fraud. This desperate tactic backfired, for on 12 May 1910 the *New York Times*, which had made the "Eusapia boom" one of the year's biggest stories, published parts of the Columbia report along with signed statements from several of the report's lead authors. This reporting exposed Eusapia as a fraud and made Carrington and James, who were mentioned in some of the stories as her backers, look foolish.[41]

The negative media coverage quickly became a public relations disaster for the cause of psychical research and for Carrington personally. This prompted James to imagine that Carrington must be having a "perfect hell of a time with all the publicity and turmoil" and that he would need "divine support."[42] But James's consolation was not enough, for the *Times* coverage not only exposed Eusapia but also discredited her in the eyes of her well-heeled supporters, who subsequently called off their private sittings with her. This dried up the funds that Carrington had started to raise to pay for her extravagant fees, which, in turn, angered Eusapia, since not only had she been publicly humiliated but she had lost the promised income that had lured her to America. "The whole thing 'fell through,'" James lamented to Théodore Flournoy. "Eusapia's trip to the U.S. will simply have spoiled her, and discredited everyone else." James could not have been more correct, especially since he was "everyone else." He had been "had," and he looked the fool. "Eusapia's type of performance is *detestable*," he complained bitterly. "If it be not fraud simulating reality, it is reality simulating fraud!"[43] Whatever it was, James had been publicly exposed for supporting a known charlatan with a long history of cheating—all in the name of legitimizing psychical research. It was probably the most humiliating and embarrassing moment of his illustrious career. Had he not abandoned his tertium quid method in favor of dogmatic support for Eusapia, he likely would have avoided it. Instead, the "Eusapia boom" became the Eusapia fiasco, discrediting him and psychical research.

After the debacle, James tried to console Carrington. Invoking words of comfort that were clearly meant as self-consolation, he told Carrington "not [to be] be upset..., that history would judge him as a serious student, and [that he] was glad that he conducted himself well in the newspapers by not losing his temper."[44] But the truth was that James had long since doubted Carrington. Two years earlier he had confided to his daughter that he found him "interesting but colorless," a far cry from how he had felt about the Sidgwick Group.[45]

Inexplicably, though, James was unable to follow his own advice to Carrington, as he continued to cling to the remote possibility that science might eventually show Eusapia's phenomena were genuine. When asked by *Cosmopolitan* magazine for his opinion, James reiterated that Eusapia's methods were "detestable" but maintained that the "uniqueness of the phenomena" justified studying her. A serious investigation, he stipulated, would require twenty-five sittings by a group of scientists, when she "may break the bounds which science hitherto has set to nature's forces."[46] Privately, he continued to argue that despite Eusapia's cheating, which he had personally witnessed on numerous occasions over the years, he still believed there were too many instances when she was not caught cheating that required explanation.[47] But the Columbia team had essentially performed those tests, and anecdotal evidence was hardly scientific. James just could not admit she was a fraud; his tertium quid approach prevented it.

Two other developments rekindled James's interest in physical mediumship during his final years. First, there were his sittings with a Spiritualist circle at George Dorr's "Oldfarm" house in Bar Harbor, Maine, in 1909.[48] "There is a new wave of advance in physical phenomena upon us," James told Piddington. "I have just got a report of table levitation from a circle ... which I attended a month ago, and where I saw something ... which awakens great confidence." James hoped that the tide of public opinion, which had turned against physical phenomena, would soon reverse its course to a more favorable position.[49] Similarly, he told Alice he had been "rewarded by the sight of an *object moving without contact*, under conditions so simple that no room for fakery seemed possible."[50] James wrote an essay providing the group's history and his analysis, noting that while the event had failed to move him emotionally and that the conditions were not very satisfactory, there was too much evidence to be dismissed outright. Offering his usual caveat that the truth would be established pragmatically in the long run, he concluded, "The levee by which scientific opinion protects nature would be cracked for me, and I should be as one watching an incipient overflow of the Mississippi of the supernatural into the fields of orthodox culture. I find, however, that I look on nature with unaltered eyes to-day, and that my orthodox habits tend to extrude this would-be levee breaker. It forms too much of an exception."[51]

Finally, there were James's erratic sittings with lesser-known mediums in New York City such as "Mrs. Beatty" and "Mrs. Mayer," the former whom he called an "excellent medium, for raps, & table & slate," and the latter convincing him of "the reality of the phenomenon as fully as was possible in a single sitting," a view that was not weakened after a follow-up sitting.[52] Several other sittings involved DeWitt Hough's "materialization," Wilson's ability to manifest a "psychic cold," Miss Crossly ("a very good medium"), and even a "voodoo lady" of "color."[53] His library also contained marked-up books on the topic.[54]

The renaissance in physical mediumship typified by the "Eusapia boom," the Bar Harbor group, and miscellaneous mediums in New York City revealed the wider, long-running debate over psychic phenomena, namely, that there would be argument without end. By 1910, for skeptics such as the authors of the Columbia report and the brass instrument psychologists, enough quality evidence had poured in. Multiple instances of verified, repeated, and consistent results had demonstrated that Eusapia and her kind failed to produce any phenomena outside the natural realm. Moreover, the cumulative body of evidence showed she and the others frequently cheated. They were simply frauds and therefore did not require further investigation. The matter was settled. But for James, who consistently held out for more effective study that might produce new and affirming evidence of supernatural quality, the matter was still open. As such, it was unwise to completely close the door on Eusapia and her ilk, no matter how "deplorable" she or they were. With the notable exception of his lapse during the Eusapia fiasco, James's tertium quid method of inquiry drove his approach to physical mediumship in these final years.

There were, however, severe limitations to this kind of intellectual justification. Clearly, it was both unrealistic and unfair, since James perpetually raised the threshold that skeptics had to pass over. The minimum number and quality of scientific studies required to prove a negative, difficult as that already was, was increased one notch every time a new report found nothing to support belief in supernormal or supernatural phenomena. This meant no amount of proof would ever convince James and thus knowledge through his model could never be attained. The tertium quid approach might have been principled, but when taken to the extreme it was self-defeating and irrational. It simply provided James with a kind of philosophical cover for a largely indefensible position. Indeed, it looked less like what Charles Peirce once called the "logic of science" and more like what he dubbed "sheer tenacity" and "stubbornness of the will."[55]

The only effective way to address this kind of stance beyond insisting the logic of science was the most rational and justified form of pragmatic inquiry was to invoke critical humor. As it turned out, Hugo Münsterberg's sitting with Eusapia in New York in 1910 provided the occasion. After Eusapia's assistant (cleverly concealed in the séance cabinet) accidently grabbed her toe instead of the wires and levers that were used to produce the desired effect, she screamed out, revealing the gig was up. The event prompted Josiah Royce, who all along had been skeptical of matters psychical and critical of James for engaging them, to write the following ditty that he wittily titled "The Search for Truth":

> Eeny, meeny, miny, mo
> Catch Eusapia by the toe;
> If she hollers, then we know—
> James's doctrines are not so![56]

Such needling made its mark, revealing just how outlandish the whole affair had become. James, however, never lost his sense of humor about psychical research and would have likely laughed along with Royce and the critics. For instance, upon declining an invitation from Smith College to give a talk, James explained, "No more lecturing in this world for WJ, though I learn from the spirits . . . thru Mrs. Piper, that 'going to lectures' is a favorite form of entertainment in the sweet bye and bye!"[57] More seriously, James would have been sympathetic to F. C. S. Schiller's view that he had "never supposed that the matter was going to be settled either way in a generation."[58]

But by 1910 almost no one in the American scientific community was listening very much. The accumulated evidence manifested in *Studies in Spiritism*, the Columbia report, and so many other investigations had severely diminished any reasonable hope for rational belief in Spiritualism. Despite James's plea for a tertium quid approach, the best phenomena Mrs. Piper and Eusapia Palladino produced had been explained naturalistically and the worst dismissed as fraud. This should have made James pause to wonder at the limits to his method of inquiry and to consider more carefully the damage that invoking it in defense of psychical research was doing to his reputation as a serious scholar. John Jay Chapman captured this point in unequivocal terms. Scolding James, he exclaimed, "O but you have done harm too—D. Miller exposing Palladino—under sofas—newspaper talk.—Who was it [that] set this fashion in higher philosophy? W. J. Miller was sick with excitement & all of them together—who started the spook hunt as a scholars' recreation? W. J."[59] This was a damning and highly accurate assessment.

So, what then were James's final views about psychic phenomena? In 1909, James tried to explain them with clarity and conviction in a popular essay cleverly titled "The Confidences of a Psychical Researcher."[60] Marion Hamilton Carter, a freelance journalist best known for her coverage of the Terranova murder trial in 1906, provided the impetus.[61] She and James maintained a correspondence during the first decade of the 1900s in which James encouraged Carter to develop her psychic abilities, while Carter, fawning over him as "St. James the Modern," described her experiences with raps and put James in contact with New York City physical mediums.[62] Carter also tried to publish an essay on Eusapia in *McClure's Magazine*, only to have it "snatched it out" of her hands at the last minute by her editor in favor of James writing it. "For heaven's sake," she implored him, "do it, or try to keep him from letting Hyslop [write it]."[63] James did write it, but for *American Magazine*, not *McClure's*. True to form, James's insecurities surfaced immediately. To his brother he proclaimed in self-amazement that "it will be queer if after all these years I have *nothing* to say!"[64] Upon completing it, James mailed copies to friends and family members to gauge their reactions.[65] Unlike William's "Report on Mrs. Piper's Hodgson-Control," Henry Jr. found this essay "most interesting & uplifting!"[66] So, too, did Carter and Emile Boutroux, who remarked that it offered more than "results"; it was mostly "a way of thinking and searching."[67] And, indeed, it was. For the final time, James expressed his psychical research in terms of a tertium quid.

The main purpose of the essay, James wrote, was to "*put my own state of mind upon record publicly*." It was to be a record not of the truth but of "*my* truth, as I now see it," he added. James expressed that truth in several long-running themes, starting with the name "psychical research," which James dubbed "ridiculous" for its inability to capture a wide spectrum of phenomena ranging from automatic writing, phantasms, and ghosts, to psychics, physical mediumship, and mental mediumship, as well as a host of explanations such as fraud, coincidence, and natural, supernormal, and supernatural abilities. After rehashing the contributions from William Crookes, William Barrett, Edmund Gurney, F. W. H. Myers, and the Sidgwicks, as well as the Eusapia Palladino case and what he called "the best manifestations of the Piper control," James revisited the SPR's tactic of adopting skepticism, which he found useful for establishing personal belief but not so much the truth. He also rehearsed the cynicism of psychical research's critics, such as Thomas Huxley's famous dismissal of the entire project as "'twaddle,'" a view James dismissed as sheer dogmatism.[68] Critically, James also invoked the language of his tender- and tough-minded dichotomy, noting the "emotionally touched" who hear the names of their recently deceased loved ones and are "'happy' to accept the revelation, and consider spiritualism 'beautiful,'" while the "hard-headed," who are disgusted by such revelations, are wont to consider them "'bosh.' Thus do two opposite sentimentalisms divide opinion between them!" Invoking his tertium quid method of inquiry, James maintained that neither approach would yield a satisfying solution. Instead, he thought "their causation is far too complex for our feelings about what is or is not romantic enough to be spiritual to throw any light upon it. The causal factors must be carefully distinguished and traced," adding that "it is unquestionable that some theory of that mixed type is required for the explanation of all mediumistic phenomena."[69]

James framed psychic phenomena as "baffling" and found their myriad of explanations unsatisfying for their inability to corroborate the known evidence. After noting that Henry Sidgwick had worried it would be quite ironic after all of his time investigating psychical matters if the evidence did not allow for "finality of decision," James proclaimed his experience was like that: "For twenty five years I have been in touch with the literature of psychical research, and have had acquaintance with numerous 'researchers.' I have also spent a good many hours (though far fewer than I ought to have spent) in witnessing (or trying to witness) phenomena. Yet I am theoretically no 'further' than I was at the beginning."[70] With regard to explaining raps, table levitating, and cabinet performances, James was right; he had not made any progress. Still, he could not abandon all hope that there might be something supernatural to them. As James encapsulated it, "I find myself believing that there is 'something in' these never ending reports of physical phenomena, although I haven't yet the least positive notion of the something."[71] In the face of the overwhelming evidence against James, this statement seems preposterous, even if he did write it before the Eusapia fiasco occurred.

Regarding mental mediumship, however, James had made progress. "The Confidences of a Psychical Researcher" recounted the key role the subconscious played in explaining Mrs. Piper's phenomena. Identifying it as the "subliminal self," James reemphasized that *there is a residuum of knowledge displayed* that can only be called supernormal" and invoked his will theory in which there is a will to communicate of some kind, either a will to deceive or a will to personate or both, *"for the phenomenon is actuated by will of some sort anyhow."* James added there were "psychological as well as 'spiritual' factors, and quite obviously, it throws open for us far more questions than it answers about our subconscious constitution." Impressed as he was with the former explanation, James could not help dwelling on the latter. As in "Report on Mrs. Piper's Hodgson-Control," James asserted his "dramatic possibility" argument, which he now claimed was a "probability," especially regarding his assertion that Mrs. Piper was like a "white crow" that disproved the maxim "all crows are black." Adding that one has to follow one's "personal sense," James stated, "My own dramatic sense tends instinctively to picture the situation as an interaction between slumbering faculties in the automatist's mind, and a cosmic environment of *other consciousness* of some sort which is able to work on them." James thus hypostatized a universe full of "diffuse soul stuff, unable of itself to get into consistent personal form, or to take permanent possession of an organism, yet always craving to do so, it might get its head into the air, parasitically so to speak, by profiting by weak spots in the armor of human minds, and slipping in and stirring up there the sleeping tendency to personate." The medium's subliminal consciousness was the conduit of that communication.[72] Surely that was theoretical progress.

At the same time, "The Confidences of a Psychical Researcher" displayed James's penchant for weak inductive arguments, especially his favorite metaphor that "weak sticks make strong faggots." As such, he was unable to prevent himself from making the most improbable of statements. Invoking his "'panpsychic' view of the universe," that is, his theory of the sublime cosmic reservoir in which psyches survive bodily death in the "mother sea of consciousness," James claimed that "there is a continuum of cosmic consciousness, against which our individuality builds but accidental fences, and into which our several minds plunge as into a mother-sea or reservoir. Our 'normal' consciousness," he explained, "is circumscribed for adaptation to our external earthly environment, but the fence is weak in spots, and fitful influences from beyond leak in, showing the otherwise unverifiable common connexion. Not only psychic research, but metaphysical philosophy and speculative biology are led in their own ways to look with favor on some such 'panpsychic' view of the universe as this."[73] In short, "The Confidences of a Psychical Researcher" repeated his major explanations and theories of psychical phenomena and called for more evidence to validate them—all in the name of his tertium quid method of inquiry.

James closed the essay with the very first question he had asked about psychic phenomena in 1869: "What is one to think of this queer chapter in human nature?" Now, after forty years of investigation, his response was the same as it had been at the start: "It is odd enough on any view." Had James learned nothing valuable during the long interim? Could he not unpack meaning from his favorite idiom "queer"?[74] As demonstrated throughout this book, he could, and he did. In fact, James was substantially further in his effort to understand and explain psychic phenomena, and his position had evolved considerably over time. During the 1880s, James groped toward the view that mediumism was a telepathic, supernormal event for which the unconscious somehow acted as a conduit. By 1890, he seemed content with that view. But that same year he also offered a supernatural explanation when he invoked a new concept, the "cosmic reservoir." For the next twenty years James vacillated between both explanations, refining the mechanisms of each theory while never dismissing outright the problems of fraud and natural explanations. Only at the end of his life did he finally suggest that a reconciliation of the supernormal and supernatural theories was possible through the sublime conscious cosmic reservoir thesis.

Thus, there was a "there" there for James, even if after four decades of exploring it he professed to have no idea of its nature, asserting he was "still in a state of *bafflement* as to all these phenomena." Claiming to be stumped by such bafflement, he confessed in exasperation, "It seems as if they were intended deliberately by the Almighty never to be either proved or disproved definitely."[75] But once again, James was being too modest. He did have a final view; it was a panpsychic one of a dynamic "pluriverse" infused with organic psyches. He just could not commit himself to it. This was not because James was fundamentally ambivalent, as some James scholars have argued over the years.[76] Rather, the lack of substantial facts and verified evidence accepted by the scientific community stopped him from proclaiming his theory true, especially since the empiricist in him understood that new evidence would roll in over time and refine or even undermine it. The rational view, James held, was to take the middle course between outright dismissal and complete acceptance. Thus, he posited a psycho-metaphysical hypothesis of consciousness returning to the cosmos upon bodily death while recognizing he might very well be wrong. As such, James concluded the "The Confidences of a Psychical Researcher" with his unique view: "The only certainty is that the phenomena are enormously complex. . . . I . . . still remain a psychical researcher waiting for more facts before concluding. . . . Hardly, as yet, has the surface of the facts called 'psychic' begun to be scratched for scientific purposes. It is through following these facts, I am persuaded, that the great scientific conquest of the coming generation will be achieved."[77] This view was the perfect expression of his tertium quid method of inquiry.

It was also not a view from nowhere. As this book has shown, James developed his third way through a lifetime fascination with and study of psychic phenomena. This intellectual proclivity originated during his boyhood experiences with the "non-normal," such as his father's ruminations on the dangers of Spiritualism, dinner conversations with his "spiritual uncles" who first investigated the Fox sisters, and James John Garth Wilkinson's "spirit cure." It was nurtured in his early manhood during the 1860s and 1870s when James first investigated levitating tables and wrote book reviews on Spiritualism and culminated when he befriended the members of the Sidgwick Group and joined the SPR and ASPR in the early 1880s. As this book has also shown, James fostered his tertium quid method of inquiry through his investigation and study of physical and mental mediums.[78] Finally, this book has demonstrated James's third way grew out of explanations of various psychic phenomena, including his notion of the subliminal self and theory of cosmic consciousness, which in turn informed his psychological and philosophical doctrines of consciousness and the will to believe, all within the framework of the tough- and tender-minded dichotomy. Indeed, the immense time and effort James devoted to psychical research—from the daily labor of running the psychical societies and conducting the investigations to his debates with the skeptics and his encouragement of numerous family members, friends, and colleagues to develop their mediumistic abilities—substantiate Ralph Barton Perry's claim that "'psychical research' was not one of his vagaries, but was central and typical" of James's life and thought.[79]

In demonstrating that James formed his tertium quid through his psychical research, this book has argued more broadly that James's intellectual disposition is best understood in the context of three major historical developments in the nineteenth century: the Victorian crisis of faith brought on by the rise of Darwinism and scientific naturalism; scientific modernism, or the collective impact of statistical thinking, the prominence of the probability calculus, the role of exact measurement, and the mathematization of natural and social phenomena; and the professionalization of the sciences with its attendant rise of specialists, experts, and codified forms of knowledge produced by the educated elite at exclusive institutions, organizations, and societies. All three altered belief formation and gave rise to cognitivism. James's third way typified this larger trend in modernist thought. Bolstered by a hybrid of German *Wissenschaft* and British empiricism, it emerged amid a unique discourse of community that emphasized historicity, temporality, and dynamism expressed across a broad transatlantic culture of inquiry rather than as a distinct social class. Its faith in progress, science, and reason offered a more hopeful alternative to the "iron cage" of modernity inside of Max Weber's imprisoned Western civilization. As such, James was a thoroughgoing modernist, committed to the view that his method would reveal the truth about psychic phenomena in the long run. His method was thus a rebuke of antimodernist disenchantment with the modern world but not an uncritical embrace of its enchantment; it was the third way.

James's confidence in the future, however, was highly overblown. The next generation of psychical researchers, who called themselves "parapsychologists" in a Jamesian attempt to yoke their research program to scientific psychology, failed to find the empirical evidence for psychic phenomena that James had gambled they would. The two most prominent such researchers in the United States were William McDougall and Joseph Rhine. They received substantial funding to conduct original research at Harvard University in the 1920s and at Duke University in the 1930s, respectively. Utilizing updated scientific methods and statistical techniques in their experimental labs, they tested for psychic phenomena. Rhine and his wife claimed to have discovered the basic psychic element of all such phenomena, which they dubbed "psi." But their work failed miserably because of fundamental mistakes they made in their use of statistics. Worse, it was later revealed that their assistants had been cheating in collaboration with some of their subjects.[80] In other words, while trying to overcome the shortcomings of pre–World War I psychical research, postwar parapsychologists ran up against the same limitations: bad science, fraud, and willful belief. James's tertium quid method of inquiry, then, might have been rational, but the research program it facilitated failed to deliver the evidence over the long run. And, while he probably would have counseled holding out still longer, doing so indefinitely was neither sound epistemology nor good science. At some point, we must all put our cards on the table, but James's third way method of inquiry prohibited this.

During his lifetime, James's psychical research was interpreted in opposing ways in the intellectual community. On the positive side, Lawrence Pearsall Jacks, an Oxford University theologian, philosopher, and novelist, found literary inspiration in James's defense of mediumship and personalized religious belief. For instance, Jacks once told James that *The Varieties of Religious Experience* and psychical research were the primary basis for his stories in a book he was sending to him. Joking that James could have written the book, he explained, "I made a very primary careful study of all Mrs. Piper's utterances 'in the waking stage' & then drew [the character] Snarly Bob as being permanently in that condition."[81] On the negative side, Friedrich von Hügel, the Roman Catholic philosopher, thought James had overemphasized the spiritual value of mediumistic phenomena. In particular, he believed psychical research had produced few facts of religious value while encouraging superstition. Like James, Hügel held that natural science methodology would add much in this light but unlike him noted that to continually invoke the names of natural scientists such as Crookes and Lodge was not an argument against the point.[82] Hügel had made a valid criticism, but blaming James for others' misreading of his tertium quid approach in favor of or against Spiritualism was surely not James's fault.

Neither was the charge that James's defense of Spiritualism made him a "spiritist" or that he believed in Spiritualism. As one of his contemporaries correctly noted, James was neither.[83] Instead, it would be more accurate to argue that James was a philosophical psychologist interested in understanding exceptional mental states. As his first intellectual biographer captured it, "His promotion of psychical research and of abnormal psychology generally, . . . his collection and description of religious experiences in all their variety, but with special emphasis on their oddity, [and] his disposition to credit mysticism as a source of knowledge, all testify to this preoccupation."[84] Not surprisingly, this reality did not prevent numerous writers throughout the twentieth century from claiming James's "spirit" spoke to them postmortem in what came to be called "channeling," a kind of modern spiritualism without the spirits or séances in which the channeler simply outpours what he or she claims is the voice of a departed person. [85]

James relinquished his lead role in psychical research in the summer of 1909. His "*active* connexion with psychical research ceases," he confessed to Henry Bowditch. It was simply "too *zeitraubend* [time-consuming] and *umständlich* [awkward], and requires quicker perceptive faculties and more memory for details than I am possessed of, to lead to anything, so I take a back seat."[86] But taking a "back seat" meant only semiretirement. For despite all those years of complaining bitterly about the daily labor, James—amazingly—kept recruiting people to the SPR to the very end.[87] He likewise maintained his friendships with his psychical brethren. For instance, while in Nauheim, Germany, where James was trying the water cure during what turned out to be his final visit to Europe, he informed his daughter that he expected "Piddington and Gerald Balfour to motor over probably tomorrow," and a month later he told his wife that he must write to Flournoy.[88] Finally, after returning to America and while on his deathbed, James summoned enough energy to dictate some of his final letters to his psychical comrades.[89]

But the ranks were thinning and had been for some time. As William exclaimed to James Sully just two years prior, "How times have changed! Of all the members of that philosophical dining club [that is, the Scratch Eight], to which you so kindly admitted me in 1882, you, he [Shadworth Hodgson] and I are the only survivors, if I remember aright. Gurney, Robertson, Stephen and Maitland are gathered in."[90] On 26 August 1910, William James thinned the ranks still further, dying from the effects of an acutely enlarged heart at the age of sixty-eight. His wife, Alice, who was with him at the end, noted in her diary there had been "no pain and no consciousness."[91] The tough-minded would likely agree with Alice, but the tender-minded might wonder whether aspects of James's consciousness were floating in the "mother sea of consciousness." James's tertium quid method of inquiry left open that possibility without committing to it. As James had once put it, "These things lie upon the knees of the gods."[92]

HISTORIOGRAPHICAL ESSAY

Explanations of William James's interest in psychical research commenced upon his death. In 1911 William McDougall, a fellow researcher at the Society for Psychical Research who was quite sympathetic to James, related it to his thought. "James'[s] active interest in 'Psychical Research,'" McDougall wrote, "was not something . . . disconnected from the main system of his activity; rather it was for him an integral part of the whole. . . . It was the expression of the same tendencies of mind which shaped all his philosophical work; to it he brought . . . just those peculiar qualities of mind that made him so original and successful in the more strictly academic fields of philosophy and psychology."[1] Four decades later, Gardner Murphy, a psychologist and psychical researcher equally sympathetic to James, revealed this explanation's staying power, stating in 1960, "William James's active interest in psychical research . . . was an integral part of the whole."[2]

In between these two statements, Ralph Barton Perry, James's junior colleague in the philosophy department at Harvard and his first intellectual biographer, offered a more expansive explanation. In 1935, in a short but exceedingly insightful chapter titled "Psychical Research" in his masterful two-volume, seven-hundred-page tome, Perry claimed, "James's interest in 'psychical research' was not one of his vagaries, but was central and typical."[3] Perry's explanation stipulated that understanding James's psychical research was essential to understanding all facets of James's life and thought, not just his theories in psychology and philosophy.

Toward that end, Perry identified eleven reasons:

(1) Psychical research embodied every psychological phenomenon out of the ordinary. "From his youth James contemplated such

'phenomena' without repulsion and with an open mind." As such, James had a "relish for the non-normal."

(2) Psychical research was associated with mental pathology. "As one who approached psychology from the side of medicine he gave attention to the pathology of mind."

(3) Psychical research offered "the possibility of a more kindly treatment of suffering humanity." If scientists could understand abnormal states, they might know better how to treat those individuals in clinical settings. And, since psychical research was associated with a number of mind cures, it might offer the possibility of relief from his own mental suffering, especially his neurasthenia.

(4) Psychical research embodied James's integrity to commitment. Once he joined the SPR and ASPR, James "became a partisan of psychical research, both as officer and as soldier in the ranks."

(5) Psychical research embodied James's sense of loyalty to those he trusted. Once James became an intimate friend with members of the SPR such as Henry Sidgwick, Frederic Myers, and Edmund Gurney, "loyalty to them implied loyalty to their cause."

(6) Psychical research was flexible and nonjudgmental of the extraordinary. As James himself proclaimed, "We should never regard [any] phenomena as 'impossible' before fully investigating it."

(7) Psychical research was all-encompassing. "James had a hypothesis for which he claimed a 'dramatic possibility'—an impression of things left upon his mind by his familiarity with the phenomena. Mrs. Piper . . . played so important a part in the unrolling 'drama' of psychical research."

(8) Psychical research was an empirical science. "Instead of being rejected as unscientific it should be welcomed as affording promise of a psychology that might be really scientific." Thus, "the rejection of phenomena for methodological reasons is an inversion of the rightful priority."

(9) Psychical research reflected the proper scientific attitude. "James felt that the critics of psychical research" obeyed "the dictates of a 'theoretic creed,' while he, on the other hand, was 'baldly empirical.'"

(10) James championed fairness and preferred the underdog. "Orthodox science was a symbol of arrogance and vulgar

success, disposed to exaggerate its claims and to abuse its power. In any dispute between science and a weaker brother [psychical research] in which it appeared that science was the aggressor, James would invariably be found intervening [on behalf of the latter]."

(11) Psychical research was central to his theory of consciousness. The idea of consciousness 'beyond the margin' or 'below the threshold' was a metaphysical hypothesis of the first importance." Thus, psychical research "afforded an experimental approach to religion" that might provide "scientific support for a supernaturalistic faith."[4]

Five decades later, Robert A. McDermott, the author of the introduction to *Essays in Psychical Research* (1986), echoed Perry's explanations and provided three additional ones:

(12) Psychical research admitted "provisional conclusions on ultimate questions," which James pursued with intellectual vigor.
(13) Psychical research "emphasized the personal and subjective character of knowledge," to which James was deeply dedicated to defending.
(14) James sought to "blur the modern, Western dualism between the mental and the physical," and psychical research afforded him that opportunity.[5]

Taken together, these fourteen explanations constitute what can be called the Perry-McDermott thesis. It offers a big-tent approach to explaining James's commitment to psychical research with regard to his familial, personal, medical, moral, scientific, psychological, philosophical, and religious interests.

The Perry-McDermott framework is useful in several respects. First, it identifies numerous reasons *why* James committed himself to psychical research. Second, it pinpoints specific *kinds* of reasons. Third, it opens the door to other scholars seeking a contextual understanding. But the framework also has some significant limitations. First, it does not actually establish *what* James believed, *how* he came to believe, or *elaborate* why he believed. That is, there is no sense of explaining the *process* of acquiring belief, which is notable since acquiring belief was always a process for James. Thus, the framework lacks full explanatory power. Second, while Perry argued James's interest in psychical research was "central and typical," he did not specify *of what* it was central and typical. The implication is his life or thought

Historiographical Essay

(or both), but what doctrines and which parts of his life are left unmentioned or undeveloped? In other words, the framework does not actually argue for the relationship between psychical research and his life and thought but rather stipulates it. Furthermore, the framework is incomplete because it offers only generalized and open-ended explanations rather than historical and philosophical ones. As such, much further explanation is required.

Many scholars across academic disciplines have developed individual elements of the Perry-McDermott framework in an attempt to provide a fuller account. Their efforts can be categorized by their research programs, methodologies, historical specialties, and theoretical commitments. James's biographers constitute the first group. Like Perry, none devote more than a chapter to psychical research. Most offer fragmented glimpses by peppering psychical research throughout their narratives, thus making it appear an epiphenomenon to other events considered more central to James's life and thought. For instance, some highlight the point that his commitment to psychical research demonstrates he was an open-minded thinker willing to consider any phenomena seriously no matter how unusual, or that he tried mind cure to alleviate the suffering his neurasthenia caused. Others emphasize the significance of James's friendships with psychical researchers, thereby personalizing his interest. This approach makes sense since biographers are obligated to cover an entire life, but it has also led to incomplete explanations.[6] Nonetheless, the biographies largely follow the Perry-McDermott framework in arguing to varying degrees that James's psychical research offered deep insights into the debates between science and religion even as they leave that claim unsupported. There is also a consensus that James believed psychical research would lead to new scientific knowledge about the nature of consciousness. Gerald E. Myers's biography *William James: His Life and Thought* made this argument persuasively by showing how James's interests in abnormal psychology and psychical research were related to his theory of consciousness, skillfully weaving together James's views with those of John Locke, Sigmund Freud, and Pierre Janet to reveal that James believed that the unconscious part of the mind provided massive potential for understanding the abnormally ill.[7]

Biographers represent but one group of scholars who have tried to explain James's interest in psychical research. Beginning in the 1930s and continuing up to the 1990s, a small group of scholars, mostly psychologists and parapsychologists overly sympathetic with James, published a small set of articles in psychical research periodicals that tried to elaborate on some of Perry's initial arguments. These scholars focused on the key role that the

SPR and ASPR played in James's commitment to psychical research, arguing that the data produced in sittings with Mrs. Leonora Piper convinced James of the reality of psychic phenomena. The only book published during this sixty-five year period was *William James on Psychical Research*, coedited by Gardner Murphy, one of the early parapsychologists who also published some of the first articles. This volume was the first of its kind to bring together some of James's key essays on psychical research. It was flanked with an introduction and an "In Retrospect" section, which mostly expounded on Murphy's claims from his earlier articles. All of these little-known works are useful for establishing some of the organizational and institutional components of the topic as well as the impact Mrs. Piper made on James's beliefs. Like the biographies, however, while providing some useful insights, they offer neither a systematic nor a historical explanation of James's interest in psychical research.[8]

Historians of psychical research compose a third group. Like the previous group, these scholars focus on the institutional and organizational aspects of the topic, but their scope is somewhat broader. In addition to the above issues, they explore the relationship between Spiritualism and psychical research. While high-quality works of history, they focus on psychical research in England rather than provide an account of James's role in the transatlantic movement.[9]

Historians of parapsychology constitute a fourth set of inquirers. Unlike the historians of psychical research, these scholars limit their focus to clairvoyance, telekinesis, and psychokinesis. These parapsychological phenomena made up one focus of psychical research, but psychical researchers studied a much broader range. Nonetheless, these scholars provide astute analysis of the historical development from the study of trance states in the nineteenth century to that of extrasensory perception in the twentieth. However, like the historians of psychical research, they discuss James only as he relates to their specific concerns.[10]

A fifth set of inquirers is comprised of historians of psychopathology. One scholar in particular, Eugene Taylor, possessed a remarkable grasp of the key role that nineteenth-century abnormal psychology played in the formation of James's thought. He demonstrated the centrality of James's work in psychopathology to his theory of consciousness beyond the margin. Unlike most of the biographers, Taylor avoided reducing James's interest in psychopathology to his mental anguish. On the other hand, since Taylor was absorbed with psychopathology, he reduced James's psychical research to it. But James's psychical research addressed many other kinds of phenomena outside of the domain of abnormal psychology. Taylor's explanation is thus useful but limited in scope.[11]

Historians of psychology constitute a sixth group. These scholars situate psychical research within the rise of modern scientific psychology. Some show a relationship between James's theories of mind, consciousness, and the will in *The Principles of Psychology* with those in his psychical research writings. Others focus on debates between James and the first generation of American experimental psychologists over whether psychical research was scientific. Since James was a leader in both fields, he occupied the center of these disputes (often to the dismay of the "brass instrument" psychologists). These scholars make compelling arguments, but they inadvertently reduce James's psychical research to a quest for scientific knowledge. As good as they are, they do not offer, or even attempt, a comprehensive history.[12]

Historians of medicine make up a seventh group. They are interested primarily in elaborating the medical reasons for James's interest in psychical research. Like their cousins the historians of psychology, they situate James's interest in psychical research within their own specialty, though their focus is much broader than any one thinker or discipline. These scholars trace the developments of alternative medicine in the nineteenth and twentieth centuries and locate its limited success within their popular appeal to a consuming public. They reveal how one aspect of James's psychical research—his interest in mind cure—emerged as part of the diverse alternative healing movements. Not surprisingly, these works also do not attempt to supply a comprehensive account of James and psychical research.[13]

Most scholars who give some attention to James and psychical research, then, cluster themselves around one major subject area with which James is associated: psychology. In that sense, they have closely followed some of the explanations in the Perry-McDermott framework. But James also made equally significant contributions to the study of religion and philosophy. Given the overlap between the study of religion and psychical research, historians of religion have argued that James's psychical research was deeply steeped in his fascination with the nature of religious belief, faith, and spirituality. These historians of religion, who compose an eighth group of scholars, seek to explain James's interest in psychical research as part and parcel of the rise of modern liberal Protestantism, or as part of his attraction to modern mysticism. In particular, they pay much attention to James's will-to-believe doctrine and the notion of the twice-born sick-soul as laid out in *The Will to Believe* and *The Varieties of Religious Experience*, respectively.[14] Like the other approaches, this one has been fruitful but also limited in scope.

The ninth group of scholars is comprised of philosophers. While generally deemphasizing the significance of psychical research in James's technical philosophy, only a few philosophers have sought connections between James's psychical research and his epistemology and metaphysics, especially his doctrines of pragmatism, radical empiricism, and pluralism. While these scholars maintain that a philosophical exploration of the former can help reveal the nature of the latter, these connections have been only suggested or at best outlined.[15]

Finally, James's interest and work in psychical research has not been without their critics and skeptics. These authors, who constitute the tenth and final group, believe that clever charlatans steeped in the ancient arts of magic and legerdemain duped James and other psychical researchers. They contend that psychical research, while semi-systematic at times, amounted to the study of fraud and therefore contained nothing whatsoever of scientific or philosophical value. As such, they argue that James and the others were naive at best and foolish at worst. Either way, the critics and skeptics contend that James's psychical research was a dead end. Since these writers represent the extreme end of an interpretive continuum—the opposite end from the parapsychologists, who are overly sympathetic to James and the phenomena—one would think that they would have done the most to offer a complete picture of James and psychical research. Unfortunately, their work amounts to a largely ahistorical and decontextualized critique, pretending only little sensitivity to the major differences between Victorian and contemporary America and England. This final group is the most egregious at failing to offer a systematic account of James and psychical research.[16]

In sum, while there exists an immense historiography of James's psychical research—ten groups of scholars, each devoted to explaining one or more aspect of it—no single group or work has provided a systematic account. Since the scholarship is scattered across a variety of disciplines, each with its own historical, methodological, and theoretical commitments, this outcome makes some sense. But while each group offers valid interpretations of James and psychical research, our understanding of the topic remains highly fragmented and incomplete. *William James: Psychical Research and the Challenge of Modernity* rectifies matters by making good on Perry's promissory note that William James's interest was "central and typical" of his life and thought.

NOTES

ABBREVIATIONS

James Family Members
AHGJ Alice Howe Gibbens James (WJ's wife)
AJ Alice James (WJ's sister)
ARJ Alexander Robertson James (WJ's youngest son)
HJ Jr. Henry James Jr. (WJ's brother, "Harry")
HJ Sr. Henry James Sr. (WJ's father)
HJ III Henry James (WJ's first son)
MMJ Margaret Mary James (WJ's daughter)
WJ William James
WJ Jr. William James (WJ's second son)

Societies and Their Publications
ASPR American Society for Psychical Research
JASPR *Journal of the American Society for Psychical Research*
PASPR *Proceedings of the American Society for Psychical Research*
SPR Society for Psychical Research
JSPR *Journal of the Society for Psychical Research*
PSPR *Proceedings of the Society for Psychical Research*

Primary Sources
CWJ *The Correspondence of William James*
ECR *Essays, Comments, and Reviews*
EP *Essays in Psychology*
EPHL *Essays in Philosophy*
EPR *Essays in Psychical Research*
ERM *Essays in Religion and Morality*
HI *Human Immortality*

HJL   *Henry James Letters*
JJGW   James John Garth Wilkinson Papers
JP   James Papers
LWJ   *The Letters of William James*
LWJTF   *Letters of William James and Théodore Flournoy*
PP   *The Principles of Psychology*
Prag.   *Pragmatism*
PU   *A Pluralistic Universe*
SPP   *Some Problems of Philosophy*
SUC   *The Selected Unpublished Correspondence*
WB   *The Will to Believe*
WWJ   *The Writings of William James*

Secondary Sources

TCWJ   *The Thought and Character of William James*

Reference Works

BDP   *Biographical Dictionary of Parapsychology*
CAT   *A Companion to American Thought*
DAB   *The Dictionary of American Biography*
DNB   *The Dictionary of National Biography*
DSB   *The Dictionary of Scientific Biography*
EOP   *Encyclopedia of Occultism and Parapsychology*
EPhil   *Encyclopedia of Philosophy*
PDS   *A Popular Dictionary of Spiritualism*
RE   *The Reader's Encyclopedia*

INTRODUCTION

1. Excerpted with quotations from *EPR*, appendix 3, "Sittings with Mrs. Piper: Kate Walsh and Baby Eliza," 436–41. See also "Weather Report."

2. *EOP*, s.v. "psychical research" and "telepathy."

3. Ibid., s.v. "Spiritualism."

4. WJ to Ralph Barton Perry, 9 September 1904, *SUC*, 348.

5. The one possible exception is Blum, *Ghost Hunters*. It is a very readable but journalistic account of the first generation of psychical researchers in the United States largely devoid of historical context, a conceptual framework, and an analytical argument. For an account of the scholarly literature, see my Historiographical Essay.

6. Perry, *TCWJ*, 2:155.

7. See Gale, *Divided Self of William James*; and W. Cooper, *Unity of William James's Thought*, especially chap. 2. Thanks to an anonymous reader of the manuscript for pointing out the latter source and argument.

8. The impetus for my argument comes from Robert A. McDermott, who wrote, "James's research concerning psychical phenomena may be understood as his effort to generate a *tertium quid*, or third position, between the equally unacceptable extremes

of skepticism and uncritical acceptance." See McDermott, introduction to *EPR*, xxix. While McDermott limited its applicability to psychology, my book develops a much broader notion of the concept. I am especially grateful to Howard Brick, who suggested the useful phrase "a tertiary synthesis of all dualisms." Some psychologists, psychiatrists, and philosophers argue that F. W. H. Myers, one of James's psychical research colleagues, took a third way approach to the study of the mind. See Kelly and Kelly et al., *Irreducible Mind*, esp. 62–63. I argue against this view in chap. 6. Thanks to one anonymous reader of the manuscript for pointing out this source.

9. *RE*, s.v. "tertium quid"; *Webster's Ninth New Collegiate Dictionary*, s.v. "tertium quid"; Chadwick, *Early Church*, 148, 157, 192–212.

10. WJ, "Thomas Davidson: Individualist," *ECR*, 89.

11. WJ to G. S. Hall, 10 October 1879, *CWJ*, 5:64. On James's rejection of Hegel and his impact on philosophy in Cambridge, see Richardson, *William James*, 213–16.

12. WJ, "On Some Hegelisms," *WB*, 216–17.

13. WJ, *Prag.*, 28; *EPhil*, s.v. "pragmatism," by H. S. Thayer.

14. Perry, *TCWJ*, 1:458–59.

15. For a contrasting view that argues "pure experience" formed James's center of vision, see Bjork, *William James*.

16. Hollinger, "William James and the Culture of Inquiry"; McDermott, introduction to *EPR*, xxxi.

17. Bowler, *Reconciling Science and Religion*, 1–24; Brooke, *Science and Religion*, chap. 8; Gregory, "The Impact of Darwinian Evolution on Protestant Theology in the Nineteenth Century."

18. Suckiel, *Heaven's Champion*.

19. J. Turner, *Without God, without Creed*, chaps. 6 and 7; F. Turner, *Between Science and Religion*, 8–37.

20. Croce, *Science and Religion in the Era of William James*, 1–26.

21. Menand, *Metaphysical Club*, 75, 90.

22. Grant, *Bible in the Church*, especially chaps. 11 and 12.

23. McDermott, introduction, *EPR*, xxxii.

24. Poovey, *History of the Modern Fact*, chap. 1.

25. Harman, *Energy, Force and Matter*; Ross, *Origins of American Social Science*.

26. Davis, "Brass Age of Psychology."

27. Boring, *History of Experimental Psychology*, chaps. 14, 15, 20, 21.

28. Camfield, "Professionalization of American Psychology"; Sokal, "Origins and Early Years of the American Psychological Association"; Coon, "Standardizing the Subject."

29. Leary, "Telling Likely Stories."

30. Leary, "William James"; Bjork, *Compromised Scientist*, 8–9, 41–43, 88–94, 114–20.

31. Ross, *G. Stanley Hall*; M. Hale, *Human Science and Social Order*; Sokal, *Education in Psychology*; Sommer, "Psychical Research and the Origins of American Psychology."

32. Bjork, *Compromised Scientist*, chap 1.

33. Taves, "Tale of Two Congresses."

34. Mauskopf and McVaugh, *Elusive Science*.

35. Coon, "Testing the Limits of Sense and Sciences."

36. J. Turner, *Without God, without Creed*, chaps. 6 and 7.

37. Butler, *Awash in a Sea of Faith*, chap. 8; B. Carroll, *Spiritualism in Antebellum America*, 4, 27, 67.

38. The phrase "aura of factuality" comes from Geertz, *Interpretation of Cultures*, 90. It was skillfully developed and applied to French spiritualism in Monroe, *Laboratories of Faith*, and heavily influences my interpretation.

39. Meyer, "American Intellectuals and the Victorian Crisis of Faith"; J. Turner, *Without God, without Creed*, chap. 6; Houghton, *Victorian Frame of Mind*, chap. 3.

40. Lears, *No Place of Grace*, 4–58.

41. Cotkin, *William James, Public Philosopher*, 40–41, 73–94.

42. Beard, *American Nervousness*, 5, 7–8.

43. Lutz, *American Nervousness, 1903*.

44. WJ to George H. Howison, 17 July 1895, *LWJ*, 2:23.

45. Gosling, *Before Freud*, 10–11.

46. Higham, "Reorientation of American Culture."

47. *Webster's Ninth New Collegiate Dictionary*, s.v. "fideism"; Perry, *TCWJ*, 2:209.

48. The best discussion of James's empiricism remains chap. 26 in vol. 2 of Perry, *TCWJ* (quoted on p. 454). My argument about the role of experience in James's empiricism should not be confused with his metaphysical doctrine of "radical empiricism." Indeed, I could find no historical relationship between James's psychical research and his radical empiricism.

49. McDermott, introduction to *EPR*, xxxii.

50. This claim should not be confused with James's pragmatic theory of meaning solution to the tough- and tender-minded dilemma. I am grateful to one anonymous reader of an early version of the manuscript for pointing out this crucial distinction.

51. WJ, *Prag.*, 13.

52. Gale, *Divided Self of William James*, 188–90.

53. WJ, *Prag.*, 11.

54. Ibid., 13.

55. Ross, "Modernism Reconsidered."

56. Hollinger, "Knower and the Artificer"; *CAT*, s.v. "scientism and cognitivism," by David. A. Hollinger.

57. Calinescu, *Five Faces of Modernity*, 41–46, 265; Bradbury and McFarlane, *Modernism*; Faulker, *Modernism*.

58. For a similar view that argues parapsychology (psychical research's successor) offered a solution to the modernity crisis in the early twentieth century, see Asprem, *Problem of Disenchantment*, especially chap. 7.

59. Hollinger brilliantly develops this concept in "Historians and the Discourse of Intellectuals."

60. Lasch, *New Radicalism in America*.

61. For a highly influential argument that invokes a *via media* interpretation for the social and political realm that is similar to my third way argument, see Kloppenberg, *Uncertain Victory*.

62. Cotkin argues, "American thinkers of this era were reluctant modernists attempting to synthesize the traditions and ideals of Victorianism with the challenges and possibilities of modernist streams of thought" (*Reluctant Modernism*, xi).

CHAPTER 1

1. Murphy and Ballou, *William James on Psychical Research*, 3.

2. The seven major biographies of James recount slightly altered versions of the standard view. See Perry, *TCWJ*; Allen, *William James: A Biography*; Feinstein, *Becoming William James*; G. Myers, *William James: His Life and Thought*; Bjork, *William James: The Center of His Vision*; Simon, *Genuine Reality: A Life of William James*; and Richardson, *William James: In the Maelstrom of American Modernism*. The classic statements that James suffered a prolonged identity crisis because of his problems with finding a suitable career are Erikson, *Identity*, 150–55; and Strout, "William James and the Twice-Born Sick Soul."

3. Allen, *William James*, 22–24.

4. Alfred Habegger, *Father*, especially 4–5, 192–96, 228–33, 247–48, 277, 307, 339–440, and 426.

5. Perry, *TCWJ*, 2:156.

6. *EOP*, s.v. "Spiritualism."

7. Oesterreich, *Possession*; and Dingwall, *Ghosts and Spirits in the Ancient World*.

8. Toksvig, *Emanuel Swedenborg*; Austin Warren, *Elder Henry James*, 241n18; Noyes, *History of American Socialisms*, 540.

9. Nordhoff, *Communistic Societies of the United States*, 117–256; Melcher, *Shaker Adventure*.

10. *DSB*, s.v. "Franz Anton Mesmer," by Robert Darnton; Buranelli; *Wizard from Vienna*; Gauld, *History of Hypnotism*.

11. Cross, *Burned-Over District*; Johnson, *Shopkeeper's Millennium*; Ryan, *Cradle of the Middle Class*; Hatch, *Democratization of American Christianity*.

12. Taves, *Fits, Trances, and Visions*.

13. Seldes, *Stammering Century*.

14. My composite of the Fox sisters is drawn from E. Lewis, "Report of the Mysterious Noises Heard in the House of Mr. John D. Fox"; Capron, *Modern Spiritualism*, 40–41, quoted from 93, 96; Podmore, *Modern Spiritualism*; Nelson, *Spiritualism and Society*, 3–85; S. Brown, *Heyday of Spiritualism*, 111–40; B. Brown, "Spiritualism in Nineteenth-Century America," especially 51; Brandon, *Spiritualists*, 1–41; and Braude, *Radical Spirits*, 17.

15. Roark et al., *American Promise*, appendix 2, "Facts and Figures," A-52.

16. Braude, *Radical Spirits*, 2, 25–31; Noyes, *History of American Socialisms*, chaps. 4 and 46; Garrison and Garrison, *William Lloyd Garrison*, 3:408; Thomas, *Liberator*, 451; B. Carroll, *Spiritualism in Antebellum America*, chap. 3.

17. S. Brown, *Heyday of Spiritualism*, 130.

18. Spann, *New Metropolis*, 94–100, 401–27.

19. Allen, *William James*, 22–23.

20. HJ Jr., *Henry James Autobiography*. *A Small Boy and Others* is contained in this edited volume.

21. Quoted in R. Lewis, *Jameses*, 67.

22. HJ Jr., *Small Boy and Others*, in *Henry James Autobiography*, 3–154; Allen, *William James*, 22–27; R. Lewis, *Jameses*, 58–70.

23. HJ Jr., *Small Boy and Others*, in *Henry James Autobiography*, 89.

24. *RE*, s.v. "Barnum."

25. Kunhardt, Kunhardt, and Kunhardt, *P. T. Barnum*, 28–131; Ashby, *With Amusement for All*, 27–40.

26. HJ Jr., *Small Boy and Others*, in *Henry James Autobiography*, 89.

27. Ibid., 95.

28. This argument was first laid out in Knapp, "James the Flâneur."

29. Bender, *New York Intellect*, chap. 4.

30. Perry, *TCWJ*, 2:155.

31. Willis, "Post-Mortuum Soiree."

32. Quoted in Nye, *George Bancroft*, 188.

33. Handlin, *George Bancroft*, 255.

34. James Fenimore Cooper to Sue Cooper, 9 June 1850, *Letters and Journals of James Fenimore Cooper*, 6:193.

35. Boynton argued in *James Fenimore Cooper* that while Cooper was curious about Spiritualism, he was "singularly hard-headed and matter-of-fact" and thus believed it could be explained by "cold reason" (373–74). By contrast, James Grossman pointed out in *James Fenimore Cooper* that Cooper's curiosity with Spiritualism belonged to his interest in "magnetic trances" and the "occult" and therefore found that it was likely Cooper "came to believe in Spiritualism" (246).

36. Dana is quoted in Wilson, *Bryant and His Friends*, 213.

37. William Cullen Bryant to Richard Henry Dana, 19 June 1852, quoted in Godwin, *Biography of William Cullen Bryant*, 2:303.

38. Quoted in Frothingham, *George Ripley*, 228.

39. Willis, "Post-Mortuum Soiree," 190, 194.

40. Greeley, *Recollections of a Busy Life*, 235, 237.

41. Quoted in B. Taylor, *Life and Letters of Bayard Taylor*, 2:194–95.

42. Greeley, *Recollections of a Busy Life*, 237–39.

43. Ibid., 239–40.

44. Quoted in W. Hale, *Horace Greeley*, 124.

45. Cornell, in *Life and Public Career of the Hon. Horace Greeley*, a campaign biography seeking to rescue Greeley from political charges that he was a Spiritualist, contended that Greeley "never believed in these vagaries and hallucinations," had no faith in "spirit-rappings" or "spiritualism," and "could spend his time much more profitably than investigating this folly" (212, 213, 221). By contrast, Ingersoll, in *Life of Horace Greeley*, maintained that Greeley treated Spiritualism like any other newsworthy event—that is, something to be investigated until the facts were exposed for the public's consumption—and therefore "did not condemn spiritualism without a hearing, and never unreservedly" (158–59).

46. Linn, *Horace Greeley*, 90–91.

47. Quoted in Habegger, *Father*, 321.

48. *New York Tribune*, 20 December 1850, 4; 26 December 1850, 3; 13 January 1851, 5.

49. Quoted in Habegger, *Father*, 321–22.

50. Ibid., 322.

51. Ibid.

52. Ibid., 307. HJ Sr. is quoted in A. Warren, *Elder Henry James*, 129.

53. HJ Jr., *Small Boy and Others*, in *Henry James Autobiography*, 133.

54. HJ Sr., "Spiritual Rappings," 419–21.

55. *DAB*, s.v. "Henry James, Sr."
56. A. Warren, *Elder Henry James*, xiv–xv.
57. Ibid., 189.
58. Kellogg, *Philosophy of Henry James*, 4–5.
59. My explication of Henry Sr.'s obtuse theology is drawn from several lucid accounts: Kellogg, *Philosophy of Henry James*, 4–29, quoted on 18; A. Warren, *Elder Henry James*, 189–95; and Young, *Philosophy of Henry James, Sr.*, 91–316.
60. Kellogg, *Philosophy of Henry James*, 15, 17–22.
61. Ibid., 26–28.
62. Ibid., 29.
63. Houghton, *Victorian Frame of Mind*, 106; D. Hall, "Victorian Connection."
64. HJ Sr., "Spiritual Rappings," 417–18.
65. Ibid., 408, and quoted in A. Warren, *Elder Henry James*, 129–30.
66. HJ Sr., "Spiritual Rappings," 415.
67. Quoted in Habegger, *Father*, 211–12, 224.
68. HJ Sr., "Spiritual Rappings," 411, 415, 417.
69. On HJ Sr. and Curtis, see Habegger, *Father*, 310–12. HJ Sr. is quoted on pages 310–11.
70. Ibid., 310–11. HJ Sr. is quoted on 311.
71. Ibid., 311.
72. HJ Sr., "Spiritual Rappings," 419.
73. See R. Lewis, *Jameses*, 491.
74. Perry, *TCWJ*, 2:156.
75. Barrow, *Independent Spirits*, 156–57.
76. C. Wilkinson, *James John Garth Wilkinson*, especially 234; *DNB*, s.v. "James John Garth Wilkinson"; Oppenheim, *Other World*, 233–34.
77. C. Wilkinson, *James John Garth Wilkinson*, 2, 6.
78. Barrow, "An Imponderable Liberator," in *Society for the Social History of Medicine Bulletin*, and an expanded version of the same title in *Studies in the History of Alternative Medicine*, 89–117.
79. JJGW.
80. Garth Wilkinson to HJ Sr., 23 January 1848, JJGW, #31. The book was by Mrs. Catherine Crowe, *The Night Side of Nature, or Ghosts and Ghost Seers* (London: T. C. Newby, 1848).
81. For one of the best discussions of this well-known development, see F. Turner, *Between Religion and Science*.
82. Garth Wilkinson to HJ Sr., 23 January 1848, JJGW, #31.
83. Ibid.
84. Ibid.
85. Garth Wilkinson to HJ Sr., 8 February 1850, JP, bMS Am 1092.9, #4063.
86. Garth Wilkinson to HJ Sr., 7 June 1850, JJGW, #66.
87. Garth Wilkinson to HJ Sr., 14 July 1850, JP, bMS Am 1092.9, #4067.
88. Garth Wilkinson to HJ Sr., 7 June 1850, JJGW, #66.
89. Ibid., 19 May 1854, #77.
90. Garth Wilkinson to HJ Sr., 13 October 1855, JP, bMS Am 1092.9, #4074.
91. Garth Wilkinson to HJ Sr., 19 May 1854, JJGW, #77.

92. Allen, *William James*, chap. 3, especially 35; Bjork, *William James*, 12; HJ Jr., *Small Boy and Others*, in *Henry James Autobiography*, 161. HJ Sr. is quoted in Le Clair, *Young Henry James*, 185.

93. Le Clair, *Young Henry James*, 188–89. As in the United States, Spiritualism developed somewhat spontaneously across different classes and regions in England during the 1850s. See Owen, *Darkened Room*, 21.

94. Owen, *Darkened Room*, 21, 79.

95. Garth Wilkinson to HJ Sr., 19 May 1854, JJGW, #77.

96. J. Wilkinson, *Improvisations from the Spirit*, 109.

97. Garth Wilkinson to HJ Sr., 13 October 1855, JP, bMS Am 1092.9, #4074.

98. HJ Sr. is quoted in Perry, *TCWJ*, 1:84–85. Perry suggested the disappointment was real but that it did not affect their friendship or their future correspondence (84 n. 3).

99. J. Wilkinson, *Homeopathy Principle Applied to Insanity*.

100. Ibid., 16, 4.

101. Ibid., 12–13.

102. Ibid., 14, 16.

103. Ibid., 5.

104. C. Wilkinson, *James John Garth Wilkinson*, 294.

105. WJ to AJ, 6 July 1891, *LWJ*, 1:310.

106. Perry, *TCWJ*, 2:157.

107. WJ to his family, 16 September 1861, *LWJ*, 2:34–35. Sir James Fitzjames Stephen, the Scottish jurist and antilibertarian, was the story's author.

108. Henry Pickering Bowditch to WJ, 10 February 1869, *CWJ*, 4:364. The book, roughly translated as "Experimental Studies of the Nervous Fluid and a Definitive Solution to the Problem of Spiritualism," was by Alphonse Chevillard (Paris: V. Masson et fils, 1869).

109. See Sargent, *Planchette*.

110. WJ to HJ Jr., 22 March 1869, JP, bMS Am 1092.9, #2568.

111. WJ, "Review of *Planchette*, by Epes Sargent," *EPR*, 1, originally published unsigned in the *Boston Daily Advertiser*, 10 March 1869.

112. Ibid., 1–2.

113. Ibid., 2.

114. WJ to Katherine Havens, 14 July 1874, JP, bMS Am 1092.1, no item number.

115. Murphy and Ballou, *William James on Psychical Research*, 3.

116. James's biographers typically invoke the 1869 book review as evidence for the starting point of James's interest in Spiritualism. See Perry, *TCWJ*, 1:294, 2:155n1; Allen, *William James*, 156; G. Myers, *William James*, 370; Simon, *Genuine Reality*, 140; and Richardson, *William James*, 99. But, as this chapter shows, the textual evidence indicates his interest began much earlier.

117. Perry, *TCWJ*, 2:156.

CHAPTER 2

1. Gauld, *Founders of Psychical Research*.

2. Perry, *TCWJ*, 2:156.

3. F. Turner, *Between Science and Religion*.

4. Aristotle, "The Varieties of Friendship," *Nicomachean Ethics*, 212.

5. On the "community of discourse" concept, see Hollinger, "Historians and the Intellectual Discourse of Intellectuals," *New Directions in American Intellectual History*, ed. Higham and Conkin, 42–63, reprinted in Hollinger, *In the American Province*.

6. Gauld, *Founders of Psychical Research*, chap. 4; Oppenheim, *Other World*, 125.

7. Annan, "Intellectual Aristocracy."

8. Ibid., 243–53, 282–84.

9. Ibid., 264.

10. See Gauld, *Founders of Psychical Research*, 88–114; Oppenheim, *Other World*, 123–35; and Haynes, *Society for Psychical Research*, 6–7.

11. On Sidgwick, see *DNB*, s.v. "Henry Sidgwick"; Sidgwick and Sidgwick, *Henry Sidgwick*; D. James, *Henry Sidgwick*; Gauld, *Founders of Psychical Research*, 46; Oppenheim, *Other World*, 81; F. Turner, *Between Science and Religion*, 38–67; Schultz, *Essays on Henry Sidgwick*, especially 1–4; and Schultz, *Henry Sidgwick*, 1–20.

12. *BDP*, s.v. "Henry Sidgwick."

13. HJ Jr. to WJ, 28 February 1877, *HJL*, 2:101.

14. George Holmes Howison to WJ, 17 November 1899, *CWJ*, 9:581.

15. F. Myers, "In Memory of Henry Sidgwick," 452, 454, 457.

16. Lodge, "In Memory of Henry Sidgwick," 464.

17. Quoted in F. Myers, "In Memory of Henry Sidgwick," 457.

18. Gauld, *Founders of Psychical Research*, 138–40.

19. WJ is quoted in D. James, *Henry Sidgwick*, 60.

20. Gauld, *Founders of Psychical Research*, 318.

21. Quoted in ibid., 97, originally from F. Myers, "Account of My Friendship with Henry Sidgwick."

22. Gauld, *Founders of Psychical Research*, 318–19.

23. Ibid., 320–21.

24. Quoted in ibid., 321.

25. Ibid., 317; Lodge, *Past Years*, 280.

26. Lodge, "In Memory of Henry Sidgwick," 463.

27. Gauld, *Founders of Psychical Research*, 56. Sidgwick is quoted in D. James, *Henry Sidgwick*, 120.

28. Quoted in D. James, *Henry Sidgwick*, 42–43.

29. F. Myers, "In Memory of Henry Sidgwick," 460.

30. Ibid., 457.

31. Quoted in Sidgwick and Sidgwick, *Henry Sidgwick*, 53.

32. WJ to AHGJ, 7 August 1889, JP, bMS Am 1092.9, #1684.

33. WJ to Josiah Royce, 8 May 1881, quoted in Perry, *TCWJ*, 2:791, and quoted in D. James, *Henry Sidgwick*, 60. James meant *The Methods of Ethics*. *The Data of Ethics*, which he was also reading at this time, was written by the English philosopher Herbert Spencer.

34. Ethel Sidgwick, *Mrs. Henry Sidgwick*; Gauld, *Founders of Psychical Research*, 104; Oppenheim, *Other World*, 120; *BDP*, s.v. "Eleanor Sidgwick"; Haynes, *Society for Psychical Research*, 191–92. On James's view that Harvard should grant PhDs to women, see Scarborough and Furumoto, *Untold Lives*, 27–30.

35. AJ, *Diary of Alice James*, 49, 152; WJ to AHGJ, 29 July 1889, JP, bMS Am 1092.9, #1680; AJ to WJ, 16 March 1890, *CWJ*, 7:10.

36. WJ to AHGJ, 24 June 1885, *CWJ*, 6:38. The friend was Margaret Oliphant Wilson, a British novelist visiting William in New Hampshire at the time. Mrs. Sidgwick's essay was "Notes on the Evidence, Collected by the Society, for Phantasms of the Dead," *PSPR* 3 (May 1885): 69–150.

37. Sidgwick is quoted in Sidgwick and Sidgwick, *Henry Sidgwick*, 160, 165.

38. Ibid., 293, 284.

39. F. Turner, *Between Religion and Science*, 39, 50–60; Schultz, *Henry Sidgwick*, 16.

40. Material for this section comes from Gauld, *Founders of Psychical Research*, 38; Oppenheim, *Other World*, 32; *DNB*, s.v. "Frederic Myers"; *BDP*, s.v. "F. W. H. Myers"; Haynes, *Society for Psychical Research*, 181–83; and F. Turner, *Between Science and Religion*, 104–33. See also Hamilton, *Immortal Longings*, especially chaps. 1 and 2, which appeared long after I wrote this section but conforms to the general pattern of my interpretation, even though Hamilton is apologetic of Myers's notable character flaws.

41. F. Turner, *Between Science and Religion*, chap. 5, quoted on 105.

42. Dixon, "In Memory of F. W. H. Myers."

43. Collins, "In Memory of F. W. H. Myers." Collins was one of the few who received a private copy of Myers's autobiography.

44. Gauld, *Founders of Psychical Research*, 330. Gurney is quoted on page 331.

45. Ibid., 329–30.

46. F. W. H. Myers to WJ, 29 November 1894, *CWJ*, 12:686; ibid., 3 January 1894, 12:684.

47. F. H. Bradley to WJ, 21 September 1897, *CWJ*, 8:311.

48. Lodge, "In Memory of F. W. H. Myers," 2, 7.

49. Ibid., 2; Lodge, *Past Years*, 288; Lodge, *Letters from Sir Oliver Lodge*, 220.

50. Gauld, *Founders of Psychical Research*, 329–34. For a more critical view of Myers that highlights his affair with Annie Marshall and alleges his youthful homosexuality, see T. Hall, *Strange Case of Edmund Gurney*, 50–51, 200–201. For a more balanced view of the affair, see F. Turner, *Between Science and Religion*, 112–14.

51. Lodge, "In Memory of F. W. H. Myers," 9–10.

52. Gauld, *History of Hypnotism*, 401n31.

53. F. Myers, *Fragments of Inner Life*, 16.

54. Ibid., 29–30.

55. F. Myers, "In Memory of Henry Sidgwick," 454.

56. Ibid., 455.

57. HJ Jr. to Thomas Sergeant Perry, 14 September 1879, *HJL*, 2:255–56; WJ to HJ Jr., 1 July 1883, *CWJ*, 2:271. James actually sailed on the *Cephalonia*, so it is unclear whether Myers joined him on that voyage.

58. F. Myers to WJ, 2 September 1889, *CWJ*, 12:683.

59. WJ to AHGJ, 24 July 1889, JP, bMS Am 1092.9, #1679.

60. WJ to AHGJ, 15 August 1892, *CWJ*, 7:312.

61. HJ Jr. to WJ, 20 August 1892, *CWJ*, 2:225.

62. WJ to HJ Jr., 24 August 1892, *CWJ*, 2:227.

63. See F. Myers, *Fragments of Inner Life*.

64. WJ to AHGJ, 18 August 1892, *CWJ*, 7:314, 315n5.

65. WJ to F. W. H. Myers, 9 July 1893, *CWJ*, 7:437.

66. Ibid., 438.

67. WJ to F. W. H. Myers, 16 July 1893, *CWJ*, 7:439.
68. WJ to F. W. H. Myers, 19 January 1897, JP, bMS Am 1092.1, no item number.
69. Sara Wyman Whitman to WJ, 10 August 1893, *CWJ*, 7:605.
70. *SUC*, 210.
71. WJ to William Wilberforce Baldwin, 1 January 1900, *CWJ*, 9:112.
72. F. W. H. Myers to WJ, 19 March 1900, *CWJ*, 12:688–89; WJ to Henry Sidgwick, 1 January 1900, *CWJ*, 9:586.
73. WJ to Karl Stumpf, 17 March 1900, *CWJ*, 9:165–66.
74. WJ to Théodore Flournoy, 1 January 1900, *CWJ*, 9:113.
75. *LWJTF*, introduction, quoted on xix.
76. WJ to Joseph Thacher Clarke, 16 February 1900, *CWJ*, 9:589.
77. WJ to Theodora Sedgwick, 21 March 1900, *CWJ*, 9:174.
78. WJ to Elizabeth Glendower Evans, 17 January 1900, *CWJ*, 9:128.
79. WJ to Josiah Royce, 8 February 1900, *CWJ*, 9:140–41.
80. The Myerses probably stayed at the chateau from 19 January through 2 March. See WJ to Richard Hodgson, 19 January 1900, *CWJ*, 9:130; and WJ to Thomas Davidson, 16 February 1900, ibid., 9:144.
81. WJ to Francis Boott, 31 January 1900, *CWJ*, 9:138.
82. WJ to MMJ, 10 March 1900, *CWJ*, 9:155.
83. WJ to F. C. S. Schiller, 6 March 1900, *CWJ*, 9:590.
84. WJ to Harriet Jackson Lee Morse, 19 February 1890, *CWJ*, 9:148.
85. WJ to Wincenty Lutoslawski, 3 March 1900, *CWJ*, 9:589.
86. For an alternative view that interprets Myers as a third way thinker, see Emily Williams Kelly, "F. W. H Myers and the Empirical Study of the Mind-Body Problem," in Kelly and Kelly, *Irreducible Mind*, 47–115. I address the shortcomings with this argument in chap. 6.
87. F. Myers, *Fragments of Inner Life*, 29–30.
88. *DNB*, s.v. "Edmund Gurney"; Gauld, *Founders of Psychical Research*, 153–85 passim; Oppenheim, *Other World*, 119; T. Hall, *Strange Case of Edmund Gurney*; and especially Epperson, *Mind of Edmund Gurney*. Eliot is quoted in Browning, *Life of George Eliot*, 116. Harrison is quoted in Harrison, *Reminiscences of a Student's Life*, 55.
89. Lady Battersea is quoted in Gauld, *Founders of Psychical Research*, 176.
90. Gurney is quoted in ibid., 156.
91. Gauld, *Founders of Psychical Research*, 157–59.
92. *BDP*, s.v. "Edmund Gurney."
93. Geikie, *Annals of the Royal Society Club*, 350–51.
94. A. Brown, *Metaphysical Society*, 247–52, quoted on 92–93. For James's participation in these clubs, see Richardson, *William James*, 233.
95. WJ to Thomas Davidson, n.d., quoted in Perry, *TCWJ*, 1:596; WJ to AHGJ, 6 February 1883, *CWJ*, 5:414.
96. T. Hall, *The Strange Case of Edmund Gurney*, 21n2; Uglow, *Lunar Men*, xv; quoted in Gladwell, "Group Think," 104.
97. Edmund Gurney to WJ, 13 December 1882, JP, bMS Am 1092, #303.
98. WJ to AHGJ, 15 December 1882, *CWJ*, 5:329.
99. Ibid., 16 December 1882, 5:332.

100. Ibid., 26 December 1882, 5:356.

101. Ibid., 13 January 1883, 5:392.

102. Ibid.,18 January 1883, 5:397, and 6 February 1883, 5:414.

103. WJ to HJ Jr., 6 February 1883, *CWJ*, 1:362.

104. Edmund Gurney to WJ, 23 September 1883, *CWJ*, 5:464.

105. Ibid.,17 February 1884, 5:492.

106. George Croom Robertson to WJ, 28 January 1884, *CWJ*, 5:485.

107. WJ to Shadworth H. Hodgson, 20 February 1885, *LWJ*, 1:242.

108. There is no history of the Scratch Eight. For sources that inform my synopsis, see Perry, *TCWJ*, 1:596–98, 606–11 and 2:12; T. Hall, *The Strange Case of Edmund Gurney*, 21n2; Allen, *William James*, 264–68; and Bjork, *William James*, 151, 298n15.

109. WJ to HJ Jr., 9 January 1883, *CWJ*, 1:345.

110. Edmund Gurney to WJ, 23 September 1883, *CWJ*, 1:461.

111. Ibid., 31 March 1885, 6:25.

112. Ibid., 8 November 1884, 5:530.

113. Ibid., 16 April 1886, 6:132.

114. Ibid., 17 February 1884, 6:492.

115. Gurney, Myers, and Podmore, *Phantasms of the Living*.

116. Edmund Gurney to WJ, 16 April 1886, *CWJ*, 6:133.

117. Ibid., 10 August 1886, 6:575.

118. Ibid., 16 January 1887, 6:190 including n. 2. On 30 October 1886, the *Times* of London reviewed *Phantasms* favorably on the whole, while only a small notice appeared in *Mind* 12 (January 1887): 135.

119. Edmund Gurney to WJ, 16 January 1887, *CWJ*, 6:193n1.

120. WJ to Karl Stumpf, 6 February 1887, quoted in Perry, *TCWJ*, 2:70.

121. For a discussion of this book, see Epperson, *Mind of Edmund Gurney*, chap. 7.

122. WJ, "*Tertium Quid*, by Edmund Gurney (1888)," *ECR*, 412–14, originally published in *Nation* 46 (April 26, 1888): 349; WJ to AHGJ, 27 April 1888, *CWJ*, 6:392.

123. See WJ to AHGJ, 24 January 1888, *CWJ*, 6:301; ibid., 6 February 1888, 6:310; ibid., 9 February 1888, 6:315; and the editor's notes to James's review of Gurney's *Tertium Quid*, *ECR*, 710.

124. WJ, "*Tertium Quid*, by Edmund Gurney (1888)," *ECR*, 413–14.

125. Edmund Gurney to WJ, 20 May 1888, *CWJ*, 6:412.

126. WJ to Henry Sidgwick, 30 April 1899, *CWJ*, 8:522.

127. Baird, *Richard Hodgson*; Gauld, *Founders of Psychical Research*, 141; Oppenheim, *Other World*, 139; Berger, *Lives and Letters in American Parapsychology*, 11–33.

128. Davies, *Sports in American Life*, 34; Rader, *American Sports*, 31, 34.

129. HJ III is quoted in Berger, *Lives and Letters in American Parapsychology*, 13–14.

130. Baird, *Richard Hodgson*, 4.

131. *BDP*, s.v. "Richard Hodgson."

132. Hodgson, "Account of Personal Investigations in India."

133. Hodgson and Davey, "Possibilities of Mal-observation."

134. Gauld, *Founders of Psychical Research*, 238, 273.

135. Hodgson, "Record of Observations of Certain Phenomena of Trance" and "Further Record of Observations of Certain Phenomena of Trance."

136. Hodgson is quoted in Berger, *Lives and Letters in American Parapsychology*, 13.
137. WJ to George Croom Robertson, 13 August 1885, *CWJ*, 6:62. The article James criticized was "The Consciousness of External Reality," *Mind* 10 (July 1885): 325–46.
138. Edmund Gurney to WJ, 16 January 1887, *CWJ*, 6:192.
139. Hodgson is quoted in Berger, *Lives and Letters in American Parapsychology*, 16.
140. WJ to George Croom Robertson, 8 August 1885, *CWJ*, 6:73.
141. Edmund Gurney to WJ, 20 May 1888, *CWJ*, 6:412.
142. WJ to AHGJ, 8 July 1890, *CWJ*, 7:54; ibid., 22 June 1891, 7:173; ibid., 18 July 1893, 7:604; ibid., 7 July 1890, 7:51; ibid., 7 February 1888, 6:594.
143. Ibid., 25 February 1888, 6:328; ibid., 30 June 1896, 8:582; ibid., 30 June 1896, 8:582; ibid., 24 January 1896, 8:124; ibid., 31 January 1888, 6:305.
144. Ibid., 18 September 1888, 6:606; ibid., 18 May 1894, 7:611; ibid., 14 August 1896, 8:583; WJ to Charles William Eliot, 7 March 1890, *CWJ*, 7:566; WJ to George Dorr, 24 March 1902[?], JP, bMS Am 1092.9, #890.
145. WJ to AHGJ, 3 or 4 April 1888, *CWJ*, 6:366; ibid., 5 April 1888, 6:600; ibid., 6 April 1888, 6:367; ibid., 3 May 1888, 6:400.
146. WJ to James Jackson Putnam, 10 August 1900, *CWJ*, 9:268; WJ to Richard Hodgson, 5 September 1900, *CWJ*, 9:291; WJ to Richard Hodgson, 14 December 1900, *CWJ*, 9:384–85; AHGJ to Richard Hodgson, 14 December 1900, *CWJ*, 9:616; WJ to Richard Hodgson, 26 December 1900, *CWJ*, 9:618.
147. WJ to Mrs. George Dorr, 11 July 1887, *CWJ*, 6:240; WJ to George Dorr, 24 March 1902[?], JP, bMS Am 1092.9, #890.
148. Prochnik, *Putnam Camp*.
149. WJ to MMJ, 11 July 1905, *CWJ*, 11:74–75; WJ to AHGJ, 4 September 1887, *CWJ*, 6:250; WJ to AHGJ, 8 September 1887, *CWJ*, 6:253; WJ to AHGJ, 11 September 1887, *CWJ*, 6:254; WJ to Richard Hodgson, 20 September 1899, *CWJ*, 8:576.
150. WJ to Richard Hodgson, 14 June 1904, *CWJ*, 10:620, and WJ to HJ III and WJ Jr., 11 September 1896, *CWJ*, 8:587.
151. Quoted in Baird, *Richard Hodgson*, 283–84.
152. WJ to HJ III, 15 June 1899, *CWJ*, 8:549. "Nichols" might be Herbert Nicols, an American psychologist who was an instructor at Harvard for a time, or Edgar Hamilton Nichols, one of two founders of the Browne and Nichols School for Boys in Cambridge. See "Biographical Register" *CWJ*, 7:636.
153. Putnam is quoted in Simon, *WJR*, 21.
154. WJ to Théodore Flournoy, 28 July 1903, JP, bMS Am 1092.1, no item number.
155. Quoted in Perry, *TCWJ*, 2:691, where Perry discusses the overall importance of friendships in James's life.
156. Ibid.
157. WJ to Richard Hodgson, 24 May 1894, *CWJ*, 7:506.
158. Perry, *TCWJ*, 2:156.

CHAPTER 3

1. Knapp, "Spatial Esotericism."
2. Perry, *TCWJ*, 2:156.

3. Gauld, *Founders of Psychical Research*, chap. 6; Oppenheim, *Other World*, chap. 4; Moore, *In Search of White Crows*, 138–42; Haynes, *Society for Psychical Research*, xiii–xv, 1–14.

4. The London Dialectical Society created a committee to investigate Spiritualism in 1869. See *EOP*, s.v. "London Dialectical Society."

5. Quoted from "Circulars of the American Society for Psychical Research," *EPR*, 5.

6. WJ to Karl Stumpf, 1 January 1886, *LWJ*, 2:248.

7. Karl Stumpf to WJ, 8 September 1886, *CWJ*, 6:574.

8. Schultz, *Henry Sidgwick*, chap 1. Sidgwick in quoted on pages 1, 29, and 332.

9. Knight, *The Nature of Science*, 82.

10. Merz, *History of European Thought in the Nineteenth Century*, 1:250.

11. Ornstein, *Role of Scientific Societies in the Seventeenth Century*, especially chaps. 4 and 5.

12. Knight, *The Nature of Science*, 97.

13. S. Mason, *History of the Sciences*, 439–40.

14. Ibid., 444.

15. Ibid., 445.

16. Knight, *The Age of Science*, 128–29.

17. Merz, *History of European Thought*, 2:239n1. Knight notes there were seven separate sections. See *The Age of Science*, 129.

18. Morrell and Thackray, *Gentlemen of Science*, chap. 1, quoted from 6, 11, 12, 17, 18, 21, 26.

19. Ibid., 29.

20. My argument that the SPR was a hybrid scientific society is based on the argument that the ASPR was. See Mauskopf, "History of the American Society for Psychical Research," especially 7–13.

21. Gauld puts the number for 1882–83 at 150. See *Founders of Psychical Research*, 140. But a careful tabulation of the roll indicates 276 members. See "Members, Associates, Honorary and Corresponding Members" in *PSPR* 1 (1882–83): 321–30 and "List of Members and Associates," *PSPR* 9 (December 1893): 372–93.

22. "Notes," *EPR*, 390–91.

23. Gladstone, untitled article.

24. F. W. H. Myers to WJ, 18 December 1893, *CWJ*, 12:684; ibid., 10 October 1894, 12:686; ibid., 31 October 1894, 12:686; ibid., 29 November 1894, 12:686–87.

25. Gauld, *Founders of Psychical Research*, 144–46.

26. F. W. H. Myers to WJ, 31 October 1894, *CWJ*, 12:686; "Proceedings of General Meetings."

27. Gauld, *Founders of Psychical Research*, 144.

28. F. W. H. Myers to WJ, 1 August 1894, *CWJ*, 12:685; ibid., 31 August 1894, 12:685; ibid., 3 November 1895, 12:687.

29. F. C. S. Schiller to WJ, 4 February 1903, *CWJ*, 10:196; Lodge, "[Third] Presidential Address," 18n17.

30. F. C. S. Schiller to WJ, 12 October 1904, *CWJ*, 10:489.

31. Edmund Gurney to WJ, 23 September 1883, *CWJ*, 5:461–62 including n. 2.

32. Ibid., 17 February 1884, 5:491.

33. Ibid., 23 September 1883, 5:462; WJ to F. W. H. Myers, 1 January 1896, JP, bMS Am 1092.1, no item number; WJ to F. W. H. Myers, 19 January 1897, JP, bMS Am 1092.1, no item number; Henry Sidgwick to WJ, 24 December 1890, JP, bMS Am 1092.9, item number illegible.

34. WJ to George Croom Robertson, 19 March 1887, JP, bMS Am1092.9, #3544.

35. WJ to HJ Jr., 12 April 1887, *CWJ*, 2:63. Note 4 indicates James probably had in mind George Trumbull Ladd's *Elements of Physiological Psychology* (1887), John Dewey's *Psychology* (1887), and Borden Parker Bowne's *Introduction to Psychological Theory* (1887). Hall did not publish a book at this point.

36. *DNB*, 136–37; *BDP*, s.v. "William Crookes"; Oppenheim, *Other World*, 338–54.

37. William Crookes, "Notes of Séances with D. D. Home" and "Address of the President before the British Association for the Advancement of Science," quoted in *BDP*, 69.

38. *BDP*, s.v. "Florence Cook"; Oppenheim, *Other World*, 16–21; Brandon, *Spiritualists*, 107–24; Gauld, *Founders of Psychical Research*, 130.

39. For samples, see Crookes, "Spiritualism Viewed by the Light of Modern Science," "Experimental Investigation of a New Force," and "Some Further Experiments on Psychic Force." His books included *Psychic Force and Modern Spiritualism*, *Researches in the Phenomena of Spiritualism*, and *Experimental Investigations of Psychic Force*.

40. Richet, *Traité de Métaphysique*, 642.

41. Trevor Hall makes a plausible case against the Cooks and Crookes in *The Spiritualists*. For supporters of Hall's argument, see Dingwall, *The Critics' Dilemma*. For criticism of Hall's evidence, see Medhurst and Goldney, "William Crookes and the Physical Phenomena of Mediumship." Skrupskelis, the associate editor of the *EPR*, accepts Hall's argument at face value. See "Notes," *EPR*, 431. For a useful discussion of the entire sordid episode, see Gauld, *Founders of Psychical Research*, 80–81.

42. See, for instance, Crookes, *Researches into the Phenomena of Modern Spiritualism*.

43. Edmund Gurney to WJ, *CWJ*, 6:25. John Tyndall, the British physicist, criticized psychical research.

44. WJ to F. W. H. Myers, 31 August 1899, *CWJ*, 9:574.

45. Edmund Gurney to WJ, 23 September 1883, *CWJ*, 5:461–62. WJ and Mrs. Piper are examined in detail in chap. 5.

46. WJ to Thomas Davidson, 1 February 1885, *CWJ*, 6:4.

47. *EOP*, s.v. "France," "Holland," "Germany," "Switzerland," and "Italy."

48. Barrett, "Prospects of Psychical Research in America," 172–78, quoted from 177.

49. Ibid., 173. The ASPR awaits a comprehensive history. For useful summaries of the early years, see Moore, *In Search of White Crows*, 142–44; Berger, "Early History of the ASPR"; Berger, *Lives and Letters in American Parapsychology*, chap. 1; and Mauskopf, "History of the American Society for Psychical Research," 10–14.

50. Gamm and Putnam, "Growth of Voluntary Associations in America."

51. Bailyn et al., *Great Republic*, 401–2; Blumin, *The Emergence of the Middle Class*, chap. 6.

52. De Tocqueville, *Democracy in America*, 95.

53. Schlesinger, "Biography of a Nation of Joiners," 24.

54. Bates, *Scientific Societies*, chap. 1; Voss, foreword to *The Pursuit of Knowledge in the Early American Republic*, vii–x; Dupree, "National Pattern of American Learned Societies."

55. Bates, *Scientific Societies*, 46.

56. Bruce, *The Launching of American Science*, chap. 19; Bates, *Scientific Societies*, 73–79.

57. Bates, *Scientific Societies*, 85.

58. Ibid., chap. 3.

59. Dexter, *History of Education in the United States*, 552, reprinted in Bates, *Scientific Societies*, 121.

60. Bates, *Scientific Societies*, table 1, category D, "associations for the study of special subjects," 121.

61. WJ, "Stanford's Ideal Destiny," *ECR*, 104, originally from *Founders' Day Addresses*, 9 March 1906 (Leland Stanford Junior University Publications, Trustees Series, no. 14, 1906): 5–8.

62. Oleson and Voss, *The Organization of Knowledge in Modern America*, xiv, xix.

63. WJ, "The Ph.D. Octopus," *ECR*, 67, originally from *Harvard Monthly* 36 (March 1903): 1–9.

64. WJ, preface, *WB*, 9.

65. "Circulars of the American Society for Psychical Research," *Circular No. 1, Issued by the Council*, *EPR*, 5. Useful information on the formation of the ASPR also comes from "Notes," *EPR*, 381–89.

66. "Request for Coöperation," 259.

67. "American Society for Psychical Research"; "The Prospects of the New Psychical Society."

68. "Constitution," 55.

69. "Request for Coöperation," 259.

70. "Circulars of the American Society for Psychical Research," *Circular No. 1, Issued by the Council*, *EPR*, 7.

71. "Circulars of the American Society for Psychical Research," *Circular No. 2, Issued by the Council*, *EPR*, 8–9.

72. "Formation of the Society."

73. "Meetings of the Society," 62.

74. Ibid.

75. "Circulars of the American Society for Psychical Research," *Circular Requesting Information on Mediumistic Phenomena*, *EPR*, 10.

76. Evidence of the extent of this work can be found in several places, including the archives of the current ASPR in New York City, which houses two filing cabinets full of reports and investigations on matters psychical. James's name appears on some of the hundreds of cases on file that range from "Apparitions" and "Haunted Houses" to "Dowsing" and "Glossographia–Glossolalia." See "Notes," *EPR*, 382–85.

77. "Circulars of the American Society for Psychical Research," *Circular No. 1, Issued by the Council*, *EPR*, 8.

78. Quoted in Newcomb, *The Reminiscences of an Astronomer*, 411.

79. WJ to Thomas Davidson, 1 February 1885, *CWJ*, 6:4; WJ to William Watson, 20 January 1886, *CWJ*, 6:570.

80. "Notes," *EPR*, 381, 385–86, 389–93.

81. "List of Members and Associates" and "Members and Associate Members."

82. WJ to William MacKintire Salter, 30 March 1886, JP, bMS Am 1092.9, #3662.

83. WJ to Thomas Davidson, 4 January 1885, *CWJ*, 6:1. John Curtis Bundy was the editor of the Chicago-based Spiritualist newspaper *Religio-Philosophical Journal*. See Biographical Registry, *CWJ*, 6:624. Bundy's name is listed on the first membership roll, so it appears that James successfully recruited him.

84. WJ to Thomas Davidson, 4 January 1885, *CWJ*, 6:1, including n. 2.
85. WJ to AJ, 24 December 1885, *CWJ*, 6:93.
86. Alfred Alexander Woodhull, a military surgeon, left the ASPR by December 1887. See *CWJ*, 2:33, and "Notes," *EPR*, 392. On Victoria Woodhull, see Goldsmith, *Other Powers*.
87. WJ to Christine Ladd-Franklin, 12 April 1888, *SUC*, 53–54.
88. Edmund Gurney to WJ, 8 November 1884, *CWJ*, 5:530; WJ to George Croom Robertson, 4 October 1886, quoted in Perry, *TCWJ*, 2:41.
89. Charles Renouvier to WJ, 5 February 1886, *CWJ*, 6:571. Renouvier was probably thinking of Charles Richet's articles.
90. WJ to Shadworth Hollway Hodgson, 16 August 1885, quoted in Perry, *TCWJ*, 2:629.
91. WJ to George Croom Robertson, 13 August 1885, *CWJ*, 6:61.
92. George Croom Robertson to WJ, 25 September 1886, *CWJ*, 6:575.
93. "The Prospects of the New Psychical Society," 44–45, quoted on 44.
94. WJ to George Croom Robertson, 13 August 1885, *CWJ*, 6:62.
95. WJ to Thomas Davidson, 24 November 1884, JP, bMS Am 1092.9, #856.
96. "Notes," *EPR*, 391–92.
97. G. S. Hall to WJ, 21 December 1886, *CWJ*, 6:578. According to the editors of *CWJ*, Hall was responding to a lost letter in which James had presumably proposed this scheme.
98. "Request for Coöperation," 259.
99. WJ to Elizabeth Stuart Phelps Ward, 24 August 1886, *CWJ*, 6:157; ibid., 25 June 1886, 6:573. The article "Psychic Wave" appeared in *Forum* 1 (June 1886): 377–88. For the *Circular Requesting Information on Mediumistic Phenomena*, see *EPR*, 10–11, originally published in the *Boston Daily Advertiser*, 9 April 1885, and the *Banner of Light*, 18 April 1885, 4.
100. WJ to AHGJ, 27 April 1888, *CWJ*, 6:392.
101. WJ to William Sturgis Bigelow, 19 January 1887, *CWJ*, 6:580.
102. WJ to John Forrester Andrew, 13 January 1887, *CWJ*, 6:189.
103. WJ to F. W. H. Myers, 15 July 1890, *CWJ*, 7:62.
104. WJ to George Croom Robertson, 13 August 1885, *CWJ*, 6:61.
105. WJ to George Croom Robertson, 29 August 1886, quoted in Perry, *TCWJ*, 1:602.
106. WJ to AHGJ, 8 August 1886, *CWJ*, 6:156.
107. WJ to Shadworth Hollway Hodgson, 12 September 1886, *LWJ*, 1:257.
108. WJ to AHGJ, 2 or 3 August 1885, *CWJ*, 6:52; ibid., 18 February 1888, 6:323; ibid., 31 March 1888, 6:361–62; ibid., 19 February 1888, 6:324.
109. Ibid., 29 August 1884, 5:521.
110. WJ to AJ, 15 June 1885, *CWJ*, 6:33.
111. WJ to HJ Jr., 23 November 1890, *CWJ*, 2:157.
112. WJ, "Address of the President before the Society to Psychical Research," *EPR*, 127.
113. WJ to F. W. H. Myers, 14 November 1892, *CWJ*, 7:340–41, including nn. 1 and 3.
114. WJ to HJ Jr., 26 January 1896, *CWJ*, 2:388–89. The talk James gave in New York was titled "Hysteria," which was part of lecture series called "Exceptional Mental States," though he had told Henry that he would give it on demonical possession, a topic he later presented in that series. James scholar Eugene Taylor brought together these lectures with his own introduction in *William James on Exceptional Mental States*. The talks at the "female" colleges were "Psychology and Relaxation," published later as "The Gospel of Relaxation" in *Talks to Teachers* (1899).

115. WJ to Richard Hodgson, 25 May 1892, *CWJ*, 7:271. The article was initially published as "What Psychical Research Has Accomplished," *Forum* 13 (August 1892): 727–42, and is reprinted in *EPR*, 89–106.

116. Benjamin Paul Blood to WJ, 22 November 1886, JP, bMS Am 1092.9, #49.

117. F. W. H. Myers to WJ, 12 December 1888, *CWJ*, 6:458.

118. Ibid., 459. Robert Pearsall Smith, a Philadelphia businessman, gave financial support to the SPR during this period, but it is unclear whether any of it went to Hodgson's salary. See note 1, F. W. H. Myers to WJ, 12 December 1888, *CWJ*; and "Notes," *EPR*, 392.

119. WJ to Christine Ladd-Franklin, 12 April 1888, *SUC*, 54–55.

120. WJ to AHGJ, 11 October 1888, *CWJ*, 6:608.

121. F. W. H. Myers to WJ, 12 December 1888, *CWJ*, 6:458–59.

122. Ibid., 28 December 1890, 7:579.

123. "Notes," *EPR*, 385.

124. WJ to AHGJ, 15 July 1890, *CWJ*, 7:61.

125. F. W. H. Myers to WJ, 12 January 1891, *CWJ*, 7:134.

126. Ibid. "Leif" was Walter Leaf, a British scholar and leading member of the SPR. "Danex" may have referred to Xavier Dariex, a French psychical researcher and editor of the *Annales des Sciences Psychiques*, which ran from 1891 through 1919. Heinrich Rudolf Hertz was a German physicist and member of the SPR. Albert Möll, known for his pioneering work in sexual psychopathology, was an early convert to hypnotism. Aleksander Nikolaevich Aksakov was a leading figure in Russian psychical research. See editor's notes to this letter.

127. For the notion of a "French-Swiss-English-and-American psychotherapeutic axis," see E. Taylor, *William James on Consciousness beyond the Margin*, 40, 95.

128. F. W. H. Myers to WJ, 12 January 1891, *CWJ*, 7:136.

129. WJ to F. W. H. Myers, 30 January 1891, *LWJ*, 1:305–6.

130. Henry Sidgwick to WJ, 24 December 1890, JP, bMS Am 1092.9, item number illegible.

131. F. W. H. Myers to WJ, 31 October 1889, *CWJ*, 12:682–83.

132. Ibid., 21 October 1890, 12:683–84; ibid., 10 November 1890, 12:684. According to the editors of *CWJ*, Myers was responding to a lost letter James had sent to him on 8 October 1890 inquiring how to proceed with the transition. The two names that Myers suggested to James for Hodgson's replacement were someone called Carey, who was a friend of Hodgson, and Arthur Peckster. It is unclear who the former was, and a search failed to find information on the latter. But it was immaterial as Hodgson did decide to stay on as the secretary of the newly formed American Branch for a least another year.

133. WJ to F. W. H. Myers, 30 January 1891, *LWJ*, 1:306.

134. WJ to AHGJ, 5 October 1890, *CWJ*, 7:575.

135. WJ to Samuel Pierpont Langley, 3 January 1891, *SUC*, 77.

136. "List of Members and Associates of the American Branch"; "Notes," *EPR*, 385; "Circular Requesting Financial Support," *EPR*, 11–12.

137. F. W. H. Myers to WJ, 24 January 1894, *CWJ*, 12:685; ibid., 1 April 1894, 12:685; ibid., 4 April 1894, 12:685; WJ to F. W. H. Myers, 4 May 1894, *CWJ*, 7:500n2; F. W. H. Myers to WJ, 8 August 1895, JP, bMS Am 1092.9, #418; F. W. H. Myers to WJ, 31 August 1894, *CWJ*, 12:685; F. W. H. Myers to WJ, 11 September 1895, JP, bMS Am 1092.9, #419; F. W. H. Myers to WJ, 3 November 1895, *CWJ*, 12:687; F. W. H. Myers to WJ, 18 November 1895, *CWJ*, 12:687.

138. WJ to Henry Sidgwick, 8 November 1895, JP, bMS Am 1092.9, #3760.
139. WJ to F. W. H. Myers, 1 January 1896, JP, bMS Am 1092.1, no item number.
140. WJ to Charles William Eliot, 14 June 1898, CWJ, 8:614.
141. "Notes," EPR, 420–21.
142. Horace Howard Furness to WJ, 19 October 1890, CWJ, 7:106–8.
143. WJ to Charles William Eliot, 14 June 1898, CWJ, 8:614. Hyslop was that time still a professor of philosophy at Columbia and seeking funds from the trustees to support psychical research.
144. WJ to George Bucknam Dorr, 24 March 1902, CWJ, 10:17.
145. F. W. H. Myers to WJ, 11 September 1895, JP, bMS Am 1092.9, #419.
146. WJ to Thomas Sergeant Perry, 6 February 1906, CWJ, 11:166.
147. F. C. S. Schiller to WJ, 4 February 1906, CWJ, 11:163.
148. Oliver Lodge to WJ, 21 December 1905, JP, bMS Am 1092, #502.
149. WJ to Théodore Flournoy, 9 February 1906, LWJTF, 174.
150. "Notice Concerning Dissolution of the American Branch," EPR, 12–13, originally published as "Dissolution of the American Branch," JASPR 1 (January 1907): 1–2, and in JSPR 12 (June 1906): 284.
151. "Notes," EPR, 388.
152. WJ to HJ Jr., 9 May 1906, CWJ, 3:316 including n. 1.
153. WJ to Théodore Flournoy, 9 February 1906, LWJTF, 174.
154. Mauskopf, "History of the American Society for Psychical Research," 13.
155. Ibid.; Perry, TCWJ, 2:155.
156. Perry, TCWJ, vol. 2, chaps. 66–68, quoted on 317.

CHAPTER 4

1. WJ to Thomas Davidson, 1 February 1885, CWJ, 6:4.
2. See, for instance, Peirce, "Logic and Spiritualism," 375.
3. Edmund Gurney to WJ, 16 April 1886, CWJ, 6:133.
4. For an insightful if at times dense account of the role of facts in modernity, see Poovey, History of the Modern Fact, especially chap. 1.
5. WJ, Prag., 13.
6. The aura of factuality in religion argument comes from Geertz, Interpretation of Cultures, 90, and is developed at length and applied insightfully for the case of France in Monroe, Laboratories of Faith, 4.
7. G. Hall, "Psychological Literature," 145.
8. WJ, "Address of the President," EPR, 132.
9. Perry, TCWJ, 2:157. McDermott concurs with Perry, writing, "James could not be more consistent in his commitment to the facts of human experience ... and [to] his corresponding rejection of a priori possibilities." See introduction to EPR, xxxi–xxxii.
10. EPhil, s.v. "Francis Bacon," by Maurice Cranston; s.v. "Auguste Comte," by Bruce Mazlish; s.v. "John Stuart Mill," by J. B. Schneewind; s.v. "positivism," by Nicola Abbagnano (translated by Nino Langiulli); s.v. "progress, the idea of," by Charles Frankel.
11. Ravetz, Scientific Knowledge and Its Social Problems, chap. 6.
12. WJ, "Philosophy and Its Critics," SPP, 15.

13. Bullard, "[First] Report of the Committee on Mediumistic Phenomena," 231. Bullard chaired the committee and wrote the report, but the sentiments show James's influence on its empirical approach.

14. Ibid.

15. *EPhil*, s.v. "empiricism," by D. W. Hamlyn.

16. Perry, *TCWJ*, 2:468.

17. Perry, *TCWJ*, 1, chap. 26. WJ is quoted on 454.

18. WJ to F. W. H. Myers, 14 November 1892, *CWJ*, 7:340.

19. F. W. H. Myers to WJ, 26 July 1890, *CWJ*, 7:73.

20. WJ to F. W. H. Myers, 30 January 1891, *LWJ*, 1:306.

21. WJ to F. W. H. Myers, 1 January 1896, JP, bMS Am 1092.1, no item number.

22. *DAB*, s.v. "Thomas Davidson," by C[harles] M. B[akewell]; WJ, "Thomas Davidson: Individualist," *ECR*, 86–96, originally published as "A Knight-Errant of the Intellectual Life," *McClure's Magazine*, May 1905, 3–11, upon which Bakewell, a onetime understudy of Davidson, clearly relies.

23. Davidson is quoted in WJ, "Thomas Davidson," *ECR*, 92.

24. WJ, "Thomas Davidson," *ECR*, 89, 86, 96, 93–94, 90, 96. For Davidson's relationship with James, see Perry, *TCWJ*, 1, chaps. 46 and 47; Allen, *William James*, 215, 264, 267–68; and Simon, *Genuine Reality*, 149–50, 278, 330.

25. WJ to Thomas Davidson, 1 February 1885, *CWJ*, 6:4.

26. George Croom Robertson to WJ, 25 September 1886, *CWJ*, 6:575.

27. *EOP*, s.v. "Spiritualism."

28. *PDS*, s.v. "mental mediumship" and "physical medium."

29. For lucid chapters on all these developments, see S. Brown, *Heyday of Spiritualism*, which is sympathetic; and Brandon, *Spiritualists*, which is critical and reveals how all these phenomena were faked. See her appendix, "The Machine in the Ghost," 255–86, and the images of famous mediums in the insets.

30. Gauld, *Founders of Psychical Research*, 124–27; Oppenheim, *Other World*, 22–23; Minot Judson Savage to WJ, 7 April 1887, *CWJ*, 6:583.

31. Gauld, *Founders of Psychical Research*, 201–7; Oppenheim, *Other World*, 139–40; Eleanor Sidgwick, "Mr. Eglinton"; Hodgson and Davey, "Possibilities of Mal-observation"; Hodgson, "Mr. Davey's Imitations"; Edmund Gurney to WJ, 16 January 1887, *CWJ*, 6:192.

32. Oppenheim, *Other World*, 159–73; "Report of the Committee Appointed to Investigate Phenomena Connected with the Theosophical Society"; Hodgson, "Account of Personal Investigations in India"; WJ to Richard Hodgson 22 January 1900, *CWJ*, 9:587–88.

33. S. Brown, *Heyday of Spiritualism*, 215–23, Truesdell, *Bottom Facts Concerning the Science of Spiritualism*.

34. Edmund Gurney to WJ, 31 July 1885, *CWJ*, 6:48; ibid., 31 July 1885, 6:49; WJ to Frederic Rowland Marvin, 19 October 1904, *CWJ*, 10:492; George C. Bartlett to WJ, 25 March 1891, *CWJ*, 7:581.

35. WJ to Shadworth Hollway Hodgson, 16 August 1885, quoted in Perry, *TCWJ*, 2:629.

36. Gauld, *Founders of Psychical Research*, 221–45.

37. F. W. H. Myers to WJ, 25 September 1892, *CWJ*, 12:684. On Eusapia, see *BDP*, s.v. "Eusapia Palladino"; Oppenheim, *Other World*, 149–52; and Brandon, *Spiritualists*, 128–36, 256–59.

38. Brandon, *Spiritualists*, 134.
39. F. W. H. Myers to WJ, 1 August 1894, *CWJ*, 12:685.
40. Charles Richet to WJ, 5 March 1895, *CWJ*, 8:565.
41. Quoted in Gauld, *Founders of Psychical Research*, 229.
42. F. W. H. Myers to WJ, 1 August 1894, *CWJ*, 12:685.
43. Ibid., 31 August 1894, 12:685.
44. Ibid.; and F. W. H. Myers to WJ, 10 October 1894, *CWJ*, 12:686.
45. WJ to AHGJ, 19 August 1895, *CWJ*, 8:572.
46. F. W. H. Myers to WJ, 20 September 1894, *CWJ*, 12:686.
47. Ibid., 13 March 1895, 12:687.
48. Quoted in Gauld, *Founders of Psychical Research*, 238.
49. F. W. H. Myers to WJ, 15 October 1895, *CWJ*, 12:687.
50. Quoted in T. Hall, *Strange Case of Edmund Gurney*, 39–40.
51. See "Eusapia Palladino," *JSPR* 7 (November 1895): 55–79.
52. For the Sidgwicks' views, see H. Sidgwick, "Eusapia Palladino."
53. Lodge, "Experience of Unusual Physical Phenomena"; Oliver Lodge to WJ, 22 September 1894, JP, bMS Am 1092, #496.
54. Oliver Lodge to WJ, 22 September 1894, JP, bMS Am 1092, #496.
55. WJ to Oliver Joseph Lodge, 4 October 1894, *CWJ*, 7:552–54. Edward Augustus Brackett, an American sculptor, poet, and investigator of Spiritualism, published a book on the medium Hannah Ross, which James informed Lodge was "based on the performance of 3 female mediums who have hoodwinked the very eyes out of his head" and damaged his reputation. The title of Brackett's book was *Materialized Apparitions: If Not Beings from Another Life, What Are They?* (Boston: Colby and Rich, 1886).
56. WJ to Oliver Joseph Lodge, 4 October 1894, *CWJ*, 7:552–54.
57. WJ to F. W. H. Myers, 29 September 1894, *CWJ*, 7:550–51.
58. Oliver Lodge to WJ, 13 October 1894, JP, bMS Am 1092, #497.
59. WJ to Oliver Lodge, 3 June 1896, JP, bMS Am 1092.1, no item number.
60. F. W. H. Myers to WJ, 8 August 1895, JP, bMS Am 1092.9, #418.
61. Ibid., 11 September 1895, #419.
62. WJ to Henry Sidgwick, 8 November 1895, JP, bMS Am 1092.9, #3760.
63. Ibid.
64. WJ to Richard Hodgson, 11 December ca. 1894, *CWJ*, 12:674, and JP, bMS Am 1092.9, #968. The editors of the *CWJ* dated this letter around 1894, and an unknown archivist dated the original copy as "possibly 1903." But the contents in the first paragraph reveal James was referencing Hodgson's remarks at a SPR General Meeting held in 1895, which suggests the letter was mostly likely written later that same year. See "General Meeting," *JSPR* 7 (October 1895): 131–38; and Baird, *Richard Hodgson*, 148.
65. Quoted in Oppenheim, *Other World*, 151.
66. Quoted in Gauld, *Founders of Psychical Research*, 242.
67. WJ to Théodore Flournoy, 30 April 1903, JP, bMS Am 1092.1, no item number.
68. According to the editors of *EPR*, the SPR reached the official conclusion that Eusapia was a fraud in 1896, but it seems it actually took until 1898. See "Notes," *EPR*, 430.
69. WJ to Katherine Prince, 1 June 1885, *CWJ*, 6:31 including n. 1.

70. *PASPR* 1 (July 1885): 49. See also WJ to Katherine Prince, 1 June 1885, *CWJ*, 6:31n1.

71. Edmund Gurney to WJ, 22 September 1885, *CWJ*, 6:82.

72. WJ to F. W. M. Myers, 14 November 1894, *CWJ*, 7:340.

73. On Diss Debar, see *EOP*, s.v. "Theodore and Laura Horos"; and Buescher, *Empress of Swindle*.

74. Moore, *In Search of White Crows*, 108–9.

75. Garland, *Tyranny of the Dark*.

76. WJ to Hamlin Garland, 25 December 1904, *CWJ*, 10:516–17.

77. WJ to AHGJ, 6 April 1888, *CWJ*, 6:367. Note 2 indicates the index to the *New York Times* contains many entries to Diss Debar in 1888 (among other years) regarding rumors, allegations, and charges of fraud. Moore confirms these reports in *In Search of White Crows*, 109n12.

78. WJ to AHGJ, 9 April 1888, *CWJ*, 6:369; ibid., 10 April 1888, 6:370.

79. Ibid., 24 April 1888, 6:388.

80. WJ to Richard Hodgson, 24 April 1888, *CWJ*, 6:601; Harry P. Place to WJ, 19 April 1888, *CWJ*, 6:601.

81. See Moore, *In Search of White Crows*, 65; and WJ to Richard Hodgson, 28 August 1896, *CWJ*, 8:188.

82. There may have been more than one set of Berry sisters who practiced Spiritualism, or at least more than one Helen Berry calling herself a medium. Conflicting locations and times regarding her whereabouts during the 1880s were reported in the *Banner of Light*. The *Banner* advertised the services of a Helen C. Berry (sometimes with her sister Gertrude as well) and sometimes of the "Berry Sisters" on different occasions. See "Notes," *EPR*, 393. It is possible, though not likely, that Helen C. Berry and Catherine Berry, the British "developing medium," were the same person, since the latter plied her trade during the 1860s and 1870s and was deceased by 1891. See *EOP*, s.v. "Catherine Berry" and "medium."

83. George Herbert Palmer, "William James," in Simon, *WJR*, 32.

84. Horace Howard Furness to WJ, 22 March 1886, *CWJ*, 6:571.

85. WJ to Horace Howard Furness, 3 June 1886, *CWJ*, 6:142–43.

86. Quoted in Allen, *William James*, 283.

87. WJ, "Report of the Committee on Mediumistic Phenomena," *EPR*, 14–18, quoted on 15, originally published in *PASPR* 1 (July 1886): 102–6.

88. J. Warren, "[Second] Report of the Committee on Mediumistic Phenomena," 321; "Notes," *EPR*, 393.

89. *Banner of Light*, 8 March 1884, 4; "Notes," *EPR*, 29–32, 393, 402–5, 457.

90. Alfred Russel Wallace to WJ, 1 June 1886, quoted in and drawn from Roback, *William James*, 98–101.

91. F. W. H. Myers to WJ, 5 October 1885, *CWJ*, 6:86.

92. Alfred Russel Wallace to WJ, 11 December 1886, *CWJ*, 6:577.

93. "A Distinguished Party at Materialization Séances," *Banner of Light*, 8 January 1887, 4, quoted in "Notes," *EPR*, 402.

94. *New York Times*, 4 February 1887, 1.

95. WJ to William Sturgis Bigelow, 19 January 1887, *CWJ*, 6:580.

96. See "Notes," *EPR*, 402.

97. WJ, "The Perception of 'Things,'" *PP*, chap. 19, 2:741–42. Since physical mediumship found its way into the *PP*, it seems James was drafting this chapter while investigating Mrs. Ross. See "Notes," *PP*, 3:1555, which makes clear James wrote this chapter between the spring of 1887 and November 1888, thus confirming the overlap.

98. WJ to Francis James Child, ca. late 1880s, *CWJ*, 12:673. Notes one and three indicate the probable date due to the reference to Mrs. Ross and confirm she lived on West Concord Street in Boston in the late 1880s.

99. Jastrow, "Psychology of Deception."

100. *Banner of Light*, 10 February 1887, 4; and WJ, "Letter on Mrs. Ross, the Medium (1887)," *EPR*, 29–32, from which the *Banner* is quoted.

101. "Notes," *EPR*, 404. Wallace seems to have believed in Spiritualism as early as 1866. See Wallace, *My Life*, 1:336.

102. *Banner of Light*, 5 March 1887, 4, quoted in "Notes," *EPR*, 404.

103. *Banner of Light*, 26 February 1887, 5, quoted in ibid., 403–4.

104. For an account of the raid and arrest, see "Notes," *EPR*, 404–5.

105. Horace Howard Furness to WJ, n.d., April 1887, *CWJ*, 6:583.

106. Ibid., n.d., April 1887, 6:214–15.

107. Ibid., 29 May 1887, 6:228. On the Seybert Commission's report on physical mediumship in 1887, see "Notes," *EPR*, 420–21. Its title was *Preliminary Report of the Commission Appointed by the University of Pennsylvania to Investigate Modern Spiritualism*.

108. Bullard, "[First] Report of the Committee on Mediumistic Phenomena," 230; Bullard, "Request for Coöperation."

109. "Gunning for Ghosts. Poor Luck of Psychical Research Society. Don't Quite Know What to Make of Spiritualistic Phenomena. But Have Some Cases of Thought Transference and Presentiments," *Boston Daily Globe*, 13 December 1887, quoted in "Notes," *EPR*, 383.

110. *Banner of Light*, 22 December 1888, 4, quoted in "Notes," *EPR*, 383.

111. Ibid.

112. Ibid.

113. J. Warren, "[Second] Report of the Committee on Mediumistic Phenomena," 321–22.

114. *Banner of Light*, 3 January 1891, 4, quoted in "Notes," *EPR*, 385. The editors of *EPR* make a similar argument. They point out that the Ross case indicates how "both mediums and skeptical investigators faced genuine risks" and thus how these cases can be viewed from a variety of perspectives. See "Notes," *EPR*, 402.

115. Jastrow, "Psychology of Spiritualism"; Jastrow, "Problems with 'Psychic Research,'" especially 80–81.

116. WJ, "The Confidences of a 'Psychical Researcher,'" *EPR*, 363.

117. WJ, "Address of the President," *EPR*, 128, 132.

118. Edmund Gurney to WJ, 16 January 1887, *CWJ*, 6:190.

119. Gardner, "Communicating with the Dead: William James and Mrs. Piper, Part I," quoted from page 20; Gardner, "Communicating with the Dead: William James and Mrs. Piper, Part 2," quoted from page 39; WJ to Richard Hodgson, 11 December ca. 1894 [1895], JP, bMS Am 1092.9, #968, partially reprinted in *CWJ*, 12:674.

120. WJ to Richard Hodgson, 11 December ca. 1895, JP, bMS Am 1092.9, #968, partially reprinted in *CWJ*, 12:674.

CHAPTER 5

1. WJ, "The Confidences of a 'Psychical Researcher,'" *EPR*, 371.
2. Perry, *TCWJ*, 2:172, 165.
3. Madden, introduction to *WB*, xv.
4. WJ, "What Psychical Research Has Accomplished," *EPR*, 97.
5. McDermott, introduction to *EPR*, xxii.
6. Ibid., xxxii.
7. *EPhil*, s.v. "fideism," by Richard H. Popkin.
8. For a useful overview of the history of theological fideism that identifies six strands, see T. Carroll, "Traditions of Fideism." Carroll makes an eloquent plea for historical clarification of the term before employing it philosophically but does not discuss the philosophical definitions. One of the major strands he identifies as the most useful is "skeptical fideism," first put forth by Popkin in *History of Skepticism*, which contextualized fideism in the history of modern philosophy.
9. *EPhil*, s.v. "fideism," by Richard H. Popkin.
10. Ibid.
11. Ibid.
12. T. Carroll, "Traditions of Fideism," 20n13.
13. Madden, introduction to *WB*, xv–xvi, xviii. One philosopher maintains Madden is mistaken in asserting James advanced two kinds of fideism and that in so doing James vacillated in a confusing way, calling this a "character assassination." See Wernham, *James's Will-to-Believe Doctrine*, 3 and 107n1. Both claims are red herrings and demonstrably false. The textual evidence of the four essays in which James advanced fideism overwhelmingly supports Madden's claim. Moreover, Madden's introduction shows the evolution of James's thought and is neither critical nor accepting but descriptive.
14. Madden, introduction to *WB*, xviii.
15. Ibid., xv. This was the stronger version of fideism that Wright had criticized.
16. Ibid., xvi, xix. The original publications were "The Sentiment of Rationality," *Mind* 4 (July 1879): 317–46, which provided the basis for four additional essays: "Rationality, Activity and Faith," *Princeton Review* 2 (July 1882): 58–86; "Reflex Action and Theism," *Unitarian Review* 16 (November 1881): 389–416; "Is Life Worth Living?," *International Journal of Ethics* 6 (October 1895): 1–24; and "The Will to Believe," *New World* 5 (June 1896): 327–47. Madden contends the first two tended toward his stronger version while the latter two tended toward the weaker, thus indicating a kind of development in which James backed away from the more extreme form of fideism that gave priority to the will over the intellect and moved toward the more moderate form that invoked the will when the intellect had done all it could to find sufficient empirical evidence for belief. However, at late as 1896 James advanced the strong version, which would seem to complicate Madden's claim. "There are, then, cases where a fact cannot come at all unless a preliminary faith exists in its coming. *And where faith in a fact can help create the fact* . . . " WJ, "The Will to Believe," *WB*, 29.
17. WJ, "The Will to Believe," *WB*, 13.
18. Ibid., 27.
19. Ibid., 20.
20. WJ to James Mark Baldwin, January 1899, *CWJ*, 8:476.

21. WJ, "The Will to Believe," *WB*, 32n4.

22. Ibid., 25.

23. Indeed, James has been accused of "wishful thinking," among other related charges. For a brief but useful account of contemporary critics, see Madden, introduction to *WB*, xx–xxiv. For a defense of James that includes more recent critics, see O'Connell, *William James on the Courage to Believe*.

24. *EPhil*, s.v. "William James," by William James Earle.

25. Quoted in Perry, *TCWJ*, 2nd ed., 208.

26. WJ, "The Sentiment of Rationality," *WWJ*, 317–18.

27. Ibid., 317.

28. WJ, "The Sentiment of Rationality," *EPHL*, 32. Simon develops this point in *Genuine Reality*, 170.

29. G. Myers, *William James*, 457.

30. Seigfried, *William James's Radical Reconstruction of Philosophy*, 26–32, quoted on 213–14. For Seigfried, the process of dismantling the traditional notion of rationality and replacing it with the sentiment of rationality was but one of many crucial steps in James's "radical reconstruction of philosophy."

31. Croce, *Science and Religion in the Era of William James*, 228–29. For Croce, this delicate balancing act reflected James's complicated relationship with modernity.

32. Perry, *TCWJ*, 2:209.

33. WJ to Elizabeth Stuart Phelps Ward, 24 August 1886, *CWJ*, 6:157.

34. *PDS*, s.v. "mental mediumship" and "trance."

35. A planchette is a small heart-shaped object supported by two felt casters at two points and a vertical pencil at a third used to spell out messages supposedly from the "other world."

36. WJ to AHGJ, 20 February 1888, 23 February 1888, *CWJ*, 6:595.

37. Ibid., 27 February 1888, 6:331. "Curtis" might refer to Allen Curtis, a Boston banker and member of the ASPR.

38. *EOP*, s.v. "mediumship."

39. WJ to Richard Hodgson, 16 May 1904, *CWJ*, 10:399 including n. 2.

40. Thomas Sawyer Spivey to WJ, 21 March 1904, *CWJ*, 10:616.

41. Hudson Tuttle to WJ, 16 February 1902, *CWJ*, 10:582.

42. WJ, "A Case of Automatic Drawing," *EPR*, 221, originally published in *Popular Science Monthly*, January 1904, 195–201.

43. Roark et al., *American Promise*, A-52.

44. For instance, see Deveney, *Paschal Beverly Randolph*; B. Carroll, *Spiritualism in Antebellum America*; and Braude, *Radical Spirits*.

45. WJ to William MacKintire Salter, 30 March 1886, JP, bMS Am 1092.9, #3662.

46. Théodore Flournoy to WJ, 18 December 1893, *CWJ*, 7:607.

47. WJ to Théodore Flournoy, 1 January 1900, *CWJ*, 9:113. Richet's medium may have been Marthe Béraud. See Haynes, *Society for Psychical Research*, 188.

48. WJ to Richard Hodgson, 14 June 1904, *CWJ*, 10:620. None of the individuals were identified by first name.

49. F. W. H. Myers to WJ, 15 July 1897, *CWJ*, 12:688; Sydney Haldane Olivier to WJ, 26 April 1904, *CWJ*, 10:617; F. W. H. Myers to WJ, 20 September 1900, *CWJ*, 12:689;

F. W. H. Myers to WJ, 9 December 1900, *CWJ*, 12:690. Mrs. Raikes was the wife of Kenneth Cochran Raikes, a British judge in Yorkshire, both of whom were SPR members. See "Biographical Register," *CWJ*, 12:710.

50. F. W. H. Myers to WJ, 1 September 1900, *CWJ*, 12:689; ibid., 20 September 1900, 12:689; WJ to F. W. H. Myers, Rome, 8 January 1901, *CWJ*, 9:409. Footnote 1 of the last letter indicates that Myers's article was published in a special issue of the *Proceedings* devoted to Mrs. Thompson (see "On the Trance-Phenomena of Mrs. Thompson," *PSPR* 17 [June 1902]: 67–74), and that Myers had read versions of the paper at the SPR meeting held on 16 July 1900 and at the International Congress of Psychology in 1900. In this paper, Myers stipulated that spirit possession explained most of Mrs. Thompson's phenomena and maintained her case was one of pseudo-possession, such as in Théodore Flournoy's medium Hélène Smith or Morton Prince's Sally Beauchamp. In this letter James told Myers, "I have read 3/4 of the *Thompson* matter and find it goes easier than seemed at first to be the case." See also WJ to Théodore Flournoy, 1 January 1900, *CWJ*, 9:113; and F. C. S. Schiller to WJ, 4 April 1900, *CWJ*, 9:594.

51. WJ to Richard Hodgson, 5 September 1900, *CWJ*, 9:29; WJ to AHGJ, 5 September 1900, *CWJ*, 9:293.

52. WJ to AHGJ, 22 February 1888, *CWJ*, 6:326.

53. Ibid., 7 March 1888, 6:343. Since James's name became synonymous with psychical research in Boston, it is not surprising that many mediums purported to manifest James's father as a disincarnate spirit.

54. WJ to Théodore Flournoy, 13 June 1902, *CWJ*, 10:57; WJ to Richard Hodgson, 17 December 1903, *CWJ*, 10:354 including n. 1, which indicates Mrs. Smith was not Hélène.

55. AHGJ to HJ Jr., 6 April 1906, *CWJ*, 3:309–10 including n. 4.

56. WJ, "Letter on Dr. Gower and Table Lifting (1907)," *EPR*, 246–47, originally from "Report on Some Recent Sittings for Physical Phenomena in America," *PSPR* 21 (October 1907): 108–9. See *EPR*, 491 and 423, which identifies the sitters, explains the events, and provides the citation of Alice Johnson's article about them in the *Proceedings*, as well as the various entries from James's diary.

57. WJ to David Starr Jordan, 4 May 1906, *CWJ*, 11:217.

58. "Biographical Register," *CWJ*, 11; David Starr Jordan to WJ, 28 April 1906, *CWJ*, 11:215; WJ to David Starr Jordan, 4 May 1906, *CWJ*, 11:217.

59. Bullard, "[First] Report of the Committee on Mediumistic Phenomena," 230.

60. J. Warren, "[Second] Report of the Committee on Mediumistic Phenomena," 320.

61. James refers to "Mrs. P" several times in "Report of the Committee on Mediumistic Phenomena," *EPR*, 14–18.

62. See *Notable American Women*, s.v. "Leonora Evelina Simonds Piper," by Gardner Murphy, 3:73–75, quoted on page 74; *EOP*, 3rd ed., s.v. "Piper, Mrs. Leonora," ed. J. Gordon Melton (Detroit: Gale Group, 1990); Bloom, "America's Most Famous Medium"; *Man, Myth, and Magic*, s.v. "Mrs. Piper," by Alan Gauld; and "Notes," *EPR*, 394–400. Four highly sympathetic contemporary accounts that support the survival hypothesis are Piper, *Life and Work of Mrs. Piper*; Robbins, *Both Sides of the Veil* and *Past and Present with Mrs. Piper*; and Sage, *Mrs. Piper and the Society for Psychical Research*. Alta Piper's work was the most shameless in making the case for her mother, while Sage's weighed the evidence in a more balanced way. Oliver Lodge, who wrote the preface to Sage's book

because he was looking for ways to popularize psychical research, endorsed the book without substantiating Sage's views.

63. *Banner of Light*, 20 October 1883, 4; "Notes," *EPR*, 399; Piper, *Life and Work of Mrs. Piper*, chap. 3; quoted in Bell, *Spiritism, Hypnotism and Telepathy*, 161.

64. Leonora is quoted in Bell, *Spiritism, Hypnotism and Telepathy*, 162.

65. See Piper, *Life and Work of Mrs. Piper*, 21–25; and "Notes," *EPR*, 397.

66. WJ, "Report of the Committee on Mediumistic Phenomena," *EPR*, 14–18, quoted from 15, 17–18, originally published in *PASPR* 1 (July 1886): 102–6.

67. WJ, "Notes on Automatic Writing," *EPR*, 37–55, originally published in *PASPR* 1 (March 1889): 548–64.

68. Mr. A. Y. to WJ, 13 June 1886, and Mr. E. D. C. to WJ, 14 June 1886, *CWJ*, 6:572–73; Joseph Estlin Carpenter to WJ, 14 December 1894, *CWJ*, 7:619, and 31 July 1898, *CWJ*, 7:617. Hodgson described these cases in "Record of Observations of Certain Phenomena of Trance," 96–97.

69. WJ, "Report of the Committee on Mediumistic Phenomena," *EPR*, 16.

70. See "Notes," *EPR*, 437–38.

71. Excerpted in and quoted from appendix 3: "Sittings with Mrs. Piper," *EPR*, 436–41. See also Hodgson, "Record of Observations of Certain Phenomena of Trance," 133–35.

72. WJ to Elizabeth Wild Blodgett, 21 June 1888, *CWJ*, 6:419.

73. WJ, "A Record of Observations of Certain Phenomena of Trance," *EPR*, 79–88, quoted from 88, originally published in *PSPR* 6 (December 1890): 651–59.

74. Ibid., 86. Hodgson described the Blodgett case in "Record of Observations of Certain Phenomena of Trance," 69–83. For James's role, see *CWJ*, 6:419–20.

75. WJ to AHGJ, 15 July 1890, *CWJ*, 7:61; WJ to F. W. H. Myers, 15 July 1890, *CWJ*, 7:62; and F. W. H. Myers to WJ, 26 July 1890, *CWJ*, 7:73.

76. WJ to Elizabeth Wild Blodgett, 21 June 1888, *CWJ*, 6:419.

77. Ibid.

78. WJ to AHGJ, 24 December 1885, *CWJ*, 6:92 including n. 2.

79. "Notes," *EPR*, 396–97.

80. Piper, *Life and Work of Mrs. Piper*, 66.

81. Myers told James that according to Hodgson, Mrs. Piper would start her voyage on 9 November. See F. W. H. Myers to WJ, 31 October 1889 and 2 September 1889, *CWJ*, 12:682–83.

82. WJ to Leonora Evelina Piper, November 1889, *CWJ*, 6:617.

83. F. W. H. Myers to WJ, 26 July 1890, *CWJ*, 7:73.

84. Ibid., 28 February 1890, 12:683.

85. Ibid., 2 April 1890, 12:683.

86. Ibid., 26 July 1890, 7:73. Instead of a special issue, major sections of volumes 6 (1890), 8 (1892), and 13 (1898) were devoted to Mrs. Piper.

87. WJ to G. S. Hall, 27 May 1894, JP, bMS Am 1092.9, #962.

88. See WJ, "A Record of Observations of Certain Phenomena of Trance," *EPR*, 79–88.

89. Piper, *Life and Work of Mrs. Piper*, 49.

90. WJ, "A Record of Observations of Certain Phenomena of Trance," *EPR*, 83.

91. Bullard, "[First] Report of the Committee on Mediumistic Phenomena," 235–36.

92. WJ, "A Record of Observations of Certain Phenomena of Trance," *EPR*, 88.

93. WJ, "What Psychical Research Has Accomplished," *EPR*, 89–106, originally published in *Forum* 13 (August 1892): 727–42.

94. WJ, "What Psychical Research Has Accomplished," *EPR*, 97.

95. WJ to Richard Hodgson, 25 May 1892, *CWJ*, 7:271.

96. F. W. H. Myers to WJ, 16 November 1893, *CWJ*, 7:468.

97. WJ to F. W. H. Myers, 17 December 1893, *CWJ*, 7:475.

98. F. W. H. Myers to WJ, 3 January 1894, JP, bMS Am 1092.9, #417.

99. WJ to F. W. H. Myers, 4 May 1894, *CWJ*, 7:500.

100. F. W. H. Myers to WJ, 11 September 1895, JP, bMS Am 1092.9, #419.

101. WJ to Henry Sidgwick, 8 November 1895, JP, bMS, Am 1092.9, #3760.

102. WJ to AHGJ, 21 May 1894, *CWJ*, 7:504.

103. Wendell Barrett to WJ, 26 May 1886, *CWJ*, 6:572; WJ to AHGJ, 23 May 1894, *CWJ*, 7:505; WJ to AHGJ, 24 May 1894, JP, bMS Am 1092.9, #1864; Hodgson, "Record of Observations of Certain Phenomena of Trance," 97.

104. WJ to James Mark Baldwin, December 1895[?], JP, bMS Am 1092.1, no item number.

105. WJ to AHGJ, 19 September 1894, *CWJ*, 7:547. For Newbold's sitting, see Newbold, "Further Record of Observations of Certain Phenomena of Trance."

106. WJ to AHGJ, 25 May 1894, JP, bMS Am 1092.9, #1865.

107. Ibid.

108. WJ to AHGJ, 28 May 1894, *CWJ*, 7:511.

109. Ibid., 27 May 1894, 7:509.

110. Ibid., 29 May 1894, 7:513. Norton is quoted in Moore, *In Search of White Crows*, 147.

111. WJ to AHGJ, 9 July 1890, *CWJ*, 7:55.

112. F. W. H. Myers to WJ, 24 January 1894, *CWJ*, 12:684–85. Mrs. Piper did not return to England at this time but did in 1906 for the SPR's cross-correspondence tests.

113. F. W. H. Myers to WJ, 1 April 1894, *CWJ*, 12:685.

114. F. W. H. Myers to WJ, 11 September 1895, JP, bMS Am 1092.9, #419.

115. F. W. H. Myers to WJ, 15 October 1895, *CWJ*, 12:687.

116. Ibid., 31 October 1894, 12:686.

117. WJ, "Address of the President before the Society for Psychical Research," *EPR*, 127–37, originally published simultaneously in *PSPR* 12 (June 1896): 2–10 and *Science*, n.s. 3 (19 June 1896): 881–88.

118. Ibid., 131.

119. Bullard, "[First] Report of the Committee on Mediumistic Phenomena," 232.

120. Huxley, 29 January 1869, quoted in *Report on Spiritualism of the Committee of the London Dialectical Society*, 229–30.

121. WJ, "The Confidences of a 'Psychical Researcher,'" *EPR*, 366.

122. WJ, "A Record of Observations of Certain Phenomena of Trance," *EPR*, 79.

123. M. Hale, *Human Science and Social Order*, 49, 102.

124. Münsterberg, "Psychology and Mysticism," 67, 78.

125. WJ to James McKeen Cattell, 18 January 1898 [1899], *CWJ*, 8:489; WJ to F. C. S. Schiller, 11 October 1899, *SUC*, 198.

126. F. W. H. Myers to WJ, 15 July 1897, *CWJ*, 12:688.

127. WJ to AHGJ, 19 May 1894, JP, bMS Am 1092.9, #1861.

128. E. B. Titchener to WJ, 28 May 1899, JP, bMS Am 1092, #1143.

129. WJ to AHGJ, 30 September 1887, *CWJ*, 6:257.

130. Ibid., 1 June 1894, 7:613.

131. Edmund Burke Delabarre, "A Student's Impressions in the Late '80s," in Simon, *William James Remembered*, 115.

132. Bullard, "[First] Report of the Committee on Mediumistic Phenomena," 234.

133. Cattell, review of "Address by the President before the Society for Psychical Research," also reprinted in *EPR*, appendix 4, 442.

134. WJ, "Psychical Research," *EPR*, 138–42, quoted on 139–40, originally published in *Psychological Review* 3 (November 1896): 649–52.

135. Cattell, "Mrs. Piper, the Medium," *Science*, n.s. 7, no. 172 (April 15, 1898): 534–35, reprinted in part in "The Text of *Essays in Psychical Research*," *EPR*, 484–85.

136. WJ, "Letter on Mrs. Piper, the Medium," *EPR*, 184–86, originally published as "Mrs. Piper, 'the Medium,'" *Science* n.s. 7, no. 175 (May 6, 1898): 640–41.

137. Ibid.

138. Cattell, "Mrs. Piper, 'The Medium.'"

139. WJ to James McKeen Cattell, 8 May 1898, quoted in *EPR*, 485.

140. WJ to James McKeen Cattell, 10 January 1898 [1899], *CWJ*, 8:483. Nichols was an American psychologist who had received his PhD from Clark University in 1891 and taught at Harvard for a while. See "Biographical Register," *CWJ*, 7:636.

141. WJ to James McKeen Cattell, 18 January 1898 [1899], *CWJ*, 8:488.

142. WJ to James McKeen Cattell, 9 July 1899, *CWJ*, 9:3.

143. Cattell, untitled editorial.

144. WJ to AHGJ, 23 May 1894, *CWJ*, 7:505. On Jackson, see "Notes," *EPR*, 391.

145. Silas Weir Mitchell to WJ, Philadelphia, 27 January 1894, JP, bMS Am 1092, #558, and *CWJ*, 12:682.

146. Horace Howard Furness to WJ, 19 October 1890, *CWJ*, 7:107.

147. George Stuart Fullerton to WJ, 1 March 1894, JP, bMS Am 1092, #275.

148. WJ to George Stuart Fullerton, 13 or 14 March 1894, *CWJ*, 7:491–92.

149. Horace Howard Furness to WJ, 19 March 1894, *CWJ*, 7:493–94.

150. George Stuart Fullerton to WJ, 19 March 1894, *CWJ*, 7:493.

151. WJ to James McKeen Cattell, 10 January 1899, *CWJ*, 8:483.

152. WJ, "A Record of Observations of Certain Phenomena of Trance," *EPR*, 88.

CHAPTER 6

1. For a reconstruction of these lectures, see E. Taylor, *William James on Exceptional Mental States*. James had initially planned to include telepathy and mediumship but changed his mind because he wanted these lectures to reflect his interest in pathology and believed references to psychical research would deter audiences from attending. "Thought-transference, the question of 'spirits' in dealing with mediumship, and other peculiarly 'psychical research' matters," he told the series founder, "would *not* be included in the course as I should give it. I should stick to the solidly ascertained parts of the subject" (emphasis added). WJ to Augustus Lowell, 18 April 1896, *CWJ*, 8:141–42.

2. Perry, *TCWJ*, 2:160.

3. WJ, "The Hidden Self," *EP*, 247.

4. *EPhil*, s.v. "unconscious," by Lancelot Law Whyte; Reed, *From Soul to Mind*, 128–30.

5. Ellenberger, *Discovery of the Unconscious*, 89–101, 143–45, 339–41; "Notes," *EPR*, 407, 412–13.

6. Perry, *TCWJ*, 2:5n9.

7. Richet, "Du somnambulisme provoque"; Charcot, "Sur les divers états nerveux," republished in *Leçons du mardi a la Salpêtrière*.

8. Janet, *De l'Automatisme psychologique*.

9. Binet, *On Double Consciousness*.

10. Ellenberger, *Discovery of the Unconscious*, 85–89, 148–51.

11. Liébeault, *Du Sommeil et des États analogues*.

12. Bernheim, *De la suggestion dans l'état hypnotique* and *De la suggestion et de ses applications a la thérapeutique*.

13. Treitel, *Science for the Soul*, chap. 2; Wolffram, *Stepchildren of Science*, 68–70.

14. Ellenberger, *Discovery of the Unconscious*, 102.

15. Wienholt, *Heilkraft des thierischen Magnetismus*, vol. 3; Werner, *Die Schutzgeister oder merkwürdige Blicke*.

16. de Chastenet de Puységur, *Du magnétisme animal*; Deleuze, *Histoire critique du magnétisme animal*.

17. de Faria, *De la cause du sommeil lucide*.

18. Elliotson, *Numerous Cases of Surgical Operations with Pain*; Esdaile, *Mesmerism in India*.

19. Braid, *Neurypnology or the Rationale of Nervous Sleep*.

20. Sunderland, *Pathetism*.

21. Gauld, *History of Hypnotism*; Crabtree, *From Mesmer to Freud*.

22. WJ, "The Hidden Self," *EP*, 247–68, originally published in *Scribner's Magazine*, March 1890, 361–73, sections of which were published elsewhere including "What Psychical Research Has Accomplished" (1892), "Address of the President before the Society for Psychical Research" (1896), "The Will to Believe" (1897), and chap. 10 in *PP*. See John J. McDermott, "Annotated Bibliography of the Writings of William James," in *WWJ*, 811–58.

23. WJ, "The Hidden Self," *EP*, 247–49.

24. Perry, *TCWJ*, 2:157.

25. WJ, "The Hidden Self," *EP*, 257–59.

26. Ibid., 263.

27. Gauld maintains this was the time and location where all three men learned of the experiments with hypnotism and the emerging theories of the "subconscious." His interpretation is supported by Frederic Myers's eulogy of Gurney, which documents Gurney's visits to France in 1883–84. See Gauld, *History of Hypnotism*, 390; and F. Myers, "Work of Edmund Gurney in Experimental Psychology."

28. Edmund Gurney to WJ, 22 September 1884, quoted in Epperson, *Mind of Edmund Gurney*, 62.

29. For a lucid account of these early experiments, see Epperson, *Mind of Edmund Gurney*, 69–70.

30. Edmund Gurney to WJ, 23 September 1883, *CWJ*, 5:462. The paper Gurney was drafting was probably "The Stages of Hypnotism," the first of six major articles on hypnotism published over the next five years.

31. Ibid., 17 February 1884, 5:491–92. Gurney published "The Problems of Hypnotism" simultaneously in *PSPR* and *Mind* in 1884.

32. Ibid., 31 March 1885, 6:25.

33. Ibid., 31 July 1885, 6:48.

34. See Gurney, "Recent Experiments in Hypnotism" and "Peculiarities of Certain Post-hypnotic States," 277.

35. F. Myers, "Work of Edmund Gurney in Experimental Psychology," 366. Gurney scholars concur with Myers. Epperson holds that Gurney's automatic writing experiments disproved Carpenter's notion of "unconscious cerebration" while simultaneously showing that the role of suggestion in the hypnotic state indicated the existence of a secondary intelligence or what Gurney and Myers had called "double consciousness." Such results allowed Gurney to assert fairly the existence not just of double consciousness or a secondary intelligence but also of "planes of consciousness." See Epperson, *Mind of Edmund Gurney*, 70–71, 74. Similarly, Gauld states Gurney's impact most succinctly: "Gurney was by far the most original and most dedicated person experimenting on hypnotism in the English-speaking world in the mid-1880s" (*History of Hypnotism*, 392).

36. Epperson, *Mind of Edmund Gurney*, 69–74. Two of Myers's key articles were "On a Telepathic Explanation of Some So-Called Spiritualistic Phenomena" and "Automatic Writing, or the Rationale of Planchette." Myers read a version of the former at the Tenth General Meeting of the SPR on 28 November 1884.

37. WJ to George Croom Robertson, 13 August 1885, *CWJ*, 6:61–62.

38. WJ to F. W. H. Myers, 25 February 1884, *CWJ*, 6:13.

39. F. Myers, "On a Telepathic Explanation of Some So-Called Spiritualistic Phenomena," 217–19.

40. F. Myers, "Work of Edmund Gurney in Experimental Psychology," 365, 369.

41. It is worth pointing out that Gurney's results have never been repeated by another hypnotist, although in 1891 Eleanor Sidgwick claimed to have identified up to eight different stages in the hypnotic subject, amounting to many more than Gurney had claimed to have discovered. However, she used the same hypnotist he had—George Albert Smith—who was later charged with being a fraud though never proven one. See Gauld, *History of Hypnotism*, 401n37. For a more sinister view that argues Smith and a small but effective group of compliant coconspirators duped Gurney from start to finish and thereby invalidated all of his research on hypnotism, see T. Hall, *Strange Case of Edmund Gurney*, especially 150–58.

42. WJ, "The Hidden Self," *EP*, 268.

43. WJ, "The Stream of Thought," *PP*, 1:233.

44. WJ, *PP*, 1:331.

45. Years of meticulous research by John J. McDermott and the editors of *The Works of William James* have demonstrated that James wrote different sections at different times over a twelve-year period, combining parts of newly drafted material with sections from earlier published articles, almost constantly changing, updating, and editing them as he went. See McDermott, "Annotated Bibliography of the Writings of William James," in *WWJ*, 811–58; and "The Text of *The Principles of Psychology*," *PP*, 3:1532–79.

46. WJ, "Two Reviews of *Principles of Mental Physiology*, by William B. Carpenter," *ECR*, 269–75, originally published in *North American Review* 119 (July 1874): 225–30. On Carpenter and "unconscious cerebration," see Epperson, *Mind of Edmund Gurney*, 69.

47. James first presented much of this content in an unsigned review of Herbert Spencer's *Data of Ethics* in the *Nation* 29 (1879): 178–79, and especially in "On Some Omissions of Introspective Psychology," *Mind* 9 (January 1884): 1–26. See "The Text of *The Principles of Psychology*," *PP*, 3:1543; and McDermott, "Annotated Bibliography of the Writings of William James," in *WWJ*, 818, 821, 827.

48. WJ, *PP*, 1:222.
49. Ibid., 223.
50. Ibid., 223, 207, 208.
51. WJ, "Notes on Automatic Writing," *EPR*, 40.
52. "The Text of *The Principles of Psychology*," *PP*, 3:1544.
53. "Do Unconscious Mental States Exist?," *PP*, 1:166–77.
54. "The Text of *The Principles of Psychology*," *PP*, 3:1557–58.
55. WJ, *PP*, 1:200–210.
56. Ibid., 201.
57. Ibid., 207.
58. Ibid., 204.
59. WJ, "Report of the Committee on Mediumistic Phenomena," *EPR*, 14–18.
60. WJ, *PP*, 1:205.
61. Ibid., 374–75.
62. WJ, "The Hidden Self," *EP*, 268.
63. WJ, *PP*, 1:372.
64. Ibid., 331.
65. Ibid., 371–72.
66. WJ, *PP*, 1:1194–1214.
67. "The Text of *The Principles of Psychology*," *PP*, 3:1555, 1566.
68. WJ, "Notes on Automatic Writing," *EPR*, 37–55.
69. WJ to AHGJ, 15 September 1898, *CWJ*, 8:435.
70. WJ, "Letter to J. G. Piddington on Mrs. Thompson in Trance," *EPR*, 229.
71. WJ to AHGJ, 29 January 1888 and 31 January 1888, *CWJ*, 6:593, 305.
72. "Automatic Writing by Mr. Arnold," 31 October 1889, JP, bMS Am 1092.9, #4528; appendix 1, "Comments on Automatic Writing," *EPR*, 433.
73. WJ, "A Case of Automatic Writing," *EPR*, 220–28, originally published in *Popular Science Monthly*, January 1904, 195–201; Leja, "William James and Automatic Drawing."
74. WJ to James McKeen Cattell, 17 November 1903, quoted in "The Text of *Essays in Psychical Research*," *EPR*, 490.
75. James McKeen Cattell to WJ, 25 November 1903, and WJ to James McKeen Cattell, 29 November 1903, quoted in "The Text of *Essays in Psychical Research*," *EPR*, 490.
76. WJ, "Notes on Automatic Writing," *EPR*, 43–45.
77. Ibid., 40.
78. Ibid., 45.
79. Ibid., 40.
80. Ibid., 45

81. WJ, "A Case of Automatic Drawing," *EPR*, 220.
82. WJ, "Notes on Automatic Writing," *EPR*, 55, 45.
83. Ibid., 37.
84. WJ, "What Psychical Research Has Accomplished," *EPR*, 89–106, originally published in *Forum* 13 (August 1892): 727–42.
85. Ibid., 102.
86. F. Myers, "On a Telepathic Explanation of Some So-Called Spiritualistic Phenomena," 218, and "Subliminal Consciousness," parts 1–5.
87. Reissued in 1919 as an abridged version by his son, Leopold Hamilton Myers, which is the edition cited hereafter.
88. F. Turner, *Between Science and Religion*, 104–33.
89. F. Myers, "Subliminal Consciousness," part 1, 305.
90. WJ, "What Psychical Research Has Accomplished," *EPR*, 98.
91. WJ to F. W. H. Myers, 14 November 1892, *CWJ*, 7:341. The editors' note five of this letter cites "Sensory Automatism and Induced Hallucinations," *PSPR* 8 (December 1892): 436–35, which was the subtitle to part 3 of Myers's series "The Subliminal Consciousness."
92. F. Myers, "Subliminal Consciousness," part 1, 305–6.
93. Hesse, *Models and Analogies in Science*.
94. F. Myers, *Human Personality*, 18–19.
95. WJ, "What Psychical Research Has Accomplished," *EPR*, 98.
96. F. Myers, *Human Personality*, 327–37.
97. Ibid., 327.
98. Ibid., 62–63, 147–49.
99. Ibid., 13–15.
100. F. Myers, "Subliminal Consciousness," part 1, 308.
101. Ibid., 301.
102. WJ, "Frederic Myers's Service to Psychology," *EPR*, 196.
103. WJ to Théodore Flournoy, 18 January 1901, Rome, JP, bMS Am 1092.1, no item number; WJ to Richard Hodgson, 18 August 1902, JP, bMS Am 1092.9, #966.
104. See F. Myers, *Human Personality*, ix–xi.
105. Ibid., 276.
106. Ibid., 46, 48, 69, 295, 327, 328, 329.
107. James is quoted in ibid., 276–77n1, originally from WJ, *PP*, 1:394.
108. WJ, "Frederic Myers's Service to Psychology," *EPR*, 195–96.
109. Ibid., 197.
110. Ibid., 199, 202.
111. WJ to Oliver Lodge, 20 December 1902, JP, bMS Am 1092.1, no item number.
112. WJ, "Review of *Human Personality and Its Survival of Bodily Death*," *EPR*, 211, 205, 204, originally published in *PSPR* 18 (June 1903): 22–33.
113. Ibid., 206, 207.
114. Ibid., 207–8, 212.
115. WJ to Richard Hodgson, 2 November 1903, quoted in "The Text of *Essays in Psychical Research*," *EPR*, 488.
116. Andrew Lang to WJ, 6 November 1903, *CWJ*, 10:326.
117. WJ, "Review of *Human Personality and Its Survival of Bodily Death*," *EPR*, 211.

118. Ibid., 213.

119. Ibid., 214.

120. Ibid., 215, 213.

121. WJ to F. C. S. Schiller, 8 April 1903, *TCWJ*, 2:376.

122. F. C. S. Schiller to WJ, 22 April 1903, *CWJ*, 10:236.

123. WJ to Théodore Flournoy, 30 April 1903, JP, bMS Am 1092.1, no item number; Théodore Flournoy to WJ, 25 June 1903, *LWJTF*, 142.

124. WJ to Théodore Flournoy, 28 July 1903, JP, bMS Am 1092.1, no item number.

125. WJ to F. C. S. Schiller, 1 May 1903, *CWJ*, 10:242–43.

126. WJ to Théodore Flournoy, 30 April 1903, *LWJTF*, 140.

127. WJ, "Frederic Myers's Service to Psychology," *EPR*, 196; WJ to Charles Eliot Norton, 26 June 1901, *CWJ*, 9:511; WJ to HJ Jr., 17 January 1901, *CWJ*, 3:157; Lodge, "In Memory of F. W. H. Myers," 5.

128. WJ to James Sully, 3 March 1901, JP, bMS Am 1092.1, no item number.

129. WJ to Frances Rollins Morse, 10 July [August] 1901, *CWJ*, 9:528.

130. The one exception was Rufus Osgood Mason, a civil war surgeon, SPR member, and popularizer of psychical research who wrote a book arguing that Myers's subliminal self theory was the key to understanding all psychical phenomena. See R. Mason, *Telepathy and the Subliminal Self*. Incredibly, some neo-Myerserian scholars sympathetic to parapsychology have recently tried to rescue Myers's system as a model for the field of psychology in the twenty-first century. See Kelly and Kelly et al., *Irreducible Mind*. My thanks to an anonymous reviewer for pointing out this text, yet it seems few psychologists have been listening to the Kellys since brain science psychology has completely overtaken introspective psychology over the past fifty years.

131. Emily Williams Kelly, "F. W. H Myers and the Empirical Study of the Mind-Body Problem," in Kelly and Kelly et al., *Irreducible Mind*, 47–115, especially 62–63, 80–83.

132. WJ, "*Cock Lane and Common-Sense*, by Andrew Lang and *Die Entdeckung der Seele durch die Geheimwissenshaften*, by Carl du Prel" (1894)," *ECR*, 501–3, quoted from 503, originally published in *Psychological Review* 1 (November 1894): 630–32.

133. WJ to Julius Goldstein, 20 January 1909, *CWJ*, 12:150.

134. Perry, *TCWJ*, 2:55, 92.

135. G. Myers, *William James*, 472, 167–68, 377.

136. E. Taylor, *William James on Exceptional Mental States*, 12, and *William James on Consciousness beyond the Margin*, 35.

CHAPTER 7

1. Lodge, "Report on Some Trance Communications Received Chiefly through Mrs. Piper," 140.

2. WJ to Shadworth Hollway Hodgson, 26 July 1889, *CWJ*, 6:515. Note 1 indicates the phrase "unseen world" referred to the title of one of Richard Hodgson's talks.

3. See Alger, *Critical History of the Doctrine of a Future Life*.

4. Perry, *TCWJ*, 2:332, 160.

5. Flew, *Body, Mind, and Death*, 1–31.

6. Descartes is quoted from *EPhil*, s.v. "immortality," by Anthony Flew.

7. *EPhil*, s.v. "immortality," by Anthony Flew.

8. Lodge, "Report on Some Trance Communications Received Chiefly through Mrs. Piper," 145.

9. Oliver Lodge to WJ, 18 October 1904, JP, bMS Am 1092, #501.0.

10. WJ to Mary Robbins Hillard, 7 December 1908, *CWJ*, 12:128.

11. Oliver Lodge to WJ, 18 October 1904, JP, bMS Am 1092, #501.0. Lodge was correct. Right after Myers died, his wife reminded James of his copy of the sealed letter. See Eveleen Myers to WJ, 25 February 1901, *CWJ*, 9:623–24.

12. Schultz, *Henry Sidgwick*, 722.

13. Eleanor Sidgwick to WJ, 26 February 1909, *CWJ*, 12:605, and quoted in Schultz, *Henry Sidgwick*, 722.

14. Schultz, *Henry Sidgwick*, 723.

15. WJ to Thomas Sergeant Perry, 5 September 1907, *CWJ*, 11:620.

16. See Piddington, "Series of Concordant Automatisms."

17. WJ to WJ Jr., 22 June 1906, *CWJ*, 11:240.

18. The use of Mrs. Verrall was highly problematical because she also wrote articles for the *Proceedings*, thus compromising her independence. See "Biographical Register," *CWJ*, 11.

19. WJ to AHGJ, 9 February 1907, *CWJ*, 11:317 including n. 7. Stickney was either Albert Stickney, a lawyer and Harvard graduate, or his son, also named Albert, a Harvard graduate (1897) and a lawyer living in New York City.

20. Eleanor Sidgwick to WJ, 21 August 1907, JP, bMS Am 1092.9, #613.

21. Eleanor Sidgwick to WJ, 26 February 1909, *CWJ*, 12:605.

22. WJ to Eleanor Sidgwick, 1 August 1907, *CWJ*, 11:405 including nn. 3 and 4. Mrs. Flemming was the real name of Mrs. Holland, one of the SPR's star mediums, and refers to Alice Kipling Flemming, Rudyard Kipling's sister. Mrs. Raikes was an SPR member listed at Beomonds, Chertsey, Surrey. It is possible she was the medium Mrs. Forbes, which was also a pseudonym.

23. Eleanor Sidgwick to WJ, 21 August 1907, JP, bMS Am 1092.9, #613.

24. WJ to F. C. S. Schiller, 16 January 1906, *SUC*, 395–96.

25. WJ to Thomas Sergeant Perry, 6 February 1906, *CWJ*, 11:166.

26. On Mrs. Soule, see "Biographical Register," *CWJ*, 11:658.

27. WJ to James H. Hyslop, 25 October 1906, quoted in Murphy and Ballou, *William James on Psychical Research*, 112, and catalogued in *CWJ*, 11:596–97.

28. WJ to Henry Pickering Bowditch, 1 February 1908, *CWJ*, 11:632.

29. WJ to Mrs. Leonora Evelina Piper, 28 November 1908, *CWJ*, 12:598.

30. WJ to Theodate Pope Riddle, 14 July 1908, *CWJ*, 12:52. Note 2 indicates that James was reading the proofs of Piddington's "A Series of Concordant Automatisms," *PSPR* 22 (October 1908): 19–416.

31. WJ to Théodore Flournoy, 9 August 1908, *CWJ*, 12:80 including n. 2. The paper was Alice Johnson's "On the Automatic Writing of Mrs. Holland," *PSPR* 21 (June 1908): 166–91.

32. WJ to Lawrence Pearsall Jacks, 14 December 1908, *CWJ*, 12:600.

33. WJ to J. G. Piddington, 1 January 1909, JP, bMS Am 1092.9, #3491, and *CWJ*, 12:139–41.

34. WJ, "Report on Mrs. Piper's Hodgson-Control," *EPR*, 253–360, originally in *PSPR* 23 (June 1909): 2–121, and *PASPR* 3 (July 1909): 470–589. The complete manuscript is preserved in Houghton Library, Harvard University, JP, bMS Am 1092.9, #4544. See "The Text of *Essays in Psychical Research*," *EPR*, 492; and *CWJ*, 3:373n4.

35. The last of James's psychical research essays was "The Confidences of a 'Psychical Researcher'" (1909), which is discussed in the conclusion.

36. See John J. McDermott in *WWJ*, 842–53.

37. WJ, "Report on Mrs. Piper's Hodgson-Control," *EPR*, 258.

38. Salter, *Trance Mediumship*, 17–18.

39. WJ to AHGJ, 30 July 1907, *CWJ*, 11:401. The "Biographical Register" for this volume could not conclusively establish Mrs. Ledyard's full identity.

40. WJ to Thomas Sergeant Perry, 1 August 1907, *CWJ*, 11:405.

41. WJ to George Bucknam Dorr, 20 March 1906, *CWJ*, 11:191; WJ to Mary Robbins Hillard, 7 or 8 December 1908, *CWJ*, 12:128–29 including n. 3. James had in mind Münsterberg's piece in *Sunday Magazine*, 3 November 1907.

42. WJ to Isaac Kauffman Funk, 15 March 1907, *CWJ*, 11:606. Funk was the author of *Widow's Mite and Other Psychic Phenomena* (New York: Funk & Wagnalls, 1904). See "Notes," *EPR*, 423.

43. WJ to John George Piddington, 13 February 1907, *CWJ*, 11:320.

44. WJ to WJ Jr., 22 June 1906, *CWJ*, 11:240.

45. WJ to ARJ, 5 November 1908, *CWJ*, 12:599; WJ to ARJ, 26 November 1908, *CWJ*, 12:124.

46. WJ to WJ Jr., 22 June 1906, *CWJ*, 12:240; WJ to F. C. S. Schiller, 24 August 1906, *CWJ*, 11:259.

47. WJ, "Report on Mrs. Piper's Hodgson-Control," *EPR*, 255.

48. Ibid., 275.

49. Ibid., 255. For the sixth explanation, James meant the spirits do not contact us; rather, we contact them, a view he noted that Eleanor Sidgwick found plausible. See *EPR*, 322n17.

50. WJ, "Report on Mrs. Piper's Hodgson-Control," *EPR*, 255. Mystical phenomena need not be supernatural.

51. Ibid., 254.

52. WJ to Giulio Cesare Ferrari, 4 December 1907, *CWJ*, 11:488–89.

53. WJ, "Report on Mrs. Piper's Hodgson-Control," *EPR*, 255.

54. Ibid.

55. WJ to Olivia Wadsworth, 19 October 1909, *CWJ*, 12:346–47.

56. WJ, "Report on Mrs. Piper's Hodgson-Control," *EPR*, 267.

57. WJ to Olivia Wadsworth, 19 October 1909, *CWJ*, 12:346–47.

58. WJ, "Report on Mrs. Piper's Hodgson-Control," *EPR*, 282.

59. Ibid., 282–83.

60. Ibid., 355.

61. Ibid.

62. Ibid., 355–56.

63. Ibid., 356.

64. Ibid., 356–57.

65. Ibid., 357.

66. Ibid., 358.
67. WJ to HJ Jr., May 1906, *CWJ*, 3:316–17.
68. WJ, "Report on Mrs. Piper's Hodgson-Control," *EPR*, 358; *PDS*, s.v. "psychometry."
69. WJ, "Report on Mrs. Piper's Hodgson-Control," *EPR*, 358–59.
70. Ibid., 356.
71. I am grateful to Fred Churchill, who pointed out James's confusion on this point.
72. WJ to Charles Lewis Slattery 21 April 1907, JP, bMS Am 1092.1, no item number.
73. WJ, "Report on Mrs. Piper's Hodgson-Control," *EPR*, 359.
74. Lodge, "Report on Some Trance Communications Received Chiefly through Mrs. Piper," especially 226–54.
75. WJ to Oliver Lodge, 4 September 1909, *CWJ*, 12:316.
76. This argument was first worked out in Knapp, "William James and Unconsciousness 'Beyond the Margin.'"
77. WJ, "Report on Mrs. Piper's Hodgson-Control," *EPR*, 277–79.
78. WJ to Charles Lewis Slattery, 21 April 1907, JP, bMS Am 1092.1, no item number.
79. WJ, "Report on Mrs. Piper's Hodgson-Control," *EPR*, 267–68.
80. WJ, "A Record of Observations of Certain Phenomena of Trance," *EPR*, 86.
81. WJ to G. S. Hall, 27 May 1894, JP, bMS Am 1092.9, #962.
82. WJ, "Review of 'A Further Record of Observations of Certain Phenomena of Trance,' by Richard Hodgson," *EPR*, 187–91, quoted from 190, 191, originally published as an unsigned review in *Psychological Review* 5 (July 1898): 420–24.
83. For its publication history, see "The Text of *Essays in Religion and Morality*," *ERM*, 233–34.
84. *EPhil*, s.v. "mind-body problem," by Jerome Shaffer.
85. WJ, *HI* in *ERM*, 81.
86. *EPhil*, s.v. "mind-body problem," by Jerome Shaffer, and s.v. "materialism," by Keith Campbell.
87. WJ, *HI* in *ERM*, 81. James quoted the medical materialists at length on pages 84–85n4.
88. See ibid., 82–83n3.
89. The view that James's defense of the brain transmission theory is related to his psychical research was first made by Perry, *TWCJ*, 2:132–33.
90. WJ, *HI* in *ERM*, 85–89.
91. WJ, *PP*, 1:325–32, quoted from 329.
92. WJ to F. C. S. Schiller, 19 August 1897, *CWJ*, 8:295. For this insight, see Perry, *TCWJ*, 2:133–34 including n. 16, which provides the Schiller and Kant references that James cited in *HI* in *ERM*, 94–95.
93. Schiller, *Riddles of the Sphinx*, 295.
94. Kant, *Critique of Pure Reason*, 618–19.
95. WJ to F. C. S. Schiller, 23 October 1897, *CWJ*, 8:317–18.
96. WJ to AJ, 6 July 1891, *LWJ*, 1:310–11.
97. AJ to WJ, 30 July 1891, quoted in Strouse, *Alice James*, 304.
98. WJ, *HI* in *ERM*, 92, 93, 94.
99. This argument was first suggested in Perry, *TWCJ*, 2:132–33. James was inconsistent about his use of capitalization of the term "mother sea." I have quoted him as he has used it in each instance but otherwise have used the lowercase.

100. Shadworth Hollway Hodgson to WJ, 25 November 1898, *CWJ*, 8:459.

101. George Holmes Howison to WJ, 18 November 1898, *CWJ*, 8:456.

102. Kennedy, "Professor William James and Human Immortality."

103. WJ to William Sloane Kennedy, 11 January 1899, *CWJ*, 8:487. James was correct; he had shown that the compatibility of his theory with transcendentalism did not entail accepting such a monistic theory of idealism. See WJ, *HI* in *ERM*, 89n5.

104. F. C. S. Schiller to WJ, 23 October 1898, *CWJ*, 8:620. See *Nation*, 1 December 1898, 416–17.

105. James Ward to WJ, *CWJ*, 8:469.

106. WJ to Théodore Flournoy, 20 October 1898, *CWJ*, 8:441. Note 1 indicates the "many-colored glass" phrase is also a reference to Shelley's *Adonaïs*, stanza 52, line 3.

107. Charles Augustus Strong to WJ, 3 December 1898, *CWJ*, 8:463 including n. 2. The poem was "Sonnet VI." See *The Complete Poems of George Santayana*, ed. William G. Holzberger (Lewisburg, Pa.: Bucknell University Press, 1979), 93.

108. James Ward to WJ, 11 December 1898, *CWJ*, 8:468.

109. WJ to Théodore Flournoy, 20 October 1898, *CWJ*, 8:441.

110. WJ to James Ward, 28 January 1899, JP, bMS Am 1092.9, #3838.

111. George Holmes Howison to WJ, 18 November 1898, *CWJ*, 8:456.

112. WJ to James Ward, 28 January 1899, *CWJ*, 8:491.

113. WJ to George Holmes Howison, 27 November 1898, *CWJ*, 8:460.

114. See Perry, *TCWJ*, 2:137.

115. WJ, "Preface to Lutoslawski's *World of Souls*," *ERM*, 105–8, quoted on 106. Lutoslawski's book in German was *Seelenmacht: Abriss einer zeitgemässen Weltanschauung* (Leipzig: W. Englemann, 1899). See "Notes," *ERM*, 187. It seems James first drafted the preface in English and then used that version to write a slightly longer one in German for the 1899 German edition, which was then retranslated into English in 1904. See "The Text of *Essays in Religion and Morality*," *ERM*, 236.

116. WJ to F. C. S. Schiller, 6 April 1900, *CWJ*, 9:182.

117. Fechner, *Zend-Avesta*. See "Notes," *EPR*, 430.

118. *EPhil*, s.v. "Fechner, Gustav Theodor," by Arnulf Zweig; Heidelberger, *Nature from Within*, chap. 1.

119. WJ, "Introduction to Fechner's *Life after Death*," *ERM*, 116–19. The original German version was *Das Büchlein vom Leben nach dem Tode* (Dresden: C. F. Grimmer, 1836). See "Notes," *ERM*, 190. The English translation was *The Little Book of Life after Death*, trans. Mary C. Wadsworth (Boston: Little, Brown, 1904). See "The Text of *Essays in Religion and Morality*," *ERM*, 242.

120. WJ, "Introduction to Fechner's *Life after Death*," *ERM*, 119.

121. WJ, *PU*; Richard J. Bernstein, introduction to *PU*, xi.

122. WJ, "Concerning Fechner," *PU*, 81.

123. Ibid., 79.

124. WJ, "Report on Mrs. Piper's Hodgson-Control," *EPR*, 358.

125. WJ, "Concerning Fechner," *PU*, 79–80.

126. WJ, "The Continuity of Experience," *PU*, 134–35.

127. WJ, "Conclusions," *PU*, 140.

128. Ibid.

129. Bixler, *Religion in the Philosophy of William James*, 26–27, 147–54, 150.
130. Morris, *William James*, 65.
131. Barnard, *Exploring Unseen Worlds*, 164–79, 189–203.

CONCLUSION

1. WJ to Henry Adams, 17 June 1910, *CWJ*, 12:555.
2. WJ to Hamlin Garland, 10 December 1908, *CWJ*, 12:132.
3. Berger, *Lives and Letters in American Parapsychology*, 47–48, 61.
4. Oliver Lodge to WJ, 31 December 1905, JP, bMS Am 1092, #503.
5. Ibid., 21 December 1905, #502.
6. WJ to Isaac Kaufman Funk, 19 February 1906, *CWJ*, 12:179–80.
7. WJ to Thomas Sergeant Perry, 6 February 1906, *CWJ*, 12:166 including n. 7. The SPR decided at its meeting on 30 March 1906 to send Piddington on its behalf. The announcement was made in the *JSPR* 12 (May 1906): 256–57.
8. WJ to Thomas Sergeant Perry, 6 February 1906, *CWJ*, 12:166; WJ to Pauline Goldmark, 8 February 1906, *CWJ*, 11:170–71.
9. WJ to AHGJ, 20 January 1906, *CWJ*, 11:149–50.
10. Ibid., 19 August 1906, 11:593; WJ to Sally Fairchild, 2 October 1906, *CWJ*, 11:275n5.
11. WJ to Theodate Pope Riddle, 27 July 1907, *CWJ*, 11:400.
12. WJ to Weston D. Bayley, 14 October 1909, *CWJ*, 12:624; WJ Jr. to WJ, 18 June 1908, *CWJ*, 12:35; WJ to ARJ, 19 March 1909, *CWJ*, 12:180; WJ to Rosamond Gregor, 14 January 1908, *CWJ*, 11:520.
13. WJ to Henry Rutgers Marshall, 16 August 1905, *SUC*, 383; WJ to John Whitehead, 17 October 1909, *SUC*, 522.
14. WJ to Théodore Flournoy, 1 April 1909, *CWJ*, 12:608; ibid., 28 September 1909, 12:334; ibid., 9 April 1910, 12:466–67; WJ to Hereward Carrington, 10 June 1910, *CWJ*, 12:550–52; WJ to Oliver Lodge, 8 August 1902, JP, bMS Am 1092.1, no item number.
15. WJ to George Bucknam Dorr, 10 March 1909, *CWJ*, 12:173; ibid., 24 March 1909, 12:188, Oliver Lodge to WJ, 29 April 1909, JP, bMS Am 1092, #505; WJ to Oliver Lodge, 4 September 1909, *CWJ*, 12:316; WJ to Oliver Lodge, 29 December 1909, *CWJ*, 12:398.
16. WJ to George Bucknam Dorr, 24 March 1909, *CWJ*, 12:188.
17. WJ to G. S. Hall, 6 July 1909, *CWJ*, 12:285–86; G. S. Hall to WJ, 8 July 1909, *CWJ*, 12:619.
18. Tanner, *Studies in Spiritism*.
19. Ibid., 267.
20. WJ to G. S. Hall, 9 November 1909, JP, bMS Am 1092, no item number.
21. Editor, *CWJ*, 12:173–74n2.
22. Hyslop, "President G. Stanley Hall's and Dr. Amy Tanner's *Studies in Spiritism*."
23. See "Notes," *EPR*, 393, 430.
24. WJ to T. S. Perry, 29 January 1909, *LWJ*, 2:320. See Flammarion, *Mysterious Psychic Forces*; Lombroso, *After Death—What?*; Morselli, *Psicologia e "Spiritismo"*; and Fielding, Baggally, and Carrington, "Report on a Series of Sittings with Eusapia Palladino." Haynes, *Society for Psychical Research*, 18, 121–22, notes that Charles Richet, Henri Bergson, and Marie and Pierre Curie also conducted tests with positive results. See also Courtier, "Rapport sur les séances d'Eusapia Palladino."

25. WJ to Hamlin Garland, 10 December 1908, *CWJ*, 12:132–33; WJ to Théodore Flournoy, 18 June 1909, *LWJ*, 2:324; WJ to Théodore Flournoy, 9 August 1908, *CWJ*, 12:80; WJ to T. S. Perry, 29 January 1909, *LWJ*, 2:320; WJ to Théodore Flournoy, 28 September 1909, *CWJ*, 12:334.

26. WJ to Henry Pickering Bowditch, 14 July 1909, *CWJ*, 12:290.

27. WJ to Eleanor Sidgwick, 1 August 1907, *CWJ*, 11:405–6; WJ to Théodore Flournoy, 28 September 1909, *CWJ*, 12:334; WJ to Oliver Lodge, 4 September 1909, JP, bMS Am 1092.1, no item number, and *CWJ*, 12:316.

28. WJ to Hamlin Garland, 10 December 1908, *CWJ*, 12:132–33.

29. WJ to Eleanor Sidgwick, 1 August 1907, *CWJ*, 11:405–6; "The Text of *Essays in Psychical Research*," *EPR*, 494–95n14.

30. *BDP*, s.v. "Hereward Hubert Lavington Carrington."

31. F. C. S. Schiller to WJ, 22 February 1909, *CWJ*, 12:163; WJ to AHGJ, 11 June 1909, *CWJ*, 12:262–63; William Sloane Kennedy to WJ, n.d., January 1910, *CWJ*, 12:632; Carrington, *Eusapia Palladino and Her Phenomena*.

32. WJ to Hereward Carrington, 8 August 1907, in Carrington, *Letters to Hereward Carrington*, 40; WJ to Theodate Pope Riddle, 2 September 1907, *CWJ*, 11:435. James was off by a year (Carrington was born in 1880).

33. Hugo Münsterberg to WJ, 21 October 1909, *CWJ*, 12:350n1; "Notes," *EPR*, 431; WJ to Hereward Carrington, 15 February 1910, *CWJ*, 12:637.

34. WJ to Théodore Flournoy, 28 September 1909, *LWJ*, 2:327; Scott in *SUC*, 498, 592n25; Carrington, *American Séances with Eusapia Palladino*; Bjork, *Compromised Scientist*, chap. 3; WJ, diary, 12 January 1910, JP, bMS Am 1092.9, #4559, abbreviated version in *CWJ*, 12:632; WJ to Charles Sanders Peirce, 12 January 1910, *CWJ*, 12:412n1.

35. William Pepperell Montague to WJ, 8 December 1909, *CWJ*, 12:380–81.

36. Some members included Dickenson Sergeant Miller, who had once tutored James's children and had taught at Harvard from 1899 to 1904; Walter Broughton Pitkin, an American educator and journalist; and Wendell T. Bush, a philosopher and co-editor of the *Journal of Philosophy*. See "Biographical Register," *CWJ*, 12:707, 709.

37. WJ to Hereward Carrington, 1 November 1909, *CWJ*, 12:626.

38. WJ to D. S. Miller, 1 November 1909, *CWJ*, 12:358.

39. Wood, "Report of an Investigation of the Phenomena Connected with Eusapia Palladino."

40. WJ to Hereward Carrington, 10 June 1910, JP, bMS Am 1092.1, no item number; *CWJ*, 12:550–52.

41. WJ to Hereward Carrington, 10 June 1910, *CWJ*, 12:550–52n2.

42. WJ to Hereward Carrington, 18 November 1909, in Carrington, *Letters to Hereward Carrington*, 42, summarized in *CWJ*, 12:628.

43. WJ to Théodore Flournoy, 9 April 1910, *CWJ*, 12:466–67.

44. WJ to Hereward Carrington, 10 March 1910, *CWJ*, 12:639.

45. WJ to MMJ, 12 January 1908, *CWJ*, 11:629–30.

46. WJ, "An Estimate of Palladino," *Cosmopolitan*, February 1910, 299.

47. WJ to Théodore Flournoy, 15 March 1910, *LWJTF*, 227–28.

48. Richardson, *William James*, 509; WJ to George Bucknam Dorr, 26 August 1909, *CWJ*, 12:621; WJ to AHGJ, 7 September 1909, *CWJ*, 12:622–23; WJ to Théodore Flournoy, 28 September 1909, *LWJ*, 2:327; WJ to ARJ, 5 November 1908, *CWJ*, 12:599.

49. WJ to J. G. Piddington, 1 January 1909, JP, bMS Am 1092.9, #3491; *CWJ*, 12:141; "Notes," *EPR*, 424.

50. WJ to AHGJ, 4 December 1908, JP, bMS Am 1092.9, #2436; *CWJ*, 12:127–28. See also "Notes," *EPR*, 424.

51. WJ, "Physical Phenomena at a Private Circle," *EPR*, 248–52, quoted from 251–52, originally published in *JASPR* 3 (February 1909): 109–13.

52. Marion Hamilton Carter to WJ, 12 March 1909, *CWJ*, 12:606, and 24 January 1907, *CWJ*, 11:602; WJ, diary, JP, bMS Am 1092.9, #4556, quoted in *CWJ*, 11:310n2; WJ to AHGJ, 7 February 1907, *CWJ*, 11:316; WJ to J. G. Piddington, 13 February 1907, *CWJ*, 11:320; Marion Hamilton Carter to WJ, 23 February 1908, *CWJ*, 11:634.

53. Marion Hamilton Carter to WJ, 10 April 1907, *CWJ*, 11:608, and 4 June 1907, *CWJ*, 11:612.

54. Two were *The Coming Science* (Boston: Small, Maynard, 1908) and *The Physical Phenomena of Spiritualism: Fraudulent and Genuine* (Boston: Herbert B. Turner, 1907). See "Notes," *EPR*, 431.

55. See Peirce, "The Fixation of Belief."

56. Quoted in Clendenning, *Life and Thought of Josiah Royce*, 317.

57. WJ to Harry Norman Gardiner, 3 March 1909, *CWJ*, 12:167.

58. F. C. S. Schiller to WJ, 26 October 1909, *CWJ*, 12:355.

59. John Jay Chapman to WJ, 19 June 1910, *CWJ*, 12:557–59.

60. WJ, "The Confidences of a 'Psychical Researcher,'" *EPR*, 361–75, originally published in *American Magazine*, October 1909, 580–89. See "The Text of *Essays in Psychical Research*," *EPR*, 535–36, especially n. 79. Early titles of this essay, begun just nine days after completing "Report on Mrs. Piper's Hodgson-Control," included "The State of Mind of One 'Psychical Researcher,'" "One 'Psychical Researcher' at the Confessional," and "Avowals of a 'Psychical Researcher.'" The title was again changed to "Final Impressions of a Psychical Researcher" in *Memories and Studies*. See John J. McDermott, *WWJ*, 850, 852.

61. The case involved Josephina Terranova, a seventeen-year-old girl who worked long hours in her uncle Gaetano Reggio's bakery. She was accused of murdering him and his wife, Concetta, after she was severely beaten for speaking English with another baker. The trial revealed Josephina was supposedly hysterical, heard voices, had not been instructed in religion, could not read or write, had never really played with other children, and was not allowed to talk with other people, including local bakers who visited the shop. Her defense was not guilty by reason of insanity. See "Insanity Plea Raised in Terranova Case." Carter was skeptical of the testimony of Austin Flint, a pathologist and psychiatrist who was paid $100 per day and judged her sane. See Marion Hamilton Carter to WJ, 9 May 1906, *CWJ*, 11:587; and "Biographical Register," *CWJ*, 12:698.

62. See the following in *CWJ* : Marion Hamilton Carter to WJ, 24 April 1906, 11:586; 15 May 1906, 11:587; 28 May 1906, 11:230; 2 October 1906, 11:595; 25 December 1906, 11:600; 31 December 1906, 11:601; 20 January 1907, 11:602; 24 January 1907, 11:602; 30 January 1907, 11:309; 12 February 1907, 11:694; 18 February 1907, 11:322; and 12 March 1909, 12:606. See also Donald McQuade, introduction to *CWJ*, 11:xli, which notes that James's side of the correspondence is lost. The Mrs. Walden depicted on the cover of this book could be one of the mediums Carter introduced to James.

63. Marion Hamilton Carter to WJ, 4 June 1907, *CWJ*, 11:612; ibid., 31 July 1909, 12:299–301.

64. WJ to HJ Jr., 24 January 1909, *CWJ*, 3:376.

65. WJ to Théodore Flournoy, 28 September 1909, *LWJ*, 2:327; WJ to T. S. Perry, 29 January 1909, *LWJ*, 2:320.

66. HJ Jr. to WJ, 31 October 1909, *CWJ*, 3:405.

67. Marion Hamilton Carter to WJ, 1 November 1909, *CWJ*, 12:626–27; Emile Boutroux to WJ, 28 October 1909, *CWJ*, 12:626.

68. WJ, "The Confidences of a 'Psychical Researcher,'" *EPR*, 361, 365, 363, 366.

69. Ibid., 365–67, 369.

70. Ibid., 370–71, 361–62.

71. Ibid., 371.

72. Ibid., 367–68, 373.

73. Ibid., 369, 371, 374.

74. Ibid., 372–73.

75. WJ to Hamlin Garland, 10 December 1908, *CWJ*, 12:132.

76. There are numerous instances in the James literature that try to explain James's ideas in terms of his ambivalent personality. For a recent version of the psychological fallacy, see Menand, *Metaphysical Club*, 75, 77.

77. WJ, "The Confidences of a 'Psychical Researcher,'" *EPR*, 374–75.

78. James also played a key multipronged role as participant in, commentator on, and analyst of experimental and mathematical telepathy and the attempt to find empirical proof for so-called hallucinations, both of which the SPR and ASPR took up during the 1880s and 1890s. James's debates with brass instrument psychologists, natural scientists, and philosophers on the epistemological value of these studies with regard to science and scientific naturalism is the focus of my next book.

79. Perry, *TCWJ*, 2:155.

80. See Mauskopf and McVaugh, *Elusive Science*.

81. Lawrence Pearsall Jacks to WJ, 5 May 1910, *CWJ*, 12:494. Note 1 indicates the book was probably *Mad Shepherds, and Other Human Studies* (1910).

82. Friedrich von Hügel to WJ, 10 May 1909, *CWJ*, 12:612–13. This summary of the letter indicates Schiller had introduced Hügel to James and that Hügel's work was *The Mystical Element of Religion* (1908).

83. Harald Höffding to WJ, 12 October 1905, *CWJ*, 12:574.

84. Perry, *TCWJ*, 2:674.

85. For a list of these works, see Skrupskelis, "James's Spirit Writings," in *William James: A Reference Guide*, 197.

86. WJ to Henry Pickering Bowditch, 14 July 1909, quoted in "The Text of *Essays in Psychical Research*," *EPR*, 497n24, originally from JP, bMS Am 1092.9, #812. See also *CWJ*, 12:289.

87. WJ to John Whitehead, 31 December 1909, *CWJ*, 12:399 including n. 1. Whitehead's name appeared on the SPR membership list by November 1910.

88. WJ to MMJ, 19 April 1910, *CWJ*, 12:474–75; WJ to AHGJ, 21 May 1910, *CWJ*, 12:644.

89. WJ to J. G. Piddington, 7 August 1910, *CWJ*, 12:649; WJ to F. C. S. Schiller, 8 August 1910, *CWJ*, 12:573.

90. WJ to James Sully, 9 November 1908, *CWJ*, 12:118.
91. Quoted in Richardson, *William James*, 520–21.
92. WJ, "Address of the President before the Society of Psychical Research," *EPR*, 137.

HISTORIOGRAPHICAL ESSAY

1. McDougall, "In Memory of William James," 12–13.
2. Murphy and Ballou, *William James on Psychical Research*, 327. Murphy initiated this argument in two earlier articles published in psychical research periodicals, "William James and Psychical Research" and "Our Pioneers, III: William James."
3. Perry, *TCWJ*, 2:155.
4. Ibid., 2:155–60, 165, 172.
5. Robert A. McDermott, introduction to *EPR*, xxxi–xxxiii.
6. See Allen, *William James*; G. Myers, *William James*; Bjork, *William James*; Simon, *Genuine Reality*; and Richardson, *William James*. Feinstein, *Becoming William James*, does not address psychical research.
7. See Allen, *William James*, 282–88, 326–27, 366–67, 378–79, 420–21, 465–66, 471–72; Bjork, *William James*, 208–213; Simon, *Genuine Reality*, 140–41, 189–95, 198–202, 224–25, 238–39, 306–8, 319–21, 342–43, 366–69; and especially G. Myers, *William James*, 369–86.
8. See Baum, "William James and Psychical Research"; Murphy, "William James and Psychical Research" and "Our Pioneers, III"; Berger, "Early History of the ASPR"; Mauskopf, "History of the American Society for Psychical Research"; Murphy and Ballou, *William James on Psychical Research*; and Schmeidler, "William James."
9. See Gauld, *Founders of Psychical Research*; Cerullo, *Secularization of the Soul*; and Oppenheim, *Other World*.
10. See Moore, *In Search of White Crows*; Mauskopf and McVaugh, *Elusive Science*; and Griffin, *Parapsychology, Philosophy, and Spirituality*.
11. See E. Taylor, "William James on Psychopathology," *William James on Exceptional Mental States*, and *William James on Consciousness beyond the Margin*.
12. See Leary, "William James, Psychical Research, and the Origins of American Psychology" and "Telling Likely Stories"; Bjork, *Compromised Scientist*; and Coon, "Testing the Limits of Sense and Science."
13. See Leahey and Leahey, *Psychology's Occult Doubles*; Burnham, *How Superstition Won*; and Whorton, *Nature Cures*.
14. See Bixler, *Religion in the Philosophy of William James*; Suckiel, *Heaven's Champion*; Barnard, *Exploring Unseen Worlds*; and especially G. Myers, *William James*, 461–80.
15. See Broad, *Religion, Philosophy, and Psychical Research*; Wheatley and Edge, *Philosophical Dimensions of Parapsychology*; Grim, *Philosophy of Science and the Occult*; and especially Ford, "William James's Psychical Research."
16. See Brandon, *Spiritualists*; and Gardner, "Communicating with the Dead: William James and Mrs. Piper," parts 1 and 2.

BIBLIOGRAPHY

A NOTE ON SOURCES

To say that the primary sources on William James are voluminous is a vast understatement. Two comprehensive works have become indispensable for James scholarship. The first is *The Works of William James*, 17 vols., edited by Frederick H. Burkhardt, Fredson Bowers, and Ignas K. Skrupskelis (Cambridge, Mass.: Harvard University Press, 1975–88), which contains all of James's published and many unpublished writings, highly insightful introductions by leading James specialists, and incredibly useful editorial notes that range from source citation to interpretation. All references and citations of James's writings will be to the relevant volumes unless otherwise indicated. The second is *The Correspondence of William James*, 12 vols., edited by Ignas K. Skrupskelis and Elizabeth M. Berkeley (Charlottesville: University Press of Virginia, 1992–2004), which contains the lion's share of James's massive tome of letters from and to him plus insightful notes and editorial commentary.

A number of James's writings on psychical research were first collected in Gardner Murphy and Robert O. Ballou, eds., *William James on Psychical Research* (New York: Viking Press, 1960), but the most comprehensive work is *Essays in Psychical Research* (Cambridge, Mass.: Harvard University Press, 1986), a volume of the *Works*, which contains major and minor essays, reports, book reviews, minutes, notes, reflections, miscellaneous arcana, key sections from many letters, and indispensable editorial notes. I rely extensively on this volume. Also quite useful from the same series is *Essays, Comments, and Reviews* (Cambridge, Mass.: Harvard University Press, 1987), which contains writings closely related to psychical research. Still others come from the sources listed below.

Despite the incredible value of the published comprehensive works, the archives were indispensable to writing this book. James's extensive letters (tens of thousands) are contained in the William James Papers, Houghton Library, Harvard University, marked by the base prefix bMS Am 1092. The *CWJ* contains or references the vast majority of these letters. Both sources are used throughout, but the archival sources are relied on especially when the *CWJ* only summarizes a letter, when there is an uncertainty in transliterating James's illegible handwriting, or when I found the original before a certain volume of the *CWJ* was published and that part of my research was already completed. Among the many collections of James letters, several useful ones are *The Letters of William James*, 2 vols., ed. Henry James III (Boston: Atlantic Monthly Press, 1920); *Selected Unpublished Correspondence, 1885–1910*, ed. Frederick J. Down Scott (Columbus: Ohio State University Press, 1986); and *The Letters of William James and Théodore Flournoy*, ed. Robert C. Le Clair (Madison: University of Wisconsin Press, 1966). These volumes were published before the *CWJ* but contain useful editorial information and in some cases better transliterations of James's penmanship. Still, the best sources remain the original letters in the archives.

Two reference works on William James were also crucial for writing this book: Ignas K. Skrupskelis, *William James: A Reference Guide* (Boston: G. K. Hall, 1977), which contains an extensive list of books and articles published on James up to 1977, and *The Writings of William James: A Comprehensive Edition*, ed. John J. McDermott (1967; repr., New York: Modern Library, 1977), which contains not only many of James's classic essays but also an annotated bibliography and timeline that was indispensable for determining the writing and publication order of James's essays.

The secondary sources on William James are even more voluminous than the primary sources. Those relevant to psychical research are listed below and cited in the notes, but two in particular deserve special mention. The first is Ralph Barton Perry, *The Thought and Character of William James*, 2 vols. (Boston: Little, Brown, 1935), on which I rely heavily. After all these years and despite six other major biographies to appear since its publication, it remains the most insightful and comprehensive interpretation of James's life and thought, including the single best chapter on psychical research. The second is Robert A. McDermott's introduction to *EPR*, which contains the second-best set of insightful although necessarily cursory remarks about James and psychical research.

PRIMARY SOURCES

Archival Collections

Berkeley, Calif.
　Center for Swedenborgian Studies, Graduate Theological Union
　　James John Garth Wilkinson Papers
Cambridge, Mass.
　Houghton Library, Harvard University
　　William James Papers

Periodicals

American Journal of Psychology
American Psychologist
Annales des Sciences Psychiques
Contemporary Review
Intellectual History Newsletter
Journal of Abnormal and Social Psychology
Journal of Interdisciplinary History
Journal of the American Society for Psychical Research
Journal of the History of the Behavioral Sciences
Journal of the Society for Psychical Research
Mind
Proceedings of the American Society for Psychical Research
Proceedings of the Society for Psychical Research
Psychological Review
Quarterly Journal of Science
Science

Magazines and Newspapers

American Magazine
American Mercury
Atlantic Monthly
Banner of Light
Boston Daily Advertiser
Boston Daily Globe
Boston Evening Transcript
Boston Herald
Conservator
Cosmopolitan
Forum
Free Inquiry
Harper's New Monthly Magazine
London Times
McClure's Magazine
Nation
New Yorker
New York Review of Books
New York Times
New York Tribune
Popular Science Monthly
Scribner's Magazine

Published Primary Sources

Alger, William Rounseville. *A Critical History of the Doctrine of a Future Life*. New York: W. J. Widdleton, 1867.
"American Society for Psychical Research." *Science* 5, no. 100 (January 2, 1885): 13.
Aristotle. *Nicomachean Ethics*. Translated by Terence Irwin. Indianapolis: Hackett, 1985.
Barrett, William F. "The Prospects of Psychical Research in America." *Journal of the Society for Psychical Research* 1 (November 1884): 172–79.

Bibliography　　　　　　　　　　　　　　　　　　　　　　　　　　　　　　　　　　357

Beard, George M. *American Nervousness: Its Causes and Consequences.* New York: G. P. Putnam's Sons, 1881.

Bell, Clark. *Spiritism, Hypnotism and Telepathy, as Involved in the Case of Mrs. Leonora Piper and the Society for Psychical Research.* 2nd ed. New York: Medico-Legal Journal, 1904.

Bernheim, Hippolyte. *De la suggestion dans l'état hypnotique et dans l'état de veille.* Paris: Doin, 1884.

——. *De la suggestion et de ses applications a la thérapeutique.* Paris: Doin, 1886.

Binet, Alfred. *On Double Consciousness: Experimental Psychological Studies.* Chicago: Open Court, 1889.

Braid, James. *Neurypnology or the Rationale of Nervous Sleep.* London: J. Churchill, 1843.

Bullard, William N. "[First] Report of the Committee on Mediumistic Phenomena." *Proceedings of the American Society for Psychical Research* 1 (December 1887): 230–36.

——. "Request for Coöperation." *Proceedings of the American Society for Psychical Research* 1 (December 1887): 266.

Capron, E. W. *Modern Spiritualism: Its Facts and Fanaticisms, Its Consistencies and Contradictions.* Boston: Bela Marsh, 1855.

Carrington, Hereward. *The American Séances with Eusapia Palladino.* 1911. Reprint, New York: Garrett Publications, 1954.

——. *Eusapia Palladino and Her Phenomena.* New York: B. W. Dodge, 1909.

——. *Letters to Hereward Carrington from Famous Psychical Researchers, Scientists, Mediums and Magicians.* 1957. Reprint, New York: Fieldcrest, n.d. [1964].

Cattell, James McKeen. "Mrs. Piper, the Medium." *Science,* n.s. 7, no. 172 (April 15, 1898): 534–35.

——. "Mrs. Piper, 'The Medium.'" *Science,* n.s. 7, no. 175 (May 6, 1898): 641–42.

——. Review of "Address by the President before the Society for Psychical Research," by William James. *Psychological Review* 3 (September 1896): 582–83.

——. Untitled editorial. *Psychological Review* 9, no. 3 (1902): 319.

Charcot, Jean-Martin. *Leçons du mardi a la Salpêtrière.* Paris: Proges Medical, 1889.

——. "Sur les divers états nerveaux determines par l'hypnotisation chex les hystériques." *Comptes-Rendus hebdomadaires des séances de l'Académie des Sciences* 94 (1882): 403–5.

Collins, Robert H. "In Memory of F. W. H. Myers." *Proceedings of the Society for Psychical Research* 17 (May 1901): 11.

"Constitution." *Proceedings of the American Society for Psychical Research* 1, no. 2 (July 1886): 55–57.

Cooper, James Fenimore. *The Letters and Journals of James Fenimore Cooper.* 6 vols. Edited by James F. Beard. Cambridge, Mass.: Belknap Press of Harvard University Press, 1968.

Courtier, Jules. "Rapport sur les séances d'Eusapia Palladino." *Bulletin de l'Institut Général Psychologique* 8 (1908): 407–578.

Crookes, William. "Address of the President before the British Association for the Advancement of Science." *Science,* n.s. 8, no. 201 (November 4, 1898): 601–12.

——. "Experimental Investigation of a New Force." *Quarterly Journal of Science* 8 (1871): 339–49.

——. *Experimental Investigations of Psychic Force.* London: J. Burns, 1874.

---. "Notes of Séances with D. D. Home." *Proceedings of the Society for Psychical Research* 6 (December 1889): 98–127.

---. *Psychic Force and Modern Spiritualism*. London: Longmans, Green, 1871.

---. *Researches in the Phenomena of Spiritualism*. London: J. Burns, 1874.

---. *Researches into the Phenomena of Modern Spiritualism*. Rochester, N.Y.: Austin, 1905.

---. "Some Further Experiments on Psychic Force." *Quarterly Journal of Science* 8 (1871): 471–93.

---. "Spiritualism Viewed by the Light of Modern Science." *Quarterly Journal of Science* 7 (1870): 316–21.

de Chastenet de Puységur, A. M. J. *Du magnétisme animal considère dans ses rapports avec diverses branches de la physique générale*. Paris: Cellot, 1806.

de Faria, J. C. *De la cause du sommeil lucide ou Étude de la nature de l'homme*. Paris: H. Jouve, 1906.

Deleuze, J. P. F. *Histoire critique du magnétisme animal*. 2 vols. Paris: Mame, 1813.

de Tocqueville, Alexis. *Democracy in America*. Edited and abridged by Richard D. Heffner. New York: Mentor Books, 1956.

Dixon, W. MacNeile. "In Memory of F. W. H. Myers." *Proceedings of the Society for Psychical Research* 17 (May 1901): 12.

Elliotson, John. *Numerous Cases of Surgical Operations with Pain in the Mesmeric State*. London: H. Bailliere, 1843.

Esdaile, James. *Mesmerism in India, and Its Practical Applications in Surgery and Medicine*. London: Longman, Brown, Green and Longmans, 1846.

Fechner, Gustav. *Zend-Avesta oder über die Dinge des Himmles und des Jenseits*. 2 vols. 2nd ed. 1851. Reprint, Hamburg: L. Voss, 1901.

Fielding, Everard, W. W. Baggally, and Hereward Carrington. "Report on a Series of Sittings with Eusapia Palladino." *Proceedings of the Society for Psychical Research* 23 (November 1909): 309–569.

Flammarion, Camille. *Mysterious Psychic Forces*. Boston: Small, Maynard, 1907.

Flournoy, Théodore. *From India to the Planet Mars: A Case of Multiple Personality with Imaginary Languages*. 1899. Reprint, Princeton: Princeton University Press, 1994.

"Formation of the Society." *Proceedings of the American Society for Psychical Research* 1, no. 1 (July 1885): 1–2.

Garland, Hamlin. *The Tyranny of the Dark*. New York: Harper and Brothers, 1905.

Gladstone, William. Untitled article. *Journal of the Society for Psychical Research* 8 (1898): 260.

Godwin, Parke. *A Biography of William Cullen Bryant, with Extracts from His Private Correspondence*. 2 vols. New York: D. Appleton, 1883.

Greeley, Horace. *Recollections of a Busy Life*. New York: J. B. Ford, 1868.

Gurney, Edmund. "Peculiarities of Certain Post-hypnotic States." *Proceedings of the Society for Psychical Research* 4 (1887): 268–323.

---. "The Problems of Hypnotism." *Mind* 9 (October 1884): 477–508.

---. "The Problems of Hypnotism." *Proceedings of the Society for Psychical Research* 2 (1884): 265–92.

---. "Recent Experiments in Hypnotism." *Proceedings of the Society for Psychical Research* 5 (1888): 3–17.

———. "The Stages of Hypnotism." *Proceedings of the Society for Psychical Research* 2 (1884): 61–72.
Gurney, Edmund, Frederic Myers, and Frank Podmore. *Phantasms of the Living*. 2 vols. London: Trübner, 1886.
Hall, G. S. "Psychological Literature." *American Journal of Psychology* 1, no. 1 (November 1887): 128–46.
Harrison, Jane. *Reminiscences of a Student's Life*. London: Hogarth Press, 1925.
Hodgson, Richard. "Account of Personal Investigations in India, and Discussion of the Authorship of the 'Koot Hoomi' Letters." *Proceedings of the Society for Psychical Research* 3 (December 1885): 207–380.
———. "A Further Record of Observations of Certain Phenomena of Trance." *Proceedings of the Society for Psychical Research* 12 (February 1898): 284–582.
———. "Mr. Davey's Imitations by Conjuring of Phenomena Sometimes Attributed to Spirit Agency." *Proceedings of the Society for Psychical Research* 8 (1892): 253–310.
———. "A Record of Observations of Certain Phenomena of Trance." *Proceedings of the Society for Psychical Research* 8 (June 1892): 1–167.
Hodgson, Richard, and S. V. Davey. "The Possibilities of Mal-observation and Lapse of Memory from a Practical Point of View." *Proceedings of the Society for Psychical Research* 4 (May 1887): 381–495.
Hyslop, J. H. "President G. Stanley Hall's and Dr. Amy Tanner's *Studies in Spiritism*." *Journal of the American Society for Psychical Research* 5 (1911): 1–98.
"Insanity Plea Raised in Terranova Case." *New York Times*, 15 May 1906, http://query.nytimes.com/gst/abstract.html?res=FB0F10F63A5A12738DDDAC0994DD405B868CF1D3. Accessed 28 April 2011.
James, Alice. *The Diary of Alice James*. Edited by Leon Edel. 1934. Reprint, New York: Dodd, Mead, 1964.
James, Henry, Jr. *Henry James Autobiography*. Edited by Frederick W. Dupee. New York: Criterion, 1956.
———. *Henry James Letters*. 5 vols. Edited by Leon Edel. Cambridge: Belknap Press of Harvard University Press, 1974–84.
James, Henry, Sr. "Spiritual Rappings." In *Lectures and Miscellanies*, 407–24. New York: Redfield, 1852.
James, William. *The Correspondence of William James*. 12 vols. Edited by Ignas K. Skrupskelis and Elizabeth M. Berkeley. Charlottesville: University Press of Virginia, 1992–2004.
———. *Essays, Comments, and Reviews. The Works of William James*. Edited by Frederick H. Burkhardt, Fredson Bowers, and Ignas K. Skrupskelis. Cambridge, Mass.: Harvard University Press, 1987.
———. *Essays in Psychical Research. The Works of William James*. Edited by Frederick H. Burkhardt, Fredson Bowers, and Ignas K. Skrupskelis. Cambridge, Mass.: Harvard University Press, 1986.
———. *Essays in Psychology. The Works of William James*. Edited by Frederick H. Burkhardt, Fredson Bowers, and Ignas K. Skrupskelis. Cambridge, Mass.: Harvard University Press, 1983.

―――. *Essays in Religion and Morality. The Works of William James.* Edited by Frederick H. Burkhardt, Fredson Bowers, and Ignas K. Skrupskelis. Cambridge, Mass.: Harvard University Press, 1982.

―――. *The Letters of William James.* 2 vols. Edited by Henry James III. Boston: Atlantic Monthly Press, 1920.

―――. *The Letters of William James and Théodore Flournoy.* Edited by Robert C. Le Clair. Madison: University of Wisconsin Press, 1966.

―――. *Memories and Studies.* Edited by Henry James Jr. New York: Longmans, Green, 1911.

―――. *A Pluralistic Universe. The Works of William James.* Edited by Frederick H. Burkhardt, Fredson Bowers, and Ignas K. Skrupskelis. Cambridge, Mass.: Harvard University Press, 1977.

―――. *Pragmatism. The Works of William James.* Edited by Frederick H. Burkhardt, Fredson Bowers, and Ignas K. Skrupskelis. Cambridge, Mass.: Harvard University Press, 1975.

―――. *The Principles of Psychology.* 3 vols. *The Works of William James.* Edited by Frederick H. Burkhardt, Fredson Bowers, and Ignas K. Skrupskelis. Cambridge, Mass: Harvard University Press, 1981.

―――. *Selected Unpublished Correspondence, 1885–1910.* Edited by Frederick J. Down Scott. Columbus: Ohio State University Press, 1986.

―――. *Some Problems of Philosophy. The Works of William James.* Edited by Frederick H. Burkhardt, Fredson Bowers, and Ignas K. Skrupskelis. Cambridge, Mass.: Harvard University Press, 1979.

―――. *The Varieties of Religious Experience. The Works of William James.* Edited by Frederick H. Burkhardt, Fredson Bowers, and Ignas K. Skrupskelis. Cambridge, Mass.: Harvard University Press, 1985.

―――. *The Will to Believe and Other Essays. The Works of William James.* Edited by Frederick H. Burkhardt, Fredson Bowers, and Ignas K. Skrupskelis. Cambridge, Mass.: Harvard University Press, 1979.

―――. *The Writings of William James: A Comprehensive Edition.* Edited by John J. McDermott. 1967. Reprint, New York: Modern Library, 1977.

Janet, Pierre. *De l'Automatisme psychologique: Essai de psychologie expérimentale sur les formes inférieures de l'activité humaine.* Paris: Alcan, 1889.

Jastrow, Joseph. "The Psychology of Deception." *Popular Science Monthly,* December 1888, 145–57.

―――. "The Psychology of Spiritualism." *Popular Science Monthly,* April 1889, 721–32.

―――. "The Problems with 'Psychic Research.'" *Harper's New Monthly Magazine,* June 1889, 76–82.

Kant, Immanuel. *Critique of Pure Reason.* Unabridged ed. Translated by Norman Kemp Smith. 1929. Reprint, New York: St. Martin's Press, 1965.

Kennedy, William Sloane. "Professor William James and Human Immortality," *Conservator* 9 (December 1898): 150–51.

Lewis, E. E. "A Report of the Mysterious Noises Heard in the House of Mr. John D. Fox, in Hydesville, Arcadia, Wayne County, Authenticated by the Certificates, Confirmed by the Statements of the Citizens of That Place and Vicinity." Canandaigua, N.Y.: E. E. Lewis, 1848.

Liébeault, Auguste Ambroise. *Du Sommeil et des États analogues, considères au point de vue de l'Action du Moral sur la Physique.* Paris: Masson, 1866.

"List of Members and Associates." *Proceedings of the American Society for Psychical Research* 1 (1885): 52–54, 571–76.

Lodge, Oliver. "Experience of Unusual Physical Phenomena Occurring in the Presence of an Entranced Person (Eusapia Palladino)." *Journal of the Society for Psychical Research* 6 (November 1894): 306–36.

———. "In Memory of F. W. H. Myers." *Proceedings of the Society for Psychical Research* 17 (May 1901): 1–12.

———. "In Memory of Henry Sidgwick." *Proceedings of the Society for Psychical Research* 15 (December 1900): 463–64.

———. *Letters from Sir Oliver Lodge: Psychical, Religious, Scientific and Personal.* Edited by J. Arthur Hill. London: Cassell, 1932.

———. *Past Years.* London: Hodder and Stoughton, 1931.

———. "Report on Some Trance Communications Received Chiefly through Mrs. Piper." *Proceedings of the Society for Psychical Research* 23 (1909): 127–285.

———. "[Third] Presidential Address before the Society for Psychical Research, January 30, 1903." *Proceedings of the Society for Psychical Research* 18 (June 1903): 1–21.

Lombroso, César. *After Death—What? Spiritistic Phenomena and Their Interpretation.* Translated by William Sloane. Boston: Small, Maynard, 1909.

Mason, Rufus Osgood. *Telepathy and the Subliminal Self: An Account of Recent Investigations Regarding Hypnotism, Automatism, Dreams, Phantasms, and Related Phenomena.* New York: Hold, 1897.

McDougall, William. "In Memory of William James." *Proceedings of the Society for Psychical Research* 25 (March 1911): 11–29.

"Meetings of the Society." *Proceedings of the American Society for Psychical Research* 1, no. 2 (July 1886): 61–62.

"Members and Associate Members." *Proceedings of the American Society for Psychical Research* 1, no. 2 (July 1886): 58–61.

"Members and Associates of the American Branch." *Proceedings of the Society for Psychical Research* 6 (December 1890): 697–707.

Morselli, Enrico. *Psicologia e "Spiritismo": Impressioni e Note Critiche sui Fenomeni Medianici di Eusapia Palladino.* 2 vols. Turin: Fratelli Bocca, 1908.

Münsterberg, Hugo. "Psychology and Mysticism." *Atlantic Monthly,* January 1899, 67–85.

Myers, F. W. H. "An Account of my Friendship with Henry Sidgwick." Unpublished.

———. "Automatic Writing, or the Rationale of Planchette." *Contemporary Review* 47 (January 1885): 233–49.

———. *Fragments of Inner Life: An Autobiographical Sketch.* 1893. Reprint, London: Society for Psychical Research, 1961.

———. *Human Personality and Its Survival of Bodily Death.* 2 vols. London: Longmans, Green, 1903.

———. *Human Personality and Its Survival of Bodily Death.* Abridged ed. Edited by Leopold Hamilton Myers. London: Longmans, Green, 1919.

———. "In Memory of Henry Sidgwick." *Proceedings of the Society for Psychical Research* 15 (December 1900): 452–62.

---. "On a Telepathic Explanation of Some So-Called Spiritualistic Phenomena." *Proceedings of the Society for Psychical Research* 2 (December 1884): 217–37.

---. "On the Trance-Phenomena of Mrs. Thompson." *Proceedings of the Society for Psychical Research* 17 (June 1902): 67–74.

---. "A Record of Observations of Certain Phenomena of Trance." *Proceedings of the Society for Psychical Research* 6 (December 1890): 436–42.

---. "The Subliminal Consciousness." Part 1. *Proceedings of the Society for Psychical Research* 7 (February 1892): 298–355.

---. "The Subliminal Consciousness." Part 2. *Proceedings of the Society for Psychical Research* 8 (July 1892): 333–404.

---. "The Subliminal Consciousness." Part 3. *Proceedings of the Society for Psychical Research* 8 (December 1892): 436–535.

---. "The Subliminal Consciousness." Part 4. *Proceedings of the Society for Psychical Research* 9 (June 1893): 3–128.

---. "The Subliminal Consciousness." Part 5. *Proceedings of the Society for Psychical Research* 11 (December 1895): 334–593.

---. "The Work of Edmund Gurney in Experimental Psychology." *Proceedings of the Society for Psychical Research* 5 (1888): 359–73.

Newbold, W. Romaine. "A Further Record of Observations of Certain Phenomena of Trance." *Proceedings of the Society for Psychical Research* 14 (December 1898): 6–49.

Newcomb, Simon. *The Reminiscences of an Astronomer*. Boston: Mifflin, 1903.

Peirce, Charles S. "The Fixation of Belief" (1877). In *Charles S. Peirce: Selected Writings (Values in a Universe of Chance)*, edited by Philip P. Wiener, 91–112. 1956. Reprint, New York: Dover, 1966.

---. "Logic and Spiritualism" (1905). In *Collected Papers of Charles Sanders Peirce*, 6 vols., edited by Charles Hartshorne and Paul Weiss, 6:375–89. Cambridge: Belknap Press of Harvard University Press, 1934.

Piddington, J. G. "A Series of Concordant Automatisms." *Proceedings of the Society for Psychical Research* 22 (October 1908): 19–416.

Podmore, Frank. *Modern Spiritualism*. 2 vols. London: Methuen, 1902.

"Proceedings of General Meetings." *Proceedings of the Society for Psychical Research* 10 (August 1894): 1.

"The Prospects of the New Psychical Society." *Science* 5, no. 102 (January 16, 1885): 44–45.

"Report of the Committee Appointed to Investigate Phenomena Connected with the Theosophical Society." *Proceedings of the Society for Psychical Research* 3 (December 1885): 201–7.

Report on Spiritualism of the Committee of the London Dialectical Society. London: Longmans, Green, Reader and Dyer, 1871.

"Request for Coöperation." *Proceedings of the American Society for Psychical Research* 1 (May 1887): 259–60.

Richet, Charles. "Du somnambulisme provoque." *Journal de l'Anatomie et de la Physiologie normales et pathologiques de l'homme et des animaux* 2 (1875): 348–78.

---. *Traité de Métaphysique*. 2nd ed. Paris: F. Alcan, 1923.

Robbins, Anne Manning. *Both Sides of the Veil: A Personal Experience*. Boston: Sherman, French, 1909.

———. *Past and Present with Mrs. Piper.* New York: Henry Holt, 1921.
Sargent, Epes. *Planchette; or, The Despair of Science.* Boston: Roberts Brothers, 1869.
———. *The Scientific Basis of Spiritualism.* Boston: Colby and Rich, 1880.
Schiller, F. C. S. *Riddles of the Sphinx: A Study in the Philosophy of Evolution.* London: Swan Sonnenshchein, 1891.
Sidgwick, Eleanor. "Mr. Eglinton." *Journal of the Society for Psychical Research* 2 (June 1886): 282–334.
———. "Results of a Personal Investigation into the Physical Phenomena of Spiritualism." *Proceedings of the Society for Psychical Research* 6 (October 1886): 45–74.
Sidgwick, Henry. "Eusapia Palladino." *Journal of the Society for Psychical Research* 7 (November 1895): 148–59.
———. *The Methods of Ethics.* 1874. Reprint, Chicago: University of Chicago Press, 1962.
Simon, Linda, ed. *William James Remembered.* Lincoln: University of Nebraska Press, 1996.
Stephens, Fitzjames. *Essays on Spirit-Rapping.* N.p., n.d.
Sunderland, La Roy. *Pathetism; with Practical Instructions.* New York: P. P. Good, 1843.
Tanner, Amy. *Studies in Spiritism.* New York: D. Appleton, 1910. Reprint, New York: Prometheus Books, 1994.
Taylor, Bayard. *Life and Letters of Bayard Taylor.* 2 vols. Edited by Marie Hansen Taylor and Horace E. Scudder. Boston: Mifflin, 1884.
Truesdell, John W. *The Bottom Facts Concerning the Science of Spiritualism.* London: G. W. Carleton, 1883.
Wallace, Alfred Russel. *My Life.* Rev. ed. London: Chapman and Hall, 1908.
Warren, Joseph W. "[Second] Report of the Committee on Mediumistic Phenomena." *Proceedings of the American Society for Psychical Research* 1 (March 1889): 320–22.
"Weather Report." *Boston Daily Advertiser,* March 6, 1889, http://infotrac.galegroup .com/itw/infomark/408/ 844/993926w16/ purl=rc1_NCNP_0_ GT3006830708&dyn=21!zoom _1?sw_aep=sain79627. Accessed 12 June 2013.
Werner, Heinrich. *Die Schutzgeister oder merkwürdige Blicke zweier Seherinnin in die Geisterwelt.* Stuttgart: J. G. Cotta, 1839.
Wienholt, Arnold. *Heilkraft des thierischen Magnetismus.* 3 vols. Lemgo: Meyer, 1806.
Wilkinson, James John Garth. *The Homeopathy Principle Applied to Insanity: A Proposal to Treat Lunacy by Spiritualism.* Boston: Otis Clapp, 1857.
———. *Improvisations from the Spirit.* New York: Charles Partridge, 1857.
Willis, Nathaniel Parker. "Post-Mortuum Soiree." In *The Rag Bag: A Collection of Ephemera,* 185–94. New York: Charles Scribner, 1855.
Wood, R. W. "Report of an Investigation of the Phenomena Connected with Eusapia Palladino." *Science* 31, no. 803 (May 10, 1910): 776–80.

SECONDARY SOURCES

Allen, Gay Wilson. *William James: A Biography.* New York: Viking Press, 1967.
Annan, Noel. "The Intellectual Aristocracy." In *Studies in Social History: A Tribute to G. M. Trevelyan,* edited by J. H. Plumb, 243–87. London: Longmans, Green, 1955.
Ashby, LeRoy. *With Amusement for All: A History of American Popular Culture since 1830.* Lexington: University Press of Kentucky, 2006.

Asprem, Egil. *The Problem of Disenchantment: Scientific Naturalism and Esoteric Discourse, 1900–1939*. Leiden, The Netherlands: Brill Academic Publishers, 2014.
Bailyn, Bernard, David Brion Davis, David Herbert Donald, John L. Thomas, Robert H. Wiebe, and Gordon S. Wood. *The Great Republic: A History of the American People*. Boston: Little, Brown, 1977.
Baird, Alexander. *Richard Hodgson: The Story of a Psychical Researcher and His Times*. London: Psychic Press, 1949.
Barnard, G. William. *Exploring Unseen Worlds: William James and the Philosophy of Mysticism*. Albany: State University of New York Press, 1997.
Barrow, Logie. "An Imponderable Liberator: J. J. Garth Wilkinson." *Society for the Social History of Medicine Bulletin* 36 (June 1985): 29–31.
———. "An Imponderable Liberator: J. J. Garth Wilkinson." In *Studies in the History of Alternative Medicine*, edited by Roger Cooter, 89–117. Oxford: Macmillan Press, 1988.
———. *Independent Spirits: Spiritualism and English Plebeians, 1850–1910*. New York: Routledge and Kegan Paul, 1986.
Bates, Ralph S. *Scientific Societies in the United States*. 3rd ed. Cambridge: MIT Press, 1965.
Baum, Maurice. "William James and Psychical Research." *Journal of Abnormal and Social Psychology* 30 (April–June 1935): 111–18.
Barzun, Jacques. *A Stroll with William James*. New York: Harper and Row, 1983.
Bender, Thomas. *New York Intellect: A History of Intellectual Life in New York City, from 1750 to the Beginnings of Our Own Time*. New York: Alfred A. Knopf, 1987.
Berger, Arthur S. "The Early History of the ASPR: Origins to 1907." *Journal of the American Society for Psychical Research* 79 (January 1985): 39–60.
———. *Lives and Letters in American Parapsychology: A Bibliographical History, 1850–1987*. Jefferson, N.C.: McFarland, 1988.
Bixler, Julius Seelye. *Religion in the Philosophy of William James*. Boston: Marshall Jones, 1926.
Bjork, Daniel W. *The Compromised Scientist*. New York: Columbia University Press, 1983.
———. *William James: The Center of His Vision*. New York: Columbia University Press, 1988.
Bloom, Murray Teigh. "America's Most Famous Medium." *American Mercury*, May 1950, 578–86.
Blum, Deborah. *Ghost Hunters: William James and the Search for Scientific Proof of Life after Death*. New York: Penguin, 2006.
Blumin, Stuart M. *The Emergence of the Middle Class: Social Experience in the American City, 1760–1900*. Cambridge: Cambridge University Press, 1989.
Boring, Edwin G. *A History of Experimental Psychology*. New York: Century, 1929.
Bowler, Peter J. *Reconciling Science and Religion: The Debate in Early-Twentieth-Century Britain*. Chicago: University of Chicago Press, 2001.
Boynton, Henry Walcott. *James Fenimore Cooper*. New York: Century, 1931.
Bradbury, Malcolm, and James McFarlane, eds. *Modernism: A Guide to European Literature, 1890–1930*. 1976. Reprint, New York: Penguin Books, 1991.
Brandon, Ruth. *The Spiritualists: The Passion for the Occult in the Nineteenth and Twentieth Centuries*. New York: Alfred E. Knopf, 1983.
Braude, Ann. *Radical Spirits: Spiritualism and Women's Rights in Nineteenth-Century America*. Boston: Beacon Press, 1989.

Broad, C. D. *Religion, Philosophy, and Psychical Research*. New York: Harcourt, Brace, 1953.
Brooke, John Hedley. *Science and Religion: Some Historical Perspectives*. Cambridge: Cambridge University Press, 1991.
Brown, A. W. *The Metaphysical Society: Victorian Minds in Conflict, 1869–1880*. New York: Columbia University Press, 1947.
Brown, Burton Gates, Jr. "Spiritualism in Nineteenth-Century America." Ph.D. diss., Boston University, 1973.
Brown, Slater. *The Heyday of Spiritualism*. New York: Hawthorn Books, 1970.
Browning, Oscar. *The Life of George Eliot*. London: W. Scott, 1890.
Bruce, Robert V. *The Launching of American Science, 1846–1876*. Ithaca: Cornell University Press, 1987.
Buescher, John Benedict. *Empress of Swindle: The Life of Ann Odella Diss Debar*. Forest Grove, Oreg.: Typhon Press, 2014.
Buranelli, Vincent. *The Wizard from Vienna: Franz Anton Mesmer*. New York: Coward, McCann and Geoghegan, 1975.
Burnham, John C. *How Superstition Won and Science Lost: Popularizing Science and Health in the United States*. New Brunswick, N.J.: Rutgers University Press, 1987.
Butler, Jon. *Awash in a Sea of Faith: Christianizing the American People*. Cambridge, Mass.: Harvard University Press, 1990.
Calinescu, Matei. *Five Faces of Modernity: Modernism, Avant-Garde, Decadence, Kitsch, Postmodernism*. Durham: Duke University Press, 1987.
Camfield, Thomas M. "The Professionalization of American Psychology, 1870–1917." *Journal of the History of the Behavioral Sciences* 9, no. 1 (January 1973): 66–75.
Carroll, Bret E. *Spiritualism in Antebellum America*. Bloomington: Indiana University Press, 1997.
Carroll, Thomas D. "The Traditions of Fideism." *Religious Studies* 44 (2008): 1–22.
Cerullo, John J. *The Secularization of the Soul: Psychical Research in Modern Britain*. Philadelphia: Institute for the Study of Human Issues, 1982.
Chadwick, Henry. *The Early Church*. Rev. ed. New York: Penguin Book, 1993.
Clendenning, John. *The Life and Thought of Josiah Royce*. Rev. ed. Nashville: Vanderbilt University Press, 1999.
Coon, Deborah J. "Standardizing the Subject: Experimental Psychologists, Introspection, and the Quest for a Technoscientific Ideal." *Technology and Culture* 34, no. 4 (October 1992); 757–83.
———. "Testing the Limits of Sense and Science: American Experimental Psychologists Combat Spiritualism, 1880–1920." *American Psychologist* 47 (February 1992): 143–51.
Cooper, Wesley. *The Unity of William James's Thought*. Nashville: Vanderbilt University Press, 2002.
Cornell, William M. *The Life and Public Career of the Hon. Horace Greeley*. Boston: Lee and Shepard, 1872.
Cotkin, George. *Reluctant Modernism: American Thought and Culture, 1880–1900*. Boston: Twayne, 1992.
———. *William James, Public Philosopher*. Baltimore: Johns Hopkins University Press, 1990.
Crabtree, Adam. *From Mesmer to Freud: Magnetic Sleep and the Roots of Psychological Healing*. New Haven: Yale University Press, 1993.

Croce, Paul Jerome. *Science and Religion in the Era of William James: The Eclipse of Uncertainty, 1820–1880*. Chapel Hill: University of North Carolina Press, 1995.

Cross, Whitney. *The Burned-Over District: The Social and Intellectual History of Enthusiastic Religion in Western New York*. Ithaca: Cornell University Press, 1950.

Davies, Richard O. *Sports in American Life: A History*. Oxford: Blackwell, 2007.

Davis, Robert C. "The Brass Age of Psychology." *Technology and Culture* 11, no. 4 (October 1970): 604–12.

Deveney, John Patrick. *Paschal Beverly Randolph: A Nineteenth-Century Black American Spiritualism Rosicrucian, and Sex Magician*. Albany: State University of New York Press, 1997.

Dexter, E. G. *History of Education in the United States*. New York: Macmillan, 1904.

Dingwall, E. J. *The Critics' Dilemma: Further Comments on Some Nineteenth Century Investigations*. Sussex: Crowhurst, 1966.

———. *Ghosts and Spirits in the Ancient World*. London: Kegan Paul, Trench, Trubner, 1930.

Dupree, A. Hunter. "The National Pattern of American Learned Societies, 1779–1863." In *The Pursuit of Knowledge in the Early American Republic: American Scientific and Learned Societies from Colonial Times to the Civil War*, edited by Alexandra Oleson and Sanborn C. Brown, 21–32. Baltimore: Johns Hopkins University Press, 1976.

Ellenberger, Henri. *The Discovery of the Unconscious: The History and Evolution of Dynamic Psychiatry*. New York: Basic Books, 1970.

Epperson. Gordon. *The Mind of Edmund Gurney*. London: Associated University Presses, 1997.

Erikson, Erik H. *Identity: Youth and Crisis*. New York: W. W. Norton, 1968.

Faulker, Peter. *Modernism*. London: Methuen, 1977.

Feinstein, Howard M. *Becoming William James*. Ithaca: Cornell University Press, 1984.

Flew, Anthony, ed., *Body, Mind, and Death*. New York: Macmillan, 1964.

Ford, Marcus. "William James's Psychical Research and Its Philosophical Implications." *Transactions of the Charles S. Peirce Society* 34 (Summer 1998): 605–26.

Frothingham, Octavius B. *George Ripley*. New York: AMS Press, 1883.

Gale, Richard M. *The Divided Self of William James*. Cambridge: Cambridge University Press, 1999.

Gamm, Gerald, and Robert D. Putnam, "The Growth of Voluntary Associations in America, 1840–1940." *Journal of Interdisciplinary History* 29, no. 4 (Spring 1999): 511–57.

Gardner, Martin. "Communicating with the Dead: William James and Mrs. Piper." Part 1. *Free Inquiry* 12 (Spring 1992): 20–27.

———. "Communicating with the Dead: William James and Mrs. Piper." Part 2. *Free Inquiry* 12 (Summer 1992): 38–48.

Garrison, Wendell Phillips, and Francis Jackson Garrison, eds. *William Lloyd Garrison, 1805–1879: The Story of His Life Told by His Children*. 4 vols. 1889. Reprint, New York: New York Times Press, 1969.

Gauld, Alan. *The Founders of Psychical Research*. New York: Schocken, 1968.

———. *A History of Hypnotism*. Cambridge: Cambridge University Press, 1992.

Geertz, Clifford. *The Interpretation of Cultures: Selected Essays*. New York: Basic Books, 1973.

Geikie, Sir Archibald. *Annals of the Royal Society Club*. London: Macmillan, 1917.
Gladwell, Malcolm. "Group Think." *New Yorker*, 2 December 2002, 102–7.
Goldfarb, Russell M., and Clare R. Goldfarb. *Spiritualism and Nineteenth-Century Letters*. London: Associated University Presses, 1978.
Goldsmith, Barbara. *Other Powers: The Age of Suffrage, Spiritualism, and the Scandalous Victoria Woodhull*. New York: Alfred A. Knopf, 1998.
Gosling, F. G. *Before Freud: Neurasthenia and the American Medical Community*. Urbana: University of Illinois Press, 1987.
Grant, Robert M. *The Bible in the Church: A Short History of Interpretation*. New York: Macmillan, 1948.
Gregory, Frederick. "The Impact of Darwinian Evolution on Protestant Theology in the Nineteenth Century." In *God and Nature: Historical Essays on the Encounter between Christianity and Science*, edited by David C. Lindberg and Ronald L. Numbers, 369–90. Berkeley: University of California Press, 1986.
Griffin, David Ray. *Parapsychology, Philosophy, and Spirituality: A Postmodern Exploration*. Albany: State University of New York Press, 1997.
Grim, Patrick, ed. *Philosophy of Science and the Occult*. 2nd ed. Albany: State University of New York Press, 1990.
Grossman, James. *James Fenimore Cooper*. New York: William Sloan Associates, 1949.
Habegger, Alfred. *The Father: A Life of Henry James, Sr.* New York: Farrar, Straus and Giroux, 1994.
Hale, Matthew, Jr. *Human Science and Social Order: Hugo Münsterberg and the Origins of Applied Psychology*. Philadelphia: Temple University Press, 1980.
Hale, William Harlan. *Horace Greeley: Voice of the People*. New York: Harper and Brothers, 1950.
Hall, David D. "The Victorian Connection." In *Victorian America*, edited by Daniel Walker Howe, 81–94. Philadelphia: University of Pennsylvania Press, 1976.
Hall, Trevor H. *The Spiritualists: The Story of Florence Cook and William Crookes*. London: Helix Press, 1962.
———. *The Strange Case of Edmund Gurney*. London: George Duckworth, 1964.
Hamilton, Trevor. *Immortal Longings: F. W. H. Myers and the Victorian Search for Life after Death*. Charlottesville: Imprint Academic, 2009.
Handlin, Lilian. *George Bancroft: The Intellectual as Democrat*. New York: Harper and Row, 1984.
Harman, P. H. *Energy, Force and Matter: The Conceptual Development of Nineteenth-Century Physics*. Cambridge: Cambridge University Press, 1982.
Hatch, Nathan O. *The Democratization of American Christianity*. New Haven: Yale University Press, 1989.
Haynes, Renée. *The Society for Psychical Research, 1882–1982: A History*. London: Macdonald, 1982.
Heidelberger, Michael. *Nature from Within: Gustav Theodor Fechner and His Psychophysical Worldview*. Translated by Cynthia Klohr. Pittsburgh: University of Pittsburgh Press, 2004.
Hesse, Mary B. *Models and Analogies in Science*. Notre Dame: University of Notre Dame Press, 1966.

Higham, John. "The Reorientation of American Culture in the 1890's." In *Writing American History*, 73–102. Bloomington: Indiana University Press, 1970.
Higham, John, and Paul Conkin, eds. *New Directions in American Intellectual History*. Baltimore: Johns Hopkins University Press, 1979.
Hollinger, David A. "Historians and the Discourse of Intellectuals." In *In the American Province: Studies in the History and Historiography of Ideas*, 130–51. Baltimore: Johns Hopkins University Press, 1985.
———. "The Knower and the Artificer, with Postscript 1993." In *Modernist Impulses in the Human Sciences, 1870–1930*, edited by Dorothy Ross, 26–53. Baltimore: Johns Hopkins University Press, 1994.
———. "William James and the Culture of Inquiry." In *In the American Province: Studies in the History and Historiography of Ideas*, 3–22. Baltimore: Johns Hopkins University Press, 1985.
Houghton, Walter E. *The Victorian Frame of Mind, 1830–1870*. New Haven: Yale University Press, 1957.
Ingersoll, L. D. *The Life of Horace Greeley*. Philadelphia: Keystone, 1890.
James, D. G. *Henry Sidgwick: Science and Faith in Victorian England*. London: Oxford University Press, 1970.
Johnson, Paul E. *A Shopkeeper's Millennium: Society and Revivals in Rochester, New York, 1815–1837*. New York: Hill and Wang, 1978.
Kellogg, Julia A. *Philosophy of Henry James: A Digest*. New York: John W. Lovell, 1883.
Kelly, Edward F., and Emily Williams Kelly, et al. *Irreducible Mind: Toward a Psychology for the 21st Century*. Lanham, Md.: Rowman and Littlefield, 2007.
Kloppenberg, James T. *Uncertain Victory: Social Democracy and Progressivism in European and American Thought, 1870–1920*. Oxford: Oxford University Press, 1986.
Knapp, Krister Dylan. "James the Flâneur." *American Scholar* 73, no. 1 (Winter 2004): 160.
———. "Spatial Esotericism: Demarcating the Geographical, Intellectual and Institutional Axes of Psychical Research from the 1880s through the 1920s." Paper presented at the meeting of the European Society for the Study of Western Esotericism, Strasbourg, France, 2–4 July 2009.
———. "William James and Unconsciousness 'Beyond the Margin.'" *Streams of William James* 3, no. 2 (Fall 2001): 1–5.
Knight, David. *The Nature of Science: The History of Science in Western Culture since 1600*. London: Andre Deutsch, 1976.
———. *The Age of Science: The Scientific World-view in the Nineteenth Century*. New York: Basil Blackwell, 1986.
Kunhardt, Philip B., Jr., Philip B. Kunhardt III, and Peter W. Kunhardt. *P. T. Barnum: America's Greatest Showman*. New York: Alfred A. Knopf, 1995.
Lasch, Christopher. *The New Radicalism in America, 1889–1963: The Intellectual as a Social Type*. New York: Norton, 1965.
Leahey, Thomas, and Grace Leahey. *Psychology's Occult Doubles*. Chicago: Nelson-Hall, 1983.
Lears, T. J. Jackson. *No Place of Grace: Antimodernism and the Transformation of American Culture, 1880–1920*. New York: Pantheon Books, 1981.
Leary, David E. "Telling Likely Stories: The Rhetoric of the New Psychology, 1880–1920." *Journal of the History of the Behavioral Sciences* 23 (October 1987): 315–31.

———. "William James, Psychical Research, and the Origins of American Psychology." Paper presented at the 88th Annual Convention of the American Psychological Association, Montreal, Quebec, Canada, September 1980.

Le Clair, Robert C. *Young Henry James, 1843–1870*. New York: Bookman Associates, 1955.

Leja, Michael. "William James and Automatic Drawing." *Intellectual History Newsletter* 23 (2001): 11–23.

Lewis, R. W. B. *The Jameses: A Family Narrative*. New York: Farrar, Straus and Giroux, 1991.

Linn, W. A. *Horace Greeley: Founder and Editor of the "New York Tribune."* New York: Appleton, 1903.

Lutz, Tom. *American Nervousness, 1903: An Anecdotal History*. Ithaca: Cornell University Press, 1991.

Mason, Stephen F. *A History of the Sciences*. Rev. ed. New York: Collier Books, 1962.

Mauskopf, Seymour. "The History of the American Society for Psychical Research: An Interpretation." *Journal of the American Society for Psychical Research* 83 (January 1989): 7–19.

Mauskopf, Seymour, and Michael R. McVaugh. *The Elusive Science: Origins of Experimental Psychical Research*. Baltimore: Johns Hopkins University Press, 1980.

Medhurst, R. G., and K. M. Goldney. "William Crookes and the Physical Phenomena of Mediumship." *Proceedings of the Society for Psychical Research* 54 (1964): 25–157.

Melcher, Margarite. *The Shaker Adventure*. Princeton: Princeton University Press, 1941.

Menand, Louis. *The Metaphysical Club*. New York: Farrar, Straus and Giroux, 2001.

Merz, John Theodore. *A History of European Thought in the Nineteenth Century*. 4 vols. 3rd ed. Edinburgh, Scotland: William Blackwood and Sons, 1913–14.

Meyer, D. H. "American Intellectuals and the Victorian Crisis of Faith." In *Victorian America*, edited by Daniel Walker Howe, 59–77. Philadelphia: University of Pennsylvania Press, 1976.

Monroe, John Warne. *Laboratories of Faith: Mesmerism, Spiritism, and Occultism in Modern France*. Ithaca: Cornell University Press, 2008.

Moore, R. Laurence. *In Search of White Crows: Spiritualism, Parapsychology, and American Culture*. New York: Oxford University Press, 1977.

Morrell, Jack, and Arnold Thackray. *Gentlemen of Science: Early Years of the British Association for the Advancement of Science*. Oxford: Clarendon Press, 1981.

Morris, Lloyd. *William James: The Message of a Modern Mind*. New York: Charles Scribner's Sons, 1950.

Murphy, Gardner. "Our Pioneers, III: William James." *Journal of the Society for Psychical Research* 39 (December 1958): 309–14.

———. "William James and Psychical Research." *Journal of the American Society for Psychical Research* 43 (July 1949): 85–93.

Murphy, Gardner, and Robert O. Ballou, eds. *William James on Psychical Research*. New York: Viking Press, 1960.

Myers, Gerald E. *William James: His Life and Thought*. New Haven: Yale University Press, 1986.

Nelson, Geoffrey K. *Spiritualism and Society*. New York: Schocken Books, 1969.

Nordhoff, Charles. *The Communistic Societies of the United States*. New York: Harper and Brothers, 1875.

Noyes, John Humphrey. *History of American Socialisms*. 1870. Reprint, New York: Hillary House, 1961.

Nye, Russell B. *George Bancroft: Brahmin Rebel*. New York: Alfred A. Knopf, 1944.

O'Connell, Robert J., SJ. *William James on the Courage to Believe*. 2nd ed. New York: Fordham University Press, 1997.

Oesterreich, T. K. *Possession, Demoniacal and Other: Among Primitive Races, in Antiquity, the Middle Ages and Modern Times*. New York: Richard R. Smith, 1930.

Oleson, Alexandra, and John Voss, eds. *The Organization of Knowledge in Modern America* Baltimore: Johns Hopkins University Press, 1979.

Oppenheim, Janet. *The Other World: Spiritualism and Psychical Research in England, 1850–1914*. Cambridge: Cambridge University Press, 1985.

Ornstein, Martha. *The Role of Scientific Societies in the Seventeenth Century*. Chicago: University of Chicago Press, 1928.

Owen, Alex. *The Darkened Room: Women, Power and Spiritualism in Late Victorian England*. London: Virago, 1989.

Perry, Ralph Barton. *The Thought and Character of William James*. 2 vols. Boston: Little, Brown, 1935.

———. *The Thought and Character of William James*. 2nd ed. Cambridge, Mass.: Harvard University Press, 1948. Reprint, Nashville: Vanderbilt University Press, 1996.

Piper, Alta. *The Life and Work of Mrs. Piper*. London: Kegan Paul, Trench, Trubner, 1929.

Poovey, Mary. *A History of the Modern Fact: Problems of Knowledge in the Sciences of Wealth and Society*. Chicago: University of Chicago Press, 1998.

Popkin, Richard. *The History of Skepticism: From Erasmus to Descartes*. Assen, The Netherlands: Royal Van Gorcum, 1960.

Prochnik, George. *Putnam Camp: Sigmund Freud, James Jackson Putnam, and the Purpose of American Psychology*. New York: Other Press, 2006.

Rader, Benjamin G. *American Sports: From the Age of Folk Games to the Age of Television*. 4th ed. Upper Saddle River, N.J.: Prentice-Hall, 1999.

Ravetz, Jerome R. *Scientific Knowledge and Its Social Problems*. Oxford: Oxford University Press, 1971.

Reed, Edward. *From Soul to Mind: The Emergence of Psychology, from Erasmus Darwin to William James*. New Haven: Yale University Press, 1997.

Richardson, Robert D. *William James: In the Maelstrom of American Modernism*. Boston: Houghton Mifflin, 2006.

Roark, James L., Michael P. Johnson, Patricia Cline Cohen, Sarah Stage, Alan Lawson, and Susan M. Hartmann. *The American Promise: A History of the United States*. Boston: Bedford Books, 1998.

Roback, A. A. *William James: His Marginalia, Personality and Contribution*. Cambridge: Sci. Art Publishers, 1942.

Ross, Dorothy. *G. Stanley Hall: The Psychologist as Prophet*. Chicago: University of Chicago Press, 1972.

———. "Modernism Reconsidered." In *Modernist Impulses in the Human Sciences, 1870–1930*, edited by Dorothy Ross, 1–25. Baltimore: Johns Hopkins University Press, 1994.

———. *The Origins of American Social Science*. Cambridge: Cambridge University Press, 1991.

Ryan, Mary P. *The Cradle of the Middle Class: The Family in Oneida County, New York, 1790–1865*. Cambridge: Cambridge University Press, 1981.
Sage, M. *Mrs. Piper and the Society for Psychical Research*. New York: Scot Thaw, 1904.
Salter, W. H. *Trance Mediumship: An Introductory Study of Mrs. Piper and Mrs. Leonard*. London: Society for Psychical Research Press, 1950.
Scarborough, Elizabeth, and Laurel Furumoto. *Untold Lives: The First Generation of American Women Psychologists*. New York: Columbia University Press, 1987.
Schlesinger, Arthur M. "Biography of a Nation of Joiners." *American Historical Review* 50, no. 1 (October 1944): 1–25.
Schmeidler, Gertrude R. "William James: Pioneering Ancestor of Modern Parapsychology." In *Reinterpreting the Legacy of William James*, edited by Margaret E. Donnelly, 339–52. Washington D.C.: American Psychological Association, 1992.
Schultz, Bart. *Henry Sidgwick: Eye of the Universe, an Intellectual Biography*. Cambridge: Cambridge University Press, 2004.
———, ed. *Essays on Henry Sidgwick*. Cambridge: Cambridge University Press, 1992.
Seigfried, Charlene Haddock. *William James's Radical Reconstruction of Philosophy*. Albany: State University of New York Press, 1990.
Seldes, Gilbert. *The Stammering Century*. New York: John Day, 1928.
Shakespeare, William. *The Tragedy of Hamlet, Prince of Denmark*. Edited by Edward Hubler. New York: Signet, 1963.
Sidgwick, A., and E. M. Sidgwick. *Henry Sidgwick: A Memoir*. London: Macmillan, 1906.
Sidgwick, Ethel M. *Mrs. Henry Sidgwick: A Memoir*. London: Sidgwick and Jackson, 1938.
Simon, Linda. *Genuine Reality: A Life of William James*. Chicago: University of Chicago Press, 1998.
Skrupskelis, Ignas K. *William James: A Reference Guide*. Boston: G. K. Hall, 1977.
Sokal, Michael M. "Origins and Early Years of the American Psychological Association, 1890–1906." *American Psychologist* 47, no. 2 (February 1992): 111–22.
———, ed. *An Education in Psychology: James McKeen Cattell's Journal and Letters from Germany and England, 1880–1888*. Cambridge, Mass.: MIT Press, 1981.
Sommer, Andreas. "Psychical Research and the Origins of American Psychology: Hugo Münsterberg, William James and Eusapia Palladino." *History of the Human Sciences* 25 (April 2012): 25–44.
Spann, Edward K. *The New Metropolis: New York City, 1840–1857*. New York: Columbia University Press, 1981.
Strouse, Jean. *Alice James: A Biography*. Boston: Houghton Mifflin, 1980.
Strout, Cushing. "William James and the Twice-Born Sick Soul." *Daedalus* 97 (Summer 1968): 1062–82.
Suckiel, Ellen Kappy. *Heaven's Champion: William James's Philosophy of Religion*. Notre Dame: University of Notre Dame Press, 1996.
Taves, Ann. *Fits, Trances, and Visions: Experiencing Religion and Explaining Experience from Wesley to James*. Princeton: Princeton University Press, 1999.
———. "A Tale of Two Congresses: The Psychological Study of Psychical, Occult, and Religious Phenomena, 1900–1909." *Journal of the History of the Behavioral Sciences* 50 (Fall 2014): 376–99.

Taylor, Eugene. *William James on Consciousness beyond the Margin*. Princeton: Princeton University Press, 1996.

———. *William James on Exceptional Mental States: The 1896 Lowell Lectures*. New York: Charles Scribner's Sons, 1982.

———. "William James on Parapsychology: The 1896 Lectures on Exceptional Mental States." "A William James Renaissance: Four Essays by Young Scholars," special issue, *Harvard Library Bulletin* 30, no. 4 (October 1982): 455–79.

Thomas, John L. *The Liberator: William Lloyd Garrison; a Biography*. Boston: Little, Brown, 1963.

Toksvig, Signe. *Emanuel Swedenborg, Scientist and Mystic*. New Haven: Yale University Press, 1948.

Treitel, Corinna. *A Science for the Soul: Occultism and the Genesis of the German Modern*. Baltimore: Johns Hopkins University Press, 2003.

Turner, Frank M. *Between Science and Religion: The Reaction to Scientific Naturalism in Late Victorian England*. New Haven: Yale University Press, 1974.

Turner, James. *Without God, without Creed: The Origins of Unbelief in America*. Baltimore: Johns Hopkins University Press, 1985.

Uglow, Jenny. *The Lunar Men*. New York: Farrar, Straus and Giroux, 2002.

Voss, John. Foreword to *The Pursuit of Knowledge in the Early American Republic: American Scientific and Learned Societies from Colonial Times to the Civil War*, edited by Alexandra Oleson and Sanborn C. Brown, vii–x. Baltimore: Johns Hopkins University Press, 1976.

Warren, Austin. *The Elder Henry James*. New York: Macmillan, 1934. Reprint, New York: Octagon Books, 1970.

Wernham, James C. S. *James's Will-to-Believe Doctrine*. Kingston, Ontario: McGill-Queen's University Press, 1987.

Wheatley, James M., and Hoyt L. Edge, eds. *Philosophical Dimensions of Parapsychology*. Springfield, Ill.: Charles C. Thomas, 1976.

Whorton, James C. *Nature Cures: The History of Alternative Medicine in America*. Oxford: Oxford University Press, 2002.

Wilkinson, Clement John. *James John Garth Wilkinson: A Memoir of His Life, with a Selection from His Letters*. London: Kegan Paul, Trench, Trübner, 1911.

Wilson, James Grant. *Bryant and His Friends: Some Reminiscences of the Knickerbocker Writers*. New York: Fords, Howard and Hulbert, 1886.

Wolffram, Heather. *The Stepchildren of Science: Psychical Research and Parapsychology in Germany, c. 1870–1939*. Amsterdam: Rodopi, 2009.

Young, Frederic Harold. *The Philosophy of Henry James, Sr.* New York: Bookman, 1951.

REFERENCE WORKS

Biographical Dictionary of Parapsychology. Edited by Helene Pleasants. New York: Helix Press, 1964.

A Companion to American Thought. Edited by Richard Wightman Fox and James T. Kloppenberg. Oxford: Blackwell, 1995.

Dictionary of American Biography. 21 vols. Edited by Allen Johnson. New York: Charles Scribner's Sons, 1928–.

Dictionary of National Biography. 66 vols. Edited by Leslie Stephen and Sidney Lee. Oxford: Oxford University Press, 1917–.

Dictionary of Scientific Biography. 16 vols. Edited by Charles Coulston Gillispie. New York: Scribner, 1970–80.

Encyclopedia of Occultism and Parapsychology. 5th ed. 2 vols. Edited by J. Gordon Melton. Detroit: Gale Research, 2001.

Encyclopedia of Philosophy. 8 vols. Edited by Paul Edwards. 1967. Reprint, London: Macmillan, 1972.

Man, Myth & Magic: The Illustrated Encyclopedia of Mythology, Religion and the Unknown. New edition. Edited by Richard Cavendish. New York: Marshall Cavendish, 1995.

Notable American Women, 1670–1950. 3 vols. Edited by Edward T. James, Janet Wilson James, and Paul S. Boyer. Cambridge, Mass: Harvard University Press, 1971.

A Popular Dictionary of Spiritualism. Edited by Norman Blunsdon. New York: Citadel Press, 1962.

The Reader's Encyclopedia. Edited by William Rose Benét. New York: Thomas Y. Crowell, 1948.

Webster's Ninth New Collegiate Dictionary. Springfield, Mass.: Merriam-Webster, 1985.

INDEX

Page numbers in italics indicate illustrations.

Abbot, Francis Ellingwood, 94–95
Abolition movement, 22, 28, 31, 114
Afterlife beliefs, 12, 104, 139–40, 143–44, 173; of Blodgett, 191–92; of Davidson, 147; of Gurney, 84; of James, 4, 170–73, 195, 251–61, 277; of Myers, 72, 74, 128, 143, 233–41. *See also* Immortality
Agassiz, Louis, 115
Aksakof, Alexander, 108, 128
American Academy of Arts and Sciences, 114
American Association for the Advancement of Science (AAAS), 102, 115
American Medical Association, 116
American Philosophical Society, 114
American Political Science Association, 116
American Psychical Society, 120
American Psychological Association, 116
American Society for Psychical Research (ASPR), 62, 101–3, 113–27; difficulties of, 122–27; dissolution of, 127–28; forming of, 2, 102, 113–14, 118–19; as independent organization, 133; medium investigations by, 123–26, 141, 144, 158–72, 182–98; membership of, 117–20; reformation of, 287
American Sociological Association, 116

Amnesia, 228
Andrew, John Albion, 120
Andrew, John Forrester, 120, 124
Anesthesia: hypnosis as, 217; during trance state, 193
"Animal magnetism," 25, 217. *See also* Mesmerism
Annan, Noel, 62–64
Anthony, Susan B., 28
Apollinaris, 6
Apostles Society, 64–65, 104
Aristotelian Society for the Systematic Study of Philosophy, 85, 114
Aristotle, 7–8, 147, 271
Arnold, John N., 229–30
ASPR. *See* American Society for Psychical Research
Astrology, 94
Athenaeum Club, 117–18
Augustine of Hippo, Saint, 173, 176–78
Automatic writing, 2, 31, 54, 172, 182–84; Ellenberger on, 217; James on, 225, 229–31, 234; Myers's on, 236; Piper's attempt at, 191; with planchettes, 56–57, 96, 182, 183, 220, 229–31, 239; related phenomena to, 182–84; "secondary self" in, 212

375

Babbage, Charles, 105
Baches, Dallas, 115
Bacon, Francis, 104, 142–43, 256
Bain, Alexander, 211, 245
Baldwin, James, 174, 196, 203
Baldwin, Wilber, 79
Balfour, Arthur, 62, 64, 65, 107
Balfour, Gerald, 62, 64, 65, 108
Bancroft, George, 31, 33
Barker, George Frederick, 119
Barnard, G. William, 283
Barnum, P. T., 28–30
Barrett, Wendell, 174, 196
Barrett, William, 106, 113, 134
Beecher, Charles, 28
Bentham, Jeremy, 143
Bernheim, Hippolyte, 215, 216, 246
Berry, Helen, 141, 158, 161–62
Bigelow, John, 31
Bigelow, William Sturgis, 123–24, 164
Binet, Alfred, 215, 226, 246
Bishop, Washington Irving, 126
Bixler, Julius, 282
Blackburn, Charles, 112
Blake, William, 47
Blavatsky, Helena Petrovna, 93, 141, 149, 152, 157
Blodgett, Elizabeth Wild, 191–92
Bloomsbury circle, 104
Boutroux, Emile, 296
Bowditch, Henry P., 56, 108, 255; as ASPR member, 117–18, 122, 127; on telepathy, 118
Boyle, Pierre, 176
Brackett, Edward Augustus, 154, 166, 167, 169
Bradley, F. H., 73–75, 279, 284
Braid, James, 25, 217, 221
British Association for the Advancement of Science (BAAS), 102, 105–8, 110–11, 115
Bryant, William Cullen, 31, 33–34
Büchner, Friedrich Karl Christian Ludwig, 250, 270
Bullard, William, 185–86

Cabanis, Pierre-Jean-Georges, 250, 270
Calvert, George Henry, 31
Calvinism, 21, 24, 25
Cambridge Apostles, 64–65, 104
Cambridge Conversazione Society, 104
Carlisle, Harvey Goodwin, 107
Carlyle, Thomas, 51, 52
Carpenter, Joseph, 189
Carpenter, William B., 211, 214, 224, 245, 250
Carqueiranne chateau, 78–81, 150–51, 184
Carrington, Hereward, 157, 286, 289–92, 290
Carroll, Lewis, 104
Carter, Marion Hamilton, 295–96
Carus, C. G., 214
Cattell, James McKeen, 10, 14, 202, 230; Piper and, 174, 199, 201–6, 261
Channing, Henry, 32
Chapman, John Jay, 295
Chapman, Temple, 46
Charcot, Jean-Martin, 211, 214–16; William James and, 245, 246; Arthur Myers and, 219
Chastenet de Puységur, A. M. J. de, 217
Chaston, Iris Jessica, 184
Chautauqua movement, 125
Chevillard, Alphonse, 56
Child, Francis, 164–65
Christian Scientists, 26
Clairvoyance, 2, 31, 159, 252; James on, 229–30, 229–31, 239; Henry James Sr. on, 37; mesmerism and, 53; parapsychologists and, 307; SPR investigations of, 252
Clifford, William, 14, 173, 271
Cocke, J. R., 186
Coleridge, Samuel Taylor, 106
Comte, Auguste, 143
Condorcet, Nicolas de, 143
Consciousness, 5, 212–13, 218–27, 244–46; altered states of, 23, 25, 26, 214; "automatic," 231; "beyond the margin," 2, 211–13, 233, 246; "double," 215, 216, 226; field of, 219; "mother sea" of, 15, 18, 249, 274–77, 280–83, 298; Myers on, 222, 234–37; Nietzsche on, 214; "postmortem," 42; stream of, 223, 227, 237–38;

"subliminal reservoir" of, 3, 249–51, 259–84, 298; "submerged," 219; supernatural, 251. *See also* Unconsciousness
Cook, Florence Eliza, 111–12, 129
Cook, Kate, 111–12
Cooper, James Fenimore, 31–33
Cooper, Wesley, 5
Correspondence, doctrine of, 41, 51
Cosmology, 277–85
Coues, Elliot, 160
Crandon, Mina Stinson "Margery," 148
Crookes, William, 110–12, 134, 289; British Association for the Advancement of Science and, 106; Society for Psychical Research and, 107–8, 128, 129
Cross-correspondence test, 253–55
Crystal gazing, 31, 139, 239
Curie, Marie, 289
Curtis, Joseph T., 45–46, 53
Cushman, Horace W., 160

Daguerreotype, 48
Dana, Richard Henry, 31, 33
Darwin, Erasmus, 85, 104
Darwin, Francis, 152
Darwinism, 9, 14, 15, 233, 270, 300
Davey, S. V., 93
Davidson, Thomas, 6–7, 120, 146–47, 171
Davis, Andrew Jackson, 53
Davis, W. S., 291
De Morgan, Sophia, 51
Delabarre, Edmund Burke, 201
Deleuze, J. P. F., 217
Descartes, René, 213, 251–52
Dessoir, Max, 108, 128, 216
D'Holbach, Baron (Paul-Henri Dietrich), 250, 270
Dialectical Society, 198
Diss Debar, Mrs. (Ann Odella), 141, 158–60
Dolbear, Amos Emerson, 120
Dorr, George Bucknam, 127; Hodgson and, 132, 258; James and, 97, 120, 132, 254, 286–88; Piper and, 254; Spiritualist circle of, 293
Douglass, Frederick, 28

Dreiser, Theodore, 12
Dreyfus, Alfred, 79, 112
Dumas, Alexandre, 160
Du Prel, Carl, 216, 244–45

Earth-soul theory, 278–83
Ectoplasm, 2, 148, 150
Edmonds, John, 28, 33
Edmunds, Lucy, 127, 129, 131
Eglinton, William, 93, 141, 149, 157
Eliot, Charles William, 131–32, 147
Eliot, George (Mary Ann Evans), 82
Ellenberger, Henri, 216–17
Elliotson, John, 217, 221
Emerson, Ralph Waldo, 53
Empiricism, 180–81, 300; fideism and, 173, 175, 177, 181–82, 194–98; pragmatic, 267–68, 277, 282, 285; radical, 5, 257, 309; skeptical, 177–78; of tertium quid method, 142–48, 157, 161
Epileptic patients, 215, 219, 242
Esdaile, James, 217, 221
Ether hypothesis, 111, 155, 179, 217
Everett, Charles Caroll, 119
"Exceptional mental states," 2, 212
Experimental psychology, 219; Charcot and, 215; development of, 10–11, 116; psychical researchers and, 141

Faith healing, 26
Faria, Abbé J. C. de, 217
Fechner, Gustav, 214, 250, 277–83
Fichte, Johann Gottlieb, 214
Fideism, 13, 175–82, 189, 192; definition of, 175; empiricism and, 173, 175, 177, 181–82, 194–98; Hume on, 176–77; philosophical, 177; will to believe and, 5, 173–74, 178, 182
Finzi, George, 153
Flew, Anthony, 252
Flournoy, Théodore, 133, ; James and, 79–80, 157, 184, 185, 243, 275
Foster, Charles H., 141, 149, 157
Fourierism, 22, 27–28, 31
Fox sisters, 23, 26–38, 299

Free love movement, 22, 28
Freud, Sigmund, 97, 306; on the unconscious, 213, 216, 217, 243, 245
Fullerton, George Stuart, 119, 122, 168, 207
Furness, Horace Howard, 167–68, 171; James and, 132, 161, 207–8; Piper and, 174, 207–8

Gale, Richard, 5
Gardiner, Edward, 122
Garland, Hamlin, 159–60, 286
Garrison, William Lloyd, 28
Ghosts, 23, 108; Henry James Sr. on, 43–45; Myers on, 76, 239; Sidgwick on, 71; Wilkinson on, 48
Gibbens, Alice. *See* James, Alice Gibbens
Giddings, Joshua, 28
Gilman, Charlotte Perkins, 12
Gladstone, William, 62, 65, 108
Godwin, Parke, 31
Goethe, Johann Wolfgang von, 213
Gower, John Henry, 185
Great Awakening, Second, 25
Greeley, Horace, 31, 34–39
Green, Thomas Hill, 63, 93
Grimké sisters, 28
Gurney, Edmund, 61–64, 81–90, 83, 109, 171; ASPR and, 121, 124; death of, 126, 248; on Hodgson, 93–94; on "hypnotic memory," 88, 212, 219–22; on hysterical patients, 246; James and, 82, 84–90, 158; on planchettes, 220; on "post-hypnotic memory," 228; on psychical research, 110, 112–13, 140, 170; spirit-return of, 267; on survival thesis, 84; on trance states, 211
Gurney, Edmund, works of: *Phantasms of the Living*, 88, 220, 235; *The Power of Sound*, 84, 85; "The Problems of Hypnotism," 220; *Tertium Quid*, 89, 222

Hahnemann, Samuel, 52
Hall, G. Stanley, 108, 141–42; as ASPR member, 117–19; Gurney and, 110; on mediums, 171; James and, 10, 14, 200, 288; Piper and, 174, 200, 269, 288;

Hallucinations, 2, 140; Gurney on, 84, 88; James on, 3, 225; Myers on, 236
Hamilton, William, 214
Harrison, Jane, 82
Havens, Katherine, 58
Hawthorne, Nathaniel, 28, 55
Hegel, G. W. F., 7, 214, 279
Helmholtz, Hermann von, 10
Herder, Johann Gottfried von, 211, 213, 245
Hertz, Heinrich, 108, 128, 129
Higginson, Thomas Wentworth, 119
Hillard, Mary Robbins, 252
Hodge, Charles, 9
Hodges, Nathaniel Dana Carlile, 119
Hodgson, Richard, 90–100, 92; American Branch of SPR and, 128–34; ASPR and, 122, 124, 126–28; death of, 132, 248, 287; empiricism of, 144; Gurney on, 93–94; James and, 1, 62, 90, 93–100, 121, 169, 184–85; on Palladino, 93, 150–52, 155, 156, 170, 289; Piper and, 93, 189–90, 193, 195–97, 203–4, 269; as Piper's control, 249, 254–67, 276, 279–84, 287–88; Sidgwick and, 90–91, 93; spirit-return of, 254–61; on Theosophy, 91–93, 149
Hodgson, Shadworth Hollway, 85, 87, 149, 274, 302
Holland, John R., 107
Home, Daniel Dunglas, 111, 112, 129, 235
Homeopathy, 31, 45, 47–48, 53
Hooper, Henry, 182
Hough, DeWitt, 293
Howells, William Dean, 12, 28; *The Undiscovered Country*, 28
Howison, George, 65, 274–77
Howitt, Mary, 51
Hume, David, 144, 173, 214, 223; on fideism, 176–77
Hutton, Richard, 107
Huxley, Thomas, 9, 14, 173, 198–99, 270
Hypnosis, 25, 108, 215–17; as anesthesia, 217; automatic writing and, 220; of hysterical patients, 215; James on, 228; Myers on, 221–22, 239, 241; role of memory in, 88, 211; somnambulism and, 214; trance

states vs., 193; Wilkinson on, 48. *See also* Mesmerism
"Hypnotic memory," 88, 212, 219–22, 228
Hyslop, James Hervey, 120, 127, 132, 133, 255; ASPR and, 287; Hall and, 288
Hysterical patients, 211–12, 215, 221, 226, 246

Idées fixes, 219
Immortality, 248–85; consciousness and, 268–77; cosmology and, 277–85; earth-soul theory of, 278–83; James on, 249, 270–74, 277, 284; Sidgwick Group on, 170, 211, 248, 249, 252–56; will and, 262–68. *See also* Afterlife beliefs; Spirit-return
International Congress for Physiological (later Experimental) Psychology, 10, 69, 77, 79

Jacks, Lawrence Pearsall, 301
Jackson, Charles Cabot, 119, 174, 208
Jackson, Frank Dutton, 158–59
James, Alice (sister), 70, 174, 273–74
James, Alice Gibbens (wife), 1, 61, 80–81, 96, 97, 98, 302; at Carqueiranne, 80–81; on Piper, 3, 174, 187
James, Henry, Jr. (brother): on P. T. Barnum, 30; early life of, 29–32; Gurney and, 84; on Myers, 77; Piper and, 174; on psychical research, 296; on Sidgwick, 65
James, Henry, Jr., works of: *Bostonians*, 28; *Notes of a Son and Brother*, 29; *A Small Boy and Others*, 29
James, Henry, III (son), 91, 98, 230
James, Henry, Sr. (father), 21–23, 31, 37–47, 40; on organized religion, 39; Wilkinson and, 48–53, 55–56
James, Margaret Mary (daughter), 97, 292, 302
James, Robertson (brother), 174, 229
James, William, 95; afterlife views of, 4, 170–73, 195, 251–61, 277; biographers of, 5; crisis of faith of, 62; early life of, 21–22, 29–32, 51, 55; egalitarian views of, 70, 117; as Harvard professor, 61; as Harvard student, 56; on "logic of presumption," 203; on planchettes, 56–57, 96, 182, 183, 229–31, 239; séances of, 150; on survival thesis, 170, 173; on "unseen world," 249; on U.S. versus British universities, 116; on women's education, 70
James, William, works of: "The Confidences of a Psychical Researcher," 295–99; *Essays in Radical Empiricism*, 257; "The Hidden Self," 218, 226–27; *Human Immortality*, 249, 270–74, 277, 284; *The Meaning of Truth*, 257, 286; "The Moral Equivalent of War," 257; "Notes on Automatic Writing," 225; *A Pluralistic Universe*, 250, 257, 279–84; *Pragmatism*, 14, 257; *The Principles of Psychology*, 125, 134–35, 164, 212–13, 223–28, 232–33, 247; "A Record of Observations of Certain Phenomena of Trance," 174, 191, 232–33, 249, 269, 273, 284; "Report on Mrs. Piper's Hodgson-Control," 249, 281–84; "Sentiment of Rationality," 180–81; *Some Problems of Philosophy*, 257; "The Substantialist Theory of the Soul," 271; *The Varieties of Religious Experience*, 8, 249–50, 284, 301, 308; "What Psychical Research Has Accomplished," 234; "Will to Believe," 8, 173–74, 178–80, 308
James, William (grandfather), 21, 22
James, William, Jr. (son), 157, 259
Janet, Pierre, 108, 128, 222, 245; on hysterical patients, 211, 215, 221, 246; on idées fixes, 219; James and, 306; on secondary consciousness, 226
Jastrow, Joseph, 122, 165, 170
John of the Cross, Saint, 176
Jung, Carl Gustav, 216
Jurieu, Pierre, 176

Kant, Immanuel, 52, 68, 147, 271; Schiller and, 272–74; transcendental idealism of, 211, 213; Transcendental Subject of, 244–45
Kardec, Allan, 148

Kelly, Emily Williams, 243–44
Kennedy, William, 275
Kierkegaard, Søren, 176
Krafft-Ebing, Richard von, 216

La Mettrie, Julien Offray de, 250, 270
Lang, Andrew, 241, 244–45
Langley, Samuel Pierpont, 120, 122
Leaf, Walter, 128, 130, 193
Leibniz, Gottfried Wilhelm, 214
Liébeault, Ambroise, 108, 215–16
Lincoln, Mary Todd, 28
Linnaean Society, 105, 115
Locke, John, 144, 223, 271, 306
Lodge, Oliver, 70, 169, 171; British Association for the Advancement of Science and, 106; on funding SPR, 109; James and, 100, 126, 132–33, 152–55, 252–53, 265, 287; on Myers, 75–76, 243; on Palladino, 150, 152–56; on Piper, 125, 193; research of, 134; Sidgwick and, 65, 67, 68, 73; on spirit-returns, 248; on survival thesis, 143
Lombroso, Cesare, 108, 150, 153–55
London Dialectical Society, 113
Loring, Katherine, 70
Lutoslawski, Wincenty, 81, 277

Magnetic Sense (Reichenbach's Experiments), 108, 118
Maitland, Frederic William, 85
Mansfield, J. V., 160
Marsh, Luther, 159
Marshall, Annie, 73, 78
Mather, Increase, 114
Mathers, S. L. Gregor, 159
Maudsley, Henry, 211, 214, 245, 250
Mauskopf, Seymour, 134
McDermott, Robert, 175, 178, 305–6, 308
McDougall, William, 241, 300–301, 303
Mediums, 1–4, 31, 289; ASPR investigations of, 123–26, 141, 144, 158–71, 182–98; levitating, 111; "secondary self" of, 212, 223–28; among Shakers, 24; SPR investigations of, 148–57, 170; of St. John's Wood, 51–52, 55, 59. *See also* Trance states *and specific persons*
Ménégoz, Eugène, 175–76
Myers, Gerald E., 306
Mesmer, Franz Anton, 25, 217
Mesmerism, 25, 31, 220; clairvoyance and, 53; crisis-state of, 53; Liébeault and, 215–16; Myers and, 76; Wilkinson and, 48–50. *See also* Hypnosis
Metaphysical Club (U.S.), 56, 114
Metaphysical Society (UK), 65, 85
Mill, John Stuart, 63, 143, 144, 214, 223; tertium quid approach of, 243
Minot, Charles, 117–19
Mitchell, Silas, 174, 203, 208
Möll, Albert, 128, 216
Montague, William Pepperell, 290–91
Montaigne, Michel de, 176
Montez, Lola, 158
Moore, G. E., 104
Morris, Lloyd, 283
Morselli, Enrico, 289
Moses, William Stainton, 107, 170, 235
Multiple personalities, 2, 212, 215, 246
Münsterberg, Hugo, 128, 129; Hyslop and, 258; James and, 10, 199–200, 258, 290; Palladino and, 294; Piper and, 174, 199–200
Murphy, Gardner, 303, 306
Myers, Arthur, 64, 109, 131, 219
Myers, Eveleen Tennant, 71, 73, 78, 80, 81
Myers, Frederic William Henry, 61–65, 72–81, 74, 109, 169, 171; afterlife views of, 72, 74, 128, 143, 233–41; American Branch of SPR and, 130–31; ASPR and, 122, 124, 127; death of, 248, 287; on ghosts, 76, 239; Hodgson and, 93; on hypnosis, 221–22, 239, 241; William James and, 77–81, 128–29, 145–46, 238–46; Henry James Jr. on, 77; Lodge on, 75–76, 243; marriage of, 71, 73, 78; on mediums, 184, 212; mesmerism and, 76; on multiple personality, 246; on Palladino, 150–53, 155, 156, 194; on Piper, 193, 195, 197, 236; Sidgwick and, 68–69, 76–77, 129;

spirit-return of, 253–55; on stream of consciousness, 237–38; on subliminal self, 212–13, 233; tertium quid approach of, 243–45; on trance states, 211, 239, 243; on unconsciousness, 222, 234–46

Myers, Frederic William Henry, works of: *Fragments of Inner Life*, 77–78; *Fragments of Prose and Poetry*, 72; *Human Personality and Its Survival of Bodily Death*, 72, 93, 233–46; *Phantasms of the Living*, 88, 220, 235

Mystical experiences, 176, 218, 282–83; "vastation" as, 45

National Academy of Sciences, 115
National Institution for the Promotion of Science, 115
Newbold, William Romaine, 132, 196, 257
Newcomb, Simon, 119, 122
Newham College for Women (Cambridge), 69
Nichols, Herbert, 205
Nietzsche, Friedrich, 214
Noel, Roden Berkeley Wriothesley, 107
Norton, Charles Eliot, 174, 196–97
Noyes, John Humphrey, 27–28

Occult, 10, 35, 37, 109, 244–45
Occultism, 23, 25, 151, 159
Ochorowicz, Julian, 150–53, 288
Ockham's razor, 261
Oken, Lorenz, 105
Olcott, Henry Steel, 149
"Orientalism," 12
Ouija boards, 182, 183. *See also* Planchettes
Owen, Richard Dale, 33–34
Owen, Robert Dale, 33–34

Palladino, Eusapia, 149–58; Carrington and, 289–92, *290*; Hodgson on, 93, 150–52, 155, 156, 170, 289; James on, 3, 141, 150, 153–56, 170, 194, 286–95; Myers on, 150–53, 155, 156, 194
Palmer, George, 161
Panpsychism, 278, 279, 281, 298, 299

Parapsychologists, 11, 300–301, 306–7, 309
Pascal, Blaise, 173, 176, 177, 179
Partridge, Charles, 159
Paul, Saint, 173, 175–78
Peirce, Benjamin, 115
Peirce, Charles, 294
Peirce, James Mills, 119, 203
Pentecostals, 25
Perkins, C. H., 229, 230
Perry, Ralph Barton, 5, 8, 22, 31, 31, 300; on empiricism, 142; on fideism, 182; on James's psychical research, 218, 303–6, 308; on psychopathology, 246
PhD programs, 10, 70, 116, 117
Pickering, Edward C., 108, 117–19
Pickering, William Henry, 119
Piddington, J. G.: James and, 133, 254–58, 286, 287
Piper, Alta, 187
Piper, Leonora, 81, 130–33, 186–98, *188*; under anesthesia, 193; Cattell and, 174, 199, 201–6, 261; critics of, 198–208; Hall and, 174, 200, 269, 288; Hodgson on, 93, 189–90, 193, 195–97, 203–4; Hodgson-control of, 249, 254–67, 276, 279–84, 287–88; Jacks and, 301; James and, 1–3, 81, 113, 131, 133, 172–75, 186–209, 212, 223–28, 232, 214, 249, 254–63, 266–69, 281–88, 295–297, 301; Lodge on, 125; Myers on, 193, 195, 197, 236; "secondary self" of, 212, 223–28
Place, Harry, 160
Planchettes, automatic writing with, 56–57, 96, 182–83, 220, 229–31, 239
Platonism, 104, 146, 250–52, 271, 284
Pluralism, 5, 250, 257, 279–84, 309; idealism and, 146; metaphysical, 268
"Pluriverse," 299
Podmore, Frank, 65, 128, 144; *Phantasms of the Living* by, 88, 220, 235
Poe, Edgar Allan, 37, 52
Pollock, Frederick, 85, 86
Popkin, Richard H., 176, 177
Positivism, 143–44, 173; agnostics and, 9; fideism and, 175; scientific naturalists and, 11

Possession, 24–26; demonic, 26, 46, 227, 231, 239. *See also* Trance states
Powell, John Wesley, 119
Pragmatism, 5–9, 293, 309; empirical, 267–68, 277, 282, 285; fideism and, 177; James's book on, 14, 141, 257; modernism and, 15; of F. C. S. Schiller, 81, 109; tertium quid method and, 6–8, 14–15
Prince, Katherine, 120
Psychical research, 2, 211–13; critics of, 14, 198–208; importance to James of, 303–6; parapsychologists and, 300; psychopathology and, 246; subjective quality of, 175, 177, 181–82
"Psycho-physiological (P-P) formula," 270, 271
Putnam, James Jackson, 97
Pythagoras, 6

Quakerism, 11, 24, 30, 63
Quincy, Josiah P., 125

Radical Club (Boston), 7, 146
Radiometer, 110
Rayleigh, John William Strutt, 62, 65, 69, 71, 107, 150
Read, Carveth, 85
Reichenbach's Experiments (Magnetic Sense), 108, 118
Renouvier, Charles, 121, 178
Rhine, Joseph, 300–301
Richardson, William Lambert, 197
Richet, Charles, 78–79, 108, 128, 145; on ectoplasm, 148; on experimental psychology, 215; on mediums, 184, 193; Arthur Myers and, 219; on Palladino, 150, 152, 153; on unconsciousness, 211, 214, 245
Rinn, Joseph F., 291
Ripley, George, 31, 34
Robertson, George Croom, 85, 87, 88, 93, 110; Myers and, 221; on Society for Psychical Research, 121
Robinson, George Blakiston, 47
Rodgers, Henry, 115
Ross, Charles, 162–64

Ross, Hannah V., 158, 192–93
Rousseau, Jean-Jacques, 213
Royal Society of London, 104, 105
Royce, Josiah, 69, 80, 279; James and, 94, 199–200, 284; Palladino and, 294; Piper and, 174
Ruskin, John, 104
Russell, Bertrand, 104, 177

Sabatier, Auguste, 175–76
Saint-Simon, Henri de, 143
Salter, Eliza "Baby Eliza," 174, 190–92
Salter, William, 183, 190, 197
Sandemanianism, 22
Santayana, George, 177, 275
Savage, Minot Judson, 120, 162, 192
Schelling, Friedrich, 214
Schiaparelli, Giordanno Virginio, 150
Schiller, F. C. S., 132, 255, 295; on brain transmission theory, 275; on funding SPR, 109; Kant and, 272–74; on Myers, 242–43; pragmatism of, 81, 109
Schlesinger, Arthur, Jr., 114
Schopenhauer, Arthur, 211, 245
Schrenck-Notzing, Albert von, 108, 128, 150–51, 216
Scratch Eight dinner club, 85–87, 104, 114, 302
Scudder, Samuel Hubbard, 119
Second sight, 2, 139, 140
"Secondary self," 212, 218, 223–28
Sellers, Coleman, 119
Sewall, May Eliza Wright, 185
Seward, Frederick William, 199
Seybert, Henry, 132, 159
Seybert Commission, 161, 167–68, 207, 208
Shadow-man doctrine, 251
Shakers, 24, 30
Shakespeare, William, 256
Shaking Quakers, 30
Shaler, Nathaniel Southgate, 174, 196, 203
Shelley, Percy Bysshe, 275
Sidgwick, Eleanor Mildred Balfour, 62, 64, 69–71, 171; James and, 99, 156, 169–71, 253, 289; on mesmerism, 220; on

Palladino, 149–50, 152, 156; on spirit-return, 253, 255
Sidgwick, Henry, 61–71, 66, 109, 171, 296; British Association for the Advancement of Science and, 106; Cambridge Apostles and, 104; death of, 248; education of, 64–65; on ghosts, 71; Hodgson and, 90–91, 93; James and, 61, 65, 69–71, 77–79, 78, 90, 99, 129, 156, 169–71, 296–97; Lodge on, 67, 68; on mesmerism, 220; Myers and, 68–69, 76–77, 129; on Palladino, 149–50, 152, 153, 156; religious views of, 71
Sidgwick, Henry, works of: *Elements of Politics*, 68; *Methods of Ethics*, 68; *Principles of Political Economy*, 68
Sidgwick Group, 12, 61–64, 99–100, 123, 128; empirical research of, 145, 239; experimental psychology and, 219; on immortality, 170, 211, 248, 249, 252–56; members of, 62
Simonds, Leonora Evelina. *See* Piper, Leonora
Slade, Henry, 141, 149, 157, 168
Slate writing, 93, 148–49, 192–93
Smith, Hélène, 80, 184, 185
Smith, Robert Pearsall, 119, 130, 155
Smith, William T., 229
Social Gospel movement, 12
Society for Psychical Research (SPR), 2, 61, 101–13; American Branch of, 128–33; ASPR support from, 123, 127; British Association for the Advancement of Science and, 105–8; establishment of, 65; funding of, 109, 129; Gurney and, 83, 84; medium investigations by, 130–33, 148–57, 170, 172, 193–97; membership of, 107–8; Myers and, 76; Sidgwick and, 65, 70, 248
Solomon, John, 158
Somnambulism, 48, 214, 217, 236
Soule, Minnie Meserve, 255
Spanish-American War (1898), 79
"Spirit-cure," 53–56, 59, 299
Spirit-return, 248, 252–56, 265; alternative explanations for, 258–62; "aura of factuality" for, 11, 169; Myers on, 242; Piper and, 267; "sublime conscious reservoir theory" of, 3, 249–51, 259–84, 298. *See also* Immortality
Spivey, Thomas, 183
SPR. *See* Society for Psychical Research
Stanton, Elizabeth Cady, 28
Stead, William Thomas, 153
Stephen, James Fitzjames, 104
Stephen, Leslie, 85, 86, 108
Stewart, Balfour, 107
Storey, Moorfield, 119
Stout, George Frederick, 241
Stowe, Harriet Beecher, 28
Strong, Charles, 275
Stumpf, Karl, 79, 89, 103
Subliminal self, 232–45, 278, 283, 297; of trance states, 212–13, 248, 260
Suffrage, woman, 22, 28
Sully, James, 85, 87
Sunderland, La Roy, 217
Survival hypothesis. *See* Afterlife beliefs
Swedenborg, Emanuel, 23–24, 34, 41
Swedenborgianism, 11, 22; creation of, 24; doctrine of correspondence in, 41, 51; Henry James Sr.'s views of, 39, 41–45, 55–56; Wilkinson's views of, 48
Symonds, John Addington, 108
Synthetic Society, 65

Tait, P. G., 178
Talmadge, N. P., 28
Tanner, Amy, 288
Tappan, Mary, 119
Taylor, Bayard, 31, 35
Taylor, Eugene, 246, 307–8
Telekinesis, 2, 151, 153, 185, 241, 307
Telepathy, 2, 3, 108, 139, 259, 260; ASPR's committee on, 118; Gurney on, 88; mathematical, 3
Temperance movement, 28, 114
Tender-minded. *See* Tough- vs. tender-minded dichotomy
Tennant, Eveleen, 71, 73, 78, 80, 81
Tennyson, Alfred, 104, 108

Tertium quid method, 6–9, 12–17, 34, 268, 289–302; Cattell on, 201; egalitarianism of, 117; empiricism of, 142–48, 157, 161; formation of, 56–60; Gurney on, 89, 222; hybrid approach of, 119, 135; of John Stuart Mill, 243; of Myers, 243–45; subjective experience in, 175, 177, 180–82

Tertullian, 176

Thackeray, William Makepeace, 51

Theobald, Florence, 51, 54–55

Theosophy, 91–94, 149

Thompson, Joseph J., 151–52

Thompson, Rosalie, 80–81, 93, 172, 184, 229

Thurston, Howard, 291

Titchener, E. B., 199–200

Tocqueville, Alexis de, 114

Tough- vs. tender-minded dichotomy, 5, 250–51, 268; psychical research and, 14, 171; will to believe and, 173

Trance states, 2, 4, 23, 182–86; anesthesia during, 193; Carpenter on, 224; dreams and, 256; fits and, 25–26; hypnosis vs., 193; James's essay on, 174, 191, 232–33, 249, 269, 273, 284; Myers on, 211, 239, 243; photographs of, *188, 290*; possession in, 24–26, 46, 227, 231, 239; subliminal self theory of, 212–13, 248, 260; unconscious and, 228. *See also* Mediums

Trowbridge, John, 119, 174, 200–201, 203

Truth, Sojourner, 28

Tuckerman, Henry, 31, 32

Tuttle, Hudson, 183

Tyndall, John, 9, 112

"Unclassified residuum," 213–18, 244–46

Unconsciousness, 211–17, 244–47; Freud's theory of, 213, 216, 217, 243, 245; James's theory of, 5, 211–13, 223–27, 233, 244–46, 297–98; Myers on, 222, 234–46. *See also* Consciousness

Unitarianism, 11, 63, 120

Universities: PhD programs at, 10, 70, 116, 117; psychical research at, 131–32; U.S. versus British, 116

Vaccination, 47

Vanderbilt, Cornelius, 159

"Vastation" (mystical experience), 45

Verrall, Margaret de Gaudrion Merrifield, 133, 172, 254

Von Hartmann, Eduard, 211, 214, 245

Voodoo, 293

Wallace, Alfred Russel, 108, 128; on Hannah Ross, 162–63, 166, 167

Walsh, Catherine, 1, 119, 174, 190–92

Ward, Elizabeth, 123

Ward, James, 275, 276

Warren, Joseph Weatherhead, 162, 186

Washington Botanical Society, 115

Watson, William, 119

Weber, Max, 16, 300

Wedgwood, Hensleigh, 107

Werner, Heinrich, 217

Whewell, William, 106

Whitman, Russell, 120

Whitman, Sara, 78

Whitman, Walt, 275

Wienholt, Arnold, 217

Wilberforce, Samuel, 9

Wild, Hannah, 174, 190–92

Wilkinson, James John Garth, 23, 46–56, 49; on ghosts, 48; homeopathy and, 47, 48, 52, 53; Henry James Sr. and, 48–53, 55–56; "spirit-cure" of, 53–56, 59, 299

Wilkinson, James John Garth, works of: *Divine Revelation and Its Works and Sciences*, 47; *The Human Body and Its Connection with Man*, 47; *Improvisations from the Spirit*, 52, 54

Wilkinson, William, 51

Will to believe, 37, 308; Bryant on, 33; fideism and, 5, 173–74, 178–82; in immortality, 262–68

Will to deceive, 262, 297
Willis, Nathaniel Parker, 31–34, 39, 42
Witchcraft, 26, 225, 227, 231
Witmer, Lightning, 196
Woman's rights, 31, 91; to education, 70; to vote, 22, 28
Woodhull, Alfred Alexander, 119
Woodhull, Victoria, 120
World's Columbian Exposition (1893), 126
Wright, Chauncey, 177
Wyckoff, Henry, 123

X-rays, 111

Zend-Avesta. See Fechner, Gustav
Zionism, 31

www.ingramcontent.com/pod-product-compliance
Lightning Source LLC
Chambersburg PA
CBHW031413230426
43668CB00007B/295